Antichrist and the New World Order

Richard G. Walker

Antichrist and the New World Order

Copyright © 2020 Richard G. Walker

All rights reserved.

ISBN:979-8-9866839-0-4

A SPECIAL WORD TO THE READER

This is a book about the future of mankind and the earth. In it, you will come to know that Jesus Christ controls history for his own glory and the eternal good of those who will inherit eternal life. There is no point to understanding the future if you become its victim. You can become a victor rather than a casualty of the last days by believing the good news that Jesus Christ was crucified, died, and was raised from the dead to pay for your sins.

John 3:16–18 (KJV 1900) 16 For God so loved the world, that he gave his only begotten Son, that whosoever believeth in him should not perish, but have everlasting life. 17 For God sent not his Son into the world to condemn the world; but that the world through him might be saved. 18 He that believeth on him is not condemned: but he that believeth not is condemned already, because he hath not believed in the name of the only begotten Son of God.

Tomorrow is coming, but it is not promised to come for you. Believe this gospel of Jesus Christ and this very moment receive forgiveness of sins and everlasting life through the new birth.

Richard G. Walker

TABLE OF CONTENTS

A SPECIAL WORD TO THE READER iii
TABLE OF CONTENTS 4
1 How To Use This Book 15
2 Are You Working For The Coming Of Jesus Christ Or The Antichrist? 17
3 Satan's Administration Of The World 20
    Dominion 21
    A Definition of The New World Order: Implications of Satan's Dominion: 22
    Good and Evil 26
    Binary Traps: Dialectical Mind Control 28
    Religion, Good and Evil 32
    The Emergence of the Antichrist 35
4 Book One: Who Is The Antichrist? 36
    Definitions 36
        What is the "Last Time [Last Hour]" 37
        Antichrist and "many antichrists" 38
        Definition of Antichrist 39
        Antichrist Promotes a Lie: 40
        Where Do Antichrists [small "a"] Come From? 49
        Some Facts About Mature Disciples 53
        The Spirit of Antichrist 55

Summary of The Concept of Antichrist 57
What Is The Mystery of Iniquity? 61
The Mystery of Iniquity and the Mystery of Godliness 64
The Mystery of Iniquity and Antichrist 66
Summary: The Mystery of Iniquity 70

5 The Character Of The Antichrist 72
Introduction: The Context of His Appearing 72
Daniel 9: Daniel's 70 Weeks: An Incredible Prophecy 73
The Prince That Shall Come 80
Who are the People of the Prince That Shall Come? 80
The 70th Week 82

6 His Character: A Rider on a White Horse: Israel in End-Time Geopolitics 87
The Timing of the Day of the Lord 88
The Beginning of Sorrows 91
Will the Real Messiah Please Stand Up? 93
Antichrist: From Statesman and Man of Government to the Assumption of Deity 95

7 His Character: The Man of Sin 98

8 His Character: The Son of Perdition, the Reanimated Man 101
Who is this Apollyon? 102

9 His Character: The Lawless One and the Conspiracy to Destroy Civilization 105
Where Does Morality Originate? 107

10 His Character: Antichrist [Against]-How This All Got Started, Satan's Motivation 110

Satan's Origin 110

Satan's Strategy 113

11 His Character: Antichrist [Instead]-Satan's Church, A New Kind of Unbeliever...115

12 His Character: The Prince That Shall Come Revisited, Government and Spiritual Warfare 118

    The Times of the Gentiles 121

    Antichrist: The State as Seat of Spiritual Power 123

13 His Character: The Little Horn and the Prophetic Symbolism of Daniel and Revelation 125

    What Can a Christian Do? 130

14 His Character: The Willful King..133

    Summary: The Character of the Antichrist 140

15 Book Two: The Career Of Antichrist 146

    Events Leading to Revelation 13...146

        The Seven Seals..147

        The Trumpet Judgments 149

        War Preparations: The Invisible Precedes the Visible 151

        The Invisible Revealed: A Vision of the Mystery of Godliness and the Mystery of Iniquity...152

        War Breaks Out In Heaven: The Invisible Precedent for the Appearance of the Beast in Revelation 13.........................154

16 The Beast..157

    The Beast Identified with Antichrist 161

        Daniel's Vision and the Two Advents of "Rome"................162

    The Beast Identified with Lucifer 162

The Beast Identified with World Government..................164

What We Should Know and Do..170

17 The Beginning Of Antichrist's Rule: Revelation 13...............173

Revelation 13.3 "And his deadly wound was healed" 173

Revelation 13.4 "And they worshipped the dragon...and they worshipped the beast" 175

The Character of Deception in the Latter Days....................177

Revelation 13.5 "And power was given him unto continue forty and two months" 179

Revelation 13.6-7 "And he opened his mouth in blasphemy against God…" 180

18 The Prime Minister of the New World Order-The False Prophet: Revelation 13 185

Revelation 13.11 "And I beheld another beast coming up out of the earth; and he had two horns like a lamb, and he spake as a dragon." 186

False Prophet-A Definition.....................................187

Revelation 13:12 "And he exerciseth all the power of the first beast before him… 189

Revelation 13:13 "And he doeth great wonders,"...................190

The False Prophet Promotes the False Messiah 191

Revelation 13:14–15 "And deceiveth them that dwell on the earth..192

Why Images..192

Why Coercion..194

The New World Order..196

What Can be Done Today? 203

19 The Mark: "From Man to Superman" Revelation 16.13-18....205
    Lucifer Will Imitate the Church 206
    The Mark..208
        The Mark is an Initiation 212
    The True Origin of the Doctrine of the Superman 212
        The Principle of Deception..213
        The Principle of Scriptural Misuse 214
        The Principle of Human Non-Culpability:.............................216
        The Principle of Occult Religion: 217
    The Superman and the New World Order 217
    Faithful Christians In the Last Days 220

20 Background to the Fall of Babylon: Revelation 16 222
    The Bowl or Vial Judgments 222

21 Disambiguating Babylon: Revelation 17 224
    Babylon the Great as the Cities of Man 226
        The City of Cain: "Enoch" 226
        The City of Enoch: The Prophet of God................................226
        The Post Flood City of Babel 227
        The City of Abraham Ur of the Chaldees [Babylon] 228
    Babylon the Great as the Capital of the New World Order 229
        Babylon Was Destroyed, But Will Live Again 229
        Capitals...230
        The Great City 231
        Jerusalem 231
        Sodom and Gomorrah..232

Babylon the First and Last Desolator of Jerusalem...............233

Prophetic Typology Makes Jerusalem Headquarters of Antichrist...............234

The Testimony of Jesus...............236

The Destruction of the Babylon the Great...............237

22 Two Aspects of Babylon-The Woman and the Beast: Revelation 17...............240

The Beast Revisited...............241

The Harlot-Spiritual Babylon: The Key to Gentile History........242

Women as Symbols of Doctrinal Systems...............243

She [Mystery Babylon] is a religious force, the mother or source of false religion: Rev 14.8; 17.5;18.3, 9, 23; 19.2.....244

The Name Mystery Babylon...............244

Mystery Babylon is the Mother of Harlots:...............246

Symbol of Harlotry: The Gold Cup...............248

Abominations...............251

23 The Woman and the Beast: The World Church...............256

An Example of Religious Babylon: The Ecumenical Movement...............256

Principles of the Ecumenical Movement...............261

Liberty in Doctrinal Interpretation:...............261

Distinction Between Doctrine And Faith:...............262

Unity Taken by Faith:...............263

Free Interpretation:...............266

Abstention from Proselytizing:...............267

24 The Woman and the Beast: World Government...............269

She [Mystery Babylon] is global in her operations and influence: Rev 17.1,2,15; 18:3, 9,11,23 269

   Understanding Good and Evil 269

   International Spiritual Adultery 270

She [Mystery Babylon] influences world politics: Rev 17.2, 15; 18.3, 9 275

An Example of Political Babylon: World Government 278

   The Reason for the Dream: "What shall be in the latter days" 280

   The Dream: One World 280

   The Dream: One Man 282

   The Dream: One Agenda 283

   The Myth of Human Progress 285

   The End of Human Government 287

   God and World Government 289

25 The Woman And The Beast: World Economics 291

   She [Mystery Babylon] is critical to international commerce: Rev 17:1-2, 15; 18: 3, 9, 11-19 291

   An Example of Economic Babylon: The Hip Hop Industry 293

      The Four Characteristics of Economic Babylon 293

      Wealth Transfer 294

      Institutional Corruption of Values 295

      Promote Luciferian Religion 297

      Political End Game 298

26 The Woman And The Beast: World Oppression 301

   She [Mystery Babylon] is a key actor in genocides, especially of believers Rev 16.6; 17.6; 18:20, 24; 19.2 301

Why is Mystery Babylon committed to the eradication of the saints and the prophets? 302

Because Mystery Babylon is opposed to the advance of the Mystery of Godliness 303

Because the prophets and the saints expose through teaching and preaching the true nature of Mystery Babylon as a demonically inspired system 304

Because Satan is specifically interested in preventing the fulfillment of the covenant promises to Abraham via regenerate Israel. God's failure to fulfill these promises would mean victory for Lucifer. 306

27 Collecting Our Thoughts Regarding Mystery Babylon 309

The Accurate Interpretation of History 309

The Accurate Understanding of Spiritual Warfare 310

What is Spiritual Warfare? 312

28 The End Of Mystery Babylon 313

Reasons for the Demise of the Harlot 313

Repercussions of the Demise of the Harlot 316

29 The End Of The Antichrist 319

Demonic Control of World Affairs 319

World System Created, Empowered and Administered by Satan 321

The Armageddon Campaign 322

Two Different Motivations for Armageddon 322

Daniel 11 and the Prophecy of the Armageddon Campaign 324

The Definition of the Armageddon Campaign 326
The Return of Christ 331
The End of Antichrist 333

30 Epilogue: What Are Our Chances? 335
The Engine of History 336
Why I am Not Optimistic for the Future of America 337
   Trend: Seeking the Kingdom of God via Government 338
   Trend: The Pneumatic Revolt, The Charismatic Movement 339
The Solution 340

Appendix 1: A God Of Forces 341
Definition 341
God as A Fortress and Refuge in the Soul 344
Lucifer as the God of Fortresses 347
Partial List of Spiritual [Theological] Strongholds or Fortresses
.... 349

Appendix 2: The Rapture 351
Definition of the Rapture 355
   Death vs. Resurrection 355
   Resurrection vs. Reincarnation 355
   The Procession of Resurrections 356
   What is the Rapture 357
   The Rapture is a Mystery 359
   The "Day of the Lord/Christ" is not the Rapture 360
Order of Events in the Thessalonian Epistles 361
   "[T]he coming of the Lord Jesus Christ, and by our gathering

together unto him" 2 Th 2.1 362

"[F]or that day shall not come, except there come a falling away first" 2 Th 3b. 364

"[A]nd that man of sin be revealed, the son of perdition;" 2 Th 2.3c 367

The Second Coming of Christ is Not the Same as the Rapture 368

   The Central Passages 368

   No Visible Signs Preceding the Rapture 368

   No Judgments before the Rapture 370

   No Kingdom Established at the Rapture 371

   Glorified Bodies Are a Part of the Rapture 371

   Believers Meet Christ in the Air in the Rapture 372

   The Role of the Angels 373

   The "Mystery" Nature of the Rapture 373

About the Restrainer 374

Appendix 3: Dispensations 381

   Dispensation: Definition 381

   Dispensation: Elements of 381

   Dispensations: Number 382

   Identifying A Change in Dispensations 382

   Dispensations and Covenants 383

   What Distinguishes Dispensationalism from Other Systems of Interpretation 383

ABOUT THE AUTHOR 384

Works Cited 385

Richard G. Walker

1
How To Use This Book

The purpose of this book is to provide the reader with the origins, plans and methodology of the devil's program to institute a New World Order headed by his protégé the Antichrist. It is also the purpose of this book to equip the *believer* with an understanding of Satan's strategy and tactics during the *Church Age*[1] to bring about the last and greatest episode in the devil's reign upon the earth. It is intended that through an understanding of the unfolding of end time events, the believer will become motivated to fight the spiritual warfare and achieve victory in his particular place in history.

This is not a book that attempts to give instruction upon the occult, or to document the many books that seek to convey the plans and methods of Satan from his own perspective. Not only are there many such books, but there is also a tendency in many believers to seek out that kind of information before they have a mastery of what the scriptures say on the subject. The Bible is an excellent source of documentation on the origin of this conspiracy, its objectives, and its salient doctrines. This book attempts to outline these categories, to communicate their impact upon the world historically, and to project their influence upon the present and the future.

This book will remind Christians of what can be done to ensure the successful prosecution of God's program in their own time. The advent of the Antichrist and the ultimate implementation of his World Order has been prophesied and will occur on schedule. However, the plan of God requires that each generation of believers execute the divine game plan in their own geography and historical context to secure the ultimate victory. Every believer, regardless of his place in history, has a contribution to make to the resolution of this ancient conflict. Understanding what Satan is specifically attempting to accomplish is an aid to the believer as he watches and engages the historical trends of his time.

The book is designed to be read from beginning to end. The initial chapters are important to understand the thesis of the book and to become oriented to the concepts necessary to prepare the reader for the biblical facts, which will often contradict his current perception of reality. Finally, the Appendices are recommended, for they will provide in depth treatment of some important themes from within the book.

2
Are You Working For The Coming Of Jesus Christ Or The Antichrist?

In writing a book about prophecy, it is easy to lose sight of what is expected of the reader. Are you to be fascinated or excited by the content? Or are you to be terrified by the prospect of experiencing the terrible trials that yet await the world?

For the pretribulational dispensationalist reader,[2] one who believes that the Lord will resurrect the Church prior to releasing His wrath upon the unbelieving world in the Day of the Lord, this question is magnified in difficulty. Of what significance are the prophecies of a distant [or not so distant] time if he will not be here to experience these events personally?

The intent of this book is that the Christian reader of these biblical prophecies discover a renewed motivation for the successful pursuit of his Christian discipleship for the duration of his life. In so doing, he will find that this pursuit requires a re-commitment to winning the spiritual warfare within his own geography and his own historical context [Heb 12.1-2]. *This is key: the plan of God is advanced by the successful execution of each Christian life.*

Every living person is involved in the spiritual conflict between the devil and the Lord as either a combatant or a casualty. You are either consciously representing the interests of Christ or the Antichrist, or you are an unconscious pawn. Pawns may be unbelievers or believers who will not submit themselves to the authority of the Lord Jesus Christ. All pawns become assets of Satan[3] and his plan to establish a New World Order and install his son, the Antichrist as the god of this

earth.

The Church Age, that period which began with the first Pentecost after the resurrection of the Lord, has consisted of successive generations of believers who may be likened to runners in a relay race [Heb 12.1]. The first flight were the apostles and their disciples who began the race and set the pace for the coming flights of runners. Each cohort passes the baton of the gospel to the next, all operating under the same Head, with the same agenda and the same objective. One Lord, one faith and one baptism, *each contributing to the ultimate victory* predicted in the prophetic books.

The devil and his angels have a competing team with runners corresponding to the saints of God who likewise are committed to one authority with one central doctrine and one mystical initiation.

The race ebbs and flows throughout the generations of human history, Satan's forces experience both victories and defeats, as do the forces of the Lord. The Bible teaches that Satan will, sometime in the future, go on a serious winning streak. He will mass an offensive against which the people of God will have no immediate defense.[4] But in the final flight of the race, the Lord will assume personal, physical leadership of the last series of battles and launch a counteroffensive of irresistible force which will bring the conflict to a conclusion.[5]

Each generation of believers plays a critical role in the development of this conflict. Our individual decisions to serve the Lord and to oppose the devil; our achievement of spiritual maturity and the mastery of the flesh which is its evidence, and our enthusiasm and commitment to the overthrow of Satan's plans via the Great Commission all have *everlasting* consequences.

The study of prophecy can galvanize these impulses. Placing prophecy in a historical context that enables the understanding of current events can help Christians see how their efforts to represent Christ in their living and verbal witness truly make a difference today and in the future.

Christian: Are you actively engaged in the spiritual warfare on Christ's behalf? *Or are you tacitly serving the coming of the Antichrist* by a halfhearted sanctification and disinterest in the eternal destiny of the souls in your periphery?

Unbeliever: Knowing the future is of no value if you will ultimately become its victim. The purpose of divine revelation is that people might be rescued from judgment. This rescue is accomplished by your acknowledgement of your rebellion against God and calling upon Him to apply the blood of Christ to your sins. By faith in the work of Christ upon the cross on your behalf you become a child of God and a beneficiary of all that Christ's sacrifice procures. You become a positive agent in God's plan for the ages.[6]

Richard G. Walker

3
Satan's Administration Of The World

Luke4:5–6 (KJV 1900)
5 And the devil, taking him up into an high mountain, shewed unto him all the kingdoms of the world in a moment of time. 6 And the devil said unto him, All this power will I give thee, and the glory of them: <u>for that is delivered unto me; and to whomsoever I will I give it</u>.

John 12:31 (KJV 1900)
31 Now is the judgment of this world: now shall the <u>prince of this world</u> be cast out.

The reality of most people is that of an agreed illusion.

This entire world has been under the temporary supervisory authority and administration of Lucifer and the fallen angels since the fall of the first humans, Adam, and Eve. This fact must be absorbed to have any accurate understanding of how and why the world functions as it does. The acknowledgement of this central fact, one that Jesus Himself acknowledged, is critical to understanding the Bible and history, the present and the future.

The Antichrist will emerge upon the stage of history because of centuries of preparation by this evil administration. That preparation may properly be said to constitute the groundwork for a New World Order. Human history is the effort of this demonic establishment and its human confederates to create an environment suitable to the emergence of the Antichrist and, at the same time, God's calling of an elect people from the midst of the devil's kingdom.

Dominion

> Genesis 1:26–28 (KJV 1900)
> 26 And God said, Let us make man in our image, after our likeness: and let them have <u>dominion</u> over the fish of the sea, and over the fowl of the air, and over the cattle, and over all the earth, and over every creeping thing that creepeth upon the earth. 27 So God created man in his own image, in the image of God created he him; male and female created he them. 28 And God blessed them, and God said unto them, Be fruitful, and multiply, and replenish the earth, and subdue it: <u>and have dominion</u> over the fish of the sea, and over the fowl of the air, and over every living thing that moveth upon the earth.

It was this status as the sovereign of the earth that mankind relinquished by obedience to the suggestion of Satan. The decision to disobey the express command of God to eat of the tree of the knowledge of Good and Evil was sufficient to break their fellowship with Him and to forfeit their dominion. The earth became the enemy of man, an adversary that would resist him until he returned to the dust in futility.

> Genesis 3:17–19 (KJV 1900)
> 17 And unto Adam he said, Because thou hast hearkened unto the voice of thy wife, and hast eaten of the tree, of which I commanded thee, saying, Thou shalt not eat of it: cursed is the ground for thy sake; in sorrow shalt thou eat of it all the days of thy life; 18 Thorns also and thistles shall it bring forth to thee; and thou shalt eat the herb of the field; 19 In the sweat of thy face shalt thou eat bread, till thou return unto the ground; for out of it wast thou taken: for dust thou art, and unto dust shalt thou return.

In the fall of humanity, Satan achieved the dual victory of temporarily confounding God's intent for mankind and catapulting himself into temporary dominion over the earth and with him his demonic host. Lucifer crowed of this authority to Christ Himself at the temptation in the wilderness:

> Luke 4:6 (KJV 1900)
> 6 And the devil said unto him, All this power will I give thee, and the glory of them: for that is delivered unto me; and to whomsoever I will I give it.

Therefore, the character of the spiritual *management* of the world is consistent with its fallen *condition*. There is now a fallen creation, inhabited by spiritually corrupted people [Jn 8.44; Eph 2.1-3] who live within a demonically ordered and directed civilization [1 Jn 2.15-16; 5.19]. There is a sympathetic cohesion and cooperation between all these elements: they work together through the agency of a single spirit, seeking the same ends and purpose.[7]

> Ephesians 2:1–2 (KJV 1900)
> 1 And you hath he quickened, who were dead in trespasses and sins; 2 Wherein in time past ye walked according to the course of this world, according to the <u>prince of the power of the air, the spirit</u> that now worketh in the children of disobedience:

The ability to understand and to accept this biblically defined reality is essential to the understanding of the past, of prophecy, and *the interpretation of current trends of history*.

It should not be assumed that this demonic dominion of the world is absolute. God is still God and overrules Satan's prerogatives whenever He chooses. Further, the devil has zero authority over anyone who has been rescued from this present darkness by faith in Christ unto salvation [Gal 1.4; 1 Jn 5.19]. God is not the source of evil, which is the result of the decisions of morally culpable beings. Despite this, God certainly works all things to his own ends which are holy, righteous, and just [Pr 19.21; Isa 46.9-10; Rom 8.28]

A Definition of The New World Order: Implications of Satan's Dominion:

The New World Order is a *spiritual* regime out of which will appear the final form of the world's political, economic, and social structures.

It will be the product of Satan's thinking applied to human organization. The preparation for this Order has been energized and directed by Satan, who at the Fall became the "god of this world" [2 Cor 4.4]

To some, the New World Order will be an optimal state, an Omega Point.[8] To others it will enable the Singularity.[9] For some it is something to be anticipated and hastened. To others it is a phrase that connotes the loss of freedom and self-determination. Students of history are unable to discern the motives for the development of the New World Order aside from the lust for wealth and power/control. Students of scripture know that the New World Order is as close as the devil will get to accomplishing his ancient plan and fulfilling his promises to fallen angels and men. It will be the kingdom sought since eternity past by the one who would be "as the Most High" ruling men and angels from "the sides of the north."

> Isaiah 14:12–14 (KJV 1900)
> 12 How art thou fallen from heaven, O Lucifer, son of the morning! How art thou cut down to the ground, which didst weaken the nations! 13 For thou hast said in thine heart, I will ascend into heaven, I will exalt my throne above the stars of God: I will sit also upon the mount of the congregation, in the sides of the north: 14 I will ascend above the heights of the clouds; I will be like the most High.

The New World Order is the *earthly objective* of the Mystery of Iniquity.[10] The New World Order is the purpose for which Mystery Babylon exists: to create the spiritual, political, and social environment suitable for the introduction of the Antichrist. Mystery Babylon is the organizational authority of the Mystery of Iniquity in the earth. It insinuates the thinking, the philosophies, and doctrines of Lucifer into every aspect of his earthly dominion. *The devil is looking to create a new kind of sinner for a new kind of world.*

The objective of Satan's world system in every generation since the Fall is the creation of a climate: socially, politically, and most importantly, spiritually that will enable the full implementation of his kingdom aspirations, a kingdom in which he will fulfill his promises to Eve and to all fallen mankind. That final kingdom: its theology, politics and social organization comprise the New World Order.

The New World Order will be a system largely sympathetic to the fallen natures of men and women. The world is philosophically and morally opposed to God. Once Christians who follow the scriptures are excluded from the discussion, everyone else: the ostensibly religious, the ethically sound or the willfully evil, are all opposed to God [Ps 14.1-3]. Their unwillingness to believe the gospel [Jn 3.16-18; 14.6] puts the lie to any claim of sensitivity towards God or identification with His purposes and agenda.[11] The purpose of the New World Order is the creation of a religious state with Lucifer as its deity; in so doing it will also "change times and laws" [Dan 7.25] by loosening the "bands and cords" of morality and by keeping, in a manner of speaking, its promise of the spiritual evolution of the human race.[12]

The New World Order is a non-biblical term which has been used by many to describe a new political order and by others to describe an evolutionary leap by humanity. In its political sense, the phrase has been used by world leaders from diverse political systems.[13] It has been used by leaders such as Mikhail Gorbachev and George H. W. Bush with reference to a new international order. It was popularized in an earlier generation by Adolph Hitler,[14] who publicly proclaimed his intent to establish his own New World Order and by Franklin Roosevelt who promised that the Allied Nations would prevent its establishment.

Earlier in history, the concept was used in connection to the movement to establish an Anglo-American world commonwealth. It was also used to describe the vision of world government sought via the League of Nations during the administration of Woodrow Wilson.[15]

Earlier still, on June 20, 1782, the reverse of the Great Seal of the United States, designed by Charles Thompson, Secretary of the Continental Congress, was adopted by that body. This seal is described as follows:

> "The motto NOVUS ORDO SECLORUM and Date, literally mean "A new order of the ages," but referred to the beginning of a New American era. The date, 1776 in Roman numerals, refers to the year of the Declaration, when the new American era began."[16]

This translation ["a new order of the ages"] of the Latin phrase has been cited in speeches by both Franklin D. Roosevelt[17] and William J. Clinton.[18]

It is likely that this phrase, NOVUS ORDO SECLORUM, has a much earlier origin. In 37 A.D, the Latin poet Vergil wrote his fourth

Eclogue, a pastoral poem which contained this same phrase, suited to his hexameter.

> "Now the last age by Cumae's Sibyl sung
> Has come and gone, and the majestic roll
> **Of circling centuries begins anew**
>   ["magnus ab integro **saeclorum nascitur ordo**"][19]
> Justice returns, returns old Saturn's reign,
> With a new breed of men sent down from heaven.
> Only do thou, at the boy's birth in whom
> The iron shall cease, the golden race arise,
> Befriend him, chaste Lucina; 'tis thine own
> Apollo reigns.[20] (Vergilius n.d.)

Virgil wrote Eclogue 4 about 37 BC; however, the poem refers to the Sibylline Books[21] ["Cumae's Sibyl" or Cumae's Prophetess] that are supposed to have been written prior to 534 B.C. The concept of a child that will be born, who will usher in a new age, a new series of centuries, when the ancient curse is reversed, a new breed of men, a golden race, infiltrates the earth, ruled by that one yet to be born, under the auspices of Saturn and Apollo, is far more ancient than even this.

It is possible that this prophecy, recorded by Vergil, originally uttered by the Sibyl of Cumae[22] is the opposite of the promise made to Eve by God [Gen 3.15]. It could be related to the promise made by Lucifer to Eve [Gen 3.4-5]. Rather than the seed of the woman who would crush the head of the serpent; this is the prophecy of the seed of the serpent, reigning and victorious over the Messiah. The son of Lucifer [Apollo/Saturn] initiates the new order of the ages, he will mitigate the curse and lead the golden race, men sent down from heaven.[23]

When we consider the biblical description of the progression of the Times of the Gentiles [Dan 2; 7], we will discover that the Gentile Age is defined by the pursuit of international dominion by nation-states through violence.[24] It is the stated plan of Lucifer to achieve a consolidated rule of heaven and earth [Isa 14.12-14] and the fulfillment of his promise of godhood to humanity [Gen 3.5]. It is therefore not surprising that fallen men have articulated a vision of a universal World Order. The creation established an earthly dominion [Gen 1.26], delegated to humanity by God, but ruined through sin. God prevented the establishment of a World Order ruled by fallen beings by barring mankind from Eden and the Tree of Life [Gen 2.22-24]. God again prevented a world government and religion at the Tower of Babel [Gen

11]. Since that time each attempt at such a program has failed.

> Acts 17:26 (KJV 1900)
> 26 And hath made of one blood all nations of men for to dwell on all the face of the earth, <u>and hath determined the times before appointed, and the bounds of their habitation</u>;

Lucifer received a limited dominion over the earth because of the fall of mankind in Eden.[25] His effort to establish a universal and permanent hegemony will result in the version of the New World Order which is the subject of this book.

Good and Evil

> Genesis 2:8–9 (KJV 1900)
> 8 And the LORD God planted a garden eastward in Eden; and there he put the man whom he had formed. 9 And out of the ground made the LORD God to grow every tree that is pleasant to the sight, and good for food; the tree of life also in the midst of the garden, and the tree of knowledge of good and evil.

God created a *test* in the Garden of Eden. He created the tree of life, to which the man and the woman had free access. He also created the tree of the knowledge of good and evil, to which He prohibited access by Adam and Eve.

> Genesis 2:16–17 (KJV 1900)
> 16 And the LORD God commanded the man, saying, Of every tree of the garden thou mayest freely eat: 17 But of the tree of the knowledge of good and evil, thou shalt not eat of it: for in the day that thou eatest thereof thou shalt surely die.

Why God created this test is somewhat outside the scope of this book, but Satan, already fallen, was permitted to tempt the first humans regarding this forbidden tree.

Adam and Eve, each for their own reasons [1Tim 2.14], ate the fruit from the tree of the knowledge of good and evil and "their eyes were opened." *From this point forward*, the world has been operated based on a dialectical system that creates opposing concepts whose conflict produces syntheses which drive the world closer to Satan's objective of the New World Order. This is the dynamic of *good and evil* in the world, but the good is not the good that one might think.

There is more than one category of good in the world.

Divine good is that good which is consistent with God's commands. Divine good submits to divine authority and seeks to advance the divine purpose and agenda. For Adam and Eve, divine good was to exercise dominion in the world per God's instructions [Gen 1.26-28] and to avoid the prohibited tree.

There was and is *another* good. This was the good symbolized in the tree of the knowledge of good and evil. This tree was prohibited to mankind for food [Gen 2.17]. To access, understand and practice the good which this tree represented, it was necessary first to transgress the divine command, to say "no" to God. *There is a category of good that cannot be experienced until one has first rejected God.*

The devil is directly associated with this category of good. The devil represented this tree as the key to enlightenment and spiritual evolution [Gen 3.5]. He convinced Eve that there is a good outside of the auspices of God. Adam was not deceived [1 Tim 2.14], but his alternate good was Eve herself and upon that basis, he also disobeyed God.

God did not commend Eve for good intentions. Both she and her husband were condemned to death and the earth itself, their dominion, was overthrown, rendered futile [Rom 8.20-22] and surrendered to a new master.

From that day on, fallen mankind practices a good that excludes God and submission to His will. This *human* good is compatible with the fallen human nature and Satan's operation of his kingdom upon the earth. As in the beginning, Satan continues to sponsor and to advance human good as an integral part of his own world rulership. Consequently, fallen men can show mercy, demonstrate kindness, philanthropy, and filial love all while rejecting God's righteousness and His solution for sin in Jesus Christ.[26]

A great deal of the good in the world has been produced by the obedience of true believers to the Word of God. Nonetheless, there is another good that has also built hospitals, relieved the hungry, clothed the naked and even built Churches and denominations. This latter good is anti-God and anti-Christ despite its motivations, proclamations, and accomplishments.

1 John 5:19[27]

We know that we are of God, and the whole world lies under the sway of the wicked one.

Binary Traps: Dialectical Mind Control

"Dialectic, also called dialectics, originally a form of logical argumentation but now a philosophical concept of evolution applied to diverse fields including thought, nature, and history." [28]

The activation of the "good and evil" [Gen 2.9, 17] paradigm has led to the proliferation of a series of opposing ideas which occupy the minds, talents, and lives of the unbelieving world. Divergent concepts regarding every sphere of life and thought place aggregations of humanity in combating ideological camps, all under the control of the devil. These conflicting concepts exist to promote the evolution of the world towards a New World Order, an objective of Satan in his ancient revolution against God. Once Adam and Eve disobeyed God, it made no difference whether they did it for the good or the evil represented by the tree; the very act of disobedience placed them outside of the will of God.

Satan rules the world by the same tactic through which he gained control of it: [Lk 4.5-7] by manipulating the thinking of mankind. Whatever the ultimate purpose of God regarding the tree of knowledge and whatever secrets it held, it has since the fall of mankind, become the source of the dialectical concept, the binary traps by which the serpent rules the world.

In our context, the binary trap is *the positing of two opposing [or apparently opposing ex.: Good and Evil] concepts where both concepts are antagonistic or irrelevant to the revealed will of God.*

The knowledge of good and evil was of less than zero value to Adam and Eve once they received it. The knowledge promised by the serpent to make them wise and like gods put them under eternal condemnation. There was no formula to be derived from this newfound knowledge of good and evil that would ever deliver them from their disastrous situation. This is the essence of the binary trap as defined here. Neither the good nor the evil of that tree provided any meaningful solutions, only insoluble problems. God has provided revelation to mankind which will lead to our earthly and heavenly security, despite the fall of our first parents. Satan engages the world in speculations in every field of thought that distract mankind from the divine solution, which is relationship to God through Jesus Christ.[29] Satan's world system provides many conflicting social, political, economic, philosophic, and theological ideas which either lead away from God's truth or place the unbeliever upon an intellectual hamster wheel of never-ending inquiry.[30]

2 Timothy 3:7 (KJV 1900)
7 Ever learning, and never able to come to the knowledge of the truth.

Aside from Bible followers, this world is essentially spiritually unified [Eph 2.1-3]. This spiritual unity leads to the observation that *all philosophical variations within Satan's world system serve identical ends*. Reduced to their simplicity, Luciferian metaphysics, epistemology, ethics, politics, aesthetics all boil down to the rejection of God [Lk 4.5-8]. The fact that the thinking of this world occurs in philosophically variegated forms prior to this reduction only exists to deceive the naïve. This does not mean that there is no good or utility in human philosophy, but that the character of that good, when it excludes submission to divine revelation, is human good.

1 John 2:15–16 (KJV 1900)
15 Love not the world, neither the things that are in the world. If any man love the world, the love of the Father is not in him. 16 For all that is in the world, the lust of the flesh, and the lust of the eyes, and the pride of life, is not of the Father, but is of the world.

1 John 4:5–6 (KJV 1900)
5 They are of the world: therefore speak they of the world, and the world heareth them. 6 We are of God: he that knoweth God heareth us; he that is not of God heareth not us. Hereby know we the spirit of truth, and the spirit of error.

Once human good and the limited function of God's righteousness through morality[31] are considered, it may be seen that all philosophies in this world conform to the single objective of the establishment of Lucifer's hegemony. This is inevitable considering the fall of mankind and the status of rebellion under which the world currently resides. Every system of thought in the world that rejects the fundamental right of God to rule *as the scriptures proclaim* that He in fact does, is a part of this rebellion [Ps 2]. Satan's world system is denominated by an innumerable number of systems which may conscientiously and sincerely oppose one another while serving his interests.

This means every philosophical or theological system at variance with scripture fits this criterion. The binary traps may involve social systems, political systems, economic systems, philosophical or theological systems. Systems that apparently oppose one another trap people into futile wrangling that does not ultimately advance God's program.[32] This principle especially applies to religious systems that call themselves Christian but significantly depart from scriptural teachings on the nature of Christ, salvation, the Bible, and the Christian life.

> 2 Corinthians 10:4–5 (KJV 1900)
> 4 (For the weapons of our warfare are not carnal, but mighty through God to the pulling down of strong holds;) 5 Casting down imaginations, and every high thing that exalteth itself against the knowledge of God, and bringing into captivity every thought to the obedience of Christ;

One sphere of spiritual warfare occurs in the realm of ideas. Doctrines and philosophies which acknowledge and extol the God of revelation are opposed by thinking which exalts itself against the God of the Bible. The conflict of these ideas has a decisive impact upon human lives and the course of history. This is the transcendent dialectical tension which will not end in synthesis, but in the unconditional defeat of the devil and the universal and permanent implementation of the Kingdom of God.

> Ephesians 6:12 (KJV 1900)
> 12 For we wrestle not against flesh and blood, but against principalities, against powers, against the rulers of the darkness of this world, against spiritual wickedness in high places.

Lucifer has built into the world system, concepts and logical processes which serve his interests by presenting false spiritual information as truth, making false application of genuine spiritual truth, or by avoiding true spiritual issues altogether. The believer cannot become ensnared in these binary controversies but must recognize that what effects lasting change in the world is the application of the spiritual principles found in the Word of God, the Bible. *True Christians must operate outside the Luciferian paradigm* by believing the gospel and obeying the truths derived from the accurate interpretation of the scriptures [Jn 7.17].

> Ezra 7:10 (KJV 1900)
> 10 For Ezra had prepared his heart to seek the law of the LORD, and to do it, and to teach in Israel statutes and judgments.

> Proverbs 3:5–6 (KJV 1900)
> 5 Trust in the LORD with all thine heart; And lean not unto thine own understanding. 6 In <u>all</u> thy ways acknowledge him, And he shall direct thy paths.

> 2 Timothy 2:15 (KJV 1900)
> 15 Study to shew thyself approved unto God, a workman that needeth not to be ashamed, rightly dividing the word of truth.

Admittedly, this book places a great burden upon the believer to rightly divide the Word of God, the Bible. This however is no greater burden than is placed upon the Christian by God Himself. God is the source of all true information regarding Himself, man, the angels, and the world. He has codified this information in the scriptures. It is only there where one can expose and circumvent the dialectical strategies by which the devil entangles the thinking of the world.

There is no man or combination of men that can outthink, overpower, or out maneuver Satan. Everyone who seeks to fight Satan on his terms ends up serving him, willingly or otherwise. Only God can overcome the devil.

> 1 John 5:4 (KJV 1900)
> 4 For whatsoever is born of God overcometh the world: and this is the victory that overcometh the world, even our faith.

We live in a time where many *believers* are fighting a futile battle against the devil from within the very philosophical constructs that he uses to rule the world. Inevitably, these believers begin to justify sinful and erroneous positions because their belief that their construct is serving the "greater good." Since there is no greater good in disobedience to the scriptures, these believers eventually find themselves under divine discipline, because they felt that the eradication of some real or apparent evil justified partial obedience to God's Word.[33]

Within the *real* world, the devil has constructed a *virtual* world of ideas which is accepted by every unbeliever and quite a few believers. The end of this artificial realm of thought is a very real Antichrist ruling a temporary yet equally real New World Order. It is the Word of God that is the key which deciphers this present darkness and discloses the real world and the Christians' place in it.

Religion, Good and Evil

> "The New World Order is more than a one world political and economic organization. *It is foremost a spiritual power* that has concrete political, economic, and social implications."

Human goodness, as opposed to the good that seeks divine approval by adherence to the scriptures, is of particular danger to the true Church. The ability of fallen man to imitate the true believer in Christ serves Satan's objective of weakening the cause of Christ in the world. Satan's efforts to compromise the true Church via *infiltration* must be considered [2 Cor 11.12-15]. There is a false Church that does good deeds, promotes ethical standards and moral behavior. The false Church can even produce an accurate doctrinal statement, *but it will not follow it*. The Church founded upon human good uses the name of Christ but will not receive him as Savior; they can read the words of scripture, but they cannot assign them their proper significance at a personal level.

Chafer describes the mechanism of Satanic deception:

> "It is evident that this partial concession of the world to the testimony of God has opened the way for counterfeit systems of truth, which, according to prophecy, are the last and most to be dreaded methods in the Satanic warfare. In this connection it must be conceded that Satan has really granted nothing from his own position, even though he be forced to acknowledge every principle of truth save that upon which salvation depends. Rather is he advantaged by such a concession; for the value and delusion of a counterfeit lies in its greatest likeness to the real. By advocating much truth, in the form of a counterfeit system of truth, Satan can satisfy all the external religious cravings of the world, and yet accomplish his own end by withholding that on which man's only hope depends. It is, therefore, no longer safe to blindly subscribe to that which promises general good, simply because it is good, and is garnished with the teachings of Scripture; for good has ceased to be all on one side and evil all on the other. In fact, that which is evil in purpose has gradually

appropriated the good until but one issue distinguishes them. Part-truth-ism has come into terrible and final conflict with whole-truth-ism, and woe to the soul that does not discern between them."[34]

This is how false Churches and false ministers can persuasively imitate true Christianity while opposing it. Part-truth-ism can be implemented in a variety of ways. One way is by presenting the genuine truths of scripture as articles of faith and then subtly contradicting them by the surreptitious introduction of other doctrines or practices.

Jude 4 (KJV 1900)
4 For there are certain men crept in unawares, who were before of old ordained to this condemnation, ungodly men, turning the grace of our God into lasciviousness, and denying the only Lord God, and our Lord Jesus Christ.

For example, alongside a stated belief in *the Trinity*, there often exists teaching which emphasizes a practical inequality in the Godhead which favors the Holy Spirit. This imbalance redefines Christ,[35] invalidating the gospel. A purported belief in the *inerrancy of scripture* is offset by a belief that the words of men have the power to create reality. This elevation of human speech devalues God's speech in the Bible. The profession of *the Church as the spiritual body of Christ* is undermined by the practice of ecumenism,[36] which includes unbelievers within the fellowship of believers. The believer's spiritual fellowship with God is predicated upon obedience to the scriptures. Believers are not free to design their own discipleship to which God must adjust.

Because of the infiltration of human good into Christendom[37], there is diminished respect for the authority of the scriptures. There is a widespread belief that the Bible is a source of *relative* truth subject to differing yet equally valid personal interpretations.[38] Each category of theology, beginning with Christology, has been undermined with the intent of replacing the true Church with a counterfeit Christianity. This apostate body, an ecumenical monstrosity consisting of every flavor of unbelief, will be the *initial* spiritual vehicle[39] that enables the appearance and success of the Antichrist. God Himself will, in judgment, assist with the deadly momentum of this doomed evolution of visible Christianity.

2 Thessalonians 2:8–12 (KJV 1900)
8 And then shall that Wicked be revealed, whom the Lord shall

consume with the spirit of his mouth, and shall destroy with the brightness of his coming: 9 Even him, whose coming is after the working of Satan with all power and signs and lying wonders, 10 And with all deceivableness of unrighteousness in them that perish; because they received not the love of the truth, that they might be saved. 11 <u>And for this cause God shall send them strong delusion, that they should believe a lie</u>: 12 That they all might be damned who believed not the truth, but had pleasure in unrighteousness. [Rom 1.28]

The New World Order is more than a one world political and economic organization. It is *foremost* a *spiritual* power that has concrete political, economic, and social implications. The historical trends which will produce conditions favorable to the appearance of the Man of Sin are simultaneously manufacturing a new kind of sinner designed to participate in his New World Order.

The Emergence of the Antichrist

Despite the worldwide, age-spanning efforts to bring the New World Order into existence, the actual emergence of it or its sovereign, the Antichrist, cannot occur until the primary spiritual obstacle blocking his appearance is removed. That obstacle is the Church, the Body of Christ.[40]

The Body of Christ,[41] the Church Universal, is the assembly of elect persons saved from Pentecost to the resurrection [Rapture][42] of the Church. The Body of Christ is formed by means of the baptism of the Holy Spirit [1 Cor 12.13][43] the spiritual action whereby the believer is incorporated in the spiritual body of Christ *at the moment of faith* in the gospel. God has identified Christ with the Church by the creation of a spiritual body with Christ as its head [Jn 14.20; Eph 5.23; Col 1.18]. The believer is made one with Christ resulting in the intensification of the many benefits of the cross and a position above the elect of other ages. Through this body, Christ is present and functioning throughout the world in every historical era since the coming of the Spirit at Pentecost.

It is because of this powerful presence that the Antichrist has not yet emerged [2 Th 2.1-7]. God is in control of the timing of the appearance of this man upon the stage of history. In the meanwhile, the devil is busy ordering his kingdom to waste no time when that moment arrives.

The Bible indicates that the body of Christ, the Church will be victorious.[44] However, that does not mean that **your** *local church* will experience that victory or survive at all. That survival is based upon your ability to distinguish true and false doctrine, your willingness to take actions to obey truth and to separate from erroneous teaching, individuals, and movements [1 Jn 4.6]. There are many Churches that know sound doctrine but are unwilling to separate from error. God will not bless spiritual compromise because we are faithful in other areas. The great king Jehoshaphat possessed very sound doctrine and did many things pleasing to the Lord, but God did not wink at his alliance with the idolater Ahab:

2 Chronicles 19:1–2 (KJV 1900)

1 And Jehoshaphat the king of Judah returned to his house in peace to Jerusalem. 2 And Jehu the son of Hanani the seer went out to meet him, and said to king Jehoshaphat, Shouldest thou help the ungodly, and love them that hate the LORD? therefore is wrath upon thee from before the LORD.

4
Book One: Who Is The Antichrist?

Definitions

> "It is the incarnation of Jesus which generally serves as the demarcation of the last days. There cannot be "many antichrists" until first there is the true Christ. It is the supernatural birth, ministry, death, resurrection, and ascension of Jesus Christ to which the devil is responding by the release of these antichrists into the world."

The writers of the New Testament agree that we are living in the latter times, the last hour, the critical season before God finally resolves the issue of sin in the world by His return.

> 1 John 2:18–22 (KJV 1900)
> 18 Little children, it is the last time: and as ye have heard that antichrist shall come, even now are there many antichrists; whereby we know that it is the last time. 19 They went out from us, but they were not of us; for if they had been of us, they would no doubt have continued with us: but they went out, that they might be made manifest that they were not all of us. 20 But ye have an unction from the Holy One, and ye know all things. 21 I have not written unto you because ye know not the truth, but because ye know it, and that no lie is of the truth. 22 Who is a liar but he that denieth that Jesus is the Christ? He is antichrist, that denieth the Father and the Son.

What is the "Last Time [Last Hour]"

> 1 John 2:18 (KJV 1900)
> 18 Little children, it is the last time: and as ye have heard that antichrist shall come, even now are there many antichrists; whereby we know that it is the last time.

John considered his time the beginning of the last time or hour.[45] It is likely that he marked time in this way because the first advent of Jesus signaled the beginning of the final dispensation of God's mercy upon sinful man prior to the beginning of judgment. Jesus is the Eschatological Man, the Last Adam; his coming to pay for sins is the beginning of the end of God's dealings with sin and evil. We now live in a time when the gospel of the grace of God is being proclaimed around the world. This age will end with the Rapture of the Church and the divine judgment of the earth will commence.

This critical season was in progress at the time of John's writing. This season is one of intensified spiritual warfare, proven by the appearance of "many antichrists."

It is the incarnation of Jesus which generally serves as the demarcation of the last days. There cannot be "many antichrists" until first there is the true Christ. It is the supernatural birth, ministry, death, resurrection, and ascension of Jesus Christ to which the devil is responding by the release of these antichrists into the world.

> 1 Timothy 3:16 (KJV 1900)
> 16 And without controversy great is the mystery of godliness: God was manifest in the flesh, justified in the Spirit, seen of angels, preached unto the Gentiles, believed on in the world, received up into glory.

Jesus is the fulfillment of God's promise to the woman Eve [Gen 3.15], the Seed of his covenant with Abraham [Gal 3.16], the prophet, like unto Moses [Dt 18.18], the Suffering Servant proclaimed by Isaiah [Isa 53], Messiah the prince, mathematically predicted by Daniel [Dan 9.25], the King that John the Baptist preached would baptize the world with the Holy Ghost or with Fire [Mt 3.11]. As such he is the Pivot upon which all history turns.

The arrival of Jesus into history from eternity was a strategic event, a statement regarding the future of evil and its champion, the devil.

> 1 John 3:8 (KJV 1900)
> 8 He that committeth sin is of the devil; for the devil sinneth from the beginning. For this purpose the Son of God was manifested, 46 that he

might destroy the works of the devil.

Hebrews 2:14 (KJV 1900)
14 Forasmuch then as the children are partakers of flesh and blood, he also himself likewise took part of the same; that through death he might destroy him that had the power of death, that is, the devil;

In this, the last hour, Jesus is not seeking to compromise or to dialogue with the devil, but to destroy both him and his works.

In view of this latest advance of Christ's program and the fact that it signifies the coming terminus of God's dealings with the devil, it is not surprising that Satan would launch his greatest offensive at this time. In this last hour, Lucifer has flooded the world with antichrists. John says that this multitude of antichrists corroborates the testimony of God in Christ that these are the last days.

Antichrist and "many antichrists"

1 John 2:18 (KJV 1900)
18 Little children, it is the last time: and as ye have heard that antichrist shall come, even <u>now</u> are there many antichrists; whereby we know that it is the last time.

The Last hour [time] is further clarified by the word *Now*. The last hour is a critical season which is unfolding at the time of John's writing.

In this verse the person of Antichrist is contrasted with the plural, antichrists. His readers had been taught ["as ye have heard"] about the doctrine of the last days and the appearance of the Antichrist, whom we will define and describe shortly. This Antichrist will appear at the end of the age[47] and his coming will signal the nearness of the return of Christ.

However, right *Now*, at the time of John's writing, there existed many antichrists. This appearance of many versions of the coming Antichrist pointed to the fact that the Last Hour was upon them. Just as Christ's appearance marked the beginning of the last days, so the appearance of junior grade antichrists confirms the same. Within the phrase "whereby we know" the word "know" [NT: 1097] *ginosko*, means to know by personal experience. The believers did not only know abstractly that there would be many antichrists, but these antichrists were right there, in their midst, as we will soon see.

Antichrist and the New World Order

Definition of Antichrist

Before we can go further, we need to define the term Antichrist.

> **"Antichrist"** 53.83 ἀντίχριστος, ου m: one who is opposed to Christ, in the sense of usurping the role of Christ—'antichrist.'[48]

> **"Antichrist"** 532 ἀντίχριστος (antichristos), ου (ou), ὁ (ho): n.masc.; ≡ Str 500; TDNT 9.493—LN 53.83 antichrist, one who opposes Christ, implying the usurping of Christ and his position 1Jn 2:18(2×), 22; 4:3; 2Jn 7+[49] (Swanson 1997)

> **"anti"** 473 ἀντί [anti /an·tee/] prep. A primary particle; TDNT 1:372; TDNTA 61; GK 505; 22 occurrences; AV translates as "for" 15 times, "because + 3639" four times, "for ... cause" once, "therefore + 3639" once, and "in the room of" once. 1 over against, opposite to, before. 2 for, instead of, in place of (something). 2A instead of. 2B for. 2C for that, because. 2D wherefore, for this cause.[50] (Strong 1995)

> **"Christ"** 53.82 Χριστός a, οῦ m; Μεσσίας, ου m: (literally 'one who has been anointed') in the NT, titles for Jesus as the Messiah—'Christ, Messiah' (but in many contexts, and especially without an article, Χριστός becomes a part of the name of Jesus; see 93.387)[51]

Anti means "against" but it also means "instead of." *Christ* is the prophesied Messiah [Isa 53; Dan 9.25-26] sent from the Father to redeem mankind [Isa 53.6; 1 Pet 3.18]. The Antichrist is one who is both opposed to Christ as well as one who seeks to usurp Christ's place.[52] The word Antichrist appears only in 1 and 2 John, but this person is identified directly as well as by allusion and type throughout the Old and New Testaments. For example:

> ➤ In Daniel he is the little "horn" (Dan 7:8); "the prince who is to come" (9:26); the willful king (11:36).
> ➤ Paul refers to the Antichrist as the Man of Sin and the Son of Perdition (2 Th 2).
> ➤ John names him Antichrist, and the Beast (1 Jn 2; 2 Jn 7, Rev 13).

The Antichrist is a person who will appear at the end of the age, prior to the second coming of Christ.

We will demonstrate in the coming chapters that, in addition to his other activities, the Antichrist will consolidate worldwide political power[53] and will convince many of the Jews that he is their Messiah.[54] Having achieved power and the trust of the world, he will reveal his true character, his commitment to Lucifer and his desire to receive worship from men on behalf of the devil.

He will then rapidly proceed to establish a spiritual and political kingdom upon the earth, based upon overtly Luciferian principles.

Satan's intent to unseat Christ [Isa 14:12-14] will ultimately necessitate the genocide of the Jews[55] to prevent God from fulfilling his unconditional promises made to Abraham[56] and to David.[57]

After a brief period of spectacular success, Antichrist and his False Prophet will be cast into the Lake of Fire at the return of Christ to the earth [Rev 19.11-16].

Antichrist Promotes a Lie:

1 John 2.22

1 John 2:22 (KJV 1900)
22 Who is a liar [NT 5583] but <u>he that denieth that Jesus is the Christ?
He is antichrist</u>, that denieth the Father and the Son.

The apostle John distinguishes The Antichrist, that person to be revealed at the end of the age, from the many antichrists in the world at the time of his writing, or "Now." If there were antichrists in John's time, then we can be sure that there are antichrists in the world today. There are persons and institutions in the world today that approximate the end-time Antichrist, in that they share his *objectives*, execute his *agenda*, and partake of his demonic *power*. In this sense they share the spirit of his enterprise, the spirit of Antichrist.

John says that an antichrist is a liar *because he denies that Jesus is the Christ*.

If the individual in question simply was *mistaken* regarding Christ, he would be ignorant, he would be incorrect, but he would not be a liar. To be a liar, the person would have to *know* the truth but tell a falsehood instead.

> "**Liar**" 5583 ψεύστης [pseustes /psyoos·tace/] n m. From 5574; TDNT 9:594; TDNTA 1339; GK 6026; 10 occurrences; AV translates as "liar" 10 times. 1 a liar. 2 one who breaks faith. 3 a false and faithless man.[58]

Lucifer, who is the god of the Antichrist, certainly broke faith when he became the adversary of God. So, if an antichrist is a liar, it means that it is his aim to intentionally deceive. This is important to remember. An antichrist attempts to deceive others into believing something about Christ that is not true. *Therefore, an antichrist will attempt to gain trust by appearing to be something that he is not.*

Antichrist and the New World Order

2 Corinthians 11:13–14 (KJV 1900)
13 For such are false apostles, deceitful workers, transforming themselves into the apostles of Christ. 14 And no marvel; for Satan himself is transformed into an angel of light.

> - *Jesus* is the prophesied king of Israel, who will fulfill God's covenants to His people, [Matt 2.2; 27.11]
> - *Jesus* is the High Priest after the order of Melchizedek who provided eternal salvation through his own blood [Heb 6.20; 9:12]
> - *Jesus* is the King of Kings and Lord of Lords who will return to the earth to vindicate his people, to judge His enemies and to rule from the throne of David with a rod of iron for 1000 years [Rev 19.16; 20.4]
> - *Jesus* is the Theanthropic Person possessing two natures in one divine Person forever. Jesus is the second person of the Godhead, equal with the Father and Spirit in eternality, in power, in righteousness as in all of His essence. [John 10:30-33; Titus 2.13]

2 Peter 2:1 (KJV 1900)
1 But there were false prophets also among the people, even as there shall be false teachers among you, who privily shall bring in damnable heresies, even denying the Lord that bought them, and bring upon themselves swift destruction.

Matthew 7:15 (KJV 1900)
15 Beware of false prophets, which come to you in sheep's clothing, but inwardly they are ravening wolves.

1 John 2:22 (KJV 1900)
22 Who is a liar but he that denieth that Jesus is the Christ? He is antichrist, that denieth the Father and the Son.

An antichrist denies that Jesus is the Christ. The "Christ" is the "Anointed One," referring to the anointing received by priests and kings, which recognized a special divine calling and empowerment. For Jesus, the Second Person of the Godhead, incarnated as the union of undiminished Deity and perfect humanity, the anointing represented His special election from the Father to become the Savior of mankind via his death and resurrection.

Luke 4:18 (KJV 1900)
18 The Spirit of the Lord is upon me, because he hath anointed me to preach the gospel to the poor; he hath sent me to heal the brokenhearted, to preach deliverance to the captives, and recovering of sight to the blind, to set at liberty them that are bruised,

Acts 10:38 (KJV 1900)
38 How God anointed Jesus of Nazareth with the Holy Ghost and with power: who went about doing good, and healing all that were oppressed of the devil; for God was with him.

These antichrists, because they deny the deity of Christ, also deny the Trinity and by this deny the Father as well

John 10:30 (KJV 1900)
30 I and my Father are one.

The antichrist denies all these assertions about Christ. He claims through subtlety and deception that Jesus is not who He claims to be, and this is: "***The Lie***".

1 John 4:1–3 (KJV 1900)
1 Beloved, believe not every spirit, but try the spirits whether they are of God: because many false prophets are gone out into the world. 2 Hereby know ye the Spirit of God: Every spirit that confesseth that Jesus Christ is come in the flesh is of God: 3 And every spirit that

<u>confesseth not that Jesus Christ is come in the flesh</u> is not of God: and <u>this is that spirit of antichrist</u>, whereof ye have heard that it should come; and even now already is it in the world.

Specifically, what is the lie that defines the spirit of Antichrist?

"The Lie" is that Jesus is not God. The devil is willing to admit that Jesus is a lot of things, but God is not one of them. We are not saying that the devil does not *know* that there is a God, nor that he does not understand, as much as is possible with creatures, what God is. The devil will lie to man and to other angels regarding the *identity* of God, he will misrepresent what God says about Himself in scripture, and this is what makes both he and the antichrists whom he has spawned to be liars.

This lie appears to have been introduced in eternity past by Satan to the angelic hosts [Eze 28.11-18]. It was first communicated by him to mankind in the Garden of Eden. Satan suggested to Eve that God had lied to her about the Tree of Knowledge and the consequences of eating from it. In so doing, he implied that God was not the Holy Being that He represented Himself as being.

Genesis 3:1–5 (KJV 1900)
1 Now the serpent was more subtil than any beast of the field which the LORD God had made. And he said unto the woman, Yea, hath God said, Ye shall not eat of every tree of the garden? 2 And the woman said unto the serpent, We may eat of the fruit of the trees of the garden: 3 But of the fruit of the tree which is in the midst of the garden, God hath said, Ye shall not eat of it, neither shall ye touch it, lest ye die. 4 And the serpent said unto the woman, Ye shall not surely die: 5 For God doth know that in the day ye eat thereof, then your eyes shall be opened, and ye shall be as gods, knowing good and evil.

The Lie can be seen at work today in the cults, the defining characteristic of which is their adherence to one of the following two positions:

Either Jesus is not God
or
Jesus and somebody else [outside the Trinity] are God.

In either case, Jesus is not what He claims to be, the Second Person of the Godhead, one with God, sharing the same essence and substance, exercising the same holiness, power, eternality, and prerogatives of the

Almighty.

John associates the spirit of antichrist with false teachers [1 Jn 4.1-3]. In the Bible, false teachers and false prophets are known by their manipulation of the truth of scripture. As in eternity past among the fallen angels and later in the Garden of Eden, a chief activity of the devil is the corruption of the Word of God. The objective in this enterprise is the propagation of the Lie.

The devil attempts to occupy the *transmission points* of the Word of God to accomplish his work of denying Christ. Just as the serpent insinuated himself between God and the woman as a transmitter and interpreter of the Word of God, the antichrists of our time secretly set themselves in the room of the professors, pastors, Bible translators and interpreters of the scriptures.

2 Corinthians 11:13–14 (KJV 1900)
13 For such are false apostles, deceitful workers, transforming themselves into the apostles of Christ. 14 And no marvel; for Satan himself is transformed into an angel of light.

An antichrist "denieth that Jesus is the Christ" [1Jn 2.22].

The devil and his representatives claim that the historical Jesus was not the *Christos*, the "Anointed One" promised by the Father in the Old Testament, was not God made flesh by means of the miraculous virgin conception[59] and birth of Christ [Lk 1.26-38]. To an antichrist, Jesus may have been a very special Jew, a great prophet, a moral leader, or an imposter who was born of fornication (as implied by the Jews in John 8.41), but he was not the Christos, the God-Man about which Isaiah wrote:

Isaiah 9:6–7 (KJV 1900)
6 For unto us a child is born, unto us a son is given: And the government shall be upon his shoulder: And his name shall be called Wonderful, Counseller, The mighty God, The everlasting Father, The prince of Peace. 7 Of the increase of his government and peace there shall be no end, Upon the throne of David, and upon his kingdom, To order it, and to establish it with judgment and with justice From henceforth even for ever. The zeal of the LORD of hosts will perform this.

The entire Bible testifies to a King who would descend from David yet possess divine authority as evidenced in his ability to decisively resolve the sins of His people, deliver them from their enemies and write his words upon their hearts.

- ➤ Daniel forecast the time of the presentation of Messiah the prince [Dan 9.25],
- ➤ King Ahaz of Judah was given a prediction that a virgin would give birth to a child whose name would mean "God with us" [Isa 7.1-16].
- ➤ God promised King David a Son who would establish his kingdom and throne *forever* [2 Sam 7.14-16]
- ➤ Jesus identified Himself as the eternal Son and Lord of David [Mt 22.41-46]

In the 4th chapter of Matthew Jesus begins to present himself as the Messiah, the Christ, and he continued to do so until his crucifixion. Jesus was finally crucified because he claimed to be the Messiah, the Christ predicted in the Old Testament scriptures:

Matthew 26:63–66 (KJV 1900)
63 But Jesus held his peace. And the high priest answered and said unto him, I adjure thee by the living God, that thou tell us whether thou be the Christ, the Son of God. 64 Jesus saith unto him, Thou hast said: nevertheless I say unto you, Hereafter shall ye see the Son of man sitting on the right hand of power,60 and coming in the clouds of heaven. 65 Then the high priest rent his clothes, saying, He hath spoken blasphemy; what further need have we of witnesses? behold, now ye have heard his blasphemy. 66 What think ye? They answered and said, He is guilty of death. [Jn 10.31-33]

1 John 4.3

Again, an antichrist "denieth that Jesus is the Christ."[61]

1 John 4:3 (KJV 1900)
3 And every spirit that confesseth not that Jesus Christ is come in the flesh is not of God: and this is that spirit of antichrist, whereof ye have heard that it should come; and even now already is it in the world.

The antichrists who precede *the* Antichrist are those operating in the sphere of the spirit of the Antichrist. This spirit was present in the world during the first century when 1 John was written, and it is the spirit of the present age.
There are a variety of ways that a person can represent the spirit of Antichrist:

By teaching that Jesus is not God.

Jesus was crucified because of his claim to be the Messiah. This is the most offensive truth to Lucifer. Just as all of history revolves on the central theme of the glory of God, the central feature of the spirit of antichrist is the denial of that glory and giving it to another who would be God.

> Isaiah 42:8 (KJV 1900)
> 8 I am the LORD: that is my name: And my glory will I not give to another, Neither my praise to graven images.

> Isaiah 47:8 (KJV 1900)
> 8 Therefore hear now this, thou that art given to pleasures, that dwellest carelessly, That sayest in thine heart, I am, and none else beside me; I shall not sit as a widow, neither shall I know the loss of children:

By denying the Trinity.

If there is no Trinity, then we do not know who exactly Jesus was. If Jesus is not equal to the Father, who then was Jesus? An antichrist will allow Christ to be God Jr. but not El Shaddai; a Jewish Prophet, but not the Eternal King of the Jews, a moral leader but not the Righteous Judge.

By killing and attempting to kill the apostles of the first century and disciples of every generation, down to this very day, who proclaim that Jesus is the Christ

> Revelation 17:6 (KJV 1900)
> 6 And I saw the woman drunken with the blood of the saints, and with the blood of the martyrs of Jesus: and when I saw her, I wondered with great admiration.

A great deal of the killing of believers in Jesus Christ is not reported or is reported as killing under another cause or motivation. This is because Satan does not wish to disclose his proxies performing Christian genocide unless it serves his purposes to reveal them.

By changing Bible manuscripts so that they do not consistently proclaim that Jesus is the Christ. The unifying principle, aside from their scant manuscript tradition, of the new translations of the 20th century is the weakening of the concept of the deity of Christ, and the Trinity.[62]

The 200+ English translations[63] produced in the past 200 years create confusion as to what exactly is the Word of God. Today's Bibles are shorter than the King James because of the passages that are truncated or omitted altogether. [e.g., Matthew 17:21; 18:11; 23:14; Mark 7:16; 9:44, 46; 11:26; 15:28; Luke 17:36; 23:17; John. 5:4; Acts 8:37; 15:34; 24:7; 28:29; Romans 16:24; 1 John 5:7.] The new translations omit portions of hundreds of other verses.

By training Bible teachers and preachers not to proclaim the scandal of the Gospel, because it is exclusive and therefore contrary to the ecumenical spirit of the age, or because you cannot grow your Church that way.

Seminaries and Bible colleges are infiltrated with men who do not believe in the inspiration of the scriptures and feel free to teach destructive heresies.[64] Scholars are joining academic societies that no longer support the inerrancy of the scriptures. Pastors are becoming part of ecumenical associations where the gospel cannot be proclaimed because it offends those who belong to gospel denying religions. The Church Growth movement has as its primary goal the attraction and maintenance of Church attendance. The weakening of the authority of the scriptures can accelerate new member growth and decrease membership loss. *Numeric growth and the desire to see the lost receive the gospel are two entirely different motivations.* The dilution of the Word of God promotes numeric growth while obstructing gospel proclamation.

By the outright denial of the work of the Cross which is the chief work of the Messiah [Isa 53]. By denying faith in Christ as the perfect and sole substitute for our sins, a person or group operates in the spirit of Antichrist.

Nationally known pastors are publicly [on NPR[65], Larry King[66] and other news shows] claiming that they do not know who will be saved and who will be lost when it comes to non-Christian religions. Others are saying that all will be saved, regardless of what they believe.[67]

2 John 7

2 John 7 (KJV 1900)
7 For <u>many deceivers</u>[68] are entered into the world, who confess not that Jesus Christ is come in the flesh. This is a <u>deceiver and an antichrist</u>.

Deceiver: This word is also found in 2 Tim 4.1 (seducing)

1 Timothy 4:1 (KJV 1900) 1 Now the Spirit speaketh expressly, that in the latter times some shall depart from the faith, giving heed to <u>seducing

spirits, and doctrines of devils;

The word *deceiver* refers to the army of false teachers that characterize the "latter times." as well as the demonic spirit [*seducing spirit*] that animates them. Thus, there is a correspondence between the legions of antichrists ["many deceivers" 2 John 7] that are already present in John's day and the demonized false teachers that Paul predicted in 1 Timothy 4. Both groups are unsaved,[69] practice deception to advance demonic doctrines, both groups pass themselves off as legitimate believers, both operate in the spirit of antichrist.

The word "confess"[70] in 2 Jn 7 is the same word as in 1 John 1.9 "If we *confess* our sins". The word means to confess, to acknowledge, to say the same thing as. It is the opposite of "to deny." The true servant of Christ confesses Him to be who He actually is, out loud, clearly, accurately and frequently.

Romans 10:9 (KJV 1900)
9 That if thou shalt confess with thy mouth the Lord Jesus, and shalt believe in thine heart that God hath raised him from the dead, thou shalt be saved.

The *deceiver* is one who represents himself as something that he is not. The reason he does this is to promote a lie. That lie is that Jesus is not God, and not the Messiah.

2 John 7 (KJV 1900)
7 For many deceivers are entered into the world, <u>who confess not that Jesus Christ is come in the flesh</u>. This is a deceiver and an antichrist.

The antichrist/deceiver denies Christ *but does not appear to do so*. One of the synonyms for deceiver [NT:4108] is *seducer*. The English definition for the word seducer is as follows:

> "1: to persuade to disobedience or disloyalty 2: to lead astray usually by persuasion or false promises"[71]

The *seducer* has as his objective the corruption of another person. Lies are his method, beginning with the impersonation of a trustworthy individual. The seducing spirit promises something that someone wants and uses that promise to get what he wants.

This is the strategy used with Eve in the garden of Eden, the promise: "ye shall be as gods."

It is critical that we understand this concept of deception as it is at work today. Most people get caught up in appearances: the attractiveness of the teacher, his teaching style, his personality, his academic credentials, the books he has written, the size of the ministry, the music, the social life of the Church; and fail to listen closely to what the teacher is saying.

This is how spiritual deception occurs. Because of a suggestion by the devil's surrogate [the serpent] that God might not be who He said He was, Eve was evicted from the garden, spiritually dead, living in a corrupted body, a corrupted marriage, and a corrupted world, mourning a murdered son.[72]

Do not allow spiritual laziness to cost you your spiritual destiny, or perhaps even send you to hell if you are not born again. Pay attention to what the preacher is saying. Check what is being said against the Bible. Ask questions: what does this Church believe? Do not accept vague answers and over-summarized doctrinal statements. Does the Church follow what it claims to believe? *A theology that is not obeyed is a theology that is not believed.*

Pay attention to your prayer life and listen to what God is telling you in your daily Bible reading.

Stop looking for social life and entertainment in the Church. The Lord has not called any true man of God to entertain you and keep you excited. Accurate Bible teaching is not always exciting.

The Antichrist of the tribulation will have the same mission of deception as his assistants today: he will come onto the scene as a statesman and as a peacemaker, when his true objective is slavery and genocide.[73] He will represent himself as the Messiah of the Jews, while he calumniates the true God.

In like manner, the many antichrists of today of whom John spoke represent themselves as believers and as teachers of the Word, when their objective is to misrepresent Christ, and to prepare the way for their master, the Antichrist. Many are being led astray today as they will be in the future.

Where Do Antichrists [small "a"] Come From?

1 John 2:18–22 (KJV 1900)
18 Little children, it is the last time: and as ye have heard that antichrist shall come, <u>even now are there many antichrists</u>; whereby we know that it is the last time. 19 <u>They went out from us</u>, but they were not of us; for if they had been of us, they would no doubt have continued with us: but they went out, that they might be made manifest that they were not all of us. 20 But ye have an unction from the Holy One, and ye know all things. 21 I have not written unto you because ye know not the truth, but because ye know it, and that no lie is of the truth. 22 Who is a liar but he that denieth that Jesus is the Christ? He is antichrist, that denieth

the Father and the Son.

John identifies the antichrists [with a small a] as *originating in the [local] Church*. Thus, the devil is attacking the Church from within, planting the unsaved like tares [Mt 13.24sq.] who incubate in the assembly and are spawned upon the world trained to deceive the elect and to pervert good morals by the corruption of the truth.

Matthew 13:24–30 (KJV 1900)
24 Another parable put he forth unto them, saying, The kingdom of heaven is likened unto a man which sowed good seed in his field: 25 But while men slept, his enemy came and sowed tares among the wheat, and went his way. 26 But when the blade was sprung up, and brought forth fruit, then appeared the tares also. 27 So the servants of the householder came and said unto him, Sir, didst not thou sow good seed in thy field? from whence then hath it tares? 28 He said unto them, An enemy hath done this. The servants said unto him, Wilt thou then that we go and gather them up? 29 But he said, Nay; lest while ye gather up the tares, ye root up also the wheat with them. 30 Let both grow together until the harvest: and in the time of harvest I will say to the reapers, Gather ye together first the tares, and bind them in bundles to burn them: but gather the wheat into my barn.

The parable of the tares is a parable of the Mysteries of the Kingdom of Heaven [Mt 13.1-53]. These are seven parables given by Jesus in Matthew 13 that describe the period between the two Advents of Christ.[74] This time frame includes Christendom as well as the period known as the Tribulation.[75]

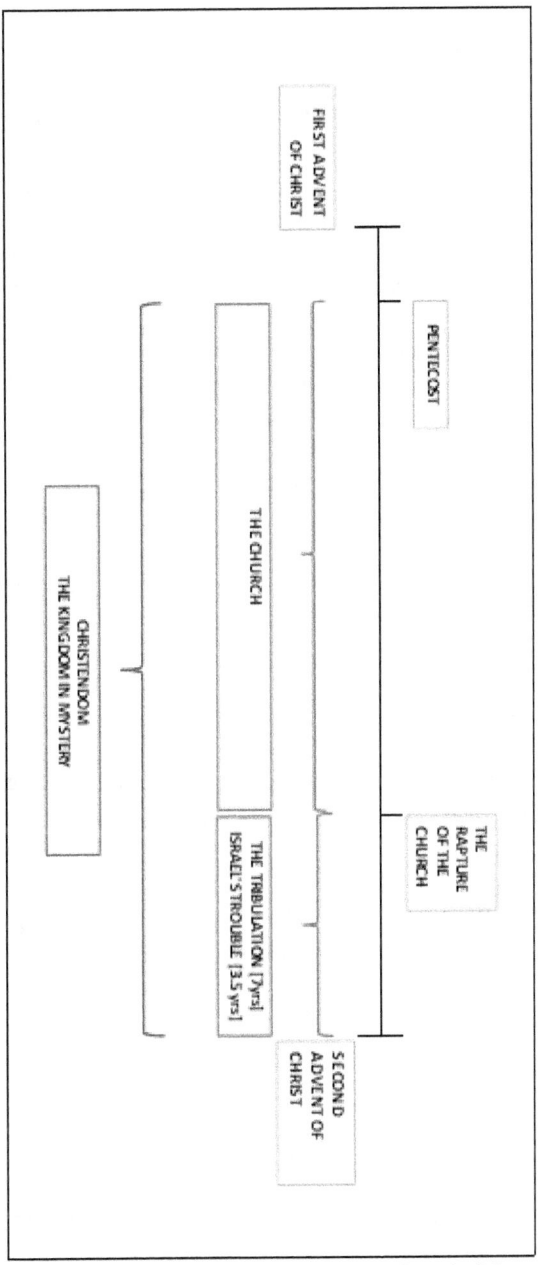

Figure 1: Christendom and the Kingdom in Mystery

From the standpoint of Christendom,[76] the world is populated by both false professors of Christ [tares] and true believers, the true Church which is the called-out body of believers from the first Pentecost following Jesus' ascension to the translation of the Church, known as the Rapture.[77] Christendom includes the Church, but is much larger than it. Christendom is the entire realm of Christian profession. It consists of all those who claim to be believers in Christ, regardless of their true spiritual identity. Thus, we see the seed of the Word of God falling on good as well as non-productive ground [Mt 13.3 sq.], we see tares which look like good grain but are not [Mt 13.24 sq.],[78] good meal and leaven [Mt 13.33 sq.], good fish and bad fish [Mt 13.47 sq.].

These parables describe the characteristics of the current age. It is an age where the spiritual Body of Christ, the Church, is being called out of the world via the new birth [Jn 3.7]. It is also an age of intensified spiritual conflict by those who have infiltrated the assemblies of believers yet serve another master ["an enemy hath done this" v28]. There are many who are masquerading as Christians ["tares"]: as pastors, evangelists, missionaries, seminary professors and regular Church members. It is the secret intent of these "tares" to subvert the work of Christ by maligning His name and by causing the malfunction of His Church. The scriptures speak of these imposters in many places.[79]

Therefore, the "tares," the emergence and proliferation of antichrists [and others opposed to Christ] is consistent with the character of this age, specifically, the resistance of the devil to the appearance of Jesus Christ, which marked the final state of the ancient spiritual conflict which will end with the return of Christ and the final incarceration of all the rebels, angelic and human, in the Lake of Fire ["Gather ye together first the tares, and bind them in bundles to burn them" v30].

The principle of spiritual conflict orchestrated by satanic agents within the local church is proclaimed throughout the Bible.

2 Corinthians 11:13–15 (KJV 1900)
13 For such are false apostles, deceitful workers, transforming themselves into the apostles of Christ. 14 And no marvel; for Satan himself is transformed into an angel of light. 15 Therefore it is no great thing if his ministers also be transformed as the ministers of righteousness; whose end shall be according to their works.

Acts 20:29–30 (KJV 1900)
29 For I know this, that after my departing shall grievous wolves enter in among you, not sparing the flock. 30 Also of your own selves shall

men arise, speaking perverse things, to draw away disciples after them.

Within the local church are "antichrists in training," who are studying the Christian and the Church.

This is the reason why a softening of the gospel and a diminishing of honest and fearless Bible teaching is a great disservice to believers and to the community at large. Frequent, accurate, systematic biblical teaching [FAST], would result in the expulsion of these antichrists into the world where they could be exposed not merely as disgruntled Christians, but as antichrists. The apostle Paul diminished the influence of these persons in the Church in Ephesus by his teaching and preaching. John had to preach them out of this Church again when he ministered there.

John says that the departure of these persons from the Church provided the opportunity for them to be manifest as antichrists.

> 1 Jn 2.19b
> "but they went out, that they might be made manifest[80] that they were not all of us"

> 1 Corinthians 11:19 (KJV 1900)
> 19 For there must be also heresies among you, that they which are approved may be made manifest among you.

Once separated, the true saints discover that these persons are dangerous, and the excluded persons themselves, having been branded as heretics, now have the opportunity to be truly saved. Unfortunately, much of today's preaching and teaching is creating a comfortable cocoon, a vacation condominium for false teachers and antichrists who await their time to advance to bigger and greater things for the devil-after they have destroyed your Church, of course.

Some Facts About Mature Disciples

> 1 John 2:18–20 (KJV 1900)
> 18 Little children, it is the last time: and as ye have heard that antichrist shall come, even now are there many antichrists; whereby we know that it is the last time. 19 They went out from us, but they were not of us; for if they had been of us, they would no doubt have continued with us: but they went out, that they might be made manifest that they were not all of us. 20 <u>But ye have an unction from the Holy One, and ye know all things</u>.

John takes the time to say a couple of things about mature disciples.

1 John 2.19 (KJV 1900)
They went out from us, but they were not of us; for if they had been of us, they would no doubt have continued with us: but they went out, that they might be made manifest that they were not all of us.

Mature disciples do not permanently depart from sound Churches. This may be the reason for the Baptist letter that is given to believers who must transfer to another Church for legitimate reasons. The Churches realize that such a believer will try to unite with another body in their new location and the former Pastor wanted to tell the new Pastor that this believer was not a heretic and could be welcomed into the new local church.

1 John 2:20 (KJV 1900)
20 But ye have an unction from the Holy One, and ye know all things.

Secondly, mature believers can take advantage of the doctrine that is in their souls to avoid being tricked by antichrists. There is, for all believers, an anointing that warns them about false teaching. This anointing is the indwelling Holy Spirit. Now verse 20 and 27 do not mean that you do not need to be taught by sound teachers, for it is God who has given the Church teachers [Eph 4.11-16]. John himself was one of the teachers provided by God to the Church. It is that *indwelling Spirit who brings genuine teaching to mind as an antidote against false teaching*. When John said you have not need of anyone to teach you, he was saying that you do not need any false prophets or antichrists to teach you.

1 John 2:27 (KJV 1900)
27 But the anointing which ye have received of him abideth in you, and ye need not that any man teach you: but as the same anointing teacheth you of all things, and is truth, and is no lie, and even as it hath taught you, ye shall abide in him.

Ephesians 4:11–12 (KJV 1900)
11 And he gave some, apostles; and some, prophets; and some, evangelists; and some, <u>pastors and teachers</u>; 12 For the perfecting of the saints, for the work of the ministry, for the edifying of the body of Christ:

John says that the Holy Spirit can bring biblical truth to the minds of believers at the proper time. John told them:

> 1 John 2:21 (KJV1900) I have not written unto you because ye know not the truth, but because ye know it, and that no lie is of the truth."

How did they know it? It did not seep miraculously into their minds, they were taught it. There is, therefore, no reason for them not to be able to tell the difference between a lie and the truth.

> John 14:26 (KJV 1900)
> 26 But the Comforter, which is the Holy Ghost, whom the Father will send in my name, he shall teach you all things, and bring all things to your remembrance, whatsoever I have said unto you.

> John 16:13 (KJV 1900)
> 13 Howbeit when he, the Spirit of truth, is come, he will guide you into all truth: for he shall not speak of himself; but whatsoever he shall hear, that shall he speak: and he will shew you things to come.

You *cannot* discern the difference between a satanic lie and the truth if you have never sat under sound teaching. A properly taught believer will know when he is hearing heresy and when he is hearing sound teaching.

The Spirit of Antichrist

> 1 John 4:1–3 (KJV 1900)
> 1 Beloved, believe not every spirit, but try[81] the spirits whether they are of God: because many false prophets are gone out into the world. 2 Hereby know ye the Spirit of God: Every spirit that confesseth that Jesus Christ is come in the flesh is of God: 3 And every spirit that confesseth not that Jesus Christ is come in the flesh is not of God: <u>and this is that spirit of antichrist</u>, whereof ye have heard that it should come; and even now already is it in the world.

The advent of Christ by his virgin conception and birth unveiled the Mystery of Godliness.

> 1 Timothy 3:16 (KJV 1900)
> 16 And without controversy great is the mystery of godliness: <u>God</u> was

manifest in the flesh, justified in the Spirit, seen of angels, preached unto the Gentiles, believed on in the world, received up into glory.

The presence of the Messiah upon the earth produced a reaction within the Mystery of Iniquity. The devil responded to the appearance of Christ with the spirit of Antichrist, which is the specific effort to nullify Christ and His testimony. The overall intensity of satanic activity in the world increased after the appearance of Jesus. Demonic resistance followed Him everywhere He ministered.[82] Satan himself entered into Judas, His betrayer [Lk 22.3]. We have seen that the local church was and is infiltrated by many antichrists. Jesus predicted a proliferation of false christ's until His return [Mt 24.23-24]. There has been a revival of the ancient Mystery Religions, and these have nourished a host of sophisticated philosophies and religious doctrines which oppose Christ. Mystery Babylon has been instrumental in coordinating all these developments throughout the centuries since the birth of Christ.

In chapter 4 of 1 John the aged apostle connects false prophets and a false spirit, which is identified as the spirit of Antichrist. According to John, this spirit energizes the false teachers of the Church Age. For the sake of clarity, a *false* teacher is not the same as an *erroneous* teacher. A teacher who is in error may be uneducated, or lazy, or even carnal, but it is not his *intent* to mislead the people with false teaching. The false teacher, on the other hand, intends to deceive. In the passage above, the chief deception which this false teacher intends to achieve is to undermine the Person and ministry of Jesus Christ.

This he does not necessarily accomplish by open and obvious means, *but by many small deceits designed to produce theological disaster in the long run*. The false teacher, in the spirit of antichrist, will question the *authority* of Christ by questioning the authority of His Word, the Bible. The false teacher will undermine the *sufficiency* of Christ by enlarging the legitimate role of the Holy Spirit until Christ is eclipsed by the Third Person [Jn 16.13-14]. The false teacher will use false interpretations of scripture [especially John 17] to encourage *ecumenism*[83] which inevitably leads to false doctrine and the diminishing of Jesus Christ. This and many other techniques are used to deceitfully damage the discipleship of believers and nullify their positive spiritual impact.

1 Timothy 4:1–5 (KJV 1900)
1 Now the Spirit speaketh expressly, that in the latter times some shall depart from the faith, giving heed to seducing spirits, and doctrines of devils; 2 Speaking lies in hypocrisy; having their conscience seared with a hot iron; 3 Forbidding to marry, and commanding to abstain from meats, which God hath created to be received with thanksgiving of them which believe and know the truth. 4 For every creature of God is

good, and nothing to be refused, if it be received with thanksgiving: 5
For it is sanctified by the word of God and prayer.

In 1 Timothy 4.1-3 we see that the spirit of antichrist is likely a demonic spirit that imitates the Holy Spirit. This false spirit empowers a special class of demon possessed teachers who exist in our time [2 Tim 2.15-3.7]. Their stock in trade is the "doctrines of devils." These doctrines were trafficked [Eze 28.14-18] in heaven before the creation of man; they were tested upon Eve in the Garden and applied to Jesus in the temptation in the wilderness [Matt 4]. We will address these doctrines specifically later.

The spirit of Antichrist is the reaction to the appearance of the Messiah and Savior, Jesus Christ. This spirit strengthens Satan's instruments and informs the spirit of the age. Its objective is to limit the effectiveness of the Mystery of Godliness through an attack upon the Word of God and Christian discipleship. God has elected to use redeemed humanity to assist in the advance of the Mystery of Godliness "preached unto the Gentiles, believed on in the world" and they are therefore a key target of Lucifer in spiritual warfare. The spirit of Antichrist is synonymous with the Mystery of Iniquity since the incarnation and prior to the appearance of the Antichrist and implementation of the New World Order.

In closing this chapter, it is important to recognize that the spirit of Antichrist does not always look like opposition to Christ. The prefix "anti" means both "against" and "instead of." The devil will maintain the illusion of a commitment to biblical Christianity as long as it serves him to do so. A significant number of apparently Christian doctrines and practices have been incorporated into local assemblies for the purpose of destabilizing believers and overturning otherwise sound Churches. The devil can appear as a roaring lion of persecution, but also an angel of light promoting deceptive doctrines that appear to be Christian but are not [Jude 4]. The local churches of our time are quite literally filled with false teachers, antichrists who resemble Bible believers in temperament and often, in teaching as well. Consequently, the true Christian must possess alertness and spiritual wisdom to discern the subtle yet massive deceptions of our time. This *sophistication of deception* is an aspect of the intensification of the spiritual conflict under the spirit of Antichrist.

Summary of The Concept of Antichrist

We know that there is an Antichrist, about whom the believers addressed by John had been taught, who had not yet appeared, but would arrive in the future. However, prior to his arrival, beginning in their own time, the world would be flooded by second class antichrists that would arise out of the local churches, sent to convince and to seduce the world into believing that Jesus is not the Christ.

1 Timothy 4:1–2 (KJV 1900)
1 Now the Spirit speaketh expressly, that in the latter times some shall depart from the faith, giving heed to seducing spirits, and doctrines of devils; 2 Speaking lies in hypocrisy; having their conscience seared with a hot iron;

In 1 John 4.1 and 1 Timothy 4 [and 2 Tim 3] we see the specific operation of the "antichrists" [small "a"] who are revealed by John and Paul. Their ministry ["speaking lies in hypocrisy"] is the powerful and popular proclamation of the doctrines of demons that will result in mass defections from sound teaching by persons so seduced [2 Th 2.1-3].

Having heard from John and from Paul, now Peter weighs in with commentary on this issue of antichrists and their ministry.

2 Peter 2:1 (KJV 1900)
1 But there were false prophets also among the people, even as there shall be false teachers among you, who privily shall bring in damnable heresies, even denying the Lord that bought them, and bring upon themselves swift destruction.

Let's close this circle with John again.

1 John 4:1–3 (KJV 1900)
1 Beloved, believe not every spirit, but try the spirits whether they are of God: because many false prophets are gone out into the world. 2 Hereby know ye the Spirit of God: Every spirit that confesseth that Jesus Christ is come in the flesh is of God: 3 And every spirit that confesseth not that Jesus Christ is come in the flesh is not of God: and this is that spirit of antichrist, whereof ye have heard that it should come; and even now already is it in the world.

There is a spiritual conspiracy in the world that seeks to dethrone Christ through the agency of false teaching. False teaching is not simply a difference of opinion, it is life and death: your life and your death. The conspiracy being executed in the spirit of antichrist is known by another name, the *Mystery of Iniquity*.

Here, near the end of the unfolding drama of history, the last hour, begins an escalation of the spiritual warfare between God and his adversary, the devil.

The appearance of Christ, his strategic victory via his substitutionary death and resurrection from the dead, was followed by the calling into being an elect group of human beings, the Church, with a unique position [as the spiritual body of Christ], and unlimited power [via the Filling of the Spirit] to glorify the Lord both in time and eternity.

The first advent has inspired a new phase in the Mystery of Iniquity, a term which we will summarize, for now, as *the prehistoric plan of Lucifer to overthrow God and to establish himself as God in His place.*

The many antichrists of our time exist to prepare the way of the coming personage identified as *the* Antichrist: the Man of Sin, the son of Perdition. The Antichrist is the final agency by which Satan seeks to secure victory and the establishment of his kingdom. The Antichrist will inaugurate the New World Order in its final form. The immediate objective of the Mystery of Iniquity is to create an environment on earth suitable for the manifestation of the Man of Sin.

The Antichrist is a usurper, he is contending for the position of Christ, his objective is the *defeat* or the *disqualification* of Jesus as God and Messiah. He denies the legitimate claim of Christ to rule the universe [Ps 2].

The Antichrist embodies the aspirations of the devil in his war against God and will be the clearest representation of Lucifer's argument and strategy.

At this point it will be helpful to introduce the concept of the Mystery of Iniquity, which is the ages old, overarching strategy of the devil in the celestial conflict which began before human history. It is within the framework of the Mystery of Iniquity that we will most profitably examine Antichrist and his pivotal role in Lucifer's end game.

Richard G. Walker

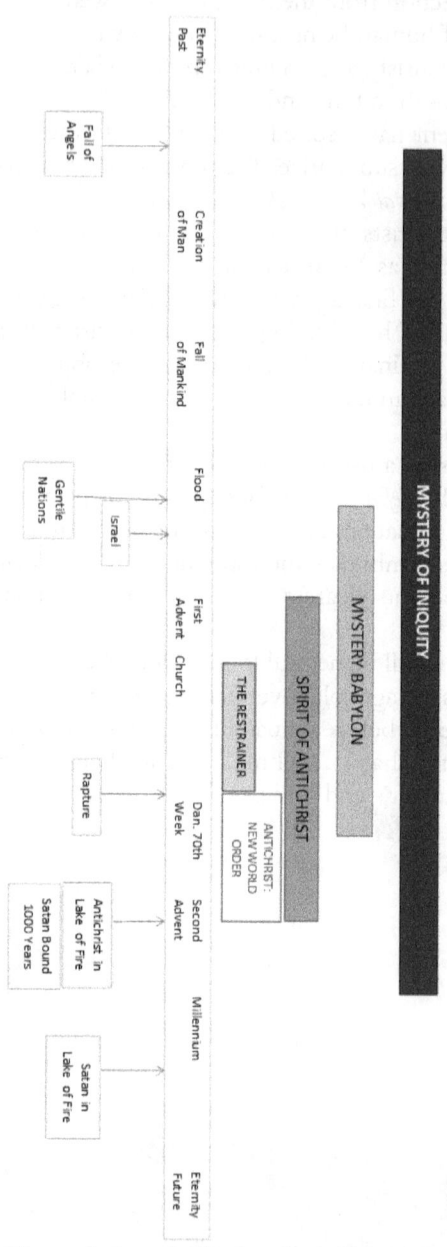

Figure 2: Satan's Eschatological Strategy

Antichrist and the New World Order

What Is The Mystery of Iniquity?

2 Thessalonians 2:1–12 (KJV 1900)
1 Now we beseech you, brethren, by the coming of our Lord Jesus Christ, and by our gathering together unto him, 2 That ye be not soon shaken in mind, or be troubled, neither by spirit, nor by word, nor by letter as from us, as that the day of Christ is at hand. 3 Let no man deceive you by any means: for that day shall not come, except there come a falling away first, and that man of sin be revealed, the son of perdition; 4 Who opposeth and exalteth himself above all that is called God, or that is worshipped; so that he as God sitteth in the temple of God, shewing himself that he is God. 5 Remember ye not, that, when I was yet with you, I told you these things? 6 And now ye know what withholdeth that he might be revealed in his time. 7 <u>For the mystery of iniquity doth already work</u>: only he who now letteth will let, until he be taken out of the way. 8 And then shall that Wicked be revealed, whom the Lord shall consume with the spirit of his mouth, and shall destroy with the brightness of his coming: 9 Even him, whose coming is after the working of Satan with all power and signs and lying wonders, 10 And with all deceivableness of unrighteousness in them that perish; because they received not the love of the truth, that they might be saved. 11 And for this cause God shall send them strong delusion, that they should believe a lie: 12 That they all might be damned who believed not the truth, but had pleasure in unrighteousness.

Iniquity

Iniquity refers to "lawlessness"

> "**Iniquity**" 88.139 ἀνομία, ας f: to behave with complete disregard for the laws or regulations of a society— 'to live lawlessly, lawlessness, lawless living.'[84]

Iniquity in the New Testament is the attitude or action of disregard for God's law, in whatever form the law may take at the time [spiritual, moral, civic]. It is sinfulness from the perspective of the rejection of law and therefore, logically, the rejection of the Author of that law.

Lawlessness or iniquity is the attitude of the angels and men who have rebelled against God. Over time lawlessness is increasing, coincident with the multiplication of false prophets and antichrists.

> Matthew 24:11–12 (KJV 1900)11
> And many false prophets shall rise, and shall deceive many. 12 And because iniquity shall abound, the love of many shall wax cold. [2Tim 3.13]

> Matthew 24:23–24 (KJV 1900)
> 23 Then if any man shall say unto you, Lo, here is Christ, or there; believe it not. 24 For there shall arise false Christs, and false prophets, and shall shew great signs and wonders; insomuch that, if it were possible, they shall deceive the very elect.

Born again believers retain a sin nature capable of being entangled in lawlessness.[85] In spiritual warfare, believers can be nullified through the encouragement of lawlessness by a variety of means.

Satan personifies the idea of iniquity. He rejects God's right to rule as the Lawgiver. He actively leads fallen creation in an effort to overthrow divine authority.[86] Lucifer is the author of the prehistoric plan to overthrow God via a synchronized coalition of fallen beings. This intergenerational conspiracy is the Mystery of Iniquity, which began before human history, but has intensified since the incarnation of Christ.

The Mystery of Iniquity is the *plan* behind the history of the fallen creation. It is organizationally complex, consisting of phases which correspond to the dispensations under which God has organized nations and peoples [Acts 17.26]. It is powerful, so powerful that since the ascension of Christ, God has seen fit to place a restraining spiritual power upon it to prevent its full expression, until an hour which He has ordained [2 Th 2.5-9].

The coming of Christ, the Seed of the woman [Gen 3.15; Gal 3.16; 4.4] has brought to light this movement to depose God via an alliance of men and angels. This campaign, though composed of many battles, will culminate in the emergence of the son of Lucifer and a New World Order. The Antichrist, the seed of the serpent, will also be known as the *Lawless* One. In the future, during the Day of the Lord,[87] there will be a final confrontation of two contrary seeds, two contrasting sons, two conflicting mysteries.

Mystery

> "Lawlessness is nothing new, but it has a purpose, a policy and authority which was undisclosed but is now revealed to the Church by the scriptures."

The word *mystery*[88] is defined as follows in the New Testament

> "**Mystery**" 28.77 μυστήριον, ου n: the content of that which has not been known before but which has been revealed to an in-group or restricted constituency—'secret, mystery.'[89]

The Mystery Iniquity is not new, but it is something unrevealed until the advent of Christ.

2 Thessalonians 2:3–7 (KJV 1900)
3 Let no man deceive you by any means: for that day shall not come, except there come a falling away first, and that man of sin be revealed, the son of perdition; 4 Who opposeth and exalteth himself above all that is called God, or that is worshipped; so that he as God sitteth in the temple of God, shewing himself that he is God. 5 Remember ye not, that, when I was yet with you, I told you these things? 6 And now ye know what withholdeth that he might be revealed in his time. 7 <u>For the mystery of iniquity doth already work</u>: only he who now letteth will let, until he be taken out of the way.

The Mystery of Iniquity is related to the Man of Sin, the Antichrist. Although the Mystery of Iniquity is currently limited in its expression ["what withholdeth…he who now letteth"], that restraint is temporary. When the restriction is removed, the Mystery of Iniquity will fully facilitate the appearance of the Antichrist and the New World Order.

Because a mystery is revealed, it does not necessarily follow that it is generally known. The concept of mystery in the New Testament pertains to that which "*has not been known before but which has been revealed to an in-group or restricted constituency.*" Why has *iniquity* been a mystery?

Iniquity is an old concept. Since the fall, mankind has sinned and openly rejected the authority of God [Ps 2]. The *Mystery* of Iniquity hides something that was secret, but also something that is *organized*. Lawlessness is nothing new, but it has a *purpose*, a *policy* and *authority* which was undisclosed but is now revealed to the Church by the scriptures.

The Mystery of Iniquity is *secret* because lawlessness has been conclusively proven to be against the best interest of man. Robbery, theft, extortion, murder, sexual molestation, racketeering, group violence, blackmail, torture have all been limited voluntarily by men in their own self- interest. The problem with lawlessness as a system [NT458 anomia] is that it is not *partial* disregard of the law, but total disregard of it. Thus, the true doctrine of lawlessness must be hidden until people are programmed to accept it under another guise. *Lawlessness needs a marketing plan*, and it has one: the New World

Order.

The Mystery of Iniquity is *clandestine* because lawlessness is not an end in itself. The purpose of lawlessness is to weaken obedience to God in preparation for obedience to another power and another law. Lawlessness is the wrecking ball used against the divine institutions of free will, marriage, family, and government; lawlessness is the controlled demolition of civilization to make way for a new kind of sinner and a new kind of world.

Mystery of Iniquity is *covert* because it is not just man who is revolting against the law of God, but the fallen angels as well. Before man was created the angels revolted against the rule of God, and it was an angel, Lucifer who, through temptation, implicated humanity in this rebellion. The big secret of the Mystery of Iniquity is the historical, conscious collaboration between fallen spirits and a portion of mankind to overthrow God. Lawlessness [Iniquity] is a short-term objective, a tactic in this warfare. The Antichrist will establish a new law, a new kingdom, and a new god.

> Daniel 7:25 (KJV 1900)
> 25 And he shall speak great words against the most High, and shall wear out the saints of the most High, and think to change times and laws: and they shall be given into his hand until a time and times and the dividing of time

The Mystery of Iniquity and the Mystery of Godliness

> 1 Timothy 3:16 (KJV 1900)
> 16 And without controversy great is the mystery of godliness: God was manifest in the flesh, justified in the Spirit, seen of angels, preached unto the Gentiles, believed on in the world, received up into glory.

The Mystery of Iniquity opposes the Mystery of Godliness. Both are anticipated in God's judgment of the serpent [Lucifer/Satan] in the Garden of Eden. God Himself will produce a Champion, the Seed of the woman, who will end the designs of Satan. However, the conflict will not be without cost to the Lord, as the seed of the Serpent will administer a blow to His heel.

> Genesis 3:15 (KJV 1900)
> 15 And I will put enmity between thee and the woman, and between thy seed and her seed; it shall bruise thy head, and thou shalt bruise his heel.

Eve ("the woman") is the mother of all living. From she and Adam proceeded a corrupted progeny who are identified with Adam according to the flesh [Gen 5.3; Rom 5.12], but Lucifer according to the spirit [Eph 2.1-2]. But God called a remnant [redeemed Israel] from the midst of fallen humanity [Is 43.1; Rom 9.6-12]. From this election came the Messiah, the Seed of the woman in that He is born of a virgin conception [Lk 1.30-35]. God is His Father. The people of Lucifer, unredeemed humanity, executed by crucifixion the Seed by the foreordination of God [Acts 2.22-23], and the instigation of Satan, who literally indwelt Christ's betrayer [Lk 22.3]. Unredeemed humanity has persecuted and killed believers throughout human history. At the cross however, a blow against Satan was struck by the punishment of Christ for the sins of mankind,[90] resulting in his strategic defeat. At the end of human history, the saints of God will crush the devil beneath their feet [Rom 16.20].

The Mystery of Godliness was hidden under types and symbols until its revelation at the first advent of Christ. The appearance of the doctrines of the New Covenant provided meaning to the types and figures, revealing the scope and magnificence of divine provision for His creation.[91]

The Mystery of Godliness is the specific plan of God to provide a solution for sin, the destruction of the works of the devil [1Jn 3.8] and the redemption of creation. Ultimately, the end of the Mystery of Godliness is doxological: God is confirmed to all as holy, all wise and omnipotent, to be glorified forever.

Daniel 9:24 (KJV 1900)
24 Seventy weeks are determined upon thy people and upon thy holy city, to finish the transgression, and to make an end of sins, and to make reconciliation for iniquity, and to bring in everlasting righteousness, and to seal up the vision and prophecy, and to anoint the most Holy.

The Mystery of Iniquity finds its origin in prehistory at the ancient rebellion of the angels [Eze 28.11-19; Rev 12.1-5]. It is the strategy and plan to install Lucifer as god and sovereign over the heavens and the earth. In human history, the Mystery of Iniquity is coincident with the Mystery of Godliness: conceiving the Fall of mankind in the Garden of Eden, orchestrating the rise of the Gentile kingdoms [Dan 2, 10], obstructing the spiritual development of the nation of Israel. Unable to present the appearance of the Messiah, the Mystery of Iniquity seeks to obscure His identity by the propagation of "The Lie" that Jesus is not the Christ. Since the incarnation of Christ, the Mystery of Iniquity is identified with the spirit of Antichrist. The terminus of these two Mysteries is the end of history, during the Day of the Lord, the confrontation between Christ and Antichrist.

Richard G. Walker

The Mystery of Iniquity and Antichrist

The Mystery of Iniquity is revealed in the midst of a discussion of the Day of Christ and the appearance of the Antichrist. The Antichrist is the chief actor during that portion of the Day of the Lord which immediately precedes the Second Advent of Christ.

> 2 Thessalonians 2:7–9 (KJV 1900)
> 7 <u>For the mystery of iniquity doth already work</u>: only he who now letteth will let, until he be taken out of the way. 8 <u>And then shall that Wicked be revealed</u>, whom the Lord shall consume with the spirit of his mouth, and shall destroy with the brightness of his coming: 9 Even him, whose coming is after the working of Satan with all power and signs and lying wonders,

There is something *working*[92] in the world that seeks as its objective the rule of Antichrist. This program, the Mystery of Iniquity, is of such wicked potential that it must be restrained by superior spiritual power. The Antichrist is a spiritual threat, a product of satanic intervention in human events. *The Mystery of Iniquity is the multifaceted strategy and blueprint of the devil's plans for heaven and earth.* The Mystery of Iniquity is revealed in scripture in the context of the Day of the Lord or the Day of Christ.[93] This "day" is the prophesied period of divine judgment upon the unbelieving world for its unbelief and its incorrigible opposition to God and to Christ.

"What Is the Day of the Lord?"

> "In order to understand the nature of the error Paul is correcting [in 2 Thessalonians-rw], it is necessary to define what is meant by the "day of the Lord." This expression is found often in the Bible. In a word, it is the period of time predicted in the Scripture when God will deal directly with human sin. It includes the tribulation time preceding the second advent of Christ as well as the whole millennial reign of Christ. It will culminate in the judgment of the great white throne. The Day of the Lord is therefore an extended period of time lasting over one thousand years. This is brought out in the events included in the Day of the Lord, presented in connection with the study of 1 Thessalonians 5."[94]

Antichrist and the New World Order

The Antichrist will appear when God unleashes His vengeance against the world. 2 Thessalonians 2 provides a timeline of the events.[95]

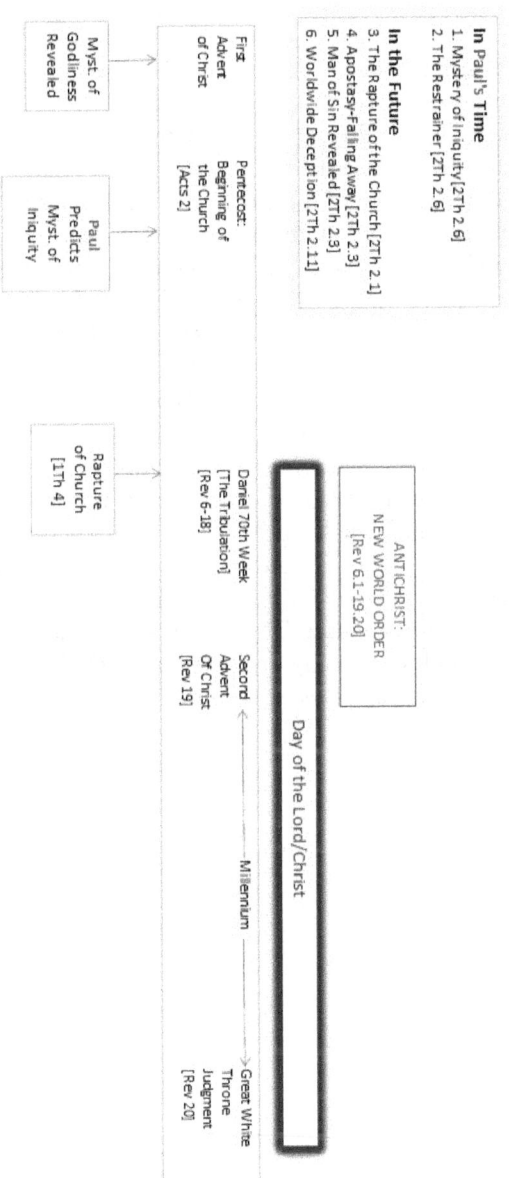

Figure 3: The Day of the Lord and Antichrist

What Is Mystery Babylon

> "Mystery Babylon is a spiritual construct; it is primarily concerned with the management of the procession of Gentile empires which follow the Flood."

A brief word regarding *Mystery Babylon*, to which we will return in later chapters. The Mystery of Iniquity, now the spirit of Antichrist, is the overarching conspiracy which finds its origin in prehistory. It began with the fall of Lucifer and his successful effort to precipitate a rebellion amongst the angelic host. This was the origin of the fallen angels and the spiritual conflict that spilled into human history at the Garden of Eden. The Mystery of Iniquity continued in human history and will continue, until it is ended by the judgment of the Antichrist, the False Prophet and at last Lucifer himself.

Mystery Babylon is a part of the historical extension of the Mystery of Iniquity. Mystery Babylon is the *modus operandi* of the Mystery of Lawlessness on the earth, specifically, after the Flood. Like the Mystery of Iniquity, Mystery Babylon is a *spiritual construct*; it is primarily concerned with the *management of the procession of Gentile empires* which follow the Flood. Mystery Babylon is characterized by the symbiosis of Church and State, it is *the religious state* [Rev 17.1-3]. It is *ecumenical*, acknowledging the validity of every false religious concept while denying and persecuting the one true Church of Jesus Christ revealed in scripture. It is *demonic*, its ritual and power based upon the invoking and evoking of fallen spirits. The *Mystery Religions* are the repository of its spiritual heritage and science. *Mystery Babylon is the thinking of Satan applied to religion, government, economics, and social organization.*

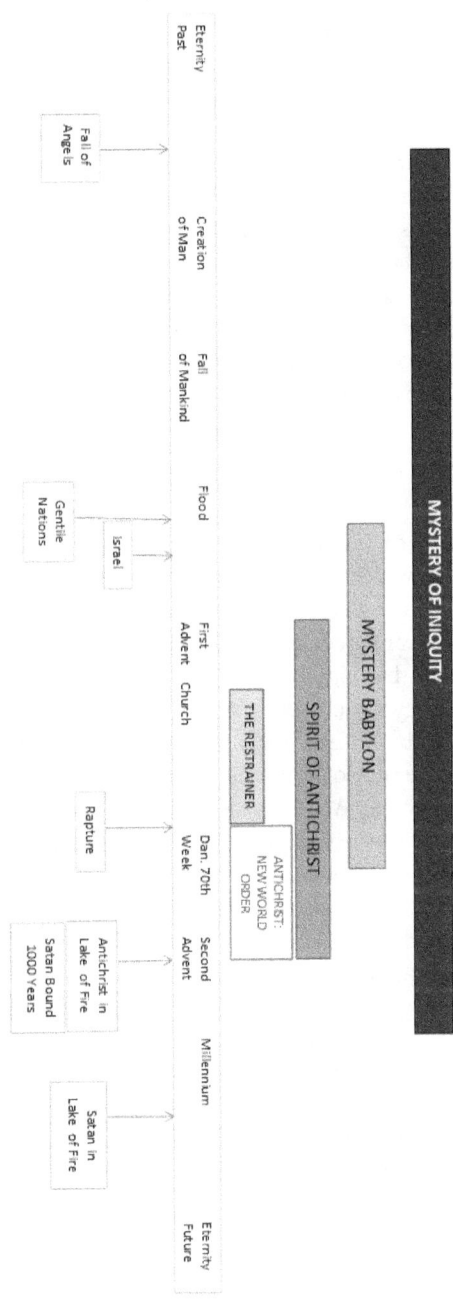

Figure 2: Satan's Eschatological Strategy

While the Mystery of Iniquity or Lawlessness is *the general plan* for the universal rule of Lucifer, *Mystery Babylon is the doctrinal substructure **and** ecclesiastical superstructure which secretly rules this world.* The Bible addresses its existence since the Flood, but its principles can be discerned in Satan's words in the Garden of Eden. The template for its general development is found in historical Babylon, which serves as a model for every subsequent Gentile world kingdom. *However, in the end, even Mystery Babylon will be revealed as a transitional ideology.* All the trappings of the ancient rites as well as the hierarchy of persons who administer them will be transitioned to the new religion or eliminated. Satan will seek to change both times and laws [Dan 7.25]. We will address Mystery Babylon in more detail later.

Summary: The Mystery of Iniquity

The Mystery of Iniquity is Satan's prehistoric, overarching plan of lawlessness by which he intends to overthrow divine rule of the heavens and the earth. It is based upon a theology that is promoted by deception and insinuated into the Church and the organs of society. At the core of this theology is The Lie. The Lie is the cornerstone of a demonic theology which seeks to overturn the Mystery of Godliness which is the truth concerning Christ and His kingdom.

The Lie is the proposition that Jesus is not the Christ [1 John 2.22], but also that Lucifer/Antichrist is God. The devil opposes the entire *Mystery of Godliness* revealed in the New Testament, the central feature of which is the deity of Jesus Christ. Lucifer's campaign against the accurate perception of the true nature of God is alluded to in his conversation with Eve, wherein he claimed that God had lied to her, and implied that perhaps He was not all that He claimed to be [Gen 3.3-5].

The Mystery of Iniquity is creating the world conditions that will lead to the kingdom of the Antichrist. These preparations are being carried out in countless ways, including the corruption of the scriptures, the dissemination of many systems of false doctrine and the infiltration of satanic agents in every facet of Christendom: local churches, the seminary, Bible translation, Christian media, and missionary societies. It is also active in the rest of the world, especially government, finance, education, and media.

The theology, priesthood and religious practice of the Mystery of Iniquity is known as Mystery Babylon. Mystery Babylon is the doctrinal and ecclesiastical structure through which the world is actually ruled.

The philosophical and theological orientation of the Mystery of Iniquity is identified with the doctrines of demons [1Tim 4.1-2] and the spirit of antichrist [1 John 4.1-3].

The Mystery of Iniquity seeks to limit the influence of righteousness, to limit the full expression of the Mystery of Godliness [1Tim 3.16], whereby God brings spiritual light into the world through Christ [Jn 8.12].

The Mystery of Iniquity exercises overwhelming power and influence due to the temporary position of the devil as the ruler of this world and the interlock of the wickedness of his world system with the fallen character of humanity [Eph 2.1-3; 1 Jn 2.15-16]. However, this power of evil is restrained from its full potential by the Spirit of God operating through the Body of Christ during the Church Age.[96] As believers advance in spiritual maturity through obedience to the Word of God, Lucifer's progress is constrained until the appropriate moment in the eschatological calendar.

God has allowed the Church Age believer to play a crucial role in the curtailing of Satan's program and the advancement of the Mystery of Godliness. As a member of the Body of Christ, the believer plays an important role of restricting the influence of the devil upon the world by living a holy life and by the evangelization and discipling of the lost. Through this *spiritual* warfare the Church is a means God uses to accomplish His purposes in the world. God has graciously allowed Church Age believers to be a factor in how every elect person will be redeemed.

When discipleship is not occurring, the local church becomes spiritually weak, and there is a corresponding loss of spiritual protection in the community and eventually in society. The proper spiritual function of the Church not only results in the salvation of the lost, but also creates morality[97] in the community as the righteousness of the Church influences the moral climate [the Church as salt and light: Matt 5.13-14; 1 Pet 2.12], ultimately strengthening the institutions of marriage, family, and government. A weak local church indirectly produces a kind of unbeliever and a kind of society that is beneficial to Lucifer's plans. Spiritual weakness and carnality in Christians due to poor discipleship causes a great deal of unnecessary misery in the world.

The devil is working to produce a new kind of unbeliever for a new kind of world. The Antichrist will not simply try to rule the world, he wants to remake it.

5
The Character Of The Antichrist

Introduction: The Context of His Appearing

The appearing of the man of sin is not the same moment as the beginning of his operations in the world.

The Antichrist will be active in the world for several years before he becomes known as the Antichrist. The removal of the Church and its restraining influence upon the Mystery of Iniquity enables the appearance of the "man of sin, son of perdition" but not in a guise that immediately betrays his true nature.

Daniel 9:27a-b (KJV 1900)
27 And he shall confirm the covenant with many for one week: and in the midst of the week he shall cause the sacrifice and the oblation to cease…

This passage refers to a prophecy to Daniel by the angel Gabriel. This prophecy pertains to the people of Israel and the city of Jerusalem [9:24].

Daniel 9:24–27 (KJV 1900)
24 Seventy weeks are determined upon thy people and upon thy holy city, to finish the transgression, and to make an end of sins, and to make reconciliation for iniquity, and to bring in everlasting righteousness, and to seal up the vision and prophecy, and to

anoint the most Holy. 25 Know therefore and understand, that from the going forth of the commandment to restore and to build Jerusalem unto the Messiah the prince shall be seven weeks, and threescore and two weeks: the street shall be built again, and the wall, even in troublous times. 26 And after threescore and two weeks shall Messiah be cut off, but not for himself: and the people of the prince that shall come shall destroy the city and the sanctuary; and the end thereof shall be with a flood, and unto the end of the war desolations are determined. 27 And he shall confirm the covenant with many for one week: and in the midst of the week he shall cause the sacrifice and the oblation to cease, and for the overspreading of abominations he shall make it desolate, even until the consummation, and that determined shall be poured upon the desolate.

Daniel 9: Daniel's 70 Weeks: An Incredible Prophecy

The purpose of this prophecy is to show Daniel the future of God's dealings with *the people of Israel* from his time until the end of human history. The prophecy is not only vast with respect to time, but it also demonstrates the dimensions of the ministry of God to and through Israel as His means of resolving the issue of evil and his dealings with sinful creatures forever. Not only does the prophecy indicate that the nation of Israel will continue as a people until the end, but that God's own righteousness will be validated through His discipline of that nation. Through Israel: its preservation, judgment and ultimate salvation, the character of God is vindicated, and the outline of His purposes become visible to those with spiritual sight.

Daniel 9:24 (KJV 1900)
24 Seventy weeks are determined upon thy people and upon thy holy city, to finish the transgression, and to make an end of sins, and to make reconciliation for iniquity,

Upon thy people and thy holy city The context of the prophecy is the people of God, Israel and their holy city, Jerusalem. The city was holy because of its selection by God and His presence within its Temple. Because of God's presence among the people, the Law of

Moses [The Mosaic Covenant] established the protocol necessary for Israel to cohabit the land with God. In fact, the entire relationship of the people to God is mediated through covenants. The Abrahamic covenant demonstrated the way of salvation, the Mosaic Covenant, the way of discipleship for Israel. Naturally, this prophecy of the future of Israel views that future through a covenantal lens.

The prophecy is a prediction of the finish, the end, or sealing up of human history, with Israel demonstrated to be the center or the key to history. God begins the prophecy with the end of "transgression…sin and iniquity" which is the promise of the New Covenant:

> Jeremiah 33:8 (KJV 1900)
> 8 And I will cleanse them from all their <u>iniquity</u>, whereby they have <u>sinned</u> against me; and I will pardon all their iniquities, whereby they have sinned, and whereby they have <u>transgressed</u> against me.

The first sentence summary of the prophecy concludes with the anointing of the Most Holy, which is both a reference to the abode of the presence of God, the Temple, as well as the One who dwelt therein.

> Matthew 23:21 (KJV 1900)
> 21 And whoso shall swear by the temple, sweareth by it, and by him that dwelleth therein.

The paramount message of the prophecy is that the Jewish nation is the nexus of history: it's foundation in Abraham, its most prominent offspring in Jesus, its judgment in the devastations of the Day of the Lord and its vindication under the covenant promises of its restoration as seat of the throne of God forever. This centrality is not due to the virtue of the Jews, but the genius and grace of God who created them out of a single man, Abram, and the sacrifice of Christ which saved a remnant from the Jews and from the Gentiles as well.

Seventy weeks are determined [*Seventy* OT 7657 *Weeks or Sevens* OT 7620] The prediction is formulated on the basis of weeks of years where one week equals seven years.[98] These weeks of years are to commence "from the going forth of the command to restore and build Jerusalem". This date may be found in Nehemiah 2.1 where the decree was given by Artaxerxes Longimanus to rebuild Jerusalem in the 20th year of his reign or in 444 BC. The first seven weeks (7x7) of years or

49 years concern the rebuilding of the city of Jerusalem. The next sixty-two weeks of years or 434 years are added for a total of 483 years until the Messiah the prince. In other words, in this prophecy, Daniel is being told the precise date that Jesus would present himself as the Messiah or the Christ. Just as Gabriel provided Daniel with this calculation [Dan 9.21-24], at the appointed time Gabriel would again appear to Zacharias and to Mary [Lk 1.19, 26] to announce the birth of He who would bring in God's own New World Order [Dan 2.44-45]. Possibly, it is by this scripture that wise men [Mt 2.1-2] and others [Lk 2.25-38] could anticipate the coming of the Lord with such precision. It is also why the scribes and Pharisees *should have* anticipated His coming.

After this, there is a remaining week of seven years which is separated from the preceding 69 weeks. This week does not fall into the timeframe, the continuous chronology of the preceding weeks.

To finish [OT 3607: to restrict, restrain, withhold] **the transgression** [OT 7322 rebellion, revolt], To end the human and angelic revolt against God. The Fall established man as the enemy of God [Rom 5.10]. The earlier fall of a portion of the angels [*earlier*, as evidenced by a fallen angel in the midst of the Garden of Eden in Genesis 3] established a heavenly antecedent to this earthly rebellion. In the mystery religions, men and fallen angels collaborate in the implementation of the Mystery of Lawlessness to achieve Lucifer's New World Order. This prophecy to Daniel designates the elect nation of Israel, the only such elect nation in human history, as the center of God's plan to resolve the issue of sin and the animosity and conflict with God that has arisen because of it. The purpose of this prophecy is to announce the coming unilateral victory of God in the cosmic conflict with evil. All the wicked, human, or angelic, will receive terminal judgment in the Lake of Fire [Rev 20.10-15].

Daniel 9:24 (KJV 1900)
24 Seventy weeks are determined upon thy people and upon thy holy city, to finish the transgression, and to make an end of sins, and to make reconciliation for iniquity,

To make an end [OT 2856 to seal or to close up] **of sins** [OT 2403 sin, wrong]. God established a covenant with Abraham that from him God would produce an innumerable progeny [Ex 17.1-7]. Later, under a separate and temporary covenant [the Law of Moses] God formally incorporated a portion of this posterity, Israel, as a *nation* of priests [Ex 19.6]. God also covenanted with Abraham that one of his heirs would be a Son who would reign in righteousness over the world forever [Jer 23.5-6; Gal 3.16-19]. The Abrahamic Covenant was a unilateral promise of God that was entered by the faith alone of Abraham and his descendants. In this covenant, specifically the portion known to us as the New Covenant, God promises to *make an end of sin altogether*, through this coming Seed. Through the New Covenant,[99] a paragraph of the Abrahamic, God promised to eliminate sin forever as an alternative for mankind.

To make reconciliation [OT 3722 to cover, purge, make atonement] **for iniquity** [OT 6411 sin, wrongdoing with a focus on the liability of guilt]. It was not sufficient for the sinless Son of God to be born and live among men. The holiness of God demanded a *satisfaction* of the debt of sin against mankind's account [Rom 3.25-26]. A perfect sacrifice was required to absorb the divine penalty of human rebellion. Therefore Jesus, the Seed of Abraham, the Son of David did not only live without sin, but also suffered and died for our sins and, having accomplished eternal redemption through His blood, was raised from the dead to reign at the right hand of the Father, in the presence of His elect saints, who are reconciled to God by this exchange of their sin for Christ's righteousness.[100] All who place their faith in this gospel will once for all be rescued from their sins and reconciled to God.[101]

> Daniel 9:24(KJV 1900)
> 24 Seventy weeks are determined upon thy people and upon thy holy city, to finish the transgression, and to make an end of sins, and to make reconciliation for iniquity, and to bring in everlasting righteousness, and to seal up the vision and prophecy, and to anoint the most Holy.

To bring in everlasting righteousness,[102] Only at the return of Jesus Christ to the earth, at the end of the seventieth week, will humanity begin to understand the difference between their own limited concepts of fairness and God's perfect righteousness. Terminally depraved humanity cannot bring and *would not* bring true righteousness even if they were able somehow to do so. The often proposed and yet future unity of the nations will not produce utopia, but Babylon as it produced Babel before: a world united in opposition to God and His Christ from beginning to end [Ps 2]. At the end of the sixty-ninth of the seventy weeks prophesied to Daniel, Christ, by his sacrifice upon the cross, provided the basis for everlasting righteousness. The believer in Christ is pardoned of his sins and will be ultimately freed from them entirely.[103] At the end of the seventieth week, a time which is in the future, the personal return of Christ to the earth will mark the proximity of the final judgment of the wicked dead [Rev 20.11-15]. There will be a permanent end to evil and its products, but only those who have received Christ by faith will see the advent of everlasting righteousness [Jn 3.3].

To seal up [OT 2856 the same as *"to make an end"* earlier in the verse] **vision and prophecy**. The purpose of vision and prophecy was to communicate divine purposes to men. Revelation 19 describes the ultimate objective of prophecy:

Revelation 19:10 (KJV 1900)
10 And I fell at his feet to worship him. And he said unto me, See thou do it not: I am thy fellowservant, and of thy brethren that have the testimony of Jesus: worship God: for the testimony of Jesus is the spirit of prophecy.

The essence of all prophecy is the "testimony of Jesus." It is this testimony which is the *spirit* behind every prophecy given to man. The epistles refer to this testimony as "the mystery of godliness."

1 Timothy 3:16 (KJV 1900)
16 And without controversy great is the mystery of godliness: God was manifest in the flesh, justified in the Spirit, seen of angels, preached unto the Gentiles, believed on in the world, received up into glory.

The activity of God among men since the Fall is the proclamation of this *testimony* in a manner appropriate to the progress of divine revelation for humanity at the time: Jesus will come [or has come] to reconcile man to God and to implement the eternal purpose of God for the earth and mankind. The testimony of Jesus is the spirit of prophecy.

The prophecy of the seventy weeks succinctly and mathematically portrays the plan for the realization of the ends and means of Jesus' testimony. Once accomplished, the purpose of prophecy is achieved and is therefore *ended* or sealed up.

And to anoint [OT 4886 *smear, rub on, i.e., smear an object with a liquid or semi-liquid as a religious activity to dedicate or consecrate a person or object for service*] **the Most Holy**. Not only redeemed Israel and the Church, but Christ Himself will be vindicated before the nations. The Antichrist who had established himself by the desecration of the Temple, having proclaimed himself Christ, is, at the end of the seventieth week, in the Lake of Fire [Rev 19.20]. The true Christ, [whose Name itself is the translation of Hebrew 'Messiah' "the anointed one" Jn 4.25] will take His place as the true creator and sovereign of the universe and every living thing. At this time there will be another Temple upon the earth which will receive its King who will then live amid a redeemed world, reminiscent of an act which He has already performed in heaven.

> Hebrews 9:12 (KJV 1900)
> 12 Neither by the blood of goats and calves, but by his own blood he entered in once into the holy place, having obtained eternal redemption for us.

This prophecy also introduces the specific timing of the appearance of the final and greatest human adversary of the Jews, "the prince who is to come."

> Daniel 9:26 (KJV 1900)
> 26 And after threescore and two weeks shall Messiah be cut off, but not for himself: and the people of the prince that shall come shall destroy the city and the sanctuary; and the end thereof shall be with a flood, and unto the end of the war desolations are determined.

Daniel is privileged to convey one of the clearest statements regarding the coming of Jesus in the Old Testament. Sixty-nine weeks [7+62] or 483 years[104] into the prophecy, the Anointed One, the Messiah will be cut off, but not for himself, speaking of the crucifixion and substitutionary atonement of Jesus Christ. When John the Baptist proclaimed: "Behold the Lamb of God, which taketh away the sin of the world" [John 1.29] it was in the full knowledge of this scripture in Daniel. This one sacrifice, the antitype to every lamb ever offered to God, was to be presented to Israel as its Messiah, prophesied over 500 years before it was to occur.

Inasmuch as *Gabriel* was conveying this message, at least at this point if not earlier, the angels became aware of this timetable and were able to anticipate how human history was to unfold not only for humanity, but for their own fallen brethren as well [Eph 3.10]. The rebellion of humanity against God has since the beginning

> **Recapitulation**
>
> The first seven sevens:
>
>> The prophecy to rebuild the city came from Artaxerxes in 444BC and using the 360 year Jewish year, 49 years
>
> The next 62 sevens:
>
>> 434 years plus the original 49 years brings us to 33AD when Jesus Christ was cut off by crucifixion.
>
> This leaves a remaining week or seven years, the 70th seven left to be fulfilled. *But there is no time in history since the crucifixion when all of the events predicted for that week have occurred*, so we believe that these events are yet future. There is a gap between the 69th and 70th week of years
>
> There is another example of a prediction having two events placed together in scripture which in fact are separated by a long period of time. In Luke 4.18-19 Jesus quotes from Isaiah 61.
>
> Isaiah 61:1-2 (KJV 1900)
>
> 1 The Spirit of the Lord GOD is upon me; Because the LORD hath anointed me to preach good tidings unto the meek; He hath sent me to bind up the brokenhearted, To proclaim liberty to the captives, And the opening of the prison to them that are bound; 2 To proclaim the acceptable year of the LORD, And the day of vengeance of our God; To comfort all that mourn;
>
> The events of Isa 61.1-2a pertain to the first advent of Jesus Christ. However the events of verse 2b and following [And the day of...] pertain to his second advent, the second coming of Christ which has not yet occurred. The intervening period between the verses, the Church age, was not disclosed in the OT because it was an unrevealed mystery. In Jesus own recitation of this passage in Luke 4:18-19 he stopped short of proclaiming "the day of vengeance of our God" because it did not apply to his purpose in the first advent.
>
> So we can see that Daniel is not the only book in which passages adjacent in the bible can be separated by long periods of time in their fulfillment.

been instigated and abetted by angels [Gen 3.1, Eph 2.2] and this illicit relationship will continue until the end. The greatest leader of fallen civilization, the Antichrist, will be a demonically possessed man, or to use modern terminology, a trans-human hybrid, the principal example of Satan's superman, the prototype of his own version of the new spiritual birth of mankind.

The Prince That Shall Come

The rejection of Messiah resulted [in 70 A.D] in the second destruction of Jerusalem and the temple [Matthew 24.2; Luke 21.24]. Already without a reigning king, Israel will have its remaining symbols of national status [its capital and temple] taken from it yet again. This desolation [Dan 9.26 c.f. Matthew 23.38[105]] will be the beginning of many that will continue until the times of Israel's sufferings are completed, at the return of Christ. In fact, His return will be to deliver the Jews from what will appear at the time to be the final desolation and end of Israel [Zech 14]

Who are the People of the Prince That Shall Come?

The defeat described in Daniel 9.26 will be accomplished by the people of the prince who will come. Determining the people and from that determining the prince is not straightforward. The book of Revelation will help us identify the people who are mentioned in Daniel 9. The identity of the prince is obscured by the passage of many centuries between the people who destroyed the "city and sanctuary" and the appearance of the prince identified with them.

Note carefully that this verse is not saying that the prince himself is participating or even present at that time that the people in verse 26 are active against Israel. In fact, the people destroyed the city and sanctuary within a few decades of the end of the 69th prophetic week. The prince will not appear until much later in time, during the 70th week which is addressed in the 27th verse.

The book of Revelation and historians such as Flavius Josephus tell us who destroyed the Temple in the first century A.D. In the description of the seven heads of the Beast of Revelation 17, the following is stated:

Revelation 17:10–11 (KJV 1900)
10 And there are seven kings: five are fallen, and one is, and the other is not yet come; and when he cometh, he must continue a short space. 11 And the beast that was, and is not, even he is the eighth, and is of the seven, and goeth into perdition.

The overall significance of this chapter will be addressed in the second half of this book. For now, it is sufficient to say that the king/kingdom which "is" *at the time of the revelation to John* is Rome. Josephus confirms that the destruction happened in August of A.D. 70 when the Roman armies of Titus, the son of Vespasian, destroyed Jerusalem and the temple and took the remaining Jews captive. Neither Titus or Vespasian were that prince of Daniel 9.26, and he *has not* yet appeared upon the scene.[106] This destruction of Jerusalem had occurred about 25 years before John received this vision.

In the visions that Daniel recorded in the 2nd chapter of his book, the second, third and fourth kingdoms which follow Babylon, "the head of gold" are left unidentified. It can be determined by an evaluation of chapter eight of Daniel that the second and third kingdoms are the Medo- Persian and the Greek empires [Dan 5.30-31 c.f. 8.17-22]. The nationality of the fourth kingdom, corresponding to the legs of iron and the feet of iron and clay, is not identified by Daniel. Neither did he disclose the national origin of the fourth beast in Daniel 7.7, 23. This issue is clarified in the book of Revelation, roughly six centuries later.

The book of Daniel addresses this fourth kingdom because its beginning occurs in the age of Israel[107] and its end, the time of the feet of iron and clay, occurs in a time in which God has resumed his dealings with the nation of Israel. It is in the latter context [the 70th week] that the "prince that shall come "appears. Between these two prophetic eras [both of which pertain to God's dealings with Israel] lies the Church, a mystery to the Old Testament prophets[108] that was revealed by Christ and given doctrinal treatment by the apostle Paul. *This era of the Church is not foreseen or addressed by Daniel, or any other Old Testament prophet.*

Armed with this knowledge, Daniel's statement regarding the *people* of the prince who will come points us in the direction of Rome. It was the people identified with the Roman empire who were responsible for the destruction of the city of Jerusalem and the Temple following the 69th week of Daniel's prophecy. The appearance of the prince has been delayed for nearly 2000 years and awaits the end of the Church Age which will occur at the resurrection or Rapture of the Body of Christ from the earth. At that time God resumes his prophetic dealings with Israel, first in judgment and culminating in salvation and fulfillment of their covenant promises. This prince is one of those judgments [Rev 6.1-2].

The identity of the prince that will come cannot be determined by resorting to the book of Daniel alone. The assumption that the prince that shall come must be a product of a revitalized Roman Empire implies that his identification with Rome must be political. What was Rome in the 1st century no longer exists today and there is no way of knowing what ethnic and geopolitical changes will transpire before the Rapture of the Church and the appearance of the kingdom in question. It is possible that this prince might be associated with Rome or its former empire ethnically, geographically, or even metaphorically. In the second half of this book, we will suggest that the 70th week of Daniel will be a time when world politics will be guided by a movement towards *global* government.[109]

The 70th Week

> Daniel 9:27 (KJV 1900)
> 27 And he shall confirm the covenant with many for one week: and in the midst of the week he shall cause the sacrifice and the oblation to cease, and for the overspreading of abominations he shall make it desolate, even until the consummation, and that determined shall be poured upon the desolate.

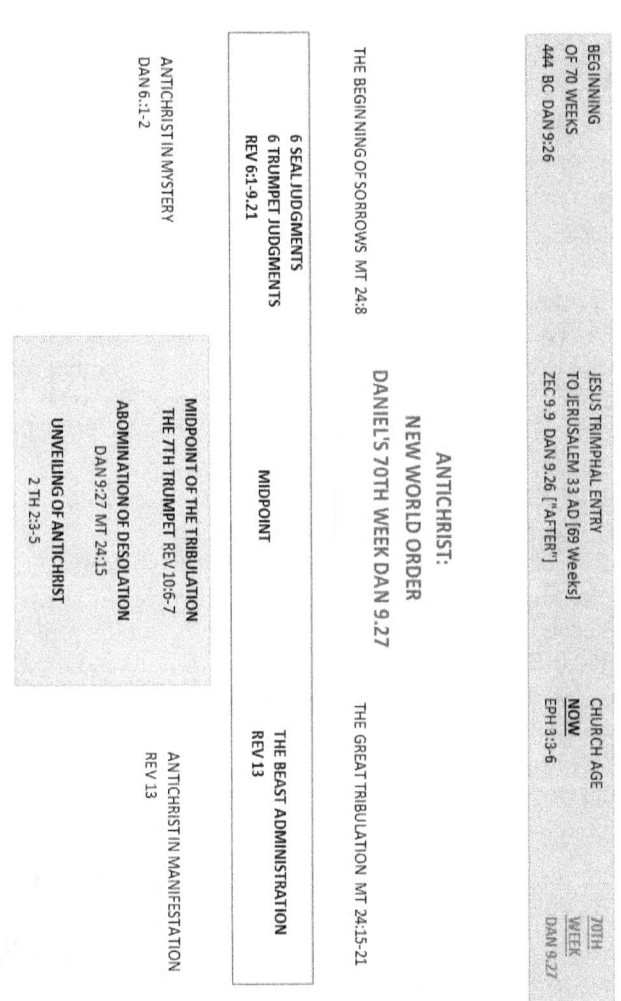

Figure 4: Daniel's 70th Week

There is a significant lapse of time between the conclusion of the 69th week [circa 33 A.D.] and the covenant to be made in the final [70th] week, mentioned in verse 27. This gap in time includes the present Church Age, which began at the Pentecost following Jesus' ascension. The duration of the Church age is unpredicted in scripture. The Church is unrevealed in the Old Testament.[110]

Daniel 9:26 (KJV 1900)
26 And <u>after</u> threescore and two [7 plus 62=69 total weeks-rw] weeks shall Messiah be cut off, but not for himself: and the people of the prince that shall come shall destroy the city and the sanctuary; and the end thereof shall be with a flood, and unto the end of the war desolations are determined.

The Triumphal Entry of Christ into Jerusalem marks the end of the 69 weeks. The existence of an interval of time between the 69th and 70th weeks is demonstrated by several things. The cutting off of the Messiah occurs *after* the 69th week but before the 70th week, indicating that there is an interval between these last two "weeks."[111] Additionally, the destruction of Jerusalem ["*the city and the sanctuary*"] occurs roughly 40 years after the end of the 69th week. The "desolations" of Daniel 9.27 also occur after the conclusion of the 69th week.

Who exactly is this prince? The word "he" in Daniel 9.27 refers back to the phrase "*the prince that shall come*" in verse 26. The prince that shall come is a reference to the Man of Sin, the Son of Perdition mentioned in 2 Thessalonians 2, the Beast in Rev 13 and the Antichrist predicted by John [1John 2]. *This prince does exactly the same things that these other men do.*

Daniel 9:27 (KJV 1900)
27 And <u>he</u> shall confirm the covenant with many for one week: and in the midst of the week he shall cause the sacrifice and the oblation to cease, and for the overspreading of abominations he shall make it desolate, even until the consummation, and that determined shall be poured upon the desolate.

The *prince that shall come* will take it upon himself to create a new form of worship to a new God. In the future, he will ravage and desecrate the Temple in the process of establishing the worship of a God whom his father's knew not [Dan 11.38]. The Bible assigns importance to this man by describing his works under several names in several biblical texts.

Another Horn/King

Daniel 7:24–25 (KJV 1900)
24 And the ten horns out of this kingdom are ten kings that shall arise: and another shall rise after them; and he shall be diverse from the first, and he shall subdue three kings. 25 <u>And he shall speak great words against the most High, and shall wear out the saints of the most High, and think to change times and laws: and they shall be given into his hand until a time and times and the dividing of time.</u>

The Man of Sin; The Son of Perdition

2 Thessalonians 2:3–4 (KJV 1900)
3 Let no man deceive you by any means: for that day shall not come, except there come a falling away first, and that man of sin be revealed, the son of perdition; 4 <u>Who opposeth and exalteth himself above all that is called God, or that is worshipped; so that he as God sitteth in the temple of God, shewing himself that he is God.</u>

The Beast

Revelation 13:1, 5-6 (KJV 1900)
1 And I stood upon the sand of the sea, and saw a beast rise up out of the sea, having seven heads and ten horns, and upon his horns ten crowns, and upon his heads the name of blasphemy…5 <u>And there was given unto him a mouth speaking great things and blasphemies; and power was given unto him to continue forty and two months.</u> 6 And he opened his mouth in blasphemy against God, to blaspheme his name, and his tabernacle, and them that dwell in heaven.

The Wilful King; That Wicked

Daniel 11:36 (KJV 1900)
36 And the king shall do according to his will; <u>and he shall exalt himself, and magnify himself above every god, and shall</u>

<u>speak marvellous things against the God of gods, and shall prosper</u> till the indignation be accomplished: for that that is determined shall be done.

2 Thessalonians 2:8 (KJV 1900)
8 And then shall <u>that Wicked be revealed</u>, whom the Lord shall consume with the spirit of his mouth, and shall destroy with the brightness of his coming:

This person is the same as the prince who is to come in Daniel 9.26. He seeks to overturn the worship of God in the earth, resulting in desolations. This person is identified with the *people*[112] [not necessarily the political entity] who will destroy Jerusalem shortly after the end of the 69th week of Daniel's prophecy. This prince will not appear until many centuries later, in a time yet future, during the seventieth week described in Daniel 9.27.

The world power, the fourth beast, or kingdom, of Daniel 7.1-8 corresponds to the legs of iron and feet of iron and clay in his vision of chapter Daniel 2:40-45. This kingdom is further explained in Rev 17: 9-11 which describes it as the sixth, seventh and eighth "heads or kingdoms." This description of the destiny of the Gentile nations to the apostle John is an in-depth explanation of something that was explained far more simply to Nebuchadnezzar in Daniel 2. That which is called "Rome," an empire in the time of John [and the *sixth* head of Rev 17.10], becomes in the latter times a designation for world government, specifically, in its development after the departure of the restraining spiritual influence of the Church and the subsequent appearance of this prince. All of this is the subject of Book Two.

The person of the Antichrist represents the culmination of Satan's efforts in the manipulation of human history since the Garden of Eden. In view of the importance of the issues that God is resolving through this supernatural conflict, the coming Antichrist, his person, and his deeds, is revealed through a number of prophecies and types in both the Old and New Testaments.

6
His Character: A Rider on a White Horse: Israel in End-Time Geopolitics

Daniel 9:27 (KJV 1900)
27 And he shall confirm the covenant with many for one week: and in the midst of the week he shall cause the sacrifice and the oblation to cease, and for the overspreading of abominations he shall make it desolate, even until the consummation, and that determined shall be poured upon the desolate.

The Timing of the Day of the Lord

The devil is having his day, or days. Evil runs rampant throughout the world. Injustice is normative, the primary institutions of the earth are undermined by evil. Human volition is compromised by addictions, gender is confused, marriage is devalued, the family is malfunctioning, and government not only fails to protect freedom but is a sponsor of oppression.

Cynical persons mock the idea of divine judgment. They observe the apparent victory of evil over good and deny the inevitability of divine justice.

> 2 Peter 3:3–4 (KJV 1900)
> 3 Knowing this first, that there shall come in the last days scoffers, walking after their own lusts, 4 And saying, Where is the promise of his coming? for since the fathers fell asleep, all things continue as they were from the beginning of the creation.

Surely, the Mystery of Lawlessness has been at work throughout history. The scoffers are unable to discern the Mystery of Godliness working within history just as surely.

> 1 Timothy 3:16 (KJV 1900)
> 16 And without controversy great is the mystery of godliness: God was manifest in the flesh, justified in the Spirit, seen of angels, preached unto the Gentiles, believed on in the world, received up into glory.

> Acts 1:9–11 (KJV 1900)
> 9 And when he had spoken these things, while they beheld, he was taken up; and a cloud received him out of their sight. 10 And while they looked stedfastly toward heaven as he went up, behold, two men stood by them in white apparel; 11 Which also said, Ye men of Galilee, why stand ye gazing up into heaven? this same Jesus, which is taken up from you into heaven, shall so come in like manner as ye have seen him go into heaven.

Scripture has promised not only the return of Christ in judgment and victory [Rev 19.11], but also the end of God's forbearance towards the sins of men. God has promised severe judgment of mankind *prior* to the return of Jesus Christ in addition to the death he will bring upon His return [Rev 19.17-20.3]. This period, beginning after the departure of the Church and continuing through the Millennium, has been referred to as the Day of the Lord[113] and it is described in detail in the book of Revelation.

Revelation describes a seven sealed book which contains the judgments against the world and its inhabitants. Only the Lamb, Jesus Christ is qualified to open the book that is in the hand of the Father [Revelation 5]. Revelation 6 relates the opening of the first seal of this book.

> Revelation 6:1 (KJV 1900)
> 1 And I saw when the Lamb opened one of the seals, and I heard, as it were the noise of thunder, one of the four beasts saying, Come and see.

The opening of the seven sealed book represents the beginning of the Day of the Lord. The judgments unsealed within the books gradually increase in severity to the point that they would destroy the earth and every life upon it if they were allowed to continue.

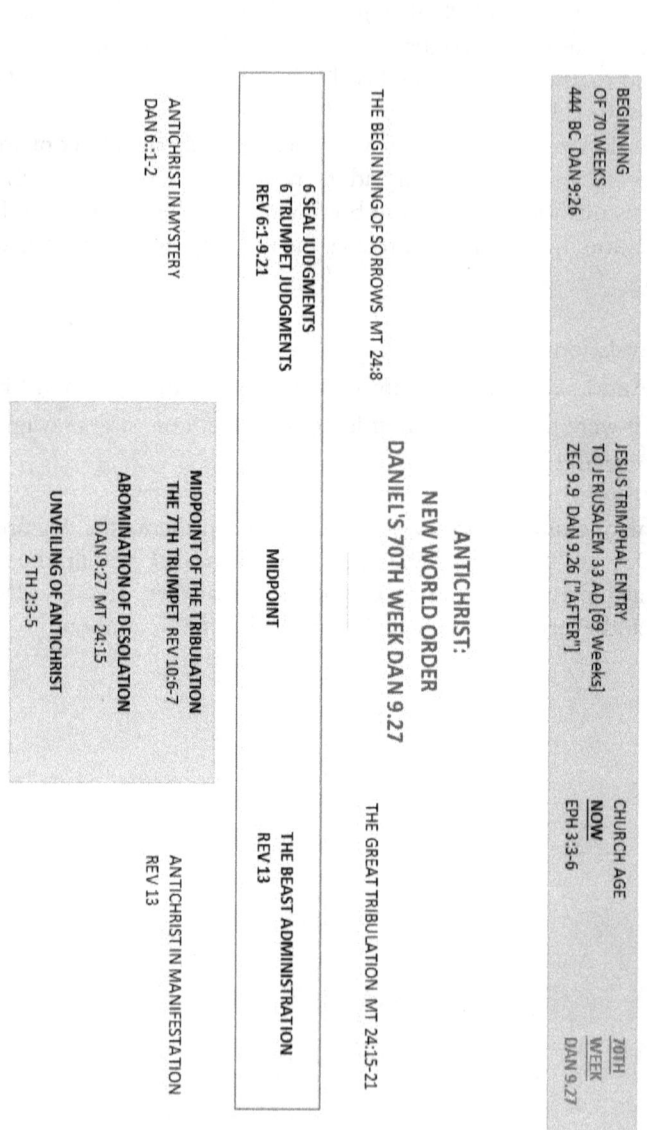

Fig 4: Daniel's 70th Week

Jesus opens the seven sealed book, but He also predicts its contents in the book of Matthew. The series of predictions in Matthew 24 parallel those of Revelation 6.

> "There is a remarkable similarity between the progress of chapter 6 as a whole and the description given by our Lord of the end of the age in Matthew 24:4–31. In both passages the order is (1) war (Matt. 24:6–7; Rev. 6:3–4), (2) famine (Matt. 24:7; Rev. 6:5–6), (3) death (Matt. 24:7–9; Rev. 6:7–8), (4) martyrdom (Matt. 24:9–10, 16–22; Rev. 6:9–11), (5) the sun darkened, the moon darkened, and the stars falling (Matt. 24:29; Rev. 6:12–14), (6) a time of divine judgment (Matt. 24:32–25:26; Rev. 6:15–17). The general features of Matthew 24 are obviously quite parallel to the events of the book of Revelation beginning in chapter 6."

The Beginning of Sorrows

Matthew 24:4–8 (KJV 1900)
4 And Jesus answered and said unto them, Take heed that no man deceive you. 5 For many shall come in my name, saying, I am Christ; and shall deceive many. 6 And ye shall hear of wars and rumours of wars: see that ye be not troubled: for all these things must come to pass, but the end is not yet. 7 For nation shall rise against nation, and kingdom against kingdom: and there shall be famines, and pestilences, and earthquakes, in divers places. 8 All these are the beginning of sorrows.

These predictions appear to correspond to the first four horsemen of Revelation 6.1-8.

Revelation 6:1–8 (KJV 1900) 1 And I saw when the Lamb opened one of the seals, and I heard, as it were the noise of thunder, one of the four beasts saying, Come and see. 2 And I saw, and behold a white horse: and he that sat on him had a bow; and a crown was given unto him: and he went forth conquering, and to conquer. 3 And when he had opened the second seal, I heard the second beast say, Come and see. 4 And there went out another horse that was red: and power was given to him that sat thereon to take peace from the earth, and that they should kill one another: and there was given unto him a great sword. 5 And when he had opened the third seal,

I heard the third beast say, Come and see. And I beheld, and lo a black horse; and he that sat on him had a pair of balances in his hand. 6 And I heard a voice in the midst of the four beasts say, A measure of wheat for a penny, and three measures of barley for a penny; and see thou hurt not the oil and the wine. 7 And when he had opened the fourth seal, I heard the voice of the fourth beast say, Come and see. 8 And I looked, and behold a pale horse: and his name that sat on him was Death, and Hell followed with him. And power was given unto them over the fourth part of the earth, to kill with sword, and with hunger, and with death, and with the beasts of the earth.

The apostle John, the writer of the book of Revelation, identifies these events as the beginning of the cataclysms to be chronicled in the Apocalypse. This is not the end, but the beginning of the Day of the Lord and the beginning of the punishments which God will pour out upon the world. Consequently, these events [Rev 6.1-8] may be placed within the first 3- and one-half years, or 42 months of Daniel's 70th week, the "beginning of sorrows."

There are other judgments revealed in Revelation that occur within the first half of the 70th week. The seventh seal is the first trumpet judgment [Rev 8.1-2]. Likewise, the seventh trumpet is the first of the seven vial or bowl judgments which conclude the judgments of the seven sealed book. The midpoint of the tribulation does not occur until the seventh trumpet judgment.[114] As of that judgment there are still seven remaining judgments [the vial or bowl judgments Rev 15.1] before the return of Jesus and yet further death and destruction [Rev 19].

We propose that the first seal of Revelation 6.1-2 is the Antichrist before his revelation as the Beast at the midpoint of the Tribulation [the Tribulation is also Daniel's 70th week]. The Man of Sin is the first manifestation of the judgment of God against the earth.

Matthew 24:5 (KJV 1900)
5 For many shall come in my name, saying, I am Christ; and shall deceive many

Revelation 6:1–2 (KJV 1900)
1 And I saw when the Lamb opened one of the seals, and I heard, as it were the noise of thunder, one of the four beasts saying, Come and see. 2 And I saw, and behold a white horse: and he that

sat on him had a bow; and a crown was given unto him: and he went forth conquering, and to conquer

Will the Real Messiah Please Stand Up?

There was a popular quiz show in the 1960's where three persons would pretend to be the same individual [let's assume his name was Smith] whose unusual occupation would be described to a panel of celebrities by the show's host. The celebrities would then ask the three persons questions, [two impostors and the real person] in an attempt to distinguish the real Mr. Smith from the imposters. At the end of the game, each celebrity would commit to the person they believed was the real Mr. Smith. The host would then dramatically ask: "**Will the real Mr. Smith please stand up.**"

The Bible describes the true Christ or Messiah, and each generation must decide who of all the pretenders is the real Christ. But this is no game. For every person, this decision is a matter of life or death. At the end of history, there will arrive upon the scene the most convincing of all the imitators of Christ.

A principal feature of the Mystery of Lawlessness is deception. This tendency will continue into the first 3.5 years that follow the Rapture or resurrection of the Church. The devil can appear as a roaring lion [1 Pet 5.8], which he will do at the midpoint of the Tribulation when the Antichrist erects the Abomination of Desolation in the Jewish Temple; but he also may appear as an angel of light [2 Cor 11.13-15]. It is as an angel of light and peace that the devil's representative will *enter* the stage of history. The Antichrist will convince many that he is the Christ because he will be an imitation that appeals to the fallen imaginations of mankind. He will appeal to the lost because they will have allowed themselves to be deceived. [2 Th 2.8-12].

In fairness, the Antichrist will resemble the true Messiah several ways. The book of Revelation highlights these similarities in its description of the true Christ and the Antichrist.

Christ Rev 19	Antichrist Rev 6	Pertaining to Antichrist in Scripture
A white horse	A white horse	
Three names: 'Faithful and True;' 'The Word of God;' 'A name written that no one knew but he himself;' 'King of Kings and Lord of Lords' [three of the four are called 'names']	Nameless	Descriptors: [but not names] Prince who shall come [Dan 9.26] Man of Sin, Son of Perdition [2Th 2], Antichrist [1Jn 2.18; 2Jn 7], Beast [Rev 13]
Judge and make war	War and death follow him Conquering and to Conquer	Victory: "the same horn made war against the saints and prevailed against them" Dan 7.21,25; 11.40-44; Rev 11.37; 13.7. He also overcame the nations Dan 11.40.44
Eyes were as fire	No physical features provided	"eyes like the eyes of man" Dan 7.8
Many crowns on his head	A crown given to him	Given: "in his estate shall he honor the god of forces" Dan 11.37 "they worshipped the dragon which gave power unto the beast" Rev 13.4
Vesture dipped in blood	Perhaps naked	
Armies follow	Alone	War follows
A sharp sword from His mouth	A bow without arrows	"a mouth speaking great things" Dan 7.8 Sword follows

Fig 5: Image of Christ and Antichrist

Christ will return to consummate the plan of God the Father, but as the Second Person of the Godhead, he comes under his own authority.

Revelation 19:15–16 (KJV 1900)
15 And out of his mouth goeth a sharp sword, that with it he should smite the nations: and he shall rule them with a rod of iron: and he treadeth the winepress of the fierceness and wrath of Almighty God. 16 And he hath on his vesture and on his thigh a name written, KING OF KINGS, AND LORD OF LORDS.

In Revelation 19, Jesus is named, he is titled, and he is clothed with the emblems of his authority. Christ is the God-man, the Son of man, undiminished deity and perfect humanity in one Person [Rev 1.13; 14.14]: he is described in some detail regarding his eyes, his head, his mouth and his thigh, as well as his vesture. Christ will demonstrate true spiritual power at His advent, destroying his enemies, he will rule the world and he will receive worship [Dan 7.13-14; Rev 19.20-20.3; Rev 21].

The Antichrist in Revelation 6.1-2, on the other hand, comes in the authority and power of another, the dragon or Satan [Dan 13.3-17]. The Antichrist is not named, not clothed, and has no human physical features described. The Antichrist will be a tool indwelt by Lucifer, whom he will worship.

Nonetheless, the Antichrist will be a reasonable facsimile of the true Christ: while Christ will conquer to bring peace, Antichrist will bring peace in order to conquer. Jesus will implement the New Covenant to redeemed Israel, while the Antichrist will negotiate a false covenant with political Israel. The Antichrist will have demonstrable spiritual power, he will rule the world, and he will be worshipped [Daniel 11.35ff; Rev 13.3-17].

Antichrist: From Statesman and Man of Government to the Assumption of Deity

During the first three- and one-half years of his covenant, the times identified with "the beginning of sorrows," Antichrist will be on the world stage unrecognized as the Man of Sin, but as a statesman who is able to do what few could do throughout history, broker a peace settlement in the Middle East. The reference to "many" in Daniel 9.27 may indicate that the covenant will involve more nations than that of Israel, including some of their neighbors and perhaps some of their allies who are factors in their geopolitical profile.

There have been Israeli peace agreements in the past, most significantly the 1949 Armistice Agreements which were negotiated by African American diplomat Ralph Bunch, for which he received the Nobel Peace Prize. These agreements were the most complete to date, including agreements with Egypt, Lebanon, Jordan, and Syria.

The two agreements that are known as the Camp David accords were signed in September of 1978 but were limited to only Egypt and Israel. This effort was initiated by Anwar El Sadat, president of Egypt, who also received the Nobel Peace Prize, jointly with Menachem

Begin, the leader of Israel. These agreements created hostility among the nations that were left out and created a power vacuum when Egypt was excluded from the Arab League.

The future agreement or covenant will surpass these in international acclaim. This covenant with Israel will apparently allow the Jews not only some assurances of peace but will also provide for their full religious expression.[115] This freedom will prove illusory when the covenant is broken a mere 42 months later, their spiritual observances condemned, and some Jews are sought out for persecution. The "beginning of sorrows" will end with this event and the Great Tribulation will begin.

According to Daniel, this breach of the peace treaty will begin with what appear to be multiple abominations pertaining to the temple and its sacrificial system.

> Daniel 9:27 (KJV 1900)
> 27 And he shall confirm the covenant with many for one week: and in the midst of the week he shall cause the sacrifice and the oblation to cease, and for the overspreading of abominations he shall make it desolate, even until the consummation, and that determined shall be poured upon the desolate.

Jesus included the temple or "holy place" in his prophecy regarding this future situation and its severity upon Israel.

> Matthew 24:15–16 (KJV 1900)
> 15 When ye therefore shall see the abomination of desolation, spoken of by Daniel the prophet, stand in the holy place, (whoso readeth, let him understand:) 16 Then let them which be in Judaea flee into the mountains: [Acts 6:13. c.f., Mark 13:14]

The prince who is to come will claim the temple and its ritual as his own dominion, now in the possession of a new god, whom he represents in a similar relation as Christ to the Godhead. As the self-proclaimed Messiah, he will claim Israel and the Jews as his possession.

> 2 Thessalonians 2:3–4 (KJV 1900)
> 3 Let no man deceive you by any means: for that day shall not come, except there come a falling away first, and that man of sin

be revealed, the son of perdition; 4 Who opposeth and exalteth himself above all that is called God, or that is worshipped; so that he as God <u>sitteth in the temple of God</u>, shewing himself that he is God.

The prince that is to come is a deceiver. He is the son of perdition who, like Judas who shares that title, deceives Israel with a promise of fidelity [Mt 26.20-22]. He will pretend to be a friend of the Jews but will harbor plans to profane their religion and to annihilate all who will not worship him and his god, the dragon, Lucifer. *Deception*, the concept which characterizes the Mystery of Lawlessness throughout history will, after the first half of the Tribulation, be replaced by the concept of *Blasphemy* which will publicly characterize the Mystery of Lawlessness from that time forward.

Richard G. Walker

7
His Character: The Man of Sin

2 Thessalonians 2:3–4 (KJV 1900)
3 Let no man deceive you by any means: for that day shall not come, except there come a falling away first, and <u>that man of sin</u> be revealed, the son of perdition; 4 Who opposeth and exalteth himself above all that is called God, or that is worshipped; so that he as God sitteth in the temple of God, shewing himself that he is God.

Daniel 11:36 (KJV 1900)
36 And the king shall do according to his will; and he shall exalt himself, and magnify himself above every god, and shall speak marvellous things against the God of gods, and shall prosper till the indignation be accomplished: for that that is determined shall be done.[116]

 The Rapture of the Church will be followed by the collision of two conflicting prophetic events: The Day of the Lord and the appearing of Satan's man, the Man of Sin. Antichrist will initially be perceived as a statesman who will broker an agreement with the Jews which will provide them with the ability to function with some degree of security and to pursue their religious obligations in the land. However, this will be a single stratagem in a campaign to situate himself in a position of power from which his true objectives will be revealed.
 The description of Antichrist as the Man of Sin clarifies his moral relation to the true Christ. Christ is holy in all his thoughts, motivations, decisions, and actions. He is entirely separate from sin, He does not

and cannot promote or condone sin in the world [1 Jn 1.5]. In His incarnation the humanity of Jesus used the power of the Spirit to resist temptation from the world and the devil [Isa 11.1-2 c.f. Mt 3.16]. His perfect humanity and absolute deity qualified Him as our Sacrifice. Jesus is not merely separate from sin; He is also positively holy in his essence. Thus, infinite righteousness and justice characterize His Person as well as His policies. Because he is positively holy, God demands holiness from His creation, the absence of which has resulted in the condemnation of the world and all who are in it. God requires holiness from redeemed humanity, a condition which he himself makes possible by the imputation of Christ's righteousness to the one who believes the gospel,[117] the death of the believer to sin,[118] the creation of a new nature[119] and the power of the indwelling Spirit[120] which produces the character of Christ in the soul of obedient believers through the Word of God [Gal 5.22-23]. In the future, this Holy Savior will establish everlasting righteousness throughout heaven and earth [Am 5.24].

By contrast, the Antichrist is the chief example of demonically indwelt, hybridized humanity. Because he will be indwelt by Lucifer[121] he will be entirely identified with the devil's rejection of everything that God has established. The simple term for this policy of opposition is sin. He is the Man of Sin.

The Antichrist is opposed to righteousness in its every manifestation because Lucifer is opposed to it. He is opposed to God's celestial and natural order, which Satan intrigued to ruin; he is opposed to all mankind because they are made in the image of God, they have been the means by which God defeated his sponsor by the incarnation of Christ as a man, and because redeemed humanity will eventually judge the angels themselves [1 Cor 6.3].[122] He is opposed to the institutions by which the orderly function of humanity is enabled: therefore, he opposes the freedom of the human soul, he opposes marriage and family and he opposes the concept of human government as they are each constituted by God. Certainly, he is against the Church, the sole means by which man is placed in right relation to God, through the gospel [Jn 3:16; Rom 10.9].

The agenda of the Antichrist is not simply to rule over what God has established, but to subvert, undermine and overthrow the existing world and replace it with a New World Order operated on the basis of satanic concepts, for the rule and worship of Lucifer as God. As sin is the demonstration of opposition to God, the Man of Sin will make sin the operating principle of his brief kingdom.

The Man of Sin will inaugurate this kingdom with the desecration of the Jewish temple which will stand at that time. The decision of the Antichrist to make himself known marks the transition out of mystery [deception and secret blasphemy] to open manifestation [desecration and open blasphemy] of the conspiracy against God. Desecration[123] has always been the center of satanic worship, but in the Antichrist, it will become universally known by this act called the "abomination of desolation." [Mk 13.14]

8
His Character: The Son of Perdition, the Reanimated Man

2 Thessalonians 2:3–4 (KJV 1900)
3 Let no man deceive you by any means: for that day shall not come, except there come a falling away first, and that man of sin be revealed, the son of perdition; 4 Who opposeth and exalteth himself above all that is called God, or that is worshipped; so that he as God sitteth in the temple of God, shewing himself that he is God.

Perdition[124] [NT; 684] means eternal destruction and torment suffered by the one who is rejected by God. The word translated "*perdition*" is in the original language the exact opposite of the word "*salvation.*"[125]

The Antichrist is prophesied as one who will experience this destiny of perdition. The Antichrist is elect unto reprobation: although he is not yet born, it is predicted that he will be eternally lost. This is the only end possible for this particular "*son*" and the one who is his "*father*"

In the scriptures, there is a class of deceivers whose end is determined to be **perdition or destruction *[NT 684]***. They operate in the same *spirit of antichrist* personified by the Son of Perdition

2 Peter 2:1–3 (KJV 1900)
1 But there were false prophets also among the people, even as there shall be false teachers among you, who privily shall bring in damnable [NT:684] heresies, even denying the Lord that bought

them, and bring upon themselves swift <u>destruction</u> [NT:684]. 2 And many shall follow their <u>pernicious</u> ways; [NT:684] by reason of whom the way of truth shall be evil spoken of. 3 And through covetousness shall they with feigned words make merchandise of you: whose judgment now of a long time lingereth not, and their <u>damnation</u> [NT:684] slumbereth not.

The Greek word that is translated *perdition* is interpreted in the book of Revelation as a *name*: **Apollyon**. Understanding this name discloses a great deal about the nature of the *Son* of Perdition. In the fifth trumpet judgment we read the following:

Revelation 9:2-3; 11 (KJV 1900)
2 And he opened the bottomless pit; and there arose a smoke out of the pit, as the smoke of a great furnace; and the sun and the air were darkened by reason of the smoke of the pit. 3 And there came out of the smoke locusts upon the earth: and unto them was given power, as the scorpions of the earth have power. 11 And <u>they had a king over them, which is the angel of the bottomless pit, whose name in the Hebrew tongue is Abaddon, but in the Greek tongue hath his name Apollyon.</u>[126]

Who is this Apollyon?

Apollyon is the key to understanding this name, Son of Perdition. His name "Apollyon" means perdition or destruction, Apollyon is the *father* of Perdition. He is the prince and angel of imprisoned spirits. He is the angel of the bottomless pit [abyss] or Hades which includes the imprisoned spirits[angels] and the souls of the lost.

Hades is the present location of Perdition, the residence of certain demons [2 Pet 2.4; Jude 6] and all lost humanity who are deceased.[127] In the future, Hades will be transferred to the Lake of Fire, the final destination of Satan, the Beast, the false prophet, demons/fallen angels and all of unbelieving humanity [Rev 20.13-14].

The bottomless pit or the *abyss* [NT:12], is also the place from which the Beast arises [Revelation 11.7]. Since the prince that shall come, the Antichrist, is a human being, this statement must refer to the one who *indwells* him, the same entity which indwelt Judas [Ps 109.6 sq.; Jn 13.21-27] *who is likewise referred to* as the son of perdition [John 17.12][128].

Apollyon is a corruption of Apollo,[129] the pagan god of the sun, and of light. Lucifer is also worshipped as the sun and as the light-bearer. The Greeks associated the name Apollo with the verb to destroy.[130]

Therefore, by way of interpretation, Apollyon is Lucifer, the Lord of the fallen angels and the sovereign of lost humanity [Jn 8.44; Eph 2.2]. He is the Father of Perdition, or everlasting destruction; he is its source and reason for being [Mt 25.41].

The notable offspring of Apollyon are Judas and the Antichrist, both called the Sons of Perdition [John 17.12; 2 Thessalonians 2.3]. Apollyon is also Apollo, the false god of the sun and of light, represented by the serpent, the lyre, **and the horseman.**[131]

A host of scholars[132] identify Apollyon as Lucifer including, C.H. Spurgeon, Warren Wiersbe, John Walvoord, Roy Zuck, Adam Clark, Jonathan Edwards.

We have stated that the *destiny* of the Antichrist is perdition. His title, Son of Perdition, also implies that his *origin* is perdition as well. Since the Antichrist will be indwelt and empowered by Lucifer, as Judas, the only other Son of Perdition, nearly all that makes him who he will be will originate in Hell.

Revelation 13:2 (KJV 1900)
2 And the beast which I saw was like unto a leopard, and his feet were as the feet of a bear, and his mouth as the mouth of a lion: and the dragon gave him his power, and his seat, and great authority.

Christ came to earth as a special incarnation, perfect humanity, and undiminished deity in one Person. Satan will also seek to produce a special creation for his greatest representative. Although the point is certainly debatable, Arthur W. Pink speculated in the early twentieth century that the Antichrist would be the reanimated Judas himself. Pink makes several points to this end, three are mentioned here:

> 1. "As we have seen, in John 17:12 Christ termed Judas "the Son of Perdition," and 2 Thessalonians 2:3 we find that the Antichrist is similarly designated—"That Man of Sin be revealed, the Son of Perdition." These are the only two places in all the Bible where his name occurs, and the fact that Judas was termed by Christ not "a son of perdition," but "the Son of Perdition," and the fact that the Man of Sin is so named prove that they are one and the same person.[133]
> 2. "In Revelation 11:7 we have the first reference to "the Beast" in the Apocalypse: "The Beast that ascendeth out of the bottomless pit." Here the Antichrist is seen issuing forth from the Abyss. What is the

Abyss? It is the abode of lost spirits, the place of their incarceration and torment—see Revelation 20:1-3, and Luke 8:31, "deep" is the "abyss" and cf. Matthew 9:28. The question naturally arises, How did he get there? and when was he sent there? We answer, When Judas Iscariot died! The Antichrist will be Judas Iscariot reincarnated. In proof of this we appeal to Acts 1:25 where we are told, "that he may take part of this ministry and apostleship from which Judas by transgression fell, that he might go to his own place." Of no one else in all the Bible is it said that at death he went "to his own place." Put these two scriptures together: Judas went "to his own place," the Beast ascends out of the Abyss."

3. "We take it, then, that what is predicted of "the Beast" in Revelation 17:8 is true of both the Roman Empire and its last head, the Antichrist: of the former, in the sense that it is infernal in its character. Viewing it now as a declaration of the Antichrist, what does it tell us about him? Four things. First, he "was." Second, he "is not." Third, he shall "ascend out of the Bottomless Pit." Fourth, he shall "go into perdition." The various time-marks here concern the Beast in his relation to the earth. First, he "was," i.e. on the earth. Second, he "is not," i.e. now on the earth (cf. Genesis 5:24, "Enoch was not for God took him;" that is, "was not" any longer on earth). Third, he shall "ascend out of the Bottomless Bit," where he is now, which agrees with Revelation 11:7. Fourth, he shall "go into perdition." We learn then from this scripture that at the time the Apocalypse was written the Beast "was not" then on the earth, but that he had been on it formerly. Further, we learn that in John's day the Beast was then in the Bottomless Pit but should yet ascend out of it.[134] Here then is further evidence that the Antichrist who is yet to appear has been on earth before." [135]

We will return to this subject in our examination of the "Beast" in Chapter 16. Whoever he turns out to be, the Beast arises geographically and ethnically out of the sea of Mediterranean nations [Revelation 13.1] but his spiritual birthright is the bottomless pit [Revelation 11.7; 17.8] as the offspring of him who is ruler of the condemned and that which is fallen. Just as Judas was indwelt by Lucifer, so will the Antichrist be possessed by his spiritual father, Apollyon.

9
His Character: The Lawless One[136] and the Conspiracy to Destroy Civilization

2 Thessalonians 2:7–10 (KJV 1900)
7 For the mystery of iniquity [NT 458] doth already work: only he who now letteth will let, until he be taken out of the way. 8 And then shall that Wicked be revealed, whom the Lord shall consume with the spirit of his mouth, and shall destroy with the brightness of his coming: 9 Even him, whose coming is after the working of Satan with all power and signs and lying wonders, 10 And with all deceivableness of unrighteousness in them that perish; because they received not the love of the truth, that they might be saved.

The "working of Satan" is the effort of Lucifer in advancing the Mystery of Iniquity throughout the ages. It is a spiritual undertaking with concrete results in the world around us. Its objective is the production of the New World Order and the emergence of the Lawless One, the Antichrist. The spirit of lawlessness is only effectively resisted by the spiritual efforts of the Body of Christ, the Church.

1 Peter 5:8–9 (KJV 1900)
8 Be sober, be vigilant; because your adversary the devil, as a roaring lion, walketh about, seeking whom he may devour: 9 <u>Whom resist</u> stedfast in the faith, knowing that the same afflictions are accomplished in your brethren that are in the world.

It is the will of God that the believer resists the devil in his own spiritual life and in his relationships with persons and institutions. The sanctification and ministry of believers is a real protection and help to the individuals and institutions in their periphery and Christians are capable of significant historical impact. The Church must resist the devil until the full company of the elect of this age is called out of this world by Christ.

The prince that shall come is "*anomos [NT 459]*" he is *without* the law, *against* the law of God. He rejects the commandments and statutes of God and operates out of pragmatism: his ends justify his means; he will pursue whatever action leads to his objective without regard for morality or righteousness. This again confirms that the Lawless One is in rebellion against God. The Antichrist is not merely a sinner, he does not simply violate God's laws; he is a *revolutionary* who rejects God's very right to rule the universe.

> Psalm 2:1–3 (KJV 1900)
> 1 Why do the heathen rage, And the people imagine a vain thing? 2 The kings of the earth set themselves, And the rulers take counsel together, Against the LORD, and against his anointed, saying, 3 Let us break their bands asunder, And cast away their cords from us.

The Bible teaches that there is a conspiracy among men to throw off the "bonds and cords" of God's law. This conspiracy mirrors its heavenly counterpart: "as above so below"[137] [Rev 12.7-9]. Mystery Babylon, a supernatural construct, is characterized by the cooperation of angels and men in rebellion against God by, among other things, an unholy symbiosis of the state and religion.

> Revelation 17:1–2 (KJV 1900)
> 1 And there came one of the seven angels which had the seven vials, and talked with me, saying unto me, Come hither; I will shew unto thee the judgment of the great whore that sitteth upon many waters: 2 With whom the kings of the earth have committed fornication, and the inhabitants of the earth have been made drunk with the wine of her fornication.

Where Does Morality Originate?

In Psalms 2, there is an emphasis upon the people and their political leaders. For the unbeliever, the *bonds* [v3] correspond to the law of conscience that is within every person and calibrated by:

1. The creation
2. The written law of God
3. The living witness of God's elect.[138]

Note that the *rulers* in Psalms 2 recognize that these bonds and cords originate in the Lord and his Anointed. God Himself is the origin of human morality through his creation of the human conscience and because of his activity in the world through saved individuals. God prepared the institution of government for the purpose of enforcing a morality based upon these divine standards [Romans 13.1-4]. Human government exists specifically to restrain human evil. The biblical disclosure that rulers of the world conspire together against God signals that government would become and has become the means by which morality is being overthrown rather than upheld. In every generation, the world rulers have chosen sides and have aligned themselves with the Lawless One. This same truth is taught in the unveiling of Mystery Babylon [Revelation 17.2; 18.3, 9].

The Lawless One is the future head of a super conspiracy which is behind all lawlessness that has ever been in the world. This conspiracy is behind the rebellions in Eden and Babel, the martyrdom of the saints of God, the crucifixion of Christ and the end time apostasy from the faith.

The institutional changes that will characterize the New World Order are being accomplished by many secular means, but these means would be unsuccessful without effective spiritual action by Satan. The *breaking and casting away* [Ps 2.3] consists in removing the moral constraints of God's law which are codified in many of the secular laws and social rules of every society. These divinely motivated guidelines are seen as shackles of divine tyranny. Since its creation, the Body of Christ, the Church, has restrained the full expression of the Mystery of Lawlessness in the world. Therefore, it is through the weakening of the Church by spiritual action that Mystery Babylon makes progress towards its objectives. The twenty-first century is the era in which it can be clearly seen that times and laws are being changed in accord with these ancient ambitions.

To make the sweeping changes sought by the devil, there must first be an undermining and then a casting away of the spiritual substructure upon which the moral, secular law is based. Morality is calibrated and maintained by another philosophical scaffold, which is the Word of God. Throughout the ages, God has supplied revelation through His prophets and the believers that have been instructed by them. The gospel commission itself demands an accurate propagation of the Word of God to believers.

"<u>Teaching them</u> [disciples] to observe <u>all things</u> whatsoever I have commanded you…" Matt 28.20a.

This supernatural influence must be weakened for the civil and social shackles to be broken. Individual Christians must be weakened in their sanctification and their gospel witness.

Enter the many antichrists of the Church Age. The function of today's antichrists includes the mass production of *false Bible teaching* [2 Pet 2.1-2]. This false teaching produces a poor quality of Christian discipleship.[139] This decline in the spiritual power of Christians is evidenced in weak marriages and families within the local church. It leads to entire Churches being nullified by sins [Rev 3.1-4]. The Church as a spiritual influence and model for how unbelievers should live under morality is diminished. This loss of spiritual protection leads to the proliferation of every category of evil in every institution of the community. The decay of these building blocks of civilization accomplishes a key tactical objective of Satan's prehistoric revolt.

Isaiah 14:12 (KJV 1900)
12 How art thou fallen from heaven, O Lucifer, son of the morning! How art thou cut down to the ground, <u>which didst weaken the nations</u>!

There is a breakdown in morality among unbelievers because *believers* lack the strong biblical commitment that leads to a powerful spiritual example. The enfeebled believer no longer exercises the same degree of spiritual influence upon society through his righteous living and verbal witness of the gospel. This results in an abating of the primary institutions upon which civilization is based. For example, the witness of Christian marriage, or the lack of it, influences every other marriage. It is through marriage and family that human capital [values, aptitudes, skills] are transferred from one generation to the next. With the breakdown of marriage and the family, these values are not transferred, resulting in the loss of a moral compass in society. Government is no stronger than the families which comprise the nation. Government inevitably reflects the values of society, which means that we ultimately get the government that we deserve.

The coming Antichrist will promote every category of *lawlessness* against God to establish *that change in times and laws* that will subsist in the New World Order.

Richard G. Walker

10
His Character: Antichrist [Against]-How This All Got Started, Satan's Motivation

This end time personage, the prince who will attempt to consummate the agenda of Satan upon the earth is called the Antichrist.

This title only occurs in 1 John 2.16-22; 1John 4.1-3; 2 John 7.

The title includes the prefix "anti"[140] which means "against". This coming individual is against Christ. But why is he against Christ?

Satan's Origin

This antipathy originates from the god of the Antichrist, which is Lucifer. It is he that is the leader of the prehistoric rebellion against Christ. When we look to discern his motivation in initiating this conspiracy, we can see but one cause intimated in scripture: *the desire for unauthorized authority*.

Ezekiel 28:15 (KJV 1900)
15 Thou wast perfect in thy ways from the day that thou wast created, till iniquity[141] was found in thee. 16a By the multitude of thy merchandise they have filled the midst of thee with violence, and thou hast sinned: … 17a Thine heart was lifted up because of thy beauty, thou hast corrupted thy wisdom by reason of thy brightness: …18a Thou hast defiled thy sanctuaries by the

multitude of thine iniquities, by the iniquity of thy <u>traffick</u>; ...

Iniquity here is wickedness, evil, injustice, or crime "*i.e., be in a state of not being right or just, often with a focus that these wrongs are harmful or damaging to others*"[142] The primary injustice here is towards God, who had blessed Lucifer and granted him a position and ministry of great honor [Eze 28.12-14]. Rather than rejoice in his close fellowship with God, he instead sought His place. Lucifer is the primordial example of the treachery of Judas as well as that of the end time Man of Sin who will betray Israel for the purpose of overthrowing their King, Jesus the Messiah.

This lust for unauthorized authority would lead to organized insurrection[143] [merchandise,[144] traffick]. It was not sufficient for Lucifer to retain these thoughts of usurpation within himself, he proceeds to defame God among the angels, enticing others to emulate his own unjust aspirations. In this he becomes the adversary [Satan] and slanderer [devil] of God. God records the ambition of Lucifer by revealing his own thoughts in the Book of Isaiah:

> Isaiah 14:13–14 (KJV 1900)
> 13 For thou hast said in thine heart, <u>I will ascend</u> into heaven, <u>I will exalt</u> my throne above the stars of God: <u>I will sit</u> also upon the mount of the congregation, in the sides of the north: 14 <u>I will ascend</u> above the heights of the clouds; <u>I will be</u> like the most High.

Upon the creation of humanity in the Garden of Eden, God provides a test to the man and the woman in the two trees planted there [Gen 2.9]. God also allows the devil access to the Garden where Satan tempts the man and woman to disobey God. These circumstances indicate that at least *one* of the purposes of the creation of mankind was to resolve the conflict caused by a rebellion of a portion of the angelic host. It is important to note that from this time forward, elect angels will become a part of every stage or dispensation of God's unfolding plan to resolve this conflict. Even now the Church is a witness to angels regarding God's character and plan [Eph 3.10].

Lucifer continues upon the earth that same *traffick* he initiated in heaven. In his temptation of Adam and Eve, Satan offers the same prize that he himself covets, unauthorized authority:

Genesis 3:5 (KJV 1900)
5 For God doth know that in the day ye eat thereof, then your eyes shall be opened, and <u>ye shall be as gods</u>, knowing good and evil.

This third instance [after 1: the original Fall of Lucifer, Isa 14; and 2: the temptation of the angelic host, Eze 28] of Satanic ambition joined humanity to the fallen angels in unified revolt against God. [145]

It is likely that Adam and Eve did not understand the *full* significance of their actions at the time. But eventually, this offer of an extraordinary, unauthorized authority via godhood would be explicitly and consciously accepted by every initiate of the Mystery Religions and advanced degrees of the secret societies, in which the secret doctrines of Lucifer are preserved until this day. These doctrines of devils comprise the secret religion of the kingdoms of this world, which are referred to in Revelation 17.

Revelation 17:1–2 (KJV 1900)
1 And there came one of the seven angels which had the seven vials, and talked with me, saying unto me, Come hither; I will shew unto thee the judgment of the great whore that sitteth upon many waters: 2 With whom the kings of the earth have committed fornication, and the inhabitants of the earth have been made drunk with the wine of her fornication.

By these things we may discern the motivation of the devil in his opposition to Christ and how this motivation is seized upon by his followers: instinctively by reason of their fallen natures, but also consciously, by those who have accepted his initiation and his doctrine. *Every attempt to entice men and women to actualize themselves outside of submission to God through Jesus Christ is another manifestation of this same temptation and a recollection of this same Fall.*

We have observed in our analysis of the Mystery of Iniquity that the central doctrine of the theology of the Antichrist is the denial that Jesus is the Christ. This is stated explicitly by the apostle John:

1 John 2:22 (KJV 1900)
22 Who is a liar but he that denieth that Jesus is the Christ? <u>He is antichrist</u>, that denieth the Father and the Son.

John 14:6 (KJV 1900)
6 Jesus saith unto him, I am the way, the truth, and the life: no man cometh unto the Father, but by me.

Satan's Strategy

Once Lucifer aspired to God's place, the very existence of a Messiah stood as the single greatest obstacle to his plans. The earliest efforts of Lucifer involve the acquisition of a following, initially a portion of the angelic host and later, via the Fall, the entire human race. The incarnation of the true Christ presupposed a people out of whom He would arise, a redeemed kingdom of believers, elect to privilege and an everlasting dominion in heaven and on earth.[146] Such a one, [the Christ, or Messiah] if his birth could not be prevented, then He *must be disqualified to rule,* and this aim is the essential center of the devil's strategy in history.

We witness in the scriptures the devil attempting to obstruct the bloodline of Christ [Gen 6]. We read of the attempt to kill the Child through the efforts of Herod the Great [Mt 2.16-18]. We behold him tempting the incarnated Lord in the wilderness [Matt 4], we find him enabling the crucifixion [Lk 22.3] and finally, we will see an all-out attempt to eliminate the Jews and prevent to fulfillment of the covenant promises made to them [Zech 14].

The Antichrist shares this hatred of the Lord since he is, as much as one can imagine, the offspring of Lucifer. Just as Jesus seeks to do the will of the Father, so too the Antichrist the will of his father.

The Antichrist is *against* the Lord. This is illustrated in his commitment to the idea that Jesus is not Lord at all. This is "The Lie" that informs the spirit of antichrist in this age.

The Antichrist is against the Lord as demonstrated by his attempts to undermine the Word of God, as we have already noted. In this he attempts to obstruct the advance of the Mystery of Godliness [1Tim 3.16] through sabotage of evangelism and Christian discipleship.

The Antichrist is against the Lord as demonstrated by his attempts to undermine the human institutions that God has established and maintains. In this he fulfills the devil's objective to "weaken the nations."

The Antichrist is against God as demonstrated in his blasphemy of the Lord. The Antichrist, under all his titles, is a blasphemer of the Lord and of His heavenly government.

2 Thessalonians 2:3–4 (KJV 1900)
3 Let no man deceive you by any means: for that day shall not come, except there come a falling away first, and that man of sin be revealed, the son of perdition; 4 Who opposeth and exalteth himself above all that is called God, or that is worshipped; so that he as God sitteth in the temple of God, shewing himself that he is God.

Revelation 13:1 (KJV 1900) 1 And I stood upon the sand of the sea, and saw a beast rise up out of the sea, having seven heads and ten horns, and upon his horns ten crowns, and upon his heads the name of blasphemy. [17.3]

Revelation 13:6 (KJV 1900)
6 And he opened his mouth in blasphemy against God, to blaspheme his name, and his tabernacle, and them that dwell in heaven.

In view of the eternal consequences, Satan and the Antichrist are fully invested in their opposition to Jesus Christ and to the Father. In this ultimate zero-sum situation, they cannot afford to lose.

11
His Character: Antichrist [Instead]-Satan's Church, A New Kind of Unbeliever

This end time personage who will attempt to consummate the agenda of Satan upon the earth, the ultimate implementer of the New World Order, is named in scripture as the Antichrist.

The title includes the prefix "anti" which means "against." The word "anti" also means "instead of." The Antichrist seeks to establish himself in the place of the true Son of God. The Antichrist will deceive the world and especially the people of Israel into thinking that he is the Messiah.

He will appeal to the thinking of unsaved people in their desire for spirituality without holiness, power without discipleship, miracles without true faith, kingdom without sacrifice.

2 Thessalonians 2:9–11 (KJV 1900)
9 Even him, whose coming is after the working of Satan with all power and signs and lying wonders, 10 And with all deceivableness of unrighteousness in them that perish; because they received not the love of the truth, that they might be saved. 11 And for this cause God shall send them strong delusion, that they should believe a lie:

The Antichrist, in his attempt to replace Christ, will *imitate* Him, the Trinity, His Church and His Kingdom. As "against" Christ, the Beast will be a blasphemer, as "instead of" Christ, he will seek to *replace*

Christ in every detail.

The kingdom of the Antichrist will fully implement a *demonic despotism*: a totally controlled society ruled by deception, force, and arbitrary judgment [recall that he is the *lawless one*]. The Book of Revelation, speaking of the False Prophet, the Prime Minister of the New World Order, who directs the worship of the Antichrist and the affairs of his kingdom, states:

> Revelation 13:14–17 (KJV 1900)
> 14 And deceiveth them that dwell on the earth by the means of those miracles which he had power to do in the sight of the beast; saying to them that dwell on the earth, that they should make an image to the beast, which had the wound by a sword, and did live. 15 And he had power to give life unto the image of the beast, that the image of the beast should both speak, and cause that as many as would not worship the image of the beast should be killed.16 And he causeth all, both small and great, rich and poor, free and bond, to receive a mark in their right hand, or in their foreheads: 17 And that no man might buy or sell, save he that had the mark, or the name of the beast, or the number of his name.

In his efforts to imitate Christ, the devil will provide his own version of the new birth and of the Church. *The new birth of the Antichrist will be demon possession achieved through initiation.* The union of all of humanity in this fashion will **imitate** *the body of Christ* where the true believer is indwelt by Christ and reciprocally dwells in Him by means of the baptism of the Holy Spirit. This initiation, administered by the False Prophet, will tie together the spiritual, the political, economic, and social spheres into a single Satanic kingdom entity, if you will, the final phase of the New World Order.

It is through the promotion of demon possession that Antichrist will change mankind by production of a *new kind of unbeliever*, the long-awaited superman, the achievement of the next evolutionary step: the *homo noeticus*, at the Omega Point.[147] It will be called transcendence to a new stage of consciousness, spiritual enlightenment, illumination, the Singularity. It will be the promised leap to a higher degree of vibration and the attainment of supernatural power: *ye shall be as gods*. The Antichrist will not tolerate the passive unbelief that the unsaved have today. He will seek, through mass initiations that are made mandatory by connecting his "new birth" to the ability to buy and sell, and the threat of death to the noncompliant, to create a new breed of demonized humanity, fully committed to himself.

> 2 Thessalonians 2:3–4 (KJV 1900)
> 3 Let no man deceive you by any means: for that day shall not come, except there come a falling away first, and that man of sin be revealed, the son of perdition; 4 Who opposeth and exalteth himself above all that is called God, or that is worshipped; so that he as God sitteth in the temple of God, shewing himself that he is God.

The Antichrist does not merely want to rule the world, he wants to *remake* the world and to remake man into a being suitable for his worship. In so doing, Satan will replicate God's plan for the kingdom. This is the essence of the meaning of Antichrist, when interpreted as *"instead of"* Christ.

The Antichrist sees himself as worthy to be God and therefore seeks permanent dominion of heaven and earth: he wants to establish times and laws; he wants worshippers, and he wants to punish transgressors to his will.

It is through the elimination of the vestiges of the worship of God and the abolition of the biblical standard of truth that he is seeking to change this world. The age-old working of Mystery Babylon will eventually result in the implementation of the pure worship of Lucifer Himself, the *Father* of Perdition.

> Revelation 13:15 (KJV 1900)
> 15 And he had power to give life unto the image of the beast, that the image of the beast should both speak, and cause that as many as would not worship the image of the beast should be killed.

We will return to the issue of the Mark and the operational details of the New World Order in Book Two, that addresses the career of the Antichrist.

12

His Character: The Prince That Shall Come Revisited, Government and Spiritual Warfare

Daniel 9:26–27 (KJV 1900)
26 And after threescore and two weeks shall Messiah be cut off, but not for himself: and the people of the prince that shall come shall destroy the city and the sanctuary; and the end thereof shall be with a flood, and unto the end of the war desolations are determined. 27 And he shall confirm the covenant with many for one week: and in the midst of the week he shall cause the sacrifice and the oblation to cease, and for the overspreading of abominations he shall make it desolate, even until the consummation, and that determined shall be poured upon the desolate.

Here is a prince who is identified with a people. This individual is the Antichrist: he will arise in the fourth kingdom, but not at the time of Christ's first advent.[148] He will be in a position to make a treaty between many peoples. He will also have the power to eventually abominate the Jewish Temple of that future time. Other scriptures pertaining to him identify his intent to be worshipped as God, as well as his spiritual deceptions and the character of his rule. He will wield political power. *The Antichrist will operate in the sphere of government.*

Daniel 9:27 indicates that the Antichrist will use governmental power as a vehicle to elevate himself to the world stage. He will make a covenant or a treaty which guarantees certain rights and protections, and then, after three- and one-half years, he will take unilateral action in the religious sphere which will result in geopolitical upheaval.

He is identified to Daniel as a "prince." The word in the original [OT:5057] speaks of official status, a ruler, leader, or prince. In Daniel 9.26, the *Messiah* who is cut off for the sake of others [KJV] is indirectly contrasted with the *prince* whose people destroy the holy city and temple, a prince who will one day declare himself Messiah. This prince will use government as a platform to assume spiritual leadership.

> *Government can restrain men, but only the gospel of Christ can change them. When Christians attempt to use government to accomplish spiritual ends, they testify to their contempt of the divine power which is at their disposal via divinely ordained means.*

God has not given human government authority in spiritual affairs.[149] Government is given to all of humanity irrespective of their spiritual disposition. The pursuit of spiritual objectives is the domain of the true Church, the Body of Christ, which is composed exclusively of the redeemed. Government can restrain men, but only the gospel of Christ can change them. When Christians attempt to use government to accomplish spiritual ends, they testify to their contempt of the divine power which is at their disposal via divinely ordained means.

Ephesians 6:12–13 (KJV 1900)
12 For we wrestle not against flesh and blood, but against principalities, against powers, against the rulers of the darkness of this world, against spiritual wickedness in high places. 13 Wherefore take unto you the whole armour of God, that ye may be able to withstand in the evil day, and having done all, to stand.

2 Corinthians 10:2–5 (KJV 1900)
2 But I beseech you, that I may not be bold when I am present with that confidence, wherewith I think to be bold against some, which think of us as if we walked according to the flesh. 3 For though we walk in the flesh, we do not war after the flesh: 4 (For the weapons of our warfare are not carnal, but mighty through God to the pulling down of strong holds;) 5 Casting down imaginations, and every high thing that exalteth itself against the knowledge of God, and bringing into captivity every thought to the obedience of Christ;

The reason that government is impotent against the true enemies of mankind is because these enemies are the fallen spiritual powers. It is this wicked spiritual regime that is at war with God and with mankind and it is not susceptible to the tools of human government. Fallen humanity is not even capable of seeing the devil in his true significance. If they did, they would recognize him as their implacable foe. The scriptures identify the spiritual weapons, the full armor of God, that is the only way for the believer to stand against the devil, his organization, and his agenda.

Unbelievers have no ability whatsoever to fight [for God] in this warfare, either individually as citizens or collectively in the form of nations. From the standpoint of believers, unbelievers are not combatants, but *casualties* of the evil one. Therefore, the believer is not commanded to be at war against sinners, but to convert them through the gospel. The fact that the visible Church today is waging war against sinners and their sins is evidence of the success of Satan's strategies in the spiritual war.

As far as believers are concerned, our support in this battle is not earthly: we should not rely upon government as our ally in the prosecution of the spiritual warfare. History has repeatedly demonstrated the folly of this strategy, as do the scriptures cited repeatedly in this book. Our citizenship is in heaven, our power is heavenly, as are our doctrine and our Captain.

The devil, on the other hand, is more than capable of using government as a means of implementing his own agenda upon unbelieving mankind.[150] The world in which we live is temporarily ruled by Satan.[151] This distasteful truth must be remembered to retain any proper orientation to reality.

Government is a secular institution with secular authority and power. Government is established by God, [Romans 13.1-2] but it is **not** established with spiritual power or duties. The prince that shall come will use government as a tool, an implement by which he would acquire political power and a stage upon which to prepare for the exercise of spiritual power upon his revelation as Antichrist, the false messiah. The following scriptures are a reminder of the political context in which the prince appears.

> Revelation 6:1–2 (KJV 1900)
> 1 And I saw when the Lamb opened one of the seals, and I heard, as it were the noise of thunder, one of the four beasts saying, Come and see. 2 And I saw, and behold a white horse: and he that sat on him had a bow; and a crown was given unto him: and he went forth conquering, and to conquer.

> Daniel 8:25 (KJV 1900)
> 25 And through his policy also he shall cause craft to prosper in his hand; and he shall magnify himself in his heart, and by peace shall destroy many: he shall also stand up against the prince of princes; but he shall be broken without hand.[152]

The Antichrist will use diplomacy and statesmanship to deceive Israel and the nations. He will use the prospect of peace to insinuate himself into a position of strategic political power. He will then use that power to oppress and ultimately attempt to destroy Israel as well as all believers in the world at that time.

The Times of the Gentiles

In the visions given to the prophet Daniel, the Times of the Gentiles[153] are depicted as a sequence of governments or kingdoms. The Times of the Gentiles is a period of the Gentile domination of Israel. It stretches from the defeat of Israel in 605 B.C. at the hands of Nebuchadnezzar and the Babylonians until the second coming of Christ. The last portion of this period is the final half of Daniel's 70th week: the three- and one-half years, the 42 months, the 1260 days, the time, times and half a time which encompasses the rule of the Antichrist as he is typically known in scripture. We live today in the Times of the Gentiles, but in a segment of this vast period not foreseen in the Old Testament.

In the vision of Nebuchadnezzar, [Dan 2] the sequence of Gentile kingdoms is depicted as a giant metal statue where each kingdom is represented as a part of the statue. The statue is that of a man, made of a metal descending in value from the head of gold to chest and arms of silver, belly and thighs of brass, legs of iron and feet of iron and clay. Here the succession of nations is seen as declining in the quality of civilization. Interestingly, God does not see technological advancement as identical to cultural advancement. This is because it is the ethical and spiritual qualities of humanity which most link them to their Creator. Man is departing further from the divine image as time passes [2 Tim 3.13].

In Daniel's next two visions [Dan 7, 8], the progression of nations is portrayed as wild beasts. The nature of each of the Gentile kingdoms is here revealed as that of a bloodthirsty predator seeking dominion of the world. Each seeks to exercise the dominion over the earth originally bequeathed to man and woman by God, but without submission to divine authority [Gen 1.26-28].

In these two visions the person of the Antichrist is presented as a horn upon an animal, which represents power and government authority.

These beasts are also governments. Understanding this fact alone should prevent the assumption that governments are equipped or qualified to perform spiritual functions in the name of Christ. Government is an institution created by God to ensure the orderly function of society [Rom 13.1-4]. The job of government is the suppression of evil so that human freedom is preserved. Therefore, government exists to enforce the morality agreed to by society in its laws. In performing this duty, the government has been given the power of capital punishment [Gen 9.6; Rom 13.4].

> The problem with government is that it is only as effective as the people who comprise it. The Fall of mankind means that, absent an external supernatural influence, such as the gospel, the tendency of *all* government is to move towards satanic forms of tyranny.

The problem with government is that it is only as effective as the people who comprise it. The Fall of mankind means that, absent an external supernatural influence, such as the gospel, the tendency of *all* governments is to move towards satanic forms of tyranny. In the devil's world, the moral deterioration of human institutions is unavoidable, and government is not exempt from this principle of corruption.

In Ps 94 we find the following:

Psalm 94:20–21 (NKJV)
20 Shall the throne of iniquity, which devises evil by law, Have fellowship with You? 21 They gather together against the life of the righteous, And condemn innocent blood.

Throughout human history, government, like every human institution, has been subject to corrupt influences and turned to serve evil purposes. In view of this tendency, we must not entrust to government the authority that belongs solely to God, nor should we expect from government blessings that can only be provided by God Himself. The Antichrist will through peace destroy many, because many will be willing to render unto Caesar that which belongs solely to God [Mk 12.17].

Antichrist: The State as Seat of Spiritual Power

Antichrist the prince will come upon the scene via political activity, secure power through the overthrow of existing political leaders of his time and consolidate world control through execution of geopolitical strategies.

However, once his position of political power is achieved, Antichrist will use this position to execute the *spiritual* domination of the world. Although Satan willingly manipulates political Christianity, the spiritual vision of the Man of Sin will not be to impose the limited and often evil concepts of politicized Christianity upon the world. His objective will be to erect the final version of Lucifer's vision, revealed by the prophet Isaiah:

Isaiah 14:12–14 (KJV 1900)
12 How art thou fallen from heaven, O Lucifer, son of the morning! How art thou cut down to the ground, which didst weaken the nations! 13 For thou hast said in thine heart, I will ascend into heaven, I will exalt my throne above the stars of God: I will sit also upon the mount of the congregation, in the sides of the north: 14 I will ascend above the heights of the clouds; I will

be like the most High.

The final stage of the divine prosecution against Lucifer[154] *anticipates* the rise of the prince who is to come. This time will be one of purging for Israel, and one of testing for the Tribulational believers. During this future reign the full character of the devil will be on display to heaven, as will be the righteousness of God.

Human history is the backdrop for the resolution of the conflict between the fallen angels and God.[155] God is demonstrating the moral culpability of volitional beings in every combination of historical circumstances [the dispensations].

In like manner God is demonstrating the sinfulness and faithlessness of man regardless of the character of revelation and responsibility provided him in any dispensation. The end of history will have exhausted the appeals of Lucifer and demonstrated the holiness and grace of God to save men in every generation despite themselves. We will revisit the issue of the Antichrist and government as we continue to examine the names applied to him in the scriptures

13
His Character: The Little Horn and the Prophetic Symbolism of Daniel and Revelation

During the last years of the Babylonian empire, Daniel received a vision of four beasts that represented the four major world empires of the Times of the Gentiles, a period which stretches from the victory of Nebuchadnezzar over Israel until the return of Christ.

In Daniel chapter 7, after describing the first three beasts, which represent the Babylonians, the Medes and Persians and the Greeks, Daniel receives instruction in a vision regarding the fourth beast, the fourth of the Gentile kingdoms:

Daniel 7:23–26 (KJV 1900)
23 Thus he said, The fourth beast shall be the fourth kingdom upon earth, which shall be <u>diverse</u> from all kingdoms, and shall devour the whole earth, and shall tread it down, and break it in pieces. 24 And the ten horns out of this kingdom are ten kings that shall arise: and another shall rise after them; and he shall be <u>diverse</u> from the first, and he shall subdue three kings. 25 And he shall speak great words against the most High, and shall wear out the saints of the most High, and think to change times and laws: and they shall be given into his hand until a time and times and the dividing of time. 26 But the judgment shall sit, and they shall take away his dominion, to consume and to destroy it unto the end.

Each of the kingdoms is represented as a carnivorous animal. However, the fourth beast is different [diverse OT:8133: changed, to be changed] from the others in that it is:

- **Different** in the *extent of its dominion*: it shall devour the whole world [v23]. Although each of the Gentile kingdoms foreseen by Daniel seeks world dominion, this final kingdom will achieve it to an extent never accomplished.
- **Different** in the *extreme character of its violence*: it will devour, trample and break in pieces. Its violence is pathological to an extreme degree. It will eat or feed upon, trample and crush to pieces. Again, each of the Gentile kingdoms operate based on brute force, but this fourth, final kingdom will surpass all its predecessors in the severity of its violence. It will not only seek to control, but it will revel in destruction for its own sake. It may be that dramatic advancements in technology will make this degree of violence possible.
- **Different** in its *governance*, having 10 horns upon its head which represent ten kings. These horns represent kings [v24] who will reign during this last kingdom of the Times of the Gentiles. After the defeat of the Babylonians by the Medes and the Persians, each successive kingdom shared rule: The Medes and the Persians and the four generals which succeeded Alexander in Greece. The final empire will divide rule between ten kings. Despite its overwhelming military power, it will be politically the weakest of the Gentile kingdoms. This weakness will create an opportunity for the Little Horn. It will be this ten-king system that becomes the *vehicle* for the Antichrist, the Little Horn, and the final iteration of Mystery Babylon [Rev 17.2-3].
- **Different** in its *claims*. Revelation 13 provides another picture of this same beast, revealing that this beast is different in its *claims*. On its ten heads it has written names of blasphemy. Blasphemy is speaking evil of God [against] or ascribing to man that which belongs to God alone [instead of]. Again, its predecessor empires were pagan and saw their kings as gods. But the fourth kingdom will openly wage war against the true God, making false and defamatory statements against Him.

- **Different** in its *sponsor*. Revelation 13 also reveals that the fourth kingdom is different regarding its *sponsor*. As the temporary ruler of this world, Satan is the sponsor of all its kingdoms [Mt 4.8-9; Jn 12.31] however the fourth kingdom is the vehicle through which the devil will attempt to consummate his objective of the overthrow of God. As such it is the ultimate and final expression of Satanic ambition.
- Out of the ten horns arises another horn which is also **different** from the others.

Daniel 7:8 (KJV 1900)
8 I considered the horns, and, behold, there came up among them another little horn, before whom there were three of the first horns plucked up by the roots: and, behold, in this horn were eyes like the eyes of man, and a mouth speaking great things.

Daniel 7:24 (KJV 1900)
24 And the ten horns out of this kingdom are ten kings that shall arise: and another shall rise after them; and he shall be diverse from the first, and he shall subdue three kings.

Another horn will arise, which will be different from the preceding ten, a little horn possessing eyes and a mouth. This horn in its arrival will eliminate three kings. These kings will not be cut off, but will be ripped out by the roots, no vestiges of them will be left. The Antichrist does not start out with complete world control.

This horn will demonstrate that his aspirations go beyond the political by blaspheming God and by oppressing his servants [Dan 7.25]. In other words, this king, the little horn, will use a government in the last days as a base of operations to wage war upon God himself. This is Antichrist. Remember, the doctrine of antichrist is that Jesus is not the Christ. He is opposed to Christ and after the midpoint of Daniel's 70th week, he will openly demonstrate his determination to replace God.

The Little Horn will intend to change times and laws. Human laws and customs generally reflect moral principles that derive from divinely established institutions such as free will, marriage, family, and government. This is because God has hard-wired conscience into the human soul and the properly functioning conscience will tend to produce rules and laws which ratify God's design for humanity and civilization [Rom 1.18-20; 2.14-15]. These laws and customs are also influenced by the presence of divine revelation that is provided to every generation of mankind. The Antichrist will attempt to obliterate the knowledge of God and His design for human civilization. He will change the fundamental laws which govern human behavior. He will also attempt to disable the conscience by promoting demon possession through mass initiations in which every individual will be compelled to pledge to worship the Beast and to accept his mark.[156]

The unprecedented violence of the fourth beast of Daniel is not without purpose. Daniel defines this purpose in his book.

Daniel 7:25 (KJV 1900)
And he shall speak great words against the most High, and shall wear out the saints of the most High, and think to change times and laws: and they shall be given into his hand until a time and times and the dividing of time.

"**change**" 5. LN 62.3–62.9 (hafel) change, set or organize a new order (Da 2:21; 7:25+)[157]

The purpose of the violence of the fourth beast, who corresponds to the Beast of Revelation 13 and 17, is to establish a *New Order*. The Beast will act with complete ruthlessness to establish that which he has always intended: a World Order with himself as its deity, demonic despotism on earth and eventually in the heavens as well [Isa 14.12-14].

To give birth to this New World Order politically, the Beast must destroy *nationalism*. To establish it spiritually, he must obliterate *all* religions and especially biblical Christianity. His great violence is for the purpose of *demolition*, one that will prepare the way for a *new order of the ages*.

This work of demolition is the immediate purpose of the Mystery of Iniquity. The confusion of gender roles and gender itself, the increasing disregard for marriage, the intergenerational effort to achieve global governance and the proximity of a one world religion based upon pagan concepts, will all ultimately lead to the changing of times and laws, the casting off the "bands and cords" [Ps 2] that God purposely built into His creation.

The only remedy to the reign of this sovereign [the Little Horn] will be the direct intervention of God. The Antichrist will succeed in many of his efforts, but his success will be short-lived. Jesus Christ, accompanied by the resurrected saints, will personally re-enter history to defeat the Little Horn and to eradicate his kingdom.

> Daniel 7:11 (KJV 1900)
> 11 I beheld then because of the voice of the great words which the horn spake: I beheld even till the beast was slain, and his body destroyed, and given to the burning flame.

> Daniel 7:26 (KJV 1900)
> 26 But the judgment shall sit, and they shall take away his dominion, to consume and to destroy it unto the end.

We will see that the horn is a part of the Beast, it directs the Beast, and is identified with and *is* the Beast. Revelation 17 represents one of several pictures of the Mystery of Iniquity in the scriptures. Each element of this conspiracy is represented in this picture: the demonic character of the Mystery of Iniquity [the Beast itself], the procession of empires [the heads], the future political system under the fourth kingdom [the horns], the Antichrist [one of the horns] and Mystery Babylon, the spiritual and ecclesiastical leadership of the movement [the woman]. Both the Beast and the horn will share the same destiny and doom. Evil will be dealt with by the destruction of the final Gentile kingdom at the personal return of Christ to the earth. This will mark the end of the Times of the Gentiles as well as the end of the Antichrist.

Let us summarize what we have learned regarding the character of the Antichrist:

Man of Sin: As the man of sin, the Antichrist is characterized by his departure from righteousness and the truth. He is the antithesis of Christ in that he is sponsored by the devil who is the author of sin, and he will promote rebellion against God as a way of life for the world.

The Lawless One: The Antichrist is not merely a sinner, he does not simply violate God's laws, he is a revolutionary who rejects God's very right to rule the universe. The Antichrist does not regard the law of God. He rejects the commandments and statutes of God and operates out of pragmatism: the ends justify the means. He will pursue whatever action leads to his objective without regard for morality or righteousness.

Antichrist: Under this name he is both against Christ and will strive to elevate himself to the place of [instead of] Christ. His doctrine is that Jesus is not the Christ, which he promotes via the Mystery of Iniquity or Lawlessness. The Antichrist will attempt to create a new world and *a new kind of sinner* to enable his worship as Christ and God.

The Prince Who is to Come: The initial appearance of the Antichrist will be as a statesman and a politician. He will operate within government to insinuate himself into the affairs of Israel and at the proper time, establish a power base through the usurpation of three kingdoms. He will both establish and maintain power through political manipulation, assisted by Lucifer.

The Little Horn: will be the most violent and ruthless ruler of the most violent and ruthless kingdom in the succession of Gentile kingdoms revealed to Daniel. He will utilize governmental power to consolidate and exercise world control for the purpose of using this planet as a base of operations for his final attempt to defeat the Most High.

What Can a Christian Do?

Before we continue with the names of the Antichrist in scripture which portray the character and strategy of this coming world ruler, we should take time to discuss what you can do as a believer with this information.

On the surface, it may appear that there is nothing that a believer can do but sit and wait for the Rapture and leave the Antichrist to the believers of the future.

It is true that the Antichrist is coming regardless of what you or I do. But it is also true that he is going to be destroyed regardless of what *he* does. Believers need to be motivated by this truth to become engaged in spiritual warfare, to get off the bench and into the contest. This information should motivate righteous anger and indignation about what the devil is doing now, today, in the world and in our communities.

There is sympathy between the human sin nature and the spirit of the age [Eph 2.1-2] which results in a temptation and tendency to fall in love with this world [1 Jn 2.15-16]. Therefore, we must resist the idea that we must ally ourselves with secular efforts to fix this world.[158]

We are drawn to schemes to improve the world, to save it. God is not going to save this world but destroy it and create a new one [2 Pet 3.10; Rev 21.1]. In the meanwhile, He is operating a rescue mission, not a renovation project. God is rescuing the elect from this perishing world, and it is our job to provide the dual witness of our lives and our lips that will call them to that destiny. Every believer should be looking to be taken out of this world, not to design and manufacture comfortable permanent quarters here. It should be a comfort to know however, that obedient, holy Christians do exercise a powerful civilizing effect upon the world, while the Church is here. Nonetheless, our primary purpose here is not to resuscitate the dying earth and its sinful inhabitants but to efficiently win and to disciple the lost in view of the coming judgment.

Most believers are like grown men watching criminals take control of their communities, businesses, homes, and children while doing nothing to stop them. When you understand the cost of losing your personal spiritual warfare: to your family and community, your children, and grandchildren, it should move you to spiritual action. The Mystery of Lawlessness may be a mystery to much of the world, but it should not be a mystery to the Christian. We are not *expecting* the Mystery of Iniquity, it is here and in full operation right now. Understanding the mechanisms of the Mystery of Iniquity and the cruelty and destruction it involves is critical to our spiritual mission today, not just to future believers. Christians must be equipped for intensified spiritual warfare during the advanced stages of spiritual apostasy that confront us in this very hour.

Victory in spiritual warfare is not defined as preventing the appearance of the Antichrist, or even defeating him once he gets here. Jesus Christ will personally defeat the Antichrist, his False Prophet and Satan at His second coming. Victory in spiritual warfare is the development of spiritual maturity in your own life and the effective ministry of the gospel unto the lost in the here and now.

> Matthew 28:18–20 (KJV 1900)
> 18 And Jesus came and spake unto them, saying, All power is given unto me in heaven and in earth. 19 Go ye therefore, and teach all nations, baptizing them in the name of the Father, and of the Son, and of the Holy Ghost: 20 Teaching them to observe all things whatsoever I have commanded you: and, lo, I am with you alway, even unto the end of the world. Amen.

The effective function of local churches creates spiritual dynamics that refresh and elevate their communities and their nation. God blesses the faithful believer, and this blessing has collateral effects upon the places they live and work.

Proverbs 14:34 (KJV 1900)
34 Righteousness exalteth a nation: But sin is a reproach to any people.

Proverbs 11:10–11 (KJV 1900)
10 When it goeth well with the righteous, the city rejoiceth: And when the wicked perish, there is shouting. 11 By the blessing of the upright the city is exalted: But it is overthrown by the mouth of the wicked.

The true Christian patriot does not attempt to make the government an organ of the Church. The true patriotic believer strives to make his local church as spiritually effective as possible. He realizes that the Church that is winning the lost and making disciples is performing the highest imaginable service to the community and to the nation. He is focused upon his own spiritual development. He is a proclaimer of the gospel. He is equipped to make disciples. He is a strong support to the elders of the Church. He is a generous giver to the ministry. He is fervent in prayer. He is focused upon his family and their spiritual and material welfare. He fearlessly stands for what is right and just. He is a defender of the weak.

The pastor/elder who would advance the cause of Christ in spiritual warfare is first advancing in his own spiritual growth and holiness. He is a fervent defender and teacher of the whole counsel of the scripture. He exposes heresies and those which advance them to the harm of the Church. He is a teacher, but also a trainer of the flock in the disciplines of the spiritual life and in how to live as believers in the world. He measures his own effectiveness not by attendance but by the number of strong marriages and families under his ministry. He is a warrior in prayer. He fearlessly rebukes unrighteousness and injustice. He is a protector of the weak.

This is Christian militancy. It is not complex, but it is hard to execute. The individual who is faithful will find the unlimited power of God to enable and to help. He will also find joy, blessing, and reward in this life and at the judgment seat of Christ.

14
His Character: The Willful King

Daniel 11:36–39 (KJV 1900)
36 <u>And the king shall do according to his will</u>; and he shall exalt himself, and magnify himself above every god, and shall speak marvellous things against the God of gods, and shall prosper till the indignation be accomplished: for that that is determined shall be done. 37 Neither shall he regard the God of his fathers, nor the desire of women, nor regard any god: for he shall magnify himself above all. 38 But in his estate shall he honour the God of forces:[159] and a god whom his fathers knew not shall he honour with gold, and silver, and with precious stones, and pleasant things. 39 Thus shall he do in the most strong holds with a strange god, whom he shall acknowledge and increase with glory: and he shall cause them to rule over many, and shall divide the land for gain.

    This passage of scripture marks the final vision to Daniel during the third year of Cyrus of Persia. Daniel is given the future of the world from his time until the end of the reign of Antiochus IV [Epiphanes] 164 BC. This Syrian king is a precursor of the Antichrist, performing an early version of many of the actions of the future Antichrist.
    In verse thirty-five of chapter 11, the story regarding Antiochus ends,[160] and in verse thirty-six, the Willful king is introduced. This individual is yet future: we know this because the events of verses 36 through 54 have not yet occurred. Thus Daniel 11, like Daniel 8 combines the prophecy of Antiochus with the revelation of another

ruler in the far distant future.

"And the king shall do according to his will"

The Antichrist will have complete authority in the political and governmental realms. Antichrist will be a governmental leader endued with supernatural ability by the devil. He will be the foremost example of the *new man*, ruling over the new state.

Government is a divinely established institution, but it is a secular institution. Government has been provided no spiritual responsibilities nor is it endowed with any spiritual capabilities. Government was not created to be an organ of the Church. Whenever Christendom has attempted to make it so, the outcome has been either religious tyranny or state tyranny. Mystery Babylon is characterized by the illicit intercourse between religion and the state [it is actually called *fornication* in Rev 17.2-3]. The attempt by the Church of Christ to make the government its servant or partner in achieving some spiritual end[161] is a mistake, if not a sin.

Antichrist, perceiving himself a god, will attempt to perfect the theocratic state. He will imitate the millennial reign of Christ. He will exercise political power with irresistible spiritual force. He will exert worldwide political authority and "do according to his will." This stands in contrast to the attitude of the true Messiah who said the following:

> John 6:38 (KJV 1900)
> 38 For I came down from heaven, not to do mine own will, but the will of him that sent me.

"(H)e shall exalt himself, and magnify himself above every god"

This is the same language used by Paul in 2 Thessalonians. Paul was not referring to Antiochus, who was long dead [two centuries] when 2 Thessalonians was written. The Antichrist will not represent himself as a superior military leader, or an emperor, but as God himself. This pride is the origin of the Satanic revolt, and it is the source of the blasphemies which he will pronounce against God.

"(A)nd shall speak marvellous things against the God of gods"

Antichrist, under the appellations of the Man of Sin and the Little Horn, is prone to blaspheme God. This is a hallmark of his rule. Although the Gentile kings of past ages were pagans who thought themselves to be gods, they often reserved a place for the God of Israel in their pantheons of deities, if for no other reason than Jehovah's ability to force them to take Him into account as he made Himself known during their rule. We see this during the lifetime of Daniel the prophet as God used him to influence both the Babylonian and Medo-Persian empires. *The Antichrist, however, is not a polytheist.* He does not believe in many gods: if he is the true god then Jehovah must be an imposter. Lucifer implies as much in his words in the Garden of Eden [Gen 3]. The Antichrist will openly proclaim what today is *the secret* of the secret societies. Deception will be displaced by open blasphemy.

The Willful King will speak "marvelous"[162] things against the God of gods. He will say things that are astonishing and extraordinary by way of disrespect to the Lord. We see a preview of this kind of outrageous blasphemy today in the Word of Faith Movement, which claims that the believer is in fact a little god and that Jesus did not claim to be Jehovah (or did not claim to be Christ/Messiah).[163]

This is the spirit of this world system, which is animated and directed by the devil.[164] It appears that every entertainment and information system requires the misuse of God's name in each and every product. The name of the Lord is cursed daily in primetime television. On the other hand, the devil is elevated and infused with heroic qualities. He even has his own television series.[165]

"[S]hall prosper till the indignation be accomplished: for that that is determined shall be done"

The Antichrist will experience success in many of his initiatives. God is prosecuting His case against Satan and the fallen angels within human history. To ask why evil should prosper, even in the short run, [Dan 8.25 "he shall cause craft to prosper in his hand"] is to also ask why Satan was allowed into the Garden of Eden [Gen 3], or why was he allowed to test Job [Job 1] or Christ [Mt 4] or why is the Church a witness to the angels [Eph 3.10]. Although the cross and blood of Christ is applied only to humanity, the destinies of angels and men are intertwined in the counsels of God. The reconciling of all things includes the just conclusion of the conflict with the fallen angels and their proper disposition in eternity. For the righteousness and wisdom of God to be permanently established and demonstrated, evil must run its course. However, it must be emphasized that although sin is a choice of moral beings, God is not the author of sin, nor are his plans advanced by the sins of men or angels. On the contrary, both human and angelic sin are consequences of the continual rejection of God's gracious provision of opportunities for right decisions and actions.

1 John 1:5–6 (KJV 1900)
5 This then is the message which we have heard of him, and declare unto you, that God is light, and in him is no darkness at all. 6 If we say that we have fellowship with him, and walk in darkness, we lie, and do not the truth:

"Neither shall he regard the God of his fathers"

Some believe this to mean that the Antichrist will be an apostate Jewish person. This makes sense if the Antichrist is to convince the Jews that he is their Messiah. He will emerge upon the scene as the deliverer of the Jews [Dan 9.27]. He will claim to have risen from the dead [Rev 13.3, 12, 14]. He will establish his headquarters in Israel [Dan 11.41; 2 Th 2.3-4]. He will repudiate Jesus as King of the Jews and will seat himself in the Jewish Temple proclaiming himself as its rightful resident.[166]

Jesus said:

Matthew 24:5 (KJV 1900)
5 For many shall come in my name, saying, I am Christ; and shall deceive many.

Matthew 24:24 (KJV 1900)
24 For there shall arise false Christs, and false prophets, and shall

shew great signs and wonders; insomuch that, if it were possible, they shall deceive the very elect.

John 5:43 (KJV 1900)
43 I am come in my Father's name, and ye receive me not: if another shall come in his own name, him ye will receive.

A false Christ is a person claiming to be Christ who is not the Christ. John uses the word antichrist and adds that such a person claims that Jesus is not the Christ

1 John 2:22–23 (KJV 1900)
²²Who is a liar but he that denieth [NT: 720 deny, disown, repudiate] that Jesus is the Christ? He is antichrist, that denieth the Father and the Son. ²³ Whosoever denieth the Son, the same hath not the Father: *(but) he that acknowledgeth the Son hath the Father also.*

Therefore, to be even a false Christ, at minimum, there must be the *pretense* of being Jewish.[167]

"Neither shall he regard…nor the desire of women"

Daniel 11:37 (KJV 1900)
37 Neither shall he regard the God of his fathers, nor the desire of women,

The context of this verse appears to be the total disregard of the Antichrist for any traditional spiritual authority be it genuine or false. This specific passage seems to be a reference to the desire of Jewish women to be the mother of the Messiah. This desire would be present at the time of Daniel's writing. In fact, his prophecies made it possible for those with such aspirations to know the precise time frame in which the Messiah was scheduled to appear [Daniel 9]. Taken in this sense the statement is possibly also a veiled reference to his (Antichrists') enemy "the seed of the woman " whose heel his sponsor has bruised.[168]

"(N)or regard any god: for he shall magnify himself above all."

This statement signals the coming end of all the false religions and false gods that have served to deceive the world under Mystery Babylon since the beginning. This means that the current efforts to establish a New World Order will eventually be superseded by an even *newer* order which will reveal to the *uninitiated* the futility of their ecumenical efforts to deliver a one world system.[169] Antichrist, in his drive to implement the purest form of Luciferian religion will eventually do away with all the false systems originally designed to obscure Christ. His patience will expire with Mystery Babylon, the ancient secret spiritual template and structure for Satan's management of the earth [Rev 17.16-17]. The current campaign to unite every shade of religion under one banner will eventually be shown to have been a satanic deception all along. This is at least a portion of the deception promised to those who reject Christ in the last days.

> 2 Thessalonians 2:11–12 (KJV 1900)
> 11 And for this cause God shall send them strong delusion, that they should believe a lie: 12 That they all might be damned who believed not the truth, but had pleasure in unrighteousness.

The desire of Lucifer is to be worshipped as God: all his strategies point to this end, all satanic deceptions terminate at this single lie, *The Lie* [1 John 2.22].

> Matthew 4:8–9 (KJV 1900)
> 8 Again, the devil taketh him up into an exceeding high mountain, and sheweth him all the kingdoms of the world, and the glory of them; 9 And saith unto him, All these things will I give thee, if thou wilt fall down and worship me. "

But in his estate shall he honour the God of forces"[170]

> Daniel 11:38 (KJV 1900)
> 38 But in his estate shall he honour <u>the God of forces</u>: and a god whom his fathers knew not shall he honour with gold, and silver, and with precious stones, and pleasant things.

The word "forces" [OT:4581] means a place of safety, strength, refuge, fortress, stronghold.

> Psalm 37:39 (KJV 1900)
> 39 But the salvation of the righteous is of the Lord: He is their

strength [OT: 4581] in the time of trouble.

Proverbs 10:29 (KJV 1900)
29 The way of the Lord is strength [OT: 4581] to the upright: But destruction shall be to the workers of iniquity.

Isaiah 25:4 (KJV 1900)
4 For thou hast been a strength [OT: 4581] to the poor, A strength [OT: 4581] to the needy in his distress, A refuge from the storm, a shadow from the heat, When the blast of the terrible ones is as a storm against the wall.

The Antichrist, the willful king, will rely upon the god who enables him to administer *irresistible strength*, of whatever kind required. The fourth beast of Daniel's vision [Dan 7.23] exercises such power, exercises it to such an extraordinary degree that it appears to be [and is] supernatural in its quality. The ability of the Antichrist to produce what has been nearly impossible: the brokering of a peace agreement that secures Israel, will be a manifestation of this strength. In another field, this strength will be demonstrated in the violent uprooting of three kings to establish his initial kingdom. A supernatural entity, whom he will honor as a god, will be the source of this strength.

Of course, this god must be Lucifer, because Antichrist has disdained and rejected all other gods as beneath him. The only god greater than himself would have to be Lucifer. In history, the worship of Lucifer has been [for the most part, until recently] a hidden, occult[171] faith and not a significant part of the parade of false religions which cover the earth. This association with a god of overwhelming power is not inconsistent with Daniel's other prophecies regarding this man and his administration, which project force in a way unknown to all previous Gentile empires.

2 Thessalonians 2:8–9 (KJV 1900)
8 And then shall that Wicked be revealed, whom the Lord shall consume with the spirit of his mouth, and shall destroy with the brightness of his coming: 9 Even him, whose coming is after the working of Satan with all power and signs and lying wonders,

This *worship of power as an absolute good* is also consistent with the devil's view of God. It appears that Satan believes that God is God primarily because He is stronger than everyone else. The devil tells Eve that she should desire to be like God, receiving secret knowledge and by implication superior authority [Gen 3.4-5]. Lucifer claims that Job serves God because of God's power to protect and to bless him [Job 1.9-11]. He also claims that the only thing preventing him from turning Job against God is God's own powerful intercession on Job's behalf [Job 2.4-5]. The devil tempts Christ by an appeal to His power to turn stones into bread [Mt 4.4]. Indeed, Satan appears to incorrectly identify Deity with power alone. *"God is Power and Power is God."* It is therefore not surprising that his "son" would acquire the same incorrect view.

In the Willful king, we see the power of the state used to advance a religious agenda. The Antichrist is a firm believer in the merger of the religious and secular authorities, and he will use the military power of government to ruthlessly implement a spiritual agenda.

> Daniel 11:39 (KJV 1900)
> 39 Thus shall he do in the most strong holds [OT: 4581] with a strange god, whom he shall acknowledge and increase with glory: and he shall cause them to rule over many, and shall divide the land for gain.

This foreign god of fortresses will enable the Antichrist to consolidate power unlike Pharaoh, Ashurbanipal, Nebuchadnezzar, Alexander, Antiochus, or any other leader in history. The god of fortresses is the father of the Antichrist, Lucifer in one of his many emanations. The power behind the cultural phenomenon of the Antichrist is demonic power. This supernatural strength also explains the massive military machine of the end time leader. It is the devil who is the source of the extraordinary violence of this final fourth kingdom.

Summary: The Character of the Antichrist

In our study of the Antichrist, we have examined the sequence of events that lead to the revelation of this pivotal end times character.

We have seen that during the Church age, the *spirit of the antichrist* is at work long centuries before the Antichrist himself is in the world. This spirit seeks as its primary objective to undermine the concept that Jesus is the Christ. This spirit also attempts to undermine the effects of the knowledge of Christ in the world. The spirit of antichrist is the operational phase of the *Mystery of Iniquity* after the incarnation of Jesus Christ. The Mystery of Iniquity is Satan's prehistoric, overarching plan of lawlessness by which he intends to overthrow divine rule of the heavens and the earth. It is based upon a theology that is promoted by deception and insinuated into the Church and the organs of society. At the core of this theology is *The Lie* that Jesus is not God. The Lie is the cornerstone of a demonic theology which seeks to overturn the *Mystery of Godliness* [1Tim 3.16] which is the truth concerning Christ and His mission.

The Mystery of Iniquity is the system of lawlessness that, since the incarnation, is administered by the many antichrists who seek to prepare a world suitable for the introduction of *the* Antichrist. Although they operate in many walks of life, a significant segment of these preliminary antichrists are *false teachers* who present doctrines of demons as legitimate Christian teaching. The primary methodology of the Mystery of Iniquity, prior to the presentation of Antichrist, is deception.

The consequence of this spirit of antichrist will be an apostasy or a falling away of followers of Christendom. Those who fall away are persons who had a profession of Christian commitment without true faith in Christ.

1 Thessalonians 2.9
Even him, whose coming is after the working of Satan with all power and signs and lying wonders, 10 And with all deceivableness of unrighteousness in them that perish; <u>because they received not the love of the truth, that they might be saved</u>. 11 And for this cause God shall send them strong delusion, that they should believe a lie: 12 <u>That they all might be damned</u> who <u>believed not the truth</u>, but had pleasure in unrighteousness.

This deception will occur upon several levels:

First, the Antichrist and his false prophet [the Prime Minister of the New World Order, who is to the Antichrist what John the Baptist was to Christ] will attempt to validate his claim to be the Messiah by means of supernatural acts. These supernatural signs and wonders will deceive many who believe that *all* manifestations of spiritual power come from God.

Secondly, there is the "deceivableness of unrighteousness." In the

Bible there is a category of deception which is the consequence of a commitment to sin. Verses 10 and 12 above confirm the love of these deceived persons for unrighteousness. Because of their rejection of righteousness, sin *itself* deceives them into believing the lie of the Antichrist. For example, once Eve had decided to disregard the divine commandment, she was then available to the deception of the serpent. Once we have given ourselves over to *"do as thou wilt,"* every type of satanic manipulation and deception becomes possible for us.

Antichrist and the New World Order

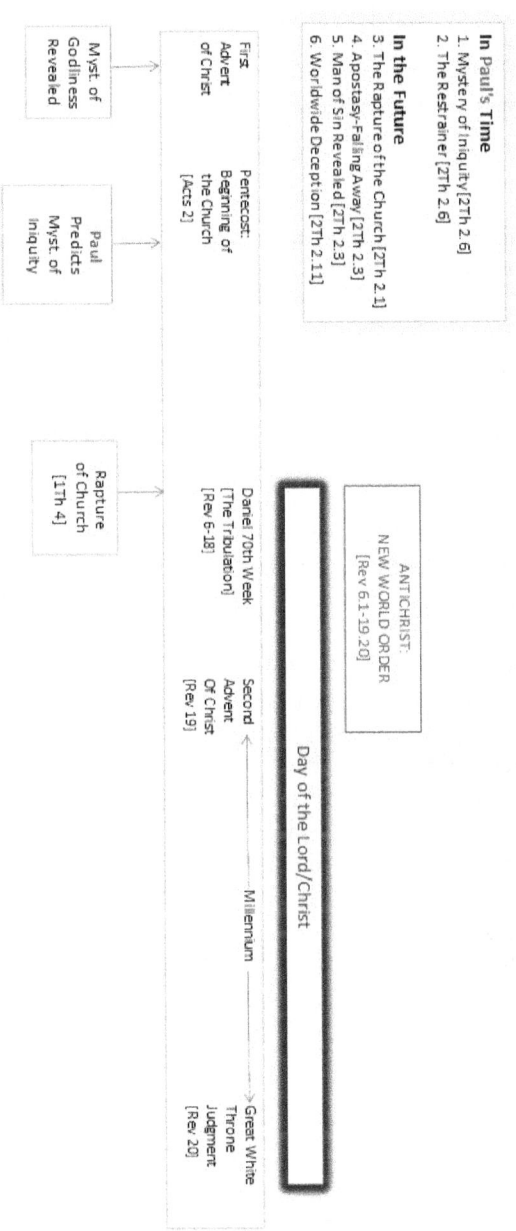

Fig 3. The Day of the Lord and Antichrist

Thirdly, there is the delusion which comes directly from God as a form of judgment. God is not the author of sin; however, God does intensify the consequences of a path already chosen. For those who have rejected the truth, and embraced demonic evil, God will send a strong or *effective* deception that will result in their acceleration along the path that they have selected. The end of this is judgment. Hence, in this strong delusion we find God fulfilling his promise to judge sinful men.

Before the apostasy, God will rescue the Church from the Day of the Lord by means of the Rapture, thereby removing the restraining power that prevents the full manifestation of the Mystery of Iniquity. The elimination of this powerful spiritual restraint will enable the appearance of the Antichrist.

The timing of the unfolding of end time events is not in the hands of the devil but is determined by God. God has predicted the end of evil in the universe [Dan 9.24]. He has defined ahead of time how far evil will advance and when it will be finally eliminated.

In the present age, the power of God operating through his Body, the true Church, exercises restraining power upon the manifestation of evil in the world. God does not allow the world to be as evil as it could be. Although the institution of government exercises a degree of physical control over evil [Rom 13.1-4], ultimately government is an institution populated by fallen men. The Church is authorized and empowered to provide a solution to evil in the world through the gospel of Jesus Christ, proclaimed through the Word and the holy lifestyle of believers. The Church is not, in this sense, a building or even an organization but an organism, a Body which executes the will and desire of the Head which is Christ.

> Colossians 1:18 (KJV 1900)
> 18 And he is the head of the body, the Church: who is the beginning, the firstborn from the dead; that in all things he might have the preeminence.

The absence of the Body of Christ on earth creates a new spiritual environment, a vacuum into which evil will flow. This new spiritual environment will be congenial to the introduction of the son of Satan, the Antichrist.

We discovered that the Antichrist will not initially come onto the scene as an overtly evil individual. But in a continuation of the strategy of the Mystery of Iniquity, he will deceive the world regarding his true intentions for a season. During this time, approximately three and one-half years, he will function as a notable statesman and politician, utilizing the institution of government to achieve a position which he will use as a springboard to world conquest.

We shall next address the timing of the revelation of the Antichrist as the Antichrist, which will coincide with the unfolding of the Vial/Bowl judgments of Revelation 15. While the Day of the Lord can be said to begin immediately after the Rapture of the Church and continue until the completion of the final judgment [Rev 20.11-15], the advent of the Beast marks an intensification of God's judgment against rebellious mankind. The Antichrist is just as much of a judgment against mankind as are the vial/bowl judgments.

We have looked at the character of the Antichrist by an examination of the extraordinary titles that are applied to him in scripture. By this examination we have also learned a great deal about his origin, destiny, and the nature of his activities in the world.

We have addressed the following names attributed to him in scripture:

- Antichrist,
- the Man of Sin,
- the Lawless One,
- the Son of Perdition,
- the Prince who is to Come,
- the Little Horn
- the Willful King.
- the Beast [we have yet to address]

15
Book Two: The Career Of Antichrist

Events Leading to Revelation 13

The revelation of the true character and agenda of the Antichrist occurs at the midpoint of the Tribulation, which is another way of saying the midpoint of Daniel's 70th week. In the first three- and one-half years of the tribulation, Antichrist has been active on the world scene but not recognized by the world for what he is.

In a similar way, the world has never comprehended who God is and has behaved as if He were not righteous, not just and not able to evaluate its conduct and punish it.

> 1 Thessalonians 5:1–3 (KJV 1900)
> 1 But of the times and the seasons, brethren, ye have no need that I write unto you. 2 For yourselves know perfectly that the day of the Lord so cometh as a thief in the night. 3 For when they shall say, Peace and safety; then sudden destruction cometh upon them, as travail upon a woman with child; and they shall not escape.

The Day of the Lord or Christ is a period which begins *after* the departure of the Church via the Rapture and continues through the Tribulation and the Millennial Kingdom. It begins with the opening of the book of seven seals, which initiates a series of increasingly destructive catastrophes which shall befall humanity.

Revelation 5:1–5 (KJV 1900)
1 And I saw in the right hand of him that sat on the throne a book written within and on the backside, sealed with seven seals. 2 And I saw a strong angel proclaiming with a loud voice, Who is worthy to open the book, and to loose the seals thereof? 3 And no man in heaven, nor in earth, neither under the earth, was able to open the book, neither to look thereon. 4 And I wept much, because no man was found worthy to open and to read the book, neither to look thereon. 5 And one of the elders saith unto me, Weep not: behold, the Lion of the tribe of Juda, the Root of David, hath prevailed to open the book, and to loose the seven seals thereof.

The Seven Seals

The seven seals contain the punishments to be released upon the God-defying world. Many have asked the question: "If there is a God, why then does he allow the wicked to go unpunished?"

God does judge the wicked, primarily at death by hell-fire, but also in history thorough means as diverse as direct historical intervention to permitting the personal sins of mankind to reach their inevitable destructive conclusion. The direct divine intervention initiated by the opening of this seven-sealed book will begin His calling of the entire world to account for its steadfast rejection of Him and its collaboration with the devil from the very dawn of human existence.

These seals unlock chastisements that reveal the righteousness of God as surely as his providing a Savior did. Just as the faith of men and women in the Gospel brings about the righteous result of justification and salvation, so also the rejection of divine mercy as revealed in Christ will bring about an equally righteous judgment of unrelenting punishment and misery upon mankind.

Galatians 6:7 (KJV 1900)
7 Be not deceived; God is not mocked: for whatsoever a man soweth, that shall he also reap.

Matthew 7:13–14 (KJV 1900)
13 Enter ye in at the strait gate: for wide is the gate, and broad is the way, that leadeth to destruction, and many there be which go in thereat: 14 Because strait is the gate, and narrow is the way, which leadeth unto life, and few there be that find it.

The first four of the seven seals release forces that result in global war and the effects that war produces: a rebalancing of political power, economic dislocations resulting in famine, and the death of one quarter of the world's population. For the large majority of the dead, death also means eternal separation from God in Hell.

Under normal situations people die in numbers and geographic distribution that allow us to avoid considering the spiritual implications of death, unless confronted with it directly via a pastor during a funeral. This future war will, in a relatively brief period, convey twenty-five percent of the world population from life on this earth to the reality of eternal damnation. At the same time the spiritual implications of death will become more apparent than ever to those who remain.

> Revelation 6:7–8 (KJV 1900)
> 7 And when he had opened the fourth seal, I heard the voice of the fourth beast say, Come and see. 8 And I looked, and behold a pale horse: and his name that sat on him was Death, and Hell followed with him. And power was given unto them over the fourth part of the earth, to kill with sword, and with hunger, and with death, and with the beasts of the earth.

The number of deaths and the suddenness of the loss of life will create tremendous dislocations economically, politically, and spiritually.

The entire sequence of judgments consisting of seals, trumpets, and bowls [vials] are contained in the seven-sealed book. The first six judgments are described as Seals, while the seventh Seal unleashes the Trumpet judgments. In like manner the seventh Trumpet judgment unleashes the seven Bowl/Vial or Plague judgments. The sixth seal is the first *physical* divine judgment, a great earthquake accompanied by fearful signs in the heavens.

> Revelation 6:12–14 (KJV 1900)
> 12 And I beheld when he had opened the sixth seal, and, lo, there was a great earthquake; and the sun became black as sackcloth of hair, and the moon became as blood; 13 And the stars of heaven fell unto the earth, even as a fig tree casteth her untimely figs, when she is shaken of a mighty wind. 14 And the heaven departed as a scroll when it is rolled together; and every mountain and island were moved out of their places.

The signs in the heavens are validation of the prophecies of the Word of God which promised such things during the Day of the Lord.[172]

These devastations will be unmistakably the work of God and men will acknowledge them as such in chapter 6 of the Book of Revelation. Nevertheless, overwhelming majority of humanity *will not* be moved to repentance but will attempt to hide from the wrath of God.

> Revelation 6:15–17 (KJV 1900)
> 15 And the kings of the earth, and the great men, and the rich men, and the chief captains, and the mighty men, and every bondman, and every free man, hid themselves in the dens and in the rocks of the mountains; 16 And said to the mountains and rocks, Fall on us, and hide us from the face of him that sitteth on the throne, and from the wrath of the Lamb: 17 For the great day of his wrath is come; and who shall be able to stand?

The final seal opens into seven more judgments, called the trumpet judgments.

The Trumpet Judgments

> Revelation 8:1–2 (KJV 1900)
> 1 And when he had opened the seventh seal, there was silence in heaven about the space of half an hour. 2 And I saw the seven angels which stood before God; and to them were given seven trumpets.

The trumpet judgments, like the seal's which preceded them, occur during the first three and one-half years of Daniel's 70th week. During forty-two months of concentrated misery, God provides unmistakable evidence of His authorship of these events through progressively severe physical upheavals in the earth.

Mankind has forgotten that God provided the earth as a stewardship [Gen 1.28], using it instead as a base of operations to serve Satan [Rom 1.18-23]. Man will be held accountable for his treatment of the physical earth, by repeated *physical* judgments whereby his destructive acts upon the earth are brought to their logical and ecological consequences. This is another example of God taking man's sinful choices and forcing him to suffer their penalties on an accelerated schedule.

Therefore, in the first four *trumpet* judgments the following occurs:

1. One third of trees are destroyed and all the green grass resulting in an ecological disaster which will upset the food chain.
2. A cataclysm in the seas results in the deaths of one third of the sea animals and the destruction of one third of the ships upon the seas, impacting both trade and military operations.
3. God will cause the loss of one third of the freshwater supply. Man will become even more aware of the fact that he has always been dependent upon the grace of God for his existence. These calamities will demonstrate to humanity that their independence was only apparent and not real. We have always been totally dependent upon the Lord. The Trumpet judgments will dramatically illustrate that dependency.
4. God will cause a malfunction in the sun, moon and stars resulting in a reduction of one third in natural light, both in the day and in the night.

The latter trumpet judgments unleash the reality of the *demonic world* upon humanity. America today behaves as if the demonic world is something that can be toyed with. Some look upon demonic entities as amoral sources of power. God will reveal that the demonic world is the implacable enemy of *all* humanity, saved or unsaved.

The sixth trumpet alone will kill another *third* of humanity. The long-desired goal of the elite class: dramatic population reduction, will be achieved, but perhaps not to their liking. After the depopulation caused by the Rapture of the Church, the seal judgments will result in a quarter of the remaining population dying by warfare and its byproducts. After this, still another third of those who remain will be killed in the 6th trumpet. Despite this evidence of the power of God there will be little repentance in those days:

Revelation 9:20–21 (KJV 1900)
20 And the rest of the men which were not killed by these plagues yet repented not of the works of their hands, that they should not worship devils, and idols of gold, and silver, and brass, and stone, and of wood: which neither can see, nor hear, nor walk: 21

Neither repented they of their murders, nor of their sorceries, nor of their fornication, nor of their thefts.

War Preparations: The Invisible Precedes the Visible

That which is observed in the world has both invisible causes and invisible effects. There is a realm of the spirit which is the true basis of our present physical and psychological reality.

2 Corinthians 4:17–18 (KJV 1900)
17 For our light affliction, which is but for a moment, worketh for us a far more exceeding and eternal weight of glory; 18 While we look not at the things which are seen, but at the things which are not seen: for the things which are seen are temporal; but the things which are not seen are eternal.

Hebrews 11:1–3 (KJV 1900)
1 Now faith is the substance of things hoped for, the evidence of things not seen. 2 For by it the elders obtained a good report. 3 Through faith we understand that the worlds were framed by the word of God, so that things which are seen were not made of things which do appear.

Events upon the earth today are influenced and often directed by spiritual forces. The nations are impacted by spiritual warfare, as revealed in the book of Daniel, and spirits are assigned to the various kingdoms in the world.

Daniel 10:12–13 (KJV 1900)
12 Then said he unto me, Fear not, Daniel: for from the first day that thou didst set thine heart to understand, and to chasten thyself before thy God, thy words were heard, and I am come for thy words. 13 But the prince of the kingdom of Persia withstood me one and twenty days: but, lo, Michael, one of the chief princes, came to help me; and I remained there with the kings of Persia.

Daniel 10:20–21 (KJV 1900)
20 Then said he, Knowest thou wherefore I come unto thee? and now will I return to fight with the prince of Persia: and when I am

gone forth, lo, the prince of Grecia shall come. 21 But I will shew thee that which is noted in the scripture of truth: and there is none that holdeth with me in these things, but Michael your prince.

This principle is also demonstrated in the invisible influence that the Church has upon the world, through its restraining power upon wickedness [2 Th 2.5-8].[173]

In the Garden of Eden, the invisible forces of wickedness invaded and impacted history when the devil indwelt the serpent, thereby influencing the destiny of every person who would ever live.

The book of Revelation reveals the *spiritual* factors which will determine the unfolding of end time events. However, we need to understand that these invisible spiritual operations are always in progress.

Perhaps this will help the believer to understand his tremendous privilege in influencing history on God's behalf through the dual witness of his life, lived in obedience to scripture and his lips by which he proclaims the grace of God towards mankind in the gospel. The believer also invisibly impacts history through his prayers to God regarding people and institutions.

The Invisible Revealed: A Vision of the Mystery of Godliness and the Mystery of Iniquity

The book of Revelation records events in heaven which precipitate the actions of both Satan and the Antichrist in the second half of the Tribulation. We are given insight into these events in Revelation 12

Revelation 12:1–7 (KJV 1900)
1 And there appeared a great wonder in heaven; a woman clothed with the sun, and the moon under her feet, and upon her head a crown of twelve stars: 2 And she being with child cried, travailing in birth, and pained to be delivered. 3 And there appeared another wonder in heaven; and behold a great red dragon, having seven heads and ten horns, and seven crowns upon his heads. 4 And his tail drew the third part of the stars of heaven[174] and did cast them to the earth: and the dragon stood before the woman which was ready to be delivered, for to devour her child as soon as it was born. 5 And she brought forth a man child, who was to rule all

nations with a rod of iron: and her child was caught up[175] unto God, and to his throne. 6 And the woman fled into the wilderness, where she hath a place prepared of God, that they should feed her there a thousand two hundred and threescore days. 7 And there was war in heaven: Michael and his angels fought against the dragon; and the dragon fought and his angels,

Verses 1-2, 5 describe the Mystery of Godliness revealed in 1 Tim 3.16. This is God's plan to provide a Savior through a nation of his own creation, Israel.

> "The woman symbolized Israel, as indicated by Genesis 37:9–11, where the sun and the moon referred to Jacob and Rachel, Joseph's parents."[176]

Verses 3, 4 are a picture of the Mystery of Iniquity and its efforts to destroy Israel, the woman, and the Child, which is Christ.

The dragon incorporates symbolic elements that reveal it as the enemy of God, the author of the angelic rebellion and source of the policy of spiritual wickedness insinuated into human institutions [Rev 12.9]. It is red[177], which identifies the dragon with the religious pretensions of its servants: Mystery Babylon, the occult theocracy that has ruled the world since the flood [Rev 17.4 *scarlet*] and the Beast, also identified as red [Rev 17.4], an allusion to the blasphemous spiritual claims of the Antichrist. The seven heads with crowns represent seven kingdoms, the religious state throughout history over which the dragon has ruled via Mystery Babylon. The ten horns identify the context of the consummation of Satan's earthly designs, his New World Order, with the last of the seven kingdoms or heads: the Iron Kingdom described by Daniel [The ten horns of the fourth beast of Dan 7.7 and the ten toes of the Iron Kingdom in the interpretation of the vision of Nebuchadnezzar Dan 2:31-34; 40-43].

The vision of Revelation 12 addresses a vast period, stretching from prehistory to the life of Christ, to the persecution and flight of redeemed Israel during the midpoint of the Tribulation period. There is a considerable lapse of time between verses 5 and 6. We are currently living during that space between the events of verses 1-5 and the events described in verse 6. The events of verse 6 [the woman fleeing into the wilderness] will not occur until the midpoint of the Tribulation when the Prince who is to Come will begin his persecution of the believing Jews.[178]

Richard G. Walker

War Breaks Out In Heaven: The Invisible Precedent for the Appearance of the Beast in Revelation 13

Revelation 12:7-12 (KJV 1900)
7 And there was war in heaven: Michael and his angels fought against the dragon; and the dragon fought and his angels, 8 <u>And prevailed not; neither was their place found any more in heaven.</u> 9 And the great dragon was cast out, that old serpent, called the devil, and Satan, which deceiveth the whole world: <u>he was cast out into the earth, and his angels were cast out with him.</u> 10 And I heard a loud voice saying in heaven, Now is come salvation, and strength, and the kingdom of our God, and the power of his Christ: for the accuser of our brethren is cast down, which accused them before our God day and night. 11 And they overcame him by the blood of the Lamb, and by the word of their testimony; and they loved not their lives unto the death. 12 Therefore rejoice, ye heavens, and ye that dwell in them. Woe to the inhabiters of the earth and of the sea! <u>for the devil is come down unto you, having great wrath, because he knoweth that he hath but a short time.</u>

Antichrist and the New World Order

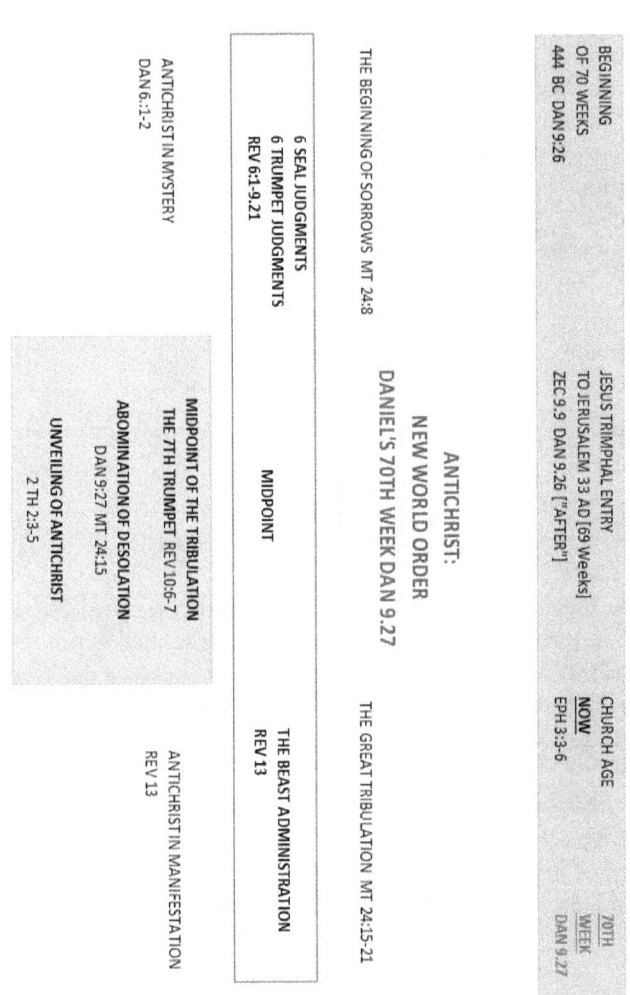

Figure 4. Daniel's 70th Week

The vision of Revelation 12 occurs after the sixth trumpet sounded [Rev 9.13]. It occurs prior to the revelation of the vision of the beast out of the sea in Revelation 13. In fact, Rev 12.14 specifically identifies the length of time the Woman will be hidden and protected from the dragon as corresponding to the last half of the Tribulation [time, and times and half a time].

We will see in our next chapter that *the beast is a person, a political entity, and a demonic spiritual being.* It is indeed possible that the indwelling of the Antichrist by Lucifer occurs immediately after the defeat suffered in Revelation 12. The eviction of the devil from heaven occurs at the midpoint of the tribulation and is coincident with the abomination of desolation[179] whereby the temple worship is halted and the temple itself is profaned. Jews and Christians unwilling to worship the Antichrist and the dragon will be subject to capital punishment [Rev 13.8, 11-12, 15].

> Daniel 9:27 (KJV 1900)
> 27 And he shall confirm the covenant with many for one week: and in the midst of the week he shall cause the sacrifice and the oblation to cease, and for the overspreading of abominations he shall make it desolate, even until the consummation, and that determined shall be poured upon the desolate.

The dragon is identified as that "old serpent, called the devil and Satan" in Rev 12.9. His mental state is also described as not just wrath, but great wrath [Rev 12.12]. This wrath exists because the long ages of God's forbearance have ended, and Satan's schemes have not produced their desired results. The Jews have not been destroyed, the worship of Lucifer has not been publicly inaugurated, and he and his angels have been defeated in warfare and cast out of heaven.

Lucifer appears on the earth in Rev 12.13; an earth which has been ravaged of its resources and depleted of much of its population by the seal and the trumpet judgments. *It is under these spiritual and physical conditions that the Antichrist is revealed to be Satan's representative.*

16
The Beast

Revelation 13:1–8 (KJV 1900)
1 And I stood upon the sand of the sea, and saw a beast rise up out of the sea, having seven heads and ten horns, and upon his horns ten crowns, and upon his heads the name of blasphemy. 2 And the beast which I saw was like unto a leopard, and his feet were as the feet of a bear, and his mouth as the mouth of a lion: and the dragon gave him his power, and his seat, and great authority. 3 And I saw one of his heads as it were wounded to death; and his deadly wound was healed: and all the world wondered after the beast. 4 And they worshipped the dragon which gave power unto the beast: and they worshipped the beast, saying, Who is like unto the beast? who is able to make war with him? 5 And there was given unto him a mouth speaking great things and blasphemies; and power was given unto him to continue forty and two months. 6 And he opened his mouth in blasphemy against God, to blaspheme his name, and his tabernacle, and them that dwell in heaven. 7 And it was given unto him to make war with the saints, and to overcome them: and power was given him over all kindreds, and tongues, and nations. 8 And all that dwell upon the earth shall worship him, whose names are not written in the book of life of the Lamb slain from the foundation of the world.

Daniel describes the 4 beasts of Daniel 7 as successive KINGDOMS [Dan 7.17]. The beast of Revelation 13 is also a kingdom: it is another explanation of the *fourth* beast of Daniel 7. The *composite* beast of Revelation 13 possesses elements of the first three beasts of Daniel: the leopard of Greece, the bear of Medo-Persia and the lion of Babylon. It should be noted that the fourth beast of Daniel 7 has the same international character of the beast of Revelation 13: having "great iron teeth" [Dan 7.7] and "nails of brass" [Dan 7.19] which, when considered in light of the image in Daniel 2, correspond to the fourth kingdom and to Greece. This beast of Revelation 13 corresponds to the fourth beast of Daniel 7. It is the final iteration of the Mystery of Iniquity, the magnum opus of Lucifer which portrays the consummation of his efforts upon the earth since the fall of mankind.

This fourth kingdom, the composite beast, will represent the devil's vision of his World Order more completely than any of its predecessors. The spirit of the dragon of Revelation 12, which animates the Beast and provides its agenda and its success [Rev 13.2] will be expressed with such fidelity in this final manifestation that *this* beast tells the entire story of the devil's activity among the nations in its physiognomy. Unlike the beasts that preceded it in history, this beast [Rev 13] has seven heads and ten crowned horns.

The four beasts of Daniel 7 correspond to four of the *heads* upon the composite beast of Revelation 13 and upon the beast of Revelation 17. There are three more heads on the New Testament beast contrasted with the beast of Daniel because Daniel was only provided a prophecy of his time [in which Babylon and then Persia ruled] forward, previous kingdoms were not in view. The *heads* are kings, or kingdoms [Rev 17.9-11], each of which are involved in blasphemy, that is, the doctrine that God is not sovereign, that Jesus is not God or Christ, the central doctrine of the Mystery of Iniquity [2 Th 2.11]. Their demotion of God is naturally accompanied by their promotion of a deity who is not God. The five kingdoms[180] preceding John the apostle which engaged in this blasphemy are: Egypt, Assyria, Babylon, Medo-Persia, and Greece.

> Revelation 17:9–12 (KJV 1900)
> [9] And here *is* the mind which hath wisdom. The seven heads are seven mountains, on which the woman sitteth. [10] And there are seven kings: five are fallen, and one is, *and* the other is not yet come; and when he cometh, he must continue a short space. [11] And the beast that was, and is not, even he is the eighth, and is of the seven, and goeth into perdition. [12] And the ten horns which thou sawest are ten kings, which have received no kingdom as yet; but receive power as kings one hour with the beast.

The kingdom [or head] which now "is," [Rev 17.10] from the standpoint of John in the first century, is Rome, the *sixth kingdom or head*. There will be a seventh head, and one which may be considered an eighth.

Heads of the Beast	Historical or Future Kingdoms	Notes	Vision of Daniel 2
Head #1	Egypt	Gentile Government after Babel and before the prophecy of Daniel	Not addressed in Daniel's vision
Head #2	Assyria		
Head #3	Babylon		Dan 2.32a "head was of fine gold"
Head #4	Medo-Persia		Dan 2.32b "breast and arms of silver"
Head #5	Greece		Dan 2.32c "belly and thighs of brass"
Head #6	Rome I	Rome in the time of John the Apostle	Dan 2.33a "Legs of Iron"
PERIOD BETWEEN PENTECOST AND RAPTURE NOT ADDRESSED IN PROPHECY			
Head #7	"Rome" IIa	Not Rome but the beginning of the geographic organization of World Government in the first 3 1/2 years of the Tribulation	Dan 2.33b "his feet part of iron and part of clay"
Head #8 [Rev 17.11]	"Rome" IIb	World Government in the final 3 1/2 years of the Tribulation-after the revelation of the World Leader as Antichrist	Dan 2.33b "his feet part of iron and part of clay"

Figure 6: The Eight Heads of the Beast of Revelation

The ten horns are of the seventh head, corresponding to the latter days of the fourth kingdom of Daniel 7.7, 23-24 and to the ten toes of the image described in Daniel 2.[181]

The Beast of Revelation is a kingdom [world government], ***a person,*** [the Little Horn, or Antichrist] ***and a spiritual entity*** [Satan or the Dragon, who indwells the Antichrist]. Remembering this is essential to comprehending the symbolism and significance of the Beast. These three concepts are intertwined and layered upon each other in the visions of Revelation concerning him. Therefore, the Beast may be identified with the Antichrist, with Lucifer and with World Government.

The Beast as the symbol of the Dragon's political management of this world in the last days has both earthly and spiritual aspects. The leadership personality of the political regime of the last days is the little horn or the Antichrist.

The Beast Identified with Antichrist

The Antichrist is a ***person*** who is identified with a ***kingdom*** or a state: specifically, the seventh and *eighth* heads of the Beast of Revelation. He is indwelt by Lucifer, a fallen angel, **a *spiritual entity*** [Rev 17.8][182]. Hence, Antichrist appears to imitate the hypostatic union of humanity and deity found in Christ.

The Beast is a human being that will be the fulfillment of all the Old Testament and New Testament predictions regarding the Antichrist. We have seen in Book One that the Antichrist considers himself greater than God, blasphemes God, demands worship, and kills believers. He will exercise governmental authority as a king, and he will seek to destroy all who will not worship him. The Antichrist is a living being who will be personally defeated by Christ at His second advent. The thirteenth, seventeenth and nineteenth chapters of Revelation reveal these same characteristics in the Beast.

It is necessary for the Beast to be a person to impersonate the Jewish Messiah. The Beast will, with Lucifer and a seducing spirit, impersonate the Trinity. He will also have his own John the Baptist in the form of the False Prophet, the miracle working Prime Minister of the New World Order. Essentially all that he will do has been disclosed in the scriptures.

According to Daniel 7.23-26 [esp. v 24] Antichrist will also represent a **kingdom**, Daniel's fourth kingdom, which is the final Gentile kingdom of the age, has *two advents*, one in the time John the apostle which is identified in history as Rome and another that appears at the end of history during the period of the Tribulation. This second advent of the Iron Kingdom is itself divided into two halves, corresponding to the two segments of Daniel's seventieth week. In the first three- and one-half years of the Tribulation, the time of the reign of the ten kings, this may be referred to as the *seventh* head or kingdom. The final three- and one-half years of the Tribulation, when the Antichrist reigns over the earth, appears to be the *eighth* head in Revelation 17.11.

Richard G. Walker

Daniel's Vision and the Two Advents of "Rome"

Revelation 17:10 (KJV 1900)
10 And there are seven kings: five are fallen, and one is, and the other is not yet come; and when he cometh, he must continue a short space.

There is a vast period which is not addressed in the Old Testament prophecies regarding this fourth kingdom of Daniel chapters 2 and 7. These prophets disclosed nothing regarding the Church, which encompasses the period from the coming of the Spirit at Pentecost [circa. 33 AD.] until the translation of the Church at the Rapture. It appears that the fourth kingdom of Daniel is divided into two portions by the Church Age: the first part corresponding to the sixth head or Rome and the second corresponding to the seventh/eighth heads in Revelation which may be unrelated to Rome as a political entity. The sixth head of the beast of Revelation 13 appears to correspond to the "legs of iron" of Nebuchadnezzar's vision, and the seventh/eights head to the "feet part of iron and part of clay." Rome no longer today constitutes a world encompassing kingdom. Prophecy does not require the reconstitution of the Roman Empire for the fulfillment of these prophecies. The seventh king/kingdom is predicted to *"continue a short space"* [Rev 17.10] and not the thousands of years that have followed the time of John. The Apostle John is given the comprehensive revelation of events partially disclosed to Daniel.

The Antichrist redirects the political and spiritual character of the fourth kingdom/seventh head after his desecration of the temple at the midpoint of the tribulation: he may in fact be seen as starting an entirely new kingdom within the seventh head and in this sense, he might be said to be an "eighth head" or eighth kingdom [Rev 17.11]. More will be said about the character of the eighth kingdom or head under the discussion of the career of the Antichrist.

The Beast Identified with Lucifer

The Beast is identified with Lucifer, the Dragon, who shares the same characteristics[183] of horns and heads [Rev 12.3 c.f. 20.2]. It is important to reiterate that the Beast is a symbol. That symbol represents simultaneously an end time political system, the chief individual identified with that system [Antichrist] and a *spiritual* entity,

Antichrist and the New World Order

Satan, who arises from the bottomless pit to empower the Antichrist.

> Revelation 17:8, 11 (KJV 1900)
> 8 The beast that thou sawest was, and is not; <u>and shall ascend out of the bottomless pit</u>, and go into perdition: and they that dwell on the earth shall wonder, whose names were not written in the book of life from the foundation of the world, when they behold the beast that was, and is not, and yet is…11 And the beast that was, and is not, even he is the eighth, and is of the seven, and goeth into perdition.

As a ***spiritual entity***, the Beast has an origin in the abyss, the bottomless pit. A political system cannot originate from this place, nor can a human being like the Antichrist who is not, in himself, supernatural. What this all means is that there will be a supernatural being who will come from this place to indwell the Antichrist and thereby guide, through him, the final Gentile world kingdom. Distinct from every other demon possessed individual who may be in government, the leader of this end time version of the fourth kingdom will be possessed by a unique spiritual entity elsewhere identified as Satan himself.[184] The Beast is described as one that "shall ascend out of the bottomless pit" [Rev 17.8]. This is a reference to the spiritual entity which we have described elsewhere as the master of the Abyss: Apollyon or Lucifer. As there is one God, subsisting in Three Persons, so Satan will imitate the Trinity by himself performing these three roles as: the animating spirit of the False Prophet [Rev 13.11 the beast of the earth], the indwelling influence of the Antichrist [Rev 13.2] and the object of worldwide worship [Rev 13.4] as the Dragon.

This spiritual dominion of the world is not unique to the end times or to Daniel's 70th week. We live in a world which is occupied by many spiritual entities and the most significant influences upon history are invisible and spiritual [Ps 127.1]. This world was created by God, a *spiritual* being [Jn 4.24] out of things which are invisible [Heb 1.3]. God created man, who possesses an immaterial, immortal, *spiritual* soul received by the breath of God [Gen 2.7; 1 Cor 15.45]. God created *spiritual* beings called angels, some of which rebelled against Him and subverted his earthly creation.[185] *The visible world is directed by spiritual entities* [Eph 6.12]. Although man has significant influence upon the world, that influence is mediated by spiritual factors including:

1. Humanity's fallen spiritual nature, a product of spiritual activity in the Garden of Eden [Rom 3.23; 5.12]
2. The dominating influence of Satan who is the god of fallen humanity [Isa 14,16-17; Eph 2.1-6; 2 Cor 4.4; Heb 2.14-15; 1 Jn 5.19]
3. The overruling action of God who preserves creation [Col 1.17], restrains the devil [2 Th 2.5-7] and saves men via the Gospel [Rom 5.10-11].

It is the blindness of most of the unbelieving world to these realities, and their lack of capacity to resist them if they could perceive them, that is critical to understanding the way in which this world functions. As stated in Chapter 1, there is no safe philosophical position in the devil's world. The entire paradigm itself must be rejected and in its place the individual must substitute a spiritually renewed nature [Jn 3.3], **only** possible through faith in the sacrifice of Christ for the world [Rom 5.8; 10.9-10]. Only then can the Word of God, the Bible, provide *the key to reality* and blueprint for personal victory[186] over Lucifer and this world system.[187]

Revelation 17:8a (KJV 1900)
The beast that thou sawest was, and is not; and shall ascend out of the bottomless pit, <u>and go into perdition</u>:

The Beast that shall go to perdition is a reference to Lucifer. He [Rev 20.1-3] will be sent to the Abyss for 1000 years and will shortly thereafter be permanently confined in the Lake of Fire [perdition]. The Antichrist [Rev 19.20] will be the first inhabitant of the Lake of Fire, [Rev 20.19] at the return of Christ to the earth.

The Beast Identified with World Government

The beast is a ***political entity***, a kingdom. Since the appearance of political organization upon the earth, political systems reflect the same fallen character of the men who inhabit and rule these systems. Political systems cannot be separated from the arrogance and lust which energize fallen humanity [Jer 17.9; Eph 2.2]. Nor can these systems operate independently from the current administrator of this world system, the devil [Jn 12.31; 2 Cor 4.4].

Government is a divine institution. God created government for the orderly function of mankind via the restraint of evil.[188] The Christian can influence government most effectively by his own discipleship and advance to spiritual maturity. This means that the believer's gospel testimony and the witness of his transformed life have a sanctifying influence upon the morality[189] of the unbelieving world [Mt 5.13-14; 1 Pet 2.12-15]. This influence impacts every human institution, including government. Believers must not withdraw from government, but function as responsible citizens. Often Christianity is used as an excuse *not* to stand for what is right in moral issues. Christian discipleship does not provide for Christian neutrality regarding issues of good and evil.

Revelation 17:8a (KJV 1900)
8 <u>The beast that thou sawest was, and is not</u>; and shall ascend out of the bottomless pit, and go into perdition:

Each of the historical heads of the Beast of Revelation [Egypt, Assyria, Babylon, Medo-Persia, Greece, Rome] was a kingdom that sought, yet did not fully achieve world rule. Since the Tower of Babel, no power has ruled the entire world. Each historical kingdom addressed in this prophecy of the Beast sought to impose *national* rule upon the world. This means one nation seeking the rule of the world in the name of its own ethnic and cultural dynasty. Therefore, we refer to their empires in *national* terms as the Babylonian or Roman empires.

The beast of Revelation chapters 13 and 17 is an *international* beast. It is different from any of the preceding historical beasts in that it eschews national designation and identifies with the whole earth. This beast is different.

Daniel 7:19–20 (KJV 1900)
19 Then I would know the truth of the fourth beast, <u>which was diverse from all the others</u>, exceeding dreadful, whose teeth were of iron, and his nails of brass; which devoured, brake in pieces, and stamped the residue with his feet; 20 And of the ten horns that were in his head, and of the other which came up, and before whom three fell; even of that horn that had eyes, and a mouth that spake very great things, whose look was more stout than his fellows.

The fourth beast is different in its destructive intent and capacity, in the appearance of the ten horns and the "other [horn] which came up," in his composition of elements of two of the previous beasts, and was different in yet another significant way from its predecessors:

Daniel 7:21 (KJV 1900)
I beheld, and the same horn made war with the saints, and prevailed against them;

The ten horns and the international composition of the beast speak to the political configuration that will exist at the end of the age. The identification of the Beast of Revelation as Rome is not an automatic assumption, as it is not openly stated in the Bible and must be inferred from texts like Daniel 9.26. The fourth beast of Daniel 7 corresponds to the period from the ancient kingdom of Rome until the second advent of Christ; the legs and feet of the image of Daniel 2. Daniel did not have the Church Age in view in his prophecies.

The unprecedented violence of the fourth beast of Daniel is not without purpose. The prophet describes this purpose in his book.

Daniel 7:25 (KJV 1900)
And he shall speak great words against the most High, and shall wear out the saints of the most High, <u>and think to **change** times and laws</u>: and they shall be given into his hand until a time and times and the dividing of time.

5. LN 62.3–62.9 (hafel) change, set **or organize a new order** (Da 2:21; 7:25+)[190]

The purpose of the violence of Daniel's fourth beast, who corresponds to the Beast of Revelation 13 and 17, is to establish a **New Order**. The Beast will act with complete ruthlessness to establish that which he has always intended: a World Order with himself as its deity, demonic despotism on earth and eventually in the heavens as well [Isa 14.12-14].

To give birth to this New World Order *politically, the beast must destroy nationalism*. To establish it *spiritually*, he must *obliterate all religions* and especially biblical Christianity. His great violence is for the purpose of *demolition*. The destruction of the present World Order is the explanation for his great violence and for his consistent blasphemy against the Lord. The ten kings represent the beginning of the beasts' *international* dominion.

There is a precedent in scripture for this coming age.

Revelation 17:8a (KJV 1900)
8 <u>The beast that thou sawest was, and is not</u>; and shall ascend out of the bottomless pit, and go into perdition:

In this verse, the Beast is something that once existed, but did not at the time of John the apostle. Lucifer certainly existed at the time of the writing of Revelation and continues to this day. The Antichrist was not present prior to that time. What was once present, but no longer, was *world government*. World government, the ideal of Satan in his administration of fallen humanity, existed at Babel, the source of Babylon of history.

Genesis 11:1–4 (KJV 1900)
1 And the <u>whole earth</u> was of one language, and of one speech. 2 And it came to pass, as they journeyed from the east, that they found a plain in the land of Shinar; and they dwelt there. 3 And they said one to another, Go to, let us make brick, and burn them throughly. And they had brick for stone, and slime had they for morter. 4 And they said, Go to, let us build us a city and a tower, whose top may reach unto heaven; and let us make us a name, lest we be scattered abroad upon the face of the whole earth.[191]

The intention of a united humanity was to reject the express command of God to repopulate the entire earth. In rebellion against God humanity sought to establish a single political entity [let us make us a name] and a single religion [a tower that at the very least would protect them from judgment by future floods and at the most would enable the worship of the heavens] in opposition to God.

We also know that this planned state was founded in disobedience to God because of His direct actions against it.

Genesis 11:4–9 (KJV 1900)
5 And the LORD came down to see the city and the tower, which the children of men builded. 6 And the LORD said, <u>Behold, the people is one</u>, and they have all one language; and this they begin to do: and now nothing will be restrained from them, which they have imagined to do. 7 Go to, let us go down, and there confound their language, that they may not understand one another's speech. 8 So the LORD scattered them abroad from thence upon the face of all the earth: and they left off to build the city. 9

Therefore is the name of it called Babel; because the LORD did there confound the language of all the earth: and from thence did the LORD scatter them abroad upon the face of all the earth.

It is possible that the *deadly blow* to world government was struck at Babel by the confusion of tongues. This divinely initiated judgment led inevitably to nationalism [Gen 10.5]. Every subsequent head or kingdom of the Beast thought of itself in national terms. The terms that we use to describe these empires today recall their geographic and ethnic identities.

Revelation 13:3–5 (KJV 1900)
3 And I saw one of his heads as it were wounded to death; and his deadly wound was healed: and all the world wondered after the beast. 4 And they worshipped the dragon which gave power unto the beast: and they worshipped the beast, saying, Who is like unto the beast? who is able to make war with him? 5 And there was given unto him a mouth speaking great things and blasphemies; and power was given unto him to continue forty and two months.

It is also possible that, as the Beast is threefold in its significance: a person, a spiritual entity, and a political configuration, so the *deadly blow* might be profitably considered this vantage point.

Since **the devil** was dealt a mortal blow at the cross of Christ, his appearance as the sole object of worship in the end times is a kind of resurrection.

Revelation 13:3 (KJV 1900)
3 And I saw one of his heads as it were wounded to death; and his deadly wound was healed: and all the world wondered after the beast.

Genesis 3:15 (KJV 1900)
And I will put enmity between thee and the woman, and between thy seed and her seed; it shall bruise thy head, and thou shalt bruise his heel.

World government was struck down at birth by the judgment of tongues, which throughout scripture is a symbol of divine judgment [Isa 28.10-12; 1 Cor 14.20-22]. World government did not exist again in history after Babel; however, it will exist in the future, briefly, and will at that time legitimately constitute a New World Order. This might also be considered a kind of resurrection.

In the *political* aspect of the Beast, World Government is of Babel, the foundation of *Babylon*. In this sense, world government is "of the seven" [Rev 17.11] and yet the eighth head, to appear during the last three- and one-half years of Gentile history, the second half of the great Tribulation.

Finally, there may be a future assassination of **the Antichrist**. In his attempt to take the place of Christ, the devil may orchestrate such a miracle on behalf of his "son" to cement his claim of deity during the second half of the Tribulation. His resuscitation could add detail to the prophecy of the eighth head.

> Revelation 17:11 (KJV 1900)
> And the beast that was, and is not, <u>even he is the eighth, and is of the seven</u>, and goeth into perdition.

The Beast of Revelation possesses traits which relate it to all the national entities referred to in Daniel 2 and 7. This beast will succeed in controlling the entire world [Rev 13.3-8]. This beast will not conquer in the name of a nationality or an ethnic group: it will be anti-nationalism, demolishing national structures worldwide.

> Revelation 13:7 (KJV 1900)
> 7 And it was given unto him to make war with the saints, and to overcome them: <u>and power was given him over all kindreds, and tongues, and nations.</u>

The fourth beast of Daniel and the Beast of Revelation will be extraordinarily violent [Dan 7.7-9]. The purpose of this violence is twofold. First, the beast will seek to destroy Christendom, both real and false Christianity, as well as every other religion.[192] All existing systems of spirituality must fall before the Luciferian world religion can be expanded upon the globe. The present ecumenical movement is a holding action doomed to elimination by Lucifer in the destruction of Mystery Babylon. Secondly, nationalism must be eliminated for world government to be fully implemented. Thus, the purpose of the great violence of this beast is demolition, the annihilation of all traces of religion and the destruction of all vestiges of national states.

What We Should Know and Do

What are we to learn from this information and how can it be applied today?

First, we must acknowledge that the nature of government, at its best, reflects the complex character of fallen men. It is therefore capable of great evil, but also of human good, which, though necessary for the orderly function of the earth, is a category of good that excludes God [Gen 2.16]. It is the purpose of government to *preserve human freedom by the restraint of evil* [Rom 13.1-4].

We must also recognize, as Daniel and the Apostle John [Revelation] demonstrate in their writings, that the principal goal of the Gentile kingdoms [governments] is to, by means of violence, consolidate world control [Dan 7.1-8; 8.1-25]. History, even the biased histories of the nations, provide ample testimony to this fact.

Government is also the seat of demonic principalities [Dan 10.12-13, 20-21] which wage war with the elect angels to determine the fortunes of nations. Lucifer uses war [both spiritual and conventional earthly wars] in his capacity as the one who "weakens the nations" [Isa 14.12]. Fallen angels, in their role as deceivers, promote wars between nations, which is partially proven by the absence of war when they are imprisoned [Rev 12.9; 20.3, 8].

These conflicting purposes explain the problems of human government.

The Christian must understand and remember that although the mission of government is to *control* evil, government has no *solution* to evil. The solution to evil lies within the domain of the Church and it is the new birth. Therefore, even born-again politicians cannot use government as an instrument of spiritual policy or as an organ of the Church. Although believers have a responsibility to be good citizens and this citizenship requires participation in government, the greatest patriotic contribution of the believer is found in his carrying out the Great Commission: evangelism and discipleship, as well as his own spiritual development. It is through these largely invisible means that the Church most powerfully influences both government and history.

The believer and his impact upon society is a subject pertaining to sanctification. The believer is a new creation possessing the life and character of Christ, and is, by definition, an advocate for righteousness *and* justice in his relationships and within the institutions with which he comes into contact. A desire for social justice, for righteous relations between men and institutions, is natural to the new creation. It is the evidence of a genetic relation to the Father whose justice is the outshining of his limitless righteousness.[193] Social justice is consistent with the believer's function as salt and light in the world and complements his mission of evangelism.

The Church cannot stop the advent of the Antichrist or the temporary operation of the New World Order upon the earth. This kingdom is prophesied, and it will occur. However, what we know about this kingdom through the prophetic scriptures can help us in this present darkness to effectively wage spiritual warfare. There is no more powerful means of historical impact than the making of disciples of Christ and being one yourself. *The spiritual life of a believer is more effective in bringing blessing or cursing to a nation than all its statesmen, wealth, and armaments.* God would have saved all of Sodom and Gomorrah for the sake of ten believers there [Gen 18]. The testimonies of Joseph, Jonah and Daniel rescued entire empires [Egypt, Nineveh, Babylon] from premature demise. Today, the invisible power of the Spirit operating through the Body of Christ via its sanctified operations in the world restrains the wickedness of Satan's entire world system [2 Th 2.6-7]. Cultural outcomes are the result of invisible spiritual victories or defeats. Gospel centered believers who pray and express their faith in righteous living exercise tremendous positive influence upon history.[194]

Finally, *the Church must stop cooperating* with the Mystery of Iniquity. The Mystery of Iniquity combats the Church by asserting its own version of spiritual truth, beginning with the false gospel that Jesus is not the Christ. It places its agents throughout Christendom in areas that enable it to inject this doctrine, and its corollaries, into the bloodstream of Christianity. Local churches, seminaries, missionary organizations, scholarly societies, Bible institutes, Bible translation societies, local churches and paraChurch organizations are some of the places where these junior grade antichrists [1 Jn 2.18-19] hide to secretly introduce heresies designed to degrade the influence of the Church and to condition society for the introduction of the Beast's reign.

Christians must identify and separate themselves from all organizations and activities which, knowingly or unknowingly, advance the agenda of Mystery Babylon including [but by no means limited to] ecumenical associations,[195] charismatic bodies[196] [which unintentionally are degrading the authority[197] of scripture and are a major channel to ecumenical unity[198]], *religious* organizations that *major* in political reform, Bible societies and seminaries that do not hold to the inerrancy[199] and authority of the scriptures, and the Emerging

Church, which has distinguished itself as another form of liberalism.

By separating from these *and other* aspects of the Mystery of Iniquity, a powerful witness is provided that will alert and equip believers and thereby strengthen the Church in its gospel mission. It is through this gospel mission, unencumbered by cooperation with the world and its religious sensibilities, that the Church exercises maximum historical impact and achieves spiritual victory in our time.

These are strong statements which will undoubtedly create hostility towards the overall message of this book. This book is about the implementation of the New World Order as the final phase of the Mystery of Iniquity. These controversial issues are the mechanisms by which the Church is weakened. A weakened local church makes the community vulnerable to spiritual influences which are harmful to the saved and unsaved alike. Either the charismatic doctrine of the Baptism of the Spirit is doctrinal, or it is not. Either the doctrine of tongues as practiced today is biblical or it is not. Ecumenism is a biblical practice, or it is not. The Bible is inerrant and infallible, or it is not.

The faithful believer will have to separate from both false and *true* believers that refuse to make the distinction between the Mystery of Godliness and the Mystery of Iniquity. A believer cannot allow himself to be condemned by God for the things that he condones. It is increasingly necessary to demonstrate Christian love and Christian separation at the same time [Dt 13.6-8].

In summary, the best thing we can do in the days leading up to the emergence of Antichrist and the Day of the Lord is to, like Josiah [2 Ch 34], finish our race with strength and endurance, that our days might be characterized by spiritual revival.

17
The Beginning Of Antichrist's Rule: Revelation 13

Revelation 13:3–8 (KJV 1900)
3 And I saw one of his heads as it were wounded to death; and his deadly wound was healed: and all the world wondered after the beast. 4 And they worshipped the dragon which gave power unto the beast: and they worshipped the beast, saying, Who is like unto the beast? who is able to make war with him? 5 And there was given unto him a mouth speaking great things and blasphemies; and power was given unto him to continue forty and two months. 6 And he opened his mouth in blasphemy against God, to blaspheme his name, and his tabernacle, and them that dwell in heaven. 7 And it was given unto him to make war with the saints, and to overcome them: and power was given him over all kindreds, and tongues, and nations.[200] 8 And all that dwell upon the earth shall worship him, whose names are not written in the book of life of the Lamb slain from the foundation of the world.

Revelation 13.3 "And his deadly wound was healed"

Revelation 13:3 (KJV 1900)
3 And I saw one of his heads as it were wounded to death; and his deadly wound was healed: and all the world wondered after the beast.

The word translated "*wounded*" means "to slay, slaughter, butcher; to put to death by violence."[201] It the same word[202] as "slain" in 13.8 referring to Christ:

> Revelation 13:8 (KJV 1900)
> 8 And all that dwell upon the earth shall worship him, whose names are not written in the book of life of the Lamb **slain** from the foundation of the world.

Recall that the beast is a symbol representing a political entity, a person, and a spiritual being. It has already been proposed that there may well be resurrections of all three of these aspects of the Beast revealed in these prophecies. Inasmuch as the devil seeks to deceive the world via an imitation of the ministry of Christ and thereby secure its worship, a resurrection serves to answer this stupendous void in the portfolio of the Antichrist when compared to Christ. It is the devil's objective to demonstrate himself, his kingdom, and his son as more deserving than God of the worship of men and angels.

> 2 Thessalonians 2:3–4 (KJV 1900)
> 3 Let no man deceive you by any means: for that day shall not come, except there come a falling away first, <u>and that man of sin be revealed</u>, the son of perdition; 4 Who opposeth and exalteth himself above all that is called God, or that is worshipped; <u>so that he as God sitteth in the temple of God, shewing himself that he is God</u>.

In the first half of the coming Tribulation, the sudden demise of the leader who will eventually become known as the Antichrist may occur. Should this person appear to [or actually] arise from the dead and proclaim himself Messiah/Christ, this would mark the end of the seventh kingdom and the beginning of the final form of the New Luciferian World Order, the eighth head, intended to replace the prophesied kingdom of Christ. In this case, the death of the precursor[203] to the Man of Sin would basically coincide with the death of the seventh kingdom/head. A "resurrection" would undoubtedly involve the spirit of Apollyon and consequently all three aspects of the beast: the man, the kingdom and the *demonic entity* would be involved in the dramatic reanimation of a *man* [Rev 13.12] and a *World Order*.

Revelation 13.4 "And they worshipped the dragon...and they worshipped the beast"

> Revelation 13:4 (KJV 1900)4 And they worshipped the dragon which gave power unto the beast: and they worshipped the beast, saying, Who is like unto the beast? who is able to make war with him?

Why will the world worship the Antichrist and the Dragon?

This passage discloses that there will be worldwide worship under a single religious concept, a one world Church, if you will [Rev 13.8,12]. The current ecumenical movement is a means of weakening biblical Christianity by amalgamation and assimilation. The hodgepodge of religions under the umbrella of ecumenism, led by the Roman Catholic Church,[204] will not be the permanent expression of the prophesied world worship. The current ecumenical movement does not agree upon doctrine, liturgy or even a single definition of God.

For the Revelation 13.4 to be fulfilled, what is currently secret must become known, that which currently restrains the Mystery of Iniquity must be removed and a significant mass delusion must be initiated.

As we have already indicated, the seventh/eighth[205] head will be directed by and possessed of an occult power far more effective than that which directed and influenced the world kingdoms that preceded it. Its primary actors, the Antichrist and the False Prophet will be indwelt by demonic entities, the Antichrist by Satan himself. This kingdom will be the focus of a previously unimaginable degree of spiritual power, made possible, in part, by the departure of the Body of Christ, the Church via the Rapture.

At the revelation of the Antichrist, in a reversal of thousands of years of policy, this power will no longer be hidden, as the word "occult" denotes, but will be publicly acknowledged and displayed.

Today, the reality of satanic control *is* occult, hidden behind a network of religions, philosophical movements, secret societies, and apparently secular organizations. The *mystery* of Mystery Babylon [Rev 17], is the secret association between men and demonic entities for the purpose of implementing a satanic New World Order that will use the earth as a base of operations to launch an offensive against God Himself. As fantastic as this sounds, it is the story that is told by passages such as Genesis 3.1-5; Isaiah 14.12-14; Psalms 2 c.f. Rev 17.2;

Daniel 8:9-14; 9.24-27; 11.36-39; Luke 22.3; John 6.70; 8.44; 1 Cor 10.20-21; 2 Thessalonians 2.3-12; Revelation 13; 17 and many other passages. The purpose of the Mystery of Iniquity and its spiritual agency, Mystery Babylon, is to produce the very worship spoken of in Revelation 13.4 in the heavens and upon the earth.

Ephesians 6:11–12 (KJV 1900)
11 Put on the whole armour of God, that ye may be able to stand against the wiles of the devil. 12 For we wrestle not against flesh and blood, but against principalities, against powers, against the rulers of the darkness of this world, against spiritual wickedness in high places.

For the worship of the Dragon and the Beast to occur, the universal but hidden dominance of the devil must become evident to all, albeit in a form that will be acceptable to the population of the world at that time.

It is not surprising that it might be difficult for the average Christian to see the reasoning above as plausible. That the world is dominated by an evil [termed *darkness*: Eph 6.12; Col 1.19; 1 Pet 2.9] directed via governmental, commercial, and ecclesiastical networks sounds like a movie, not reality. But a comprehensive examination of the Bible can lead to no other conclusion. The *appearance* of things, as generally presented to the people of the nations of the world, is not the *reality* of things.

As an example, this illicit and secret cooperation with Mystery Babylon is why the political and economic news and explanations we receive daily are mostly incomprehensible to normal, rationally thinking people. These pronouncements, even the political science and economics classes that students take in high school and college, make little sense *because the public objectives of government [and especially national government] are often not it's true objectives*. Consequently, the explanation of the motives and goals of government provided to the public cannot possibly jibe with the outcomes that we see in the economy and in world affairs. The government [and its complicit news media] cannot say: "Well, of course we are involved in fornication with harlot of Mystery Babylon [Rev 17.1-2], and here is what we actually mean by that…" However, in the days of the emergence of the Antichrist *as* the Antichrist, Lucifer will be proclaimed as the true god, straight with no chaser. His doctrine and objectives will synchronize with the management of his kingdom, including its spiritual initiatives. There will be worldwide worship of the Dragon and the Beast.

The occult *collaboration* between the kingdoms of history, down to the present moment, and the ecclesiastical system which administers Satan's Church *is* the *Mystery* of Mystery Babylon. Mystery Babylon is the religion of the Mystery of Iniquity, its system of orthodoxy and orthopraxy. It is the science of blasphemy and desecrations. It was perhaps the clear revelation of this relationship that was the terrifying aspect of the vision of the Gentile kingdoms seen by Nebuchadnezzar [Dan 2.31" *terrible*"[206]]: that the kingdoms of this world are but a vehicle of the implementation of the Mystery of Iniquity. Nebuchadnezzar had to see this collaboration functioning within his own government [Dan 2.2]. The underlying religion of every kingdom on earth[207] is some form of Mystery Babylon.

The worship of the Dragon and the Beast involves the externalization of a system that in its entirety imitates the Plan of God for mankind and the angels, while at the same time blaspheming the God that created that Plan. It will require a great deal of spiritual delusion for the world to accept such a kingdom and that deception will be put into place at the proper moment.

This delusion begins with the self-deception of Lucifer himself. The apparent basis of the devil's desire for worship was his own incorrect self-assessment [Eze 28.17] and his incorrect assessment of God's character [Gen 3:1-5]. On a certain level, it may be that he actually believes what he said to Eve about God. Does he not appear to resent that he has failed to receive the worship and recognition that he believes that he deserved from God, angels, and men? Does he not appear to see his condemnation as capricious and unjust?

So, the world of the last days will be faced with an irrational proposition that they will not be able to universally accept without supernatural deception. The devil will blaspheme God, seek to take His place of sovereignty over men and angels, yet imitate Jehovah in every detail of his demonically powered kingdom.[208]

The Character of Deception in the Latter Days

Deception, coercion, and the promise of power will convince the world to enthusiastically support the Beast, the Dragon, and their global institutional reset. We will address deception here and the other motivations in upcoming chapters.

The departure of the Church will deprive the world of its key witness[209] to spiritual reality. It is the witness of the Church through its obedience to and proclamation of the Word of God that provides the unbelieving world with reality orientation in the spiritual and every other sphere of existence.

Following this, three categories of delusion will afflict the unbelievers of the Tribulation period. The self-delusion which is the lot of all unbelievers [the "deceivableness of unrighteousness" 2 Th 2.10] will be augmented by the "power, signs and lying wonders" of the False Prophet [2 Th 2.9 c.f. Rev 13.11-15]. Finally, the third delusion will be sent from God Himself, resulting in their "believing a lie" [2 Th 2.11-12] and all the corollaries of that lie. This lie, of course, is *the Lie* that Jesus is not God, the same lie which was the main issue in the Garden of Eden[210] and at the Crucifixion.[211] Having already believed the primary doctrine of the Mystery of Iniquity, it will be a natural progression to the worship of Lucifer as God and the Beast/Antichrist as the Son of God.

To motivate worship, we will see that the beast will be recommended by miracles and signs. Those who reject the Word of God are always susceptible to both apparent and real manifestations of spiritual power and spiritual experiences. They fail to realize that all manifestations and experiences do not originate with God. They also fail to realize that any manifestation or experience that involves a rejection or modification of God's Word is not of God [Dt 13.1-5].

The population of the world that worships the Beast and the Dragon will do so because they are unbelievers who have rejected the truth of the gospel [2 Th 2.9-12].

Revelation 13:8 (KJV 1900)
And all that dwell upon the earth shall worship him, whose names <u>are not written</u> in the book of life of the Lamb slain from the foundation of the world.

The motivations of coercion and the promise of power will be administered by the Prime Minister of the New World Order, also known as the Beast of the earth, or the False Prophet [Rev 13.11 sq.]. We will address this man in Chapter 18.

Revelation 13.5 "And power was given him unto continue forty and two months"

Revelation 13:5 (KJV 1900)
5 And there was given unto him a mouth speaking great things and blasphemies; and power was given unto him to continue forty and two months.

This duration of influence [42 months] will not and could not be granted by the devil. The physical and temporal boundaries of peoples and kingdoms belong to God [Acts 17.26]. No creature would be capable of imposing upon God in this manner. Although the Antichrist may decide to do evil and to seek to change times and laws [establish a New World Order], it is God who determines the times and the seasons.

Acts 1:6–7 (KJV 1900)
6 When they therefore were come together, they asked of him, saying, Lord, wilt thou at this time restore again the kingdom to Israel? 7 And he said unto them, It is not for you to know the times or the seasons, <u>which the Father hath put in his own power</u>.

Acts 17:26 (KJV 1900)
26 And hath made of one blood all nations of men for to dwell on all the face of the earth, and hath <u>determined the times before appointed, and the bounds of their habitation</u>

This of course begs the question: "Why then allow this period of Satanic rule to transpire at all?" This may be briefly addressed by asking additional questions. Why did God allow Satan to continue to exist after his initial sin in eternity past? Why did God allow Satan into the Garden of Eden? Why did God allow Adam and Eve to exist after the Fall? Why has God allowed *you* to continue to exist despite your sins?

God has created human beings with free moral agency and decision-making capacity to exercise the creation mandate [Gen 1.28-30]. He has allowed human [as well as angelic] decisions to have consequences and has held these beings responsible for the choices that they made, up to and including their eternal destiny. Through this process, God is revealing Himself: his character and his plan, to both the angels and to mankind [Eph 3.10; Rom 9.22-24]. Men and angels are, within certain limits, free to decide, however God controls the environment and the timing in which these decisions must occur.[212] For example, God established the Garden in Eden and the test of the two trees. God appointed a test for Job but limited its parameters. God allows Satan to make his case against Himself within the context of human history but appoints how far he can go and for how long.

In the evil times predicted in Revelation, there will be many righteous purposes accomplished. In the kingdom of the Beast, many unbelievers will be saved, and many believers will prove their fidelity to God by their martyrdom. The violence and depravity of Lucifer will demonstrate the perverseness of his claims against God to the entire angelic world. In the end, the righteousness and the justice of God and His plan will be confirmed, and sin will be defeated in all its forms and effects. The eternal reign of God over the elect under the conditions prophesied will take effect, to last forever.

Revelation 13.6-7 "And he opened his mouth in blasphemy against God..."

> Revelation 13:6–7 (KJV 1900)
> 6 And he opened his mouth in blasphemy against God, to blaspheme his name, and his tabernacle, and them that dwell in heaven. 7 And it was given unto him to make war with the saints, and to overcome them: and power was given him over all kindreds, and tongues, and nations.

God is sovereign. God sets the boundaries and limits upon what can and cannot be done by everyone at all times. The decision to kill believers is made by Lucifer of his own free will. His ability to succeed at doing so is allowed, for a time, by God. Our ability to approve God's actions or to find fault with them is not in view as we do not have the intellectual or spiritual capacity to judge God even if we had all the facts, which we do not.

The devil has made a reputation of incorporating the abuse and murder of believers in his plans from the very beginning.

> John 8:44 (KJV 1900)
> 44 Ye are of your father the devil, and the lusts of your father ye will do. <u>He was a murderer from the beginning</u>, and abode not in

the truth, because there is no truth in him. When he speaketh a lie, he speaketh of his own: for he is a liar, and the father of it.

1 John 3:11–12 (KJV 1900)
11 For this is the message that ye heard from the beginning, that we should love one another. 12 Not as Cain, <u>who was of that wicked one, and slew his brother</u>. And wherefore slew he him? Because his own works were evil, and his brother's righteous.

Satan realizes that the Mystery of Godliness and the Mystery of Iniquity cannot coexist. One must finally fall to the other. The New Order sought by the devil is not primarily secular but spiritual. The blaspheming of God and the killing of the saints are elements of this attempt at the spiritual conquest of the earth.

Satan, as a fallen and condemned creature, has the option of killing the saints of God or killing their witness. One is accomplished by persecution, the other by assimilation. One is accomplished by Satan as a roaring lion [1 Pet 5.8], the other by Satan as an angel of light [1 Cor 11.14].

In the era of the Church, Satan has used the *state* as an agency[213] by which the deaths of believers have been accomplished. For example, the Roman Empire through its persecutions attempted to destroy the apostolic Church.

> "The piety of Romulus and Numa was believed to have laid the foundation of the power of Rome. To the favor of the deities of the republic, the brilliant success of the Roman arms was attributed. The priests and Vestal virgins were supported out of the public treasury. The emperor was ex-officio the pontifex maximus, and even an object of divine worship. The gods were national; and the eagle of Jupiter Capitalinus moved as a good genius before the world-conquering legions. Cicero lays down as a principle of legislation, that no one should be allowed to worship foreign gods, unless they were recognized by public statute.1 Maecenas counselled Augustus: "Honor the gods according to the custom of our ancestors and compel others to worship them. Hate and punish those who bring in strange gods.""[214]

The Roman Empire persecuted the saints of the apostolic Church well into the 4th century. Many were martyred and many more were deprived of their possessions, tortured, mutilated, imprisoned, and enslaved. Under Galerius [311 A.D.] and Constantine [323 A.D.], Christianity went from being an unauthorized religion and enemy of the Roman state to a tolerated religion.[215] Under Theodosius [383]

Christianity became the new state religion of Rome.[216] It was as the state religion of Rome that a portion[217] of the Church acquired, through assimilation[218] with Roman idolatry, an idolatrous character of its own, eventually persecuting and martyring many more persons than did the Roman Emperors over the first 250 years of the Church.[219] Persecution of Christianity was followed by its assimilation, followed by greater persecutions of Christianity by the assimilated "Church."

The Mystery of Iniquity seeks to reverse God's intent wherever it is found. Although government is an institution established by God,[220] the Antichrist will use the state to annihilate the Tribulation saints.

At bottom, there are only two faiths in the world. The Mystery of Iniquity is opposed to the Mystery of Godliness. Satan attempts to eliminate believers who represent a competing worship and who actively evangelize his servants. Bible *following* Christians are the only human threat to Satan on earth. Christian worship requires a holy lifestyle that repudiates the Mystery of Iniquity by validating the Mystery of Godliness. A lifestyle characterized by the worship of the true God is, in itself, a most powerful form of evangelism.

The devil indeed kills believers.[221] Violence is a kind of anti-evangelism that not only eliminates believers but discourages those who might be interested in investigating Christianity. In addition to violence, the devil also deceives and assimilates Christians. He assimilates Christians via movements such as that of ecumenism. We will see that the ecumenical movement, a key initiative of Mystery Babylon, forbids evangelization of unbelievers[222] by true Christians.

Mystery Babylon is the ancient and current operational agency of the Mystery of Iniquity. It is directly identified by Scripture as the authority behind the murder of believers, the chief architect of their deaths and the false deity to whom they are sacrificed.

Revelation 17:5–6 (KJV 1900)
5 And upon her forehead was a name written, MYSTERY, BABYLON THE GREAT, THE MOTHER OF HARLOTS AND ABOMINATIONS OF THE EARTH. 6 And I saw the woman drunken with the blood of the saints, and with the blood of the martyrs of Jesus: and when I saw her, I wondered with great admiration [amazement, astonishment-rw].

Revelation 18:24 (KJV 1900)
24 And in her [Babylon the Great Rev 18.2] was found the blood of prophets, and of saints, And of all that were slain upon the

earth.

It is the devil's consistent reliance upon violence and death as a means of advancing his kingdom that reveals the illegitimacy of his claims to Deity and kingdom. Although murder and violence have been the hallmark of his activity, Satan has not and will not accomplish his purposes. He has failed to destroy Israel, he has not eliminated the influence of the Church [although he has, in all fairness, diminished it at times], he has yet to establish his public rule of the earth and he has not overtaken God's throne, his goal. Satan has not and will not ultimately prevail against Israel or the Church. The Abrahamic Covenant has not been abridged: those who curse him [Israel] shall be cursed [Gen 12.3]. God has promised victory for the Church, as distinct from Israel. Jesus has promised that the gates of Hell will not prevail against the Church [Mt 16.18 c.f. Rom 16.20].

Although Satan enjoys limited will rule today and will taste universal human worship in the future, his rule will be brief and culminate in his eternal destruction. All the *believers* who were victims of the devil's violence, those saints who suffered for the sake of Christ, will be resurrected to see Satan's incarceration in the Lake of Fire.[223] They will also be rewarded for their faithfulness unto death [Rev 2.10; 7.14].

It should be briefly noted that the "saints" in Revelation 13.7 do not include unregenerate Israel, at least not at the beginning of the final three and one-half years of the Tribulation. The devil has a definite interest in the elimination of the Jews; however, this aim is not directly addressed in this passage. It is not obviously apparent that even the Antichrist knows the full extent of Lucifer's plans for Israel. Revelation 12 indicates that the dragon will seek to destroy the remainder of the *seed* of the Woman.

Revelation 12:17 (KJV 1900)
17 And the dragon was wroth with the woman, and went to make war with <u>the remnant of her seed, which keep the commandments of God, and have the testimony of Jesus Christ</u>.

This satanic activity follows the devil's expulsion from heaven and is thus contemporaneous with the events of the first verses of chapter 13. It is therefore clear that he is not yet here seeking to destroy every Jew, but those who are followers of Christ, irrespective of their genetic origins.

Galatians 3:16 (KJV 1900)
16 Now to Abraham and his seed were the promises made. He saith not, And to seeds, as of many; but as of one, And to thy seed, which is Christ.

Antichrist seeks the worship of the Jews, which he will receive from many [Rev 13.8,12,14]. Though he will certainly kill the noncompliant [Rev 13.15], it is difficult to find evidence of his desire to destroy his worshippers. Satan, on the other hand, recognizes the destruction of Israel, regenerate or not, as a strategic objective essential to his defeat of Jehovah. He will set the "final solution" into operation in Revelation 16.13-14 [Zech 12.1-3].

18
The Prime Minister of the New World Order- The False Prophet: Revelation 13

Revelation 13:11–17 (KJV 1900)
11 And I beheld <u>another beast</u> coming up out of the earth; and he had two horns like a lamb, and he spake as a dragon. 12 And he exerciseth all the power of the first beast before him, and causeth the earth and them which dwell therein to worship the first beast, whose deadly wound was healed. 13 And he doeth great wonders, so that he maketh fire come down from heaven on the earth in the sight of men, 14 And deceiveth them that dwell on the earth by the means of those miracles which he had power to do in the sight of the beast; saying to them that dwell on the earth, that they should make an image to the beast, which had the wound by a sword, and did live. 15 And he had power to give life unto the image of the beast, that the image of the beast should both speak, and cause that as many as would not worship the image of the beast should be killed. 16 And he causeth all, both small and great, rich and poor, free and bond, to receive a mark in their right hand, or in their foreheads: 17 And that no man might buy or sell, save he that had the mark, or the name of the beast, or the number of his name.

Revelation 13.11 "And I beheld another beast coming up out of the earth; and he had two horns like a lamb, and he spake as a dragon."

Four characteristics are given of this person which will aid us in discovering who he is. First, he is called a beast. This identifies him with the first beast and shows that they share a similar nature. This means that the beast from the earth is also a demonically controlled human being. Secondly, he comes up from the earth. The first beast [personally and politically] came up out of the sea [Mediterranean] of men and nations. This second beast arises from the earth, which may be understood to mean from *beneath* the earth. In fact, even the first beast will be identified in a similar way in Rev 17.

> Revelation 17:8 (KJV 1900)
> 8 The beast that thou sawest was, and is not; <u>and shall ascend out of the bottomless pit</u>, and go into perdition: and they that dwell on the earth shall wonder, whose names were not written in the book of life from the foundation of the world, when they behold the beast that was, and is not, and yet is.

Again, although the first beast is a man, he is indwelt by Lucifer. We noted earlier that the name the "Son of Perdition" seems to be associated with persons so indwelt [Lk 22.3 c.f. Jn 17.12]. Just as the humanity of Christ was controlled by the Holy Spirit, the Antichrist will be controlled by the devil or Apollyon. This means that the second beast, who shares the nature of the first beast, is similarly possessed by a demonic entity of the bottomless pit. Demon control enables the imitation of true prophetic gifts, and more, by those so controlled.[224]

Thirdly, he will have horns like a lamb. A lamb is a clean ceremonial animal. The lamb is associated with the priesthood. This individual will be a man of religion, he will have both the position and power of a prophet.[225] Thus, while the Antichrist is the King of the Earth, the False Prophet is both Prophet and Priest. The Antichrist, False Prophet and Dragon are a false trinity.

Fourthly, the beast from the earth speaks like a dragon. He shares, as the first beast, the aims and agenda of the Dragon, or the devil. He will glorify the Beast. This also means that, like the beast from the sea, he is a blasphemer. The Holy Spirit glorifies Christ; what the Spirit says reflects the thinking of the Godhead:

> John 16:14–15 (KJV 1900)
> 14 He shall glorify me: for he shall receive of mine, and shall shew it unto you. 15 All things that the Father hath are mine: therefore said I, that he shall take of mine, and shall shew it unto you.

The false prophet speaks like or glorifies the devil. When you hear him, you are hearing the thinking of Lucifer. He will speak like a dragon.

False Prophet-A Definition

> Jeremiah 23:28–32 (KJV 1900)
> 28 The prophet that hath a dream, let him tell a dream; and he that hath my word, let him speak my word faithfully. What is the chaff to the wheat? saith the LORD. 29 Is not my word like as a fire? saith the LORD; and like a hammer that breaketh the rock in pieces? 30 Therefore, behold, I am against the prophets, saith the LORD, that steal my words every one from his neighbour. 31 Behold, I am against the prophets, saith the LORD, that use their tongues, and say, He saith. 32 Behold, I am against them that prophesy false dreams, saith the LORD, and do tell them, and cause my people to err by their lies, and by their lightness; yet I sent them not, nor commanded them: therefore they shall not profit this people at all, saith the LORD.

The tool of the prophet is the divine revelation. Today, in the times of the New Covenant, it is the revealed and completed scripture, the Bible, which is in the hand of God's authorized servant. That revelation is the power of God that changes individuals and nations for better or for worse. God's Word always accomplishes God's purposes, whether we can comprehend them or not.

We can see in Jeremiah 23 above that God does not need *volunteer* prophets. Every true spokesman for the Lord is called and authorized by Him: in the Old Testament, personally and today, through the plurality of elders in the local church, to proclaim an accurate message from scripture.

All false prophets seek to appear to serve the Lord but deliver a word which is from the devil. This end time false prophet will operate upon a variation of this theme by openly rejecting the Lord with the claim that the first Beast, the Antichrist, is in fact the *true* sovereign of heaven and earth.

The ancient role of the false prophet continues to this present day [1 Jn 4.1]. Our difficulty in perceiving their existence is because:

- ➤ **Believers** often do not know what the Bible says and are easily deceived.
- ➤ **Believers** who do not know the Word of God are impressed by good music, speaking ability and apparent success in the form of large and wealthy ministries.
- ➤ **Believers** who do not know the scriptures are impressed by appeals to their felt needs, prejudices, and carnal ambitions, presented as legitimate spiritual aspirations by the false teacher.
- ➤ **Believers** who do not know their Bibles are deceived by signs and wonders, unable to discern their source.

2 Peter 2:1 (KJV 1900)
[1] But there were false prophets also <u>among the people</u>, even as <u>there shall be false teachers among you</u>, who <u>privily shall bring in</u>[226] damnable heresies, even denying the Lord that bought them, and bring upon themselves swift destruction.

The traditional false prophet exists "among the people" because his primary duty is to obstruct the spiritual function of the people of God. He may give lip service to the Gospel, but his objective is not salvation but to derail God's program by the introduction of false teaching among the flock. He will introduce these heresies secretly, mixing them with biblical and, more often, moral truths. He will affect a personality and bearing that resembles holiness and piety so as to make his true identity and purpose difficult to perceive by those who are unequipped to evaluate his false message. The false teacher of today also avoids detection by the unwillingness of true pastors to identify him as a teacher of falsehoods. For a variety of inadequate reasons, pastors allow the false teacher to continue to destroy believers and local churches undisturbed, often even befriending and ministering together with the wolf.

The False Prophet of the end times will be of another order because he will be the prophet of the final representative of the devil, the Antichrist. He will not attempt to hide his allegiance or his true doctrine. He will flatly proclaim the devil as God and the Antichrist as his Son. He will be a deceiver as he will represent the Antichrist and himself as something [worthy, right, just] that they are not. However, he *will not* represent himself or the beast as representatives of Jehovah, which is the normal *modus operandi* of false prophets. Further, this false prophet will not hesitate to kill those who will not submit to this doctrine and the Order which is built upon it.

The final false prophet will be to his predecessors what John the Baptist was to the true prophets that preceded him.

Matthew 11:11 (NKJV)
11 "Assuredly, I say to you, among those born of women there has not risen one greater than John the Baptist;

The greatest false prophet of all time is yet to appear upon the scene.

Revelation 13:12 "And he exerciseth all the power of the first beast before him...

Revelation 13:12 (KJV 1900)
12 And he exerciseth all the power of the first beast before him, and causeth the earth and them which dwell therein to worship the first beast, whose deadly wound was healed.

It is the job of the 'beast from the earth' to promote the kingdom, the agenda, and the worship of the Antichrist in the world. This individual operates in an executive role to accomplish the objectives of his sovereign, the Beast. Thus, the title: *Prime Minister of the New World Order.*

The word *power* in v12 is a word meaning *authority.*[227] The False Prophet has received delegated authority from the Beast. He is actively advancing the interests of the Antichrist and directing his worship in the world. If the deadly wound applies to the person of the Antichrist as the *king* of the seventh/eighth head, then the repetition of the deadly wound in this verse and verse 14 may imply that the false prophet devotes himself to the proclamation of the resurrection of the Beast from the dead.

The "earth and them which dwell therein" will eventually worship the Beast. This group excludes the believers of that time, who will choose death or have it thrust upon them because of their faith.[228] There will be a *one world Church*, superintended by the False Prophet with the Beast and the Dragon as its objects of worship.

Revelation 13:13 "And he doeth great wonders,"

Revelation 13:13 (KJV 1900)13 And he doeth great wonders, so that he maketh fire come down from heaven on the earth in the sight of men,

The beast from the earth is a priest, overseeing worship, but he is also a prophet who proclaims the name of his deity. He demonstrates the power of a prophet and of an apostle. Elijah was able to bring fire down upon men and the apostles performed mighty works. The two tribulational prophets of God will also demonstrate a similar ability [Rev 11.5].

The miracles of the apostles were designed to authenticate their message regarding God and his plan for mankind. The power of the beast from the earth will be to authenticate the person and the program of the Antichrist.

The Bible labels this miracle ministry as deception, a word we have used repeatedly when dealing with the Antichrist and his administration. The Bible teaches that even genuine miracles cannot always be trusted.

Deuteronomy 13:1–5 (KJV 1900)
1 If there arise among you a prophet, or a dreamer of dreams, and giveth thee a sign or a wonder, 2 <u>And the sign or the wonder come to pass</u>, whereof he spake unto thee, saying, Let us go after other gods, which thou hast not known, and let us serve them; 3 Thou shalt not hearken unto the words of that prophet, or that dreamer of dreams: for the LORD your God proveth you, to know whether ye love the LORD your God with all your heart and with all your soul. 4 Ye shall walk after the LORD your God, and fear him, and keep his commandments, and obey his voice, and ye shall serve him, and cleave unto him. 5 And that prophet, or that dreamer of dreams, shall be put to death; because he hath spoken to turn you away from the LORD your God, which brought you out of the land of Egypt, and redeemed you out of the house of bondage, to thrust thee out of the way which the

LORD thy God commanded thee to walk in. So shalt thou put the evil away from the midst of thee.

Matthew 24:24 (KJV 1900)
24 For there shall arise false Christs, and false prophets, <u>and shall shew great signs and wonders</u>; insomuch that, if it were possible, they shall deceive the very elect.

These signs, wonders and miracles will be used to confirm that the Antichrist is the Messiah.

The False Prophet Promotes the False Messiah

The beast from the earth will promote the Antichrist as the Messiah of Israel and the Christ of all men:

- ➢ Because the Jews rejected the Messiah, [John 1.11; 5.43] they will be sent the Antichrist.
- ➢ Those Gentiles and Jews who reject the truth will be sent strong delusion to believe the lie that the Antichrist is the Messiah [2 Th 2.7].
- ➢ The title Antichrist can mean, "instead of Christ."
- ➢ The chief doctrine of the Antichrist is that Jesus is not the Christ. If Jesus is not the Messiah, then who is?
- ➢ The Antichrist seeks to make a covenant with Israel [Dan 9.27]
- ➢ The Antichrist will seat himself in the Jewish temple [not in a mosque, or a Buddhist shrine or in a Church] representing himself as God [Dan 9.27; 2 Th 2.4]

The Antichrist will seek that all worship him as the son of God. Because people accept miracles without questioning their source, many will accept these miracles as evidence that the Antichrist is in fact the prophesied Messiah.

Revelation 13:14–15 "And deceiveth them that dwell on the earth

Revelation 13:14–15 (KJV 1900)
14 And deceiveth them that dwell on the earth by the means of those miracles which he had power to do in the sight of the beast; saying to them that dwell on the earth, that they should make an image to the beast, which had the wound by a sword, and did live. 15 And he had power to give life unto the image of the beast, that the image of the beast should both speak, and cause that as many as would not worship the image of the beast should be killed.

This passage takes us back to the beginning of the Times of the Gentiles and the kingdom of Nebuchadnezzar the Babylonian [Dan 3]. His rule was a type, a facsimile of the end-time kingdom of the Antichrist. He created a super cult under which all the native religions of his subjects were subsumed. He provided an image as the focal point of this new religion and demanded that all worship this new religion under the threat of death.

This leads naturally to the questions: Why worship an image and Why coerce that worship?

Why Images

God prohibits the worship of images.

Exodus 20:1–4 (KJV 1900)
1 And God spake all these words, saying, 2 I am the LORD thy God, which have brought thee out of the land of Egypt, out of the house of bondage. 3 Thou shalt have no other gods before me. 4 Thou shalt not make unto thee any graven image, or any likeness of any thing that is in heaven above, or that is in the earth beneath, or that is in the water under the earth:

God is far greater than anything that can be represented by the mind of man. Anything created to represent God will either start out as a false God or quickly become one.[229]
An image of "god" always ends up being a disguise for something

or someone who is not God. The case of the Antichrist is no different. Lucifer has had a long career of hiding behind idols and symbols and images. The ancient world was overpopulated with statues and images representing false gods [Acts 17.16]. An image allows the devil to control what is portrayed and therefore what is believed. Just like our pictures of Jesus, an idol portrays what the *artist* wants portrayed. The devil wants the Antichrist portrayed as a person of personal attractiveness, charismatic leadership, spiritual power, and an image makes this focus possible.

The alternative to the image is what God requires, which is faith. God provides faith as a system of perception which comprehends what the eyes cannot see.

Hebrews 11:1 (KJV 1900)
1 Now faith is the substance of things hoped for, the evidence of things <u>not seen</u>.

Hebrews 11:24 (KJV 1900)
24 By faith Moses, when he was come to years, refused to be called the son of Pharaoh's daughter. 27 By faith he forsook Egypt, not fearing the wrath of the king: for he endured, <u>as seeing him who is invisible</u>.

2 Corinthians 5:7 (KJV 1900)
7 (For we walk by faith, <u>not by sight</u>:)

Lucifer, the Antichrist, and the False Prophet cannot call upon their followers to exercise this kind of perception. First of all, their followers are unsaved and do not have biblical faith. Secondly, even if the followers of the Antichrist possessed spiritual vision through faith, they would then perceive the true nature of the Antichrist. True faith comprehends the inner quality that proves One worthy of worship.

So then, even if it were possible to give them faith, the devil would withhold it because biblical faith is not consistent with an agenda of deception.

Matthew 24:24 (KJV 1900)
24 For there shall arise false Christs, and false prophets, and shall shew great signs and wonders; insomuch that, if it were possible, they shall deceive the very elect.

Thus, an image enables deception because it allows the creator of the image to manage perception and simultaneously cause the worshiper to blaspheme God via direct disobedience to the Bible. The False Prophet will use images to *market* the Antichrist and to unite all humanity under impious unbelief. Beware of religious images, even the Protestant ones.

Why Coercion

Revelation 13:15 (KJV 1900)
15 And he had power to give life unto the image of the beast, that the image of the beast should both speak, and cause that as many as would not worship the image of the beast should be killed.

Why force worship under the pain of death? This is a page out of the playbook of Nebuchadnezzar, who gave the three Hebrew friends of Daniel to the flames because they would not worship the image that he had made [Dan 3]. The devil would probably argue that God Himself forces worship since all who do not believe in him are sent to Hell. "Isn't this forced worship?" he might argue.

No, it is not. Once a person freely rejects Christ as Savior, the only thing left is to face the reality of existence without God. When a dependent child rebels against his parents and leaves the home, he himself has chosen poverty and insecurity thereafter. The problem is a misunderstanding of reality. When we understand that everything that sustains life is here because God put it here; everything that is truly lovely and worthy of praise has the Almighty as its source; our very habitation of this sphere of existence is due to the forbearance and kindness of the Creator, then we will understand is to reject Him is to end our personal probation and enter the only possible alternative.

That alternative includes eternal darkness, despair, torment, all that is left after the subtraction of God. Add to this the fact that in the beginning, humanity threw in its lot with Satan and therefore must share his destiny when he fails in his revolution against God. This makes the unbeliever a two-time loser: a loser first in the Garden of Eden [original sin], and a loser again when he ratified the decision of his original parents by rejecting the offer of eternal life in Christ. Meanwhile, the unbeliever enjoys all the benefits of God's grace provided during his probation here on earth, despite his status quo of rebellion against Him. No, God does not force worship, he simply allows human decisions to have consequences.

The devil, on the other hand, *must* force worship because most of mankind is only interested in worshiping themselves, or that which serves them. We are interested in our needs, our desires, our aspirations. Satan has represented himself since the beginning as the enabler of human freedom, as the one who will free man to actualize these desires, needs and aspirations. Unfortunately, this strategy does not produce worshippers, any more than the overindulgence of children produces thankful, gracious adults.

Therefore, to receive worship, Satan has had to use force. Babylon did it, Rome did it and the Antichrist will do it. Consequently, throughout history we see the state as the agent of religious tyranny. The false Church, like the mystery religions, cries out to government to enforce its precepts upon mankind and to exclude *true* Christianity. By contrast, the true God enables worship by first providing faith, which empowers the believer to accurately perceive Him as entirely and exclusively worthy of worship.

Isaiah 42:8 (KJV 1900)
8 I am the LORD: that is my name: And my glory will I not give to another, Neither my praise to graven images.

In summary, the Antichrist will use an image to control perceptions of himself, to make himself appear worthy of worship. The image is yet another deception. He forces worship under threat of death because of the human selfishness that the devil himself has sponsored for so long and is unable to change. The Antichrist, nor his sponsor the devil, are worthy of worship and only deception and coercion will produce it.

Richard G. Walker

The New World Order

The Antichrist will not merely attempt to improve upon the current systems of religion and social organization. The Antichrist seeks to create a **New World Order** which revolves around a new god and a new theology. He will create a *new theocratic administration of the earth* under a satanic trinity of the devil, the false prophet and himself.

> Revelation 13:4–5 (KJV 1900)
> 4 And they worshipped the dragon which gave power unto the beast: and they worshipped the beast, saying, Who is like unto the beast? who is able to make war with him? 5 And there was given unto him a mouth speaking great things and blasphemies; and power was given unto him to continue forty and two months.

Today, the devil is the "god of this world" [2 Cor 4.4] but he has not yet been able to establish the quality of control that he desires. To the extent that there are efforts to create a "New World Order" today, they are either conscious or unwitting efforts to pave the way for the appearance of the Antichrist, the son of Satan. It is this end time personality who will implement the New World Order in its truest sense. Until that time, Lucifer exerts significant power and influence in this world, but he is not formally recognized as the sovereign of the earth by most of mankind.

The spiritual influence of Satan is limited by the Church, the body of Christ, referred to as the Restrainer or "he who now letteth" [2 Th 2.6-7].[230] The spiritual body of Christ exercises real spiritual power in the world through the proclamation of the Word of God and the living testimony of true believers.

Once the restraining power of God dwelling within the true Church is removed, the devil will be free to fully implement his plans for the New World Order, beginning with the establishing of his management team, consisting of the Antichrist and the False Prophet, who is the second beast, the beast from the earth.

Just as the Holy Spirit administers the plan of God and glorifies Christ, so this False Prophet will manage the New World Order and supervise the worship of the Antichrist. His job will be to glorify the son of Satan, who has been elevated to the place of prominence by the devil. In this way the Man of Sin will be made to seem to a deceived world as the true Christ.

The False Prophet will be the Prime Minister of the New World Order, exercising the authority and power of the first beast on his behalf.

- He proclaims satanic doctrine [speaks like a dragon]
- He has power to perform signs
- He organizes idolatrous worship
- He administers a system of commerce that requires a commitment to the first beast.

This second beast operates as a priest in that he is an intercessor between man and the false Christ and supervises his worship. He is a prophet in that he proclaims the word of the false Christ and exercises power that validates his message.

The second beast is authorized to use both deception and coercion to create worship for the Antichrist.

During the reign of these two end time rulers, every human institution will openly promote the greater glory of Antichrist and his father, Lucifer.

This same agenda is in the world today, covertly. This program is directed by the occult [or hidden[231]] management of the many antichrists who are embedded throughout the world in every generation. Every human institution is under satanic attack to adjust its values to coincide with the values of Lucifer, labeled the 'doctrines of demons' in 1 Timothy 4.

There is a quiet revolution taking place all over the world where the conspiracy of Psalm 2 is being worked out: in theology and religion, in government and politics, in commerce and finance, in the arts, media, and education. What will in the future become open and evident to all today is being advanced under the cloak of hypocrisy and secrecy.

This agenda is based upon the Lie that "Jesus is not God." This lie is infiltrated into civilization by all the means mentioned above. There is a philosophy, a theology which is interwoven into the fabric of the culture of this world which exalts the devil and demotes Christ. This system of thought finds its expression in every nation, every culture, and every generation of humanity.

The following is a portion of the substructure of lies which are used to build the edifice of Luciferian doctrine founded upon that central Lie. Upon these secondary falsehoods are built the superstructure of philosophy and theology which dominates thought in the world.[232]

These are the fundamental elements of the doctrines of demons, the raw material from which are derived the multifaceted systems of falsehood which compose the ideology of the "kosmos" or world system. These principles are derived from the direct statements of the devil in scripture.

The Substructure of Luciferian Doctrine

Principle of Deception: Genesis 3.1 If you ever encounter Lucifer, you will not recognize him. Lucifer modifies his appearance and manner to deceive men.

Principle of The Lie: Genesis 3.4-5 Matthew 4.3a Lucifer denies that Jehovah is who He claims to be in scripture. He denies that Jesus is Christ. He claims that God lied to Adam and Eve to prevent their spiritual progress.

Principle of Occult Religion: Genesis 3.4-5 Lucifer represents himself as the benefactor of man, the champion of freedom and the conductor of souls to spiritual evolution and godhood.

Principle of Human Non-Culpability: Genesis 3.4 Lucifer claims that disobedience to God leads not to death but to spiritual evolution.

Principle of Scriptural Misuse: Gen 3.1 Matthew 4.1-10 Satan uses his mastery of the scriptures to deceive man by their misuse. Satan attempted to use God's own words to control Him.

Principle of the Superhero: Matt 4.3-10 Lucifer represents spiritual power, spiritual gifts and spiritual ministry as ours to use as we please.

Principle of Prosperity: Job 1.1-11; 2.3-7 Lucifer argues to God that man serves Him because it is in his best interests to do so. Man serves God to receive blessings and protection alone. The inverse of this argument is that man is entitled to prosperity [health, wealth, and protection] at all times as a servant of God. [Job 2.7-10].

Principle of Pragmatism: Genesis 3.4-5 Matthew 4.8-10 Satan deceives men by the claim that God's plan can be advanced by the violation of His Word. Man is the judge of scripture. His ends justify his means.

Figure 7 Substructure of Luciferian Doctrine

The doctrines of demons are effective because they easily harmonize with our fallen natures. Because of this harmony, there is a spiritual sympathy between the indwelling sin natures of men, the constructs of the world system administered by Satan [the world-kosmos/aion[233]] and the spirit of Satan himself [Jn 8.44; Eph 2.2] that is working in fallen humanity. Because of this sympathy, the sin nature is strengthened in its rejection of both the revelation of God in nature and the accurate proclamation of scripture.

Ephesians 2:1–2 (KJV 1900)
1 And you hath he quickened, <u>who were dead</u> in trespasses and sins; 2 Wherein in time past ye walked according to the course of this world, according to the prince of the power of the air, <u>the spirit that now worketh</u> in the children of disobedience:

Because of this rejection of truth, the entire unbelieving human race suffers from a disorientation to reality. This deficiency is nourished and exploited by the devil [2 Cor 4.4] but is overcome by the new birth and Christian discipleship.

Acts 26:17–18 (KJV 1900)
17 Delivering thee from the people, and from the Gentiles, unto whom now I send thee, 18 To open their eyes, and to turn them from darkness to light, and from the power of Satan unto God, that they may receive forgiveness of sins, and inheritance among them which are sanctified by faith that is in me.

The New World Order, the earthly objective of the Mystery of Iniquity, will be the outcome of the effort by chosen men and demonic principalities to guide history on behalf of Lucifer. This Order was the intent of the effort at Bab-el [Gen 11.1-6], sought openly and peacefully by cooperation among men. It was also the esoteric[234] aim of the Gentile empires as revealed to Daniel, beginning with the Babylon of his own time. Esoteric in the sense that, whatever the motivations of the individual Gentile rulers, Mystery Babylon and its initiates are working behind the scenes, providing intergenerational continuity, moving the plans of the Mystery of Iniquity towards the goal of the New World Order. These initiates are aided and abetted by the demonic principalities that are assigned to these nations for that purpose [Dan 10.12-13, 20-21]. Nebuchadnezzar's Babylon, the "head of gold," is the kingdom template used by Mystery Babylon for the duration of the times of the Gentiles: that is, world conquest achieved by violence and false religion imposed by means of demonic despotism.[235]

The New World Order will not merely be a reorganization of political powers, but the rejection of human society as originally organized by God. Humanity's disorientation to reality is a consequence of its rejection of God but it is also a conscious choice by a world guided by the philosophical systems of Lucifer.

Mystery Babylon has successfully guided the transformation of values that will enable the collapse of the divine institutions which form the basis of civilization

Short Term Priorities of the New World Order
The recalibration of conscience resulting in a new morality.
The redefinition of gender.
The demolition of biblical standards for marriage and family.
The expansion of racism, terrorism, war, medical and ecological crisis to promote world government.
The maintenance of the global ecumenical movement to bring about a one world church.
The completion of the infiltration of Christian churches and seminaries with false teaching.
The control of national governments: COMPLETED.
The control of international finance and commerce: COMPLETED.

Figure 8: Short Term Objectives-New World Order

It is the intergenerational and global cooperation of the "kings of the earth" that makes this progress possible. [236]

Revelation 17:1–2 (KJV 1900)
1 And there came one of the seven angels which had the seven vials, and talked with me, saying unto me, Come hither; I will shew unto thee the judgment of the great whore that sitteth upon many waters: 2 <u>With whom the kings of the earth have committed fornication</u>, and the inhabitants of the earth have been made drunk with the wine of her fornication.

Revelation 17:18 (KJV 1900)
18 And the woman which thou sawest is that great city, <u>which reigneth over the kings of the earth</u>.

This means that the collective mind of world Gentile leadership [as well as apostate Judaism] is synchronized with the agenda of the devil and operates in a manner consistent with his doctrine and methods. This reality is inconceivable to people today, who do not acknowledge the existence of an *organized* spiritual kingdom of evil.

The point of the revelation given to Daniel was that there was an *organized* evil upon the earth, opposed to the people of God and to God Himself. This evil would be ordered under the successive Gentile kingdoms, whom God likened to wild beasts, and illustrated via a statue of a man of such countenance that its image terrified the king Nebuchadnezzar [Dan 2.21]. The succession of Gentile kingdoms would increase in savagery and demonic strength, ultimately to be permanently destroyed by God Himself [Dan 7.1-14].

It is the *implications* of these truths that must be understood by the believer if he is to understand the New World Order.

First, this organized evil is sponsored by a *spiritual* power that manipulates every human institution. Therefore, its influence is often invisible, but indestructible by any merely human means.

Secondly, it is a *global* power; there is no nation today that is outside of its influence and control.

1 John 5:19 (KJV 1900)
19 And we know that we are of God, and the whole world lieth in wickedness.

Thirdly, it is a *demonic* power which is in opposition to God, His Word, and His people. Any appearances to the contrary are deceptions. By demonic power, it is meant that the key actors who direct the action in the various theaters of this warfare are not only following a demonically scripted playbook but are demonically indwelt themselves.[237] Under the description of "the Mark" we will investigate this further.

The New World Order is a social order which accurately reflects the thinking of Satan, superintended by those empowered by demonic entities. All aspects of this order: social, economic, political, and spiritual will operate on the basis of a theology that is preserved in the ancient mysteries and secret societies but is identified in the Bible as 'doctrines of demons' and 'the deep things of Satan' [Rev 2.24]. This Order will use deception, coercion, and the promise of power to enforce its hegemony upon the whole earth.

What Can be Done Today?

There is no spiritual action that can be taken to *prevent* the Antichrist's dominion and his New World Order. The Lord Himself will destroy this kingdom at His second advent [Rev 19.11-21]. However, each believer and each true local church can participate in God's resistance movement against the Satanic program.

The very existence of the spiritual body of Christ upon the earth restrains the devil from the full execution of his plans in time. Local churches led by true men of God exist to fulfill the Great Commission, producing spiritually mature disciples [Eph 4.11-15; 2 Pet 3.18] who by their sanctified lives, glorify God and impact history.

Each generation of believers, by the exercise of their faith within the institutions of society, project the righteousness and justice of God, influencing those institutions for good. It is by their testimony that the consciences of the unsaved are calibrated and the divine model for marriage, family and government are preserved. Every generation of believers, by their verbal proclamation of the gospel [Mk 16.15], win the lost and produce yet another generation of Christian soldiers. By these actions not only are the lost born again, but the world is rescued from unnecessary suffering that would occur if the devil was allowed free reign prematurely.

The critical, essential resource for the execution of our spiritual resistance to the devil's program is the frequent, accurate and systematic teaching of the Word of God, the Bible. The scriptures, when obeyed, enlighten, and empower the Church. Biblically equipped Christians resist the devil by exposing the false Church. Biblically equipped Christians bring wisdom and holy perspective to every organization and every community where they are found.

Because of the potency of sound biblical teaching there is, during the Church Age, an unprecedented spiritual effort to make sound teaching unavailable by the outpouring of false doctrine via a glut of highly competent false teachers[238] who have appeared around the world.

1 John 4:1 (KJV 1900)
1 Beloved, believe not every spirit, but try the spirits whether they are of God: because <u>many</u> false prophets are gone out into the world.

Romans 16:17–18 (KJV 1900)

17 Now I beseech you, brethren, mark them which cause divisions and offences contrary to the doctrine which ye have learned; and <u>avoid them</u>. 18 For they that are such serve not our Lord Jesus Christ, but their own belly; and by good words and fair speeches deceive the hearts of the simple.

Just because the devil is seeking to implement a future kingdom under the Antichrist, one should not assume that he is not equally committed to the spiritual subversion of every generation until that time. As the temporary god of this world, Lucifer is consolidating his rule and influence in every era of human civilization. Christians must resist him daily, beginning with our own spiritual discipline.

It is by the frequent, accurate and systematic teaching and preaching of the Word of God that our institutions are purified, and civilization is maintained until the time that this great evil is imposed upon the world. We are fighting, not to prevent the appearance of the Antichrist, but for the salvation of men and women, we are fighting for our own spiritual victory, we are fighting for the overall health and well-being of our families, community, and nation. Satan is not your friend; he is the implacable enemy of every human being, both saved and unsaved. When we proclaim and live out the Word of Truth, we are nation building, we are winning the lost, and we are performing true worship.

19
The Mark: "From Man to Superman"
Revelation 16.13-18

Revelation 13:16–18 (KJV 1900)
16 And he causeth all, both small and great, rich and poor, free and bond, to receive a mark in their right hand, or in their foreheads: 17 And that no man might buy or sell, save he that had the mark, or the name of the beast, or the number of his name. 18 Here is wisdom. Let him that hath understanding count the number of the beast: for it is the number of a man; and his number is Six hundred threescore and six.

One of the core doctrines of the devil is that through the rejection of God's authority, man begins his ascent to deity [Principle of Occult Religion]. The lie that man can be God is the carrot which is counter-poised with the stick of death to those who oppose Satan's plans.

Genesis 3:4–5 (KJV 1900)
4 And the serpent said unto the woman, Ye shall not surely die: 5 For God doth know that in the day ye eat [i.e. disobey rw] thereof, then your eyes shall be opened, and ye shall be as gods, knowing good and evil.

During Daniel's 70th week, there will be many who will willingly follow the Antichrist in full knowledge of his true identity and origin. Just as at the birth of Christ there were those who awaited and sought his coming [Lk 2.25-38] there are multiplied millions of people who are waiting for *a* Christ but not Jesus Christ. These people are waiting for the fulfillment of a promise made to Eve and to many since her; the promise that man can become superman, that the mortal can achieve godhood. These are those who seek to participate in what was once known as the Greater Mysteries.

Lucifer has a plan to fulfill this promise of godhood. He will do so by imitating the body of Christ, the Church.

Lucifer Will Imitate the Church

John 14:15–20 (KJV 1900)
15 If ye love me, keep my commandments. 16 And I will pray the Father, and he shall give you another Comforter, that he may abide with you for ever; 17 Even the Spirit of truth; whom the world cannot receive, because it seeth him not, neither knoweth him: but ye know him; for he dwelleth with you, <u>and shall be in you</u>. 18 I will not leave you comfortless: I will come to you. 19 Yet a little while, and the world seeth me no more; but ye see me: because I live, ye shall live also. 20 <u>At that day ye shall know that I am in my Father, and ye in me, and I in you.</u>

In the Church, God accomplished the unprecedented. He established a spiritual union between Himself and a person who places his faith in Christ as redeemer. This union is *spiritual*, it is *organic*, and it is *reciprocal*.

It is a *spiritual* union, it is not physical, and could not be, as God is Spirit [Jn 4.24] and what is permanent about mankind is also spirit. As a spiritual union it partakes of the invisible essence of both man and God.

This union between God and man is *organic*, and by this is meant that God creates a new spiritual entity [Rom 6.1-5; 2 Cor 5.17], known as the Church which is the Body and Bride of Christ[239] This new organism has the character of both redeemed man and of God.[240]

This union is *reciprocal*, that is, God is in redeemed man and redeemed man resides in turn within God.

God resides within the redeemed man through the mechanism of the Indwelling of the Holy Spirit [Rom 8.9; Col 1.27]. This operation is permanent.

Man resides within God by means of the Baptism of the Holy Spirit.[241] By this operation an individual becomes permanently a part of the Church. Every person born again since Pentecost[242] has been made a part of this spiritual organism and is now a member of a new spiritual order of creation [2 Cor 5.17].

Such a person, the born-again believer of the Church age, has access to divine omnipotence for the specific purposes of holy living and effective ministry as God has commanded for all believers [1 Th 4.3-4; Acts 1.8].

The born-again believer can understand the Word of God and know the will of God for their lives.[243]

The spiritually mature believer has a disproportionate impact upon their generation through their alignment to God and his plan.[244] Believers are lights that illuminate God's plan for salvation as well as the divine design for marriage, family, and the state. Through these means the body of Christ exercises tremendous historical impact, purifying and stabilizing civilization.

The criterion for becoming a part of the Church, this body of Christ, is faith in Jesus as the Savior of mankind and our Substitute, who suffered the punishment that we should have suffered, paying the entire debt of our sin.

1 John 5:11–13 (KJV 1900)
11 And this is the record, that God hath given to us eternal life, and this life is in his Son. 12 He that hath the Son hath life; and he that hath not the Son of God hath not life. 13 These things have I written unto you that believe on the name of the Son of God; that ye may know that ye have eternal life, and that ye may believe on the name of the Son of God.

Belief implies both an assent to the facts of the gospel as well as a desire that those facts be applied in your case. Faith in Christ will continue after the resurrection of the Church at the rapture, but the body of Christ will have been completed and withdrawn as an option for future believers.

It is by the *simulation* of this spiritual template that the devil will seek to fulfill his promise to mankind of human evolution to godhood. The priest-prophet of the Antichrist, the Prime Minister of the New World Order, will be the one to supervise *the ritual to receive the Mark* to every person in his kingdom.

It should be re-emphasized that the sole purpose of the False Prophet will be the management of the worship of the first beast. This man is not a politician, or a financier or a military man. He is a religious leader who exercises temporal power to accomplish his spiritual duties. *The False Prophet will use the economic system as a mechanism to support the mass possession of the end time population with demon spirits.* In this way man will become superman. It is the realization of the promise of Eden[245] and the secret of the Mysteries. This is the significance of the Mark.

It is not the job of the False Prophet to organize the economic activity of the Antichrist's kingdom. It is his job to administer its worship and spiritual activities. His use of the power of buying and selling as a vehicle for coercing the world into the worship of the Beast will ensure the achievement of the **primary objective** of the Son of Perdition:

> 2 Thessalonians 2:3–4 (KJV 1900)
> 3 Let no man deceive you by any means: for that day shall not come, except there come a falling away first, and that man of sin be revealed, the son of perdition; 4 <u>Who opposeth and exalteth himself above all that is called God, or that is worshipped</u>; so that he as God sitteth in the temple of God, <u>shewing himself that he is God</u>.

The Antichrist will use his control of world financial systems to force a commitment to his leadership not as a human leader but as Deity.

There is nothing new about this kind of thing: Nebuchadnezzar required the worship of an idol representation of himself and his kingdom; Caesar required the burning of incense and the affirmation of his godhood ["kaisar kurios"] and National Socialism made the State into God. Consistent with the spirit of lawlessness, many, many earthly rulers have declared themselves at least partially divine.

None of these previous kingdoms however, required or could require what the Antichrist will demand, which is universal spiritual identification with himself through a mark which is the external sign of a new internal, or spiritual reality. The mark itself will be the sign of a *decision*, a *commitment* to receive Lucifer's son as Christ and Messiah.

The Mark

> Revelation 13:16–18 (KJV 1900)
> 16 And he causeth all, both small and great, rich and poor, free and bond, <u>to receive a mark in their right hand, or in their foreheads</u>: 17 And that no man might buy or sell, save he that had the <u>mark</u>, or the <u>name</u> of the beast, or the <u>number of his name</u>. 18 Here is wisdom. Let him that hath understanding count the number of the beast: for it is the number of a man; and his

number is Six hundred threescore and six.

A mark [NT:5480] is a stamp or an imprint.[246] There will be a choice between

- ➢ The **Mark** [NT:5480] [*charagma*] perhaps a symbol
- ➢ The **Name** [NT:3686] of the Beast [*onoma*] a personal name or title
- ➢ The **Number** [NT:706] of his name [*arithmos*] an arithmetic code 666

The modern translations have a Greek construction that indicates that the mark is either the name or the number of the Beast. The King James and the New King James have Greek that includes the word "or" after the word "mark" and after the word "beast"; therefore, it is rendered: "that no man might buy or sell save he that had the mark, **or** the name of the beast, **or** the number of his name." The KJV and the NKJV set up three options for the recipient:

- ➢ **The Mark**
- ➢ **The Name**
- ➢ **The Number**

There will also be the option of placing the mark upon either the right hand or the forehead. These three types of mark and two locations for placing the mark set up multiple combinations of options for the recipient depending upon the symbols used and where they are placed.

For example, one might have the mark on the hand or the forehead, or the name, or number. One might have the name on the hand or the forehead, or the number on the hand and forehead. Or perhaps, one mark on the hand and the name or number on the forehead.

There's no way to know for certain, but there may be a way of determining, by the type of mark and its location, the level of commitment and status of the person so identified.

The concept of a mark or seal by which a person is identified with God is not original to Satan.[247]

For example, no person living during the Church age, which is the period between the first Pentecost after the resurrection of Christ, until the Rapture of the Church, will enter heaven who does not possess the *seal* of the Holy Spirit.

Ephesians 1:13 (KJV 1900)
13 In whom ye also trusted, after that ye heard the word of truth, the gospel of your salvation: in whom also after that ye believed, ye were sealed with that holy Spirit of promise, [Eph 4.30]

A seal, [NT:4973 *sphragis*] though a different word, is also a mark, stamp, inscription

In this passage the Church age believer is identified as belonging to God by the seal of the indwelling presence of the Spirit of God. In other words, God himself is the seal, the imprint, the stamp of divine ownership upon the believer.

In the same way, the false prophet will ensure that no person is allowed to function within the kingdom of Antichrist without his seal *and his spirit*. It will not be the mark alone that is the seal of membership into this kingdom, *but what the mark represents*.

The idea of a symbolic act representing a real spiritual transaction is illustrated by water baptism. No one is going to heaven because he underwent water baptism. It is the real spiritual transformation to which the baptism points that is important. Likewise, no one is married simply because he or she has been given a ring: it is the spiritual and legal obligations [the covenant] that are represented by the ring that constitute marriage. Both water baptism and wedding rings are symbols or seals, if you will, that denote a real transaction which has taken place. This is the significance of the mark.

Even the concept of the marking the *forehead* is not unique to this situation in scripture.

Revelation 7:2–4 (KJV 1900)
2 And I saw another angel ascending from the east, <u>having the seal of the living God</u>: and he cried with a loud voice to the four angels, to whom it was given to hurt the earth and the sea, 3 Saying, Hurt not the earth, neither the sea, nor the trees, <u>till we have sealed the servants of our God in their foreheads</u>. 4 And I heard the number of them which were sealed: and there were sealed an hundred and forty and four thousand of all the tribes of the children of Israel. [Eze 9.4-6]

Also,

Exodus 28:36–38 (KJV 1900)
36 And thou shalt make a plate of pure gold, and grave upon it,

like the engravings of a signet, HOLINESS TO THE LORD. 37 And thou shalt put it on a blue lace, that it may be upon the mitre; upon the forefront of the mitre it shall be. 38 <u>And it shall be upon Aaron's forehead</u>, that Aaron may bear the iniquity of the holy things, which the children of Israel shall hallow in all their holy gifts; <u>and it shall be always upon his forehead</u>, that they may be accepted before the LORD.

Ezekiel 9:3–5 (KJV 1900)
3 And the glory of the God of Israel was gone up from the cherub, whereupon he was, to the threshold of the house. And he called to the man clothed with linen, which had the writer's inkhorn by his side; 4 And the LORD said unto him, Go through the midst of the city, through the midst of Jerusalem, <u>and set a mark upon the foreheads</u> of the men that sigh and that cry for all the abominations that be done in the midst thereof. 5 And to the others he said in mine hearing, Go ye after him through the city, and smite: let not your eye spare, neither have ye pity:

Finally,

Revelation 17:3–5 (KJV 1900)
3 So he carried me away in the spirit into the wilderness: and I saw a woman sit upon a scarlet coloured beast, full of names of blasphemy, having seven heads and ten horns. 4 And the woman was arrayed in purple and scarlet colour, and decked with gold and precious stones and pearls, having a golden cup in her hand full of abominations and filthiness of her fornication: 5 <u>And upon her forehead was a name written</u>, MYSTERY, BABYLON THE GREAT, THE MOTHER OF HARLOTS AND ABOMINATIONS OF THE EARTH.

In each case the seal or mark upon the forehead was symbolic for something *real*: the imputed righteousness of the 144 thousand evangelists, the real holiness of those who opposed the idolatry and sin of Judah in Ezekiel's time, the real status of holiness granted to the High Priest and the real and actual wickedness of the whore, Mystery Babylon. In like manner, the seal administered by the False Prophet on behalf of the Antichrist will represent *a true spiritual transaction*, whereby spiritual allegiance is pledged, and a new spirit is received. <u>The mark of the beast represents an initiation.</u>

The Mark is an Initiation

"The Latin initium means beginning, as in our "initial"; initiatus, the participle from the verb initiare, referred to any act incident to the beginning or introduction of a thing. The word came widely into use in mysteries and sacred rites, whence it has come into [our] Masonic nomenclature. Back of it, [as used by us], is the picture of birth, so that the Masonic initiation means that a candidate has been born into the Masonic life, making the same kind of beginning therein that a babe makes when born into the world." [248]

The Mark is a symbol which is the visible evidence on an invisible initiation.

"In the context of ritual magic and esotericism, an initiation is considered to cause a fundamental process of change to begin within the person being initiated. The person conducting the initiation (the *initiator*), being in possession of a certain power or state of being, transfers this power or state to the person being initiated..... The initiation process is often likened to a simultaneous death and rebirth, because as well as being a beginning it also implies an ending as existence on one level drops away in an ascension to the next."[249] [emphasis added]

"*Initiation* is the "process of undergoing an expansion [toward higher levels] of consciousness"[250]

The mark is the symbol which is the visible evidence of an invisible initiation. This initiation is the delivery upon a promise: that man can become as God.

The True Origin of the Doctrine of the Superman[251]

Genesis 3:1–5 (KJV 1900)
1 Now the serpent was more subtil than any beast of the field which the LORD God had made. And he said unto the woman, Yea, hath God said, Ye shall not eat of every tree of the garden? 2 And the woman said unto the serpent, We may eat of the fruit of the trees of the garden: 3 But of the fruit of the tree which is in the midst of the garden, God hath said, Ye shall not eat of it, neither shall ye touch it, lest ye die. 4 And the serpent said unto the woman, Ye shall not surely die: 5 For God doth know that in the day ye eat thereof, then your eyes shall be opened, and ye shall

<u>be as gods, knowing good and evil.</u>

The recorded portion of this conversation is very brief. This statement by Satan is only two sentences. It may be brief, but it is very effective. We will concisely review this exchange between he and Eve to disclose the doctrines of demons, or the thinking of Satan that forms the foundation of his philosophy and his agenda. While we will not address every principle that is present in this exchange, we will establish those which will be prominent in the development of the kingdom of Antichrist in the last days.

The claim was made to Adam and Eve was that a species of godhood was available to mankind, but that God had withheld this status from them. The idea of unauthorized authority, of spiritual advancement and secret knowledge was the temptation offered and accepted by Eve. The scripture says that Adam was not deceived by the devil [1Tim 2.14], however, his love for his wife was greater than his love for God and he deliberately chose what he knew to be a lie for the sake of that relationship. It was the first love story.

The Principle of Deception

Satan is coming to you in a way that you would not expect, in a way that you will willingly receive him. Evil isn't always ugly [Gen 3.1].

Genesis 3:1a (KJV 1900)
1 Now the serpent was more subtil than any beast of the field which the LORD God had made. And he said unto the woman,

The fact that this conversation between Eve and the serpent takes place at all is noteworthy. The existence of a talking, thinking [*subtil* OT:6175] animal that called God a liar, should have been doubly disturbing to the first humans.

The very first act of the devil in *human* history was to perpetrate an outrageous deception. He did not appear as a fallen angel, or as an angel at all, but as a talking animal [Rev 12.9]. The principle here is the Principle of Deception: that Satan does not present himself as he is, but in a way that we will readily receive him.

2 Corinthians 11:13–14 (KJV 1900)
13 For such are false apostles, deceitful workers, <u>transforming themselves into the apostles of Christ</u>. 14 And no marvel; for

Satan himself is <u>transformed into an angel of light</u>.

Satan is very effective in packaging himself as the "good," but his "good" is always short of the will of God. It is because human beings believe that all that is "good" is of God, that we fail to comprehend the misuse of the good. The tree of knowledge provided access to a "good" that was only possible after God was disobeyed. *The principle of deception allows for all the good necessary to deceive.* Therefore, we can find Satan in all the following disguises:

- A handsome and gifted preacher
- A humanitarian who sacrifices his life for those in need
- A cultured and sophisticated woman of the world who speaks for those who have no voice
- A fearless crusader for morality
- A brilliant and charismatic world leader

Or, if necessary, a talking animal.

The antidote to the believers' deception is twofold: a thorough understanding of the Word of God [2 Tim 2.15] and a daily walk with Him in prayer and obedience [Gal 5.16]. The devil can only proclaim a portion of the Word since his intent is to propagate a lie. Spiritual discernment based upon an understanding of what the Bible teaches arms the Christian to avoid deception, Eve's downfall. Spiritual maturity enables the believer to prioritize the glory of God, Adam's demise.

Satan has and will in the future mesmerize the world with appearances that resonate with our fallen sensibilities. Unbelievers will believe in him because of his message, his miraculous person and the threat of violence that lurks behind his program. Regardless of his disguise, a careful examination of his words and his works will disclose his identity, for he cannot support God's Word or God's Son, beyond superficial assent.

The Principle of Scriptural Misuse

Lucifer uses his mastery of the Word of God to create misleading arguments based upon the misuse of the scripture [Gen 3.1b].

Genesis 3:1 (KJV 1900)
1 Now the serpent was more subtil than any beast of the field

which the LORD God had made. And he said unto the woman, Yea, hath God said, Ye shall not eat of every tree of the garden?

Satan reversed what God had said [Gen 2.16-17]. By doing this he positioned God as possibly unfair and thereby prepared Eve[252] for his next argument. We are especially susceptible to this tactic today because we are not listening to our teachers as closely as we should.

Many are open to deceptions based upon Satan's misuse of the Bible. This manipulative question engaged Eve in a debate with a talking animal about something that was cut and dried: the question of what could or couldn't be eaten in the garden.

Satan is the author of a multifaceted offensive against the Word of God, the Bible.

1. The creation of spurious methods of biblical **textual criticism**[253]
2. The denial of the **perspicacity** of the scriptures: the assertion that the meaning of the Bible cannot be known with accuracy, or that the meaning can change based upon the individual's perception of it.[254]
3. The denial of the **inerrancy** of the scriptures.[255]
4. A rejection of the scriptures as the ultimate **authority** for the faith and practice of believers

Satan, by the restatement of what God said, implied that God was withholding something from her that was for her good. The serpent's skilled questioning brought about the desired response.

Genesis 3:2–3 (KJV 1900)
2 And the woman said unto the serpent, We may eat of the fruit of the trees of the garden: 3 But of the fruit of the tree which is in the midst of the garden, God hath said, Ye shall not eat of it, neither shall ye touch it, lest ye die.

This is not exactly what God said. Having absorbed the suggestion of God as a tyrant, Eve added her own thoughts to the statement of God. The words "nor shall you touch it" reveal the way that Eve *felt* about the instruction, rather than a simple restatement of the divine command. Further, the word "lest" makes contingent what God stated absolutely: Eve introduces the *possibility* of death where God's warning was absolute Gen 2.17b "for in the day that thou eatest thereof thou shalt surely die."[256]

Even though God provided every possible delight in the garden and prohibited only one tree, Eve's thoughts are drifting closer to the arguments of the talking serpent.

The Principle of Human Non-Culpability:

Satan claims that the wages of sin is not death [Gen 3.4].

Genesis 3:4 (KJV 1900)
4 And the serpent said unto the woman, Ye shall not surely die:

Satan suggests that Eve can deliberately reject God's command without negative consequences ["do as thou wilt"]. Today the notion is becoming more and more popular that Hell does not exist, and if it does, nearly no one will be going there. The doctrines of soul sleep, soul annihilation, the transmigration of souls, purgatory and the possibility of universal salvation all deny that the wages of sin are death.

Revelation 20:15 (KJV 1900)
15 And whosoever was not found written in the book of life was cast into the lake of fire.

Ezekiel 18:4 (KJV 1900)
4 Behold, all souls are mine; as the soul of the father, so also the soul of the son is mine: the soul that sinneth, it shall die.

The serpent flatly argued that God was misleading Eve about sin and death. The implication, at this point, is that either God did not know that He was wrong, or He lied about the Tree of Knowledge. Perhaps God is also misleading her as to His own identity. If he is a liar, then he is not holy, not righteous, and not just. If He is mistaken, perhaps this is even worse. Satan has already shed doubt upon what God has said, he now suggests an alternate explanation as to who God is! This is the basis of "The Lie:" the claim that God is not who he says he is, and neither is Jesus.

Satan attempts to remove a foundational component of human spiritual motivation: the fear of God.

Proverbs 1:7 (KJV 1900)
7 The fear of the LORD is the beginning of knowledge: But fools despise wisdom and instruction.

The Principle of Occult Religion:

Satan presents himself to Eve as the benefactor of mankind, the source of secret knowledge, the champion of human freedom, the conductor of souls to spiritual evolution [Gen 3.5].

Genesis 3:5 (KJV 1900)
5 For God doth know that in the day ye eat thereof, then your eyes shall be opened, and ye shall be as gods, knowing good and evil.

Inasmuch as God saw fit, according to the devil, to withhold wisdom and godhood from humanity, Satan takes it upon himself to disclose these things to man. Since it is through him that Eve is being made aware of God's true intentions and the true interpretation His words, then Lucifer represents himself as the true spiritual benefactor of mankind, the true *conductor of souls* to spiritual evolution. This is the doctrine of the New Age Movement: that man can become God, that man is in fact God already. This is the doctrine of the superman, the promise to mankind that the devil will attempt to make good for humanity at the appearing of the Antichrist.

How many people today are seeking knowledge and power through, initiations, invocations, incantations, positive confessions, spiritism and astrology: in other words, through the devil? The serpent convinced Eve that secret knowledge accessed through Satan and the forbidden tree was of greater value than fellowship with God. Eve could not have one without forsaking the other. The *violation* of the prohibition laid down by God regarding the tree is the *initiation* which she must undergo to qualify for "godhood."

The Superman and the New World Order

The Man of Sin will attempt to make good on the promise of the superman. To achieve the godhood promised by Lucifer, a number of conditions must be met, and a number of lies must be accepted as truth. These original deceits underlie Mystery Babylon, and they will become the basis of the promise made to end time humanity by the Antichrist.

We have already established that the Antichrist will use deception and force to rule his kingdom. His initiation will promise the godhood that he accused the Lord of withholding from mankind. However, this initiation will result in demon possession, which while making man more powerful in some respects, is a far cry from godhood. *God is not God merely because he is powerful*, but because of his eternality, absolute holiness, and his infinite love as well as the coordinated function of these and all his other divine attributes. Lucifer has today and will in the future convince fallen mankind that God is Power, and that Power is God.

In the satanic initiation, power will come at the cost of that imprint which identifies man as the handiwork of God: *his ability to know and to act according to the dictates of conscience and morality*. You cannot be indwelt by demons and maintain this capacity for moral function.

1 Timothy 4:1–2 (KJV 1900)
1 Now the Spirit speaketh expressly, that in the latter times some shall depart from the faith, giving heed to seducing spirits, and doctrines of devils; 2 Speaking lies in hypocrisy; <u>having their conscience seared with a hot iron;</u>

In the time of the end, the Antichrist will force a satanic initiation upon the people of the world. This initiation will be symbolized by a mark which can be worn on the flesh. All, every person regardless of rank or station, will be required to receive this initiation or they will be unable to eat, or to provide shelter or medical care for themselves or their families.

This initiation will be a fulfillment of Satan's offer of godhood to Eve in the garden of Eden. It will provide a measure of power and intelligence.[257] It will provide the Antichrist with an unprecedented level of social control via the demonic spirits who will indwell humanity.

This initiation will form the basis of Satan's efforts to consolidate his control of the earth for its use as a base of operations to wage a counterattack upon the heaven from which he has been recently expelled by force [Rev 12]. His goal is to produce *a new kind of sinner in a new kind of world*. Humanity will become a hybridized new creation with inhuman powers and capacities brought about via demon possession and advanced biological technology[258].

Lucifer will imitate the Church, a body spiritually united with Christ and provided with unlimited power for sanctification and ministry, by manufacturing a spiritual organism united to himself via demon possession and thereby exercising considerable spiritual power. The world will for a time be united under the rule of Antichrist in a facsimile of the Kingdom over which Christ is scheduled to rule. The devil is not an amillennialist.

This plan will succeed, but only briefly, as the initiation will result in horrible suffering for all those who receive it. Satan's kingdom building efforts will finally end in eternal judgment in the Lake of Fire where the Antichrist, the False Prophet and all "spiritually evolved" humanity will accompany him.

Revelation 14:9–11 (KJV 1900)
9 And the third angel followed them, saying with a loud voice, If any man worship the beast and his image, and receive his mark in his forehead, or in his hand, 10 The same shall drink of the wine of the wrath of God, which is poured out without mixture into the cup of his indignation; and he shall be tormented with fire and brimstone in the presence of the holy angels, and in the presence of the Lamb: 11 <u>And the smoke of their torment ascendeth up for ever and ever</u>: and they have no rest day nor night, who worship the beast and his image, <u>and whosoever receiveth the mark</u> of his name.

Revelation 16:2 (KJV 1900)
2 And the first went, and poured out his vial upon the earth; and there fell a noisome and grievous sore upon the men which had the mark of the beast, and upon them which worshipped his image.

Revelation 19:20 (KJV 1900)
20 And the beast was taken, and with him the false prophet that wrought miracles before him, with which he deceived them that had received the mark of the beast, and them that worshipped his image. These both were cast alive into a lake of fire burning with brimstone.

Richard G. Walker

Faithful Christians In the Last Days

The implication of Revelation 14.9-11 is that believers will accept death rather than receive the Mark. Tribulation believers appear in heaven soon after the opening of the seven sealed book in Rev 5.

> Revelation 6:9–11 (KJV 1900) 9 And when he had opened the fifth seal, I saw under the altar the souls of them that were slain for the word of God, and for the testimony which they held: 10 And they cried with a loud voice, saying, How long, O Lord, holy and true, dost thou not judge and avenge our blood on them that dwell on the earth? 11 And white robes were given unto every one of them; and it was said unto them, that they should rest yet for a little season, <u>until their fellowservants also and their brethren, that should be killed as they were, should be fulfilled</u>.

The 144,000 are martyred in Rev 14.

How can the behavior of Christians today be reconciled with the devotion to Christ which will send every believer that the Antichrist can locate to their deaths?

Perhaps genuine Christians have simply been obscured by the hordes of pretenders. Many professing Christians will defect from the local church during the apostasy that occurs at the beginning of the tribulation. There will be a worldwide ecumenical Church movement that will draw away false believers, permitting the remaining true Christians to demonstrate a clear testimony of faithfulness.

Perhaps the cleansing power of persecution itself will eliminate the millions of false Christians that are crammed into Churches today. Much of the misbehavior we witness among Christians and even pastors is being performed by unbelievers posing as believers in Christ. Later, there will be persecutions of believers by the Antichrist that will frighten away the unfaithful. These complementary actions will purge the local churches of pretenders.

Perhaps this incredible display of spirituality will be caused by the arrival of a special group of teachers who will effectively combat the false teaching of the end times. We know that God will, in addition to the 144,000 evangelists, send the two witnesses who will have a powerful worldwide influence [Rev 11]. The Tribulation may be the greatest era of *accurate* Bible teaching ever.

Perhaps these believers will experience special grace from God that will strengthen them and enlighten them to resist the temptation to value their own lives over Christ. In this they would imitate the martyrs of the Church who did the same throughout its history. The martyrs of past ages were willing to die rather than to provide even verbal assent to false teaching.

Richard G. Walker

20
Background to the Fall of Babylon: Revelation 16

The Bowl or Vial Judgments

Chapter 16 of Revelation portrays the final and most severe series of judgments unleashed against a hostile world.

The seven plagues or bowls are devastating, beginning with the loathsome sores which shall appear on each person who has received the mark of the Beast. This judgment will be followed by the turning of the seas and the fresh waters into blood. What will be severely limited water supplies because of the trumpet judgments are now eliminated altogether.

The fourth bowl will cause reactions in the sun which will cause unbearable heat upon the earth. The fifth bowl will be limited to the kingdom of the Beast. Recall that the Beast will attain his kingdom through the uprooting of three of the Ten Kingdoms. This bowl will turn off the lights in the Beasts' domain, resulting in atmospheric effects [darkness] that will mirror the spiritual condition of its inhabitants.

The sixth bowl will dry the Euphrates River, which will enable a reversal of age-old geopolitical realities, opening the west to the military designs of the kings of the east. Antichrist's imposition of world government will be unstable. This instability was predicted in the dual composition of the toes of the image dreamt by Nebuchadnezzar and interpreted by Daniel [Dan 2.41-44].The seventh and final bowl releases multiple catastrophic disasters upon the world. The worst earthquake of all time alters the configuration of the land masses of the earth and results in the destruction of all the major cities of the world.

As if the earthquake were not enough, the wrath of God will be further demonstrated by the crisis of hail weighing from 100 to 200 pounds per hailstone falling upon the earth.

> Revelation 16:18–21 (KJV 1900)
> 18 And there were voices, and thunders, and lightnings; and there was a great earthquake, such as was not since men were upon the earth, so mighty an earthquake, and so great. 19 And the great city was divided into three parts, and the cities of the nations fell: and great Babylon came in remembrance before God, to give unto her the cup of the wine of the fierceness of his wrath. 20 And every island fled away, and the mountains were not found. 21 And there fell upon men a great hail out of heaven, every stone about the weight of a talent: and men blasphemed God because of the plague of the hail; for the plague thereof was exceeding great.

Richard G. Walker

21
Disambiguating Babylon:
Revelation 17

It is in the context of the devastations of Revelation 16 that the Bible introduces the concept of Mystery Babylon the Great. Mystery Babylon is depicted as a woman riding upon a now familiar beast, in a wilderness. She is independent of the beast, but she is also in a cooperative relationship with it. Just as the beast is more than one thing, comprising temporal, earthly and spiritual meaning, so also the "great harlot" [Rev 17.1] relates concepts that are terrestrial and spiritual.

Disambiguation is the process of separating concepts with the same or similar meanings. Mystery Babylon the Great contains multiple concepts, each of which possess multiple scriptural referents. Each concept is important to understanding our times and the end of the Gentile era.

The Whore [Rev 17.1] *Spiritual Babylon*, the *religious* aspect of the devil's post flood world system including its [mystery] doctrine, ecclesiastical organization, and strategies of world control. The whore entices both kings and kingdoms into God-rejecting idolatry in service to Satan.[259] This seduction is accomplished by the promise of power: spiritual evolution garnished with worldly pleasure, wealth, and influence. Mystery Babylon in this sense is the Greater and Lesser Mystery religions which represent the distilled essence of Lucifer's thinking and plan.

The Beast[260] *Political Babylon* represents the *governmental* structure of the devil's kingdom upon the earth, consisting of a series of post-flood

Gentile empires or kingdoms. It is the historical, visible World Order. While post-flood Babel is the root, its posterity, the Babylon of Nebuchadnezzar is the head, the gold standard and template which forms the blueprint for each of the future Gentile kingdoms.[261] Technically, this world political and economic system, symbolized as the Beast in Revelation 13 and 17 [c.f. Dan 7.1-8, 19-26], is distinct from the whore/harlot, but their relationship is symbiotic: each depends upon the other throughout history. This interdependence is illustrated by the depiction in Revelation 17 of the harlot and the beast together and headed in the same direction. Although the harlot is the creation and agent of Lucifer, he and the ten kings will eliminate her halfway through the Tribulation period to establish the final form of demonic despotism that this book refers to as the New World Order.

Many Waters[262] This term signifies the *geographic* reach of the devil's world system. Mystery Babylon is worldwide: excepting the theocratic kingdom of Israel in the Old Testament, there is no nation or people that is outside the direct control of this system. Since its implementation after the Flood, Mystery Babylon has maintained an uninterrupted international supremacy.

That Great City [Rev 17.18]: The demolition of Ancient Babylon was accompanied by the divine promise that it shall never be rebuilt.[263] If this is so, what then is the Babylon of the Book of Revelation? We will attempt to demonstrate that the terrestrial scope of Babylon the Great involves many cities and possibly *also*, a single city which is the spiritual manifestation of ancient Babylon and the earthly headquarters of the Antichrist.

Strictly speaking, Mystery Babylon is a spiritual construct. It is the outworking of the Mystery of Iniquity since the judgment wrought upon the world through the Flood. The flood of Noah's era was the final expression of God's wrath against the world that was. The family of Noah began a new dispensation, wherein man received another covenant [Gen 9.8-17] and Satan recommenced operations upon the earth under Mystery Babylon.

Revelation 17.18 refers to Mystery Babylon the Great as "that great city." The term "mystery" means that the concept of "Babylon" is a spiritual one: the whore and the beast are symbols of a spiritual reality. The designation "Babylon" can communicate a spiritual truth about the spiritual system that dominates the world, without specifically designating the *historical* city of Babylon, which today consists of ruins.

Richard G. Walker

Babylon the Great as the Cities of Man

The history of **cities** as recorded in the scriptures, provides an explanation of their significance and meaning in our end time context. To discern our first definition of the statement, "that great city," we must briefly examine the first organized cities, beginning with the city established by Cain, before the Deluge.

The City of Cain: "Enoch"

> Genesis 4:16–17 (KJV 1900)
> 16 And Cain went out from the presence of the LORD, and dwelt in the land of Nod, on the east of Eden. 17 And Cain knew his wife; and she conceived, and bare Enoch: and he builded a city, and called the name of the city, after the name of his son, Enoch.

Cain established the first city in history and named it after his firstborn Enoch, whose name means "dedicated." Cain, before his condemnation as the murderer of his brother Abel, was free to express faith in Jehovah and to offer an appropriate sacrifice, but he refused. Consequently, like his parents, he "went out from the presence of the Lord" [Gen 4.16] to the *east* of Eden, an area that could have been the site of the future Babel.

There Cain constructed a *city* built on the premise of a future [a future represented by naming the city after his son] without God. He had a marriage without God, a son without God and a city without God. Cain established this city as the home of a continuing, progressing people without God, *dedicated* to man for man's sake.

The City of Enoch: The Prophet of God

There is another Enoch, a prophet born later, but prior to the flood.

> Genesis 5:20–24 (KJV 1900)
> 20 And all the days of Jared were nine hundred sixty and two years: and he died. 21 And Enoch lived sixty and five years, and begat Methuselah: 22 And Enoch walked with God after he begat Methuselah three hundred years, and begat sons and daughters: 23 And all the days of Enoch were three hundred sixty and five years:

24 And Enoch walked with God: and he was not; for God took him.

This Enoch was a prophet [Jude 14] who was not identified with any earthly city. He was also 'dedicated' and so obeyed God that God "took him." He was to inherit a city, but "an heavenly," whose "builder and maker is God" [Heb 11.10, 13-16].

The Post Flood City of Babel

It is by the comparison and contrast of these cities we will determine our first definition of that great city, Babylon the Great. The first city established after the flood was Babel.

> Genesis 11:1–4 (KJV 1900)
> 1 And the whole earth was of one language, and of one speech. 2 And it came to pass, as they journeyed from[264] the east, that they found a plain in the land of Shinar; and they dwelt there. 3 And they said one to another, Go to, let us make brick, and burn them throughly. And they had brick for stone, and slime had they for morter. 4 And they said, Go to, let us build us a city and a tower, whose top may reach unto heaven; and let us make us a name, lest we be scattered abroad upon the face of the whole earth.

Like Cain, these people built a city while journeying *to* the east. They built this city in *dedication* to man: "let *us* build a city," "let *us* make *a name*," even as Cain sought to perpetuate his name and his creed by naming his city for his son. The trust and hope of the people of Babel was in man and his wisdom, skill, and destiny apart from God. In fact, the tower [skyscraper/temple] was to reach "into heaven" not to be near God, but to circumvent God's command to disperse, and to thwart future judgment, apparently in unbelief of God's covenant with Noah that there would never be another worldwide flood [Gen 9.9-15].

Unlike the days of Cain, this population of Babel was not offset by godly individuals and families. God said: "Behold, the people is one" [Gen 11.6]. Babel leveraged the power of universal [ecumenical] unity which God Himself acknowledged as a powerful force for evil [Gen 11.6-9].

The City of Abraham Ur of the Chaldees[265] [Babylon]

> Genesis 11:31 (KJV 1900)
> 31 And Terah took Abram his son, and Lot the son of Haran his son's son, and Sarai his daughter in law, his son Abram's wife; and they went forth with them <u>from</u> Ur of the Chaldees, to go into the land of Canaan; and they came unto Haran, and dwelt there.

God calls Abraham from Ur, the city of the dead and home of the moon goddess, *west* to Canaan. However, He provides him with no city and no immediate inheritance for himself or for his sons [Acts 7.4-5]. Like Enoch the prophet, Abram [Gen 20.7] did not receive a "continuing city" [Heb 11.9; 13.14] but one with "foundations" whose builder and maker is God [Heb 11.10].

> Hebrews 11:13–16 (KJV 1900)
> 13 These all died in faith, not having received the promises, but having seen them afar off, and were persuaded of them, and embraced them, <u>and confessed that they were strangers and pilgrims on the earth</u>. 14 For they that say such things declare plainly that they seek a country. 15 And truly, if they had been mindful of that country from whence they came out, they might have had opportunity to have returned. 16 But now they desire a better country, that is, an heavenly: wherefore God is not ashamed to be called their God: <u>for he hath prepared for them a city</u>.

From a spiritual perspective, there are *two kinds of cities* delineated in scripture. There is an invisible city; one which is real yet perceived only by the faith of the righteous. This heavenly city is only entered via resurrection, the hope of the heroes of faith in Hebrews 11.

There are also, by contrast, physical, continuing cities, "dedicated" to men and raised up for the glory of man in opposition to God. These earthly cities are dedicated to territorial expansion, material wealth and intellectual progress. These earthly cities have a theological orientation based upon the rejection of God and the worship of false gods which are demons.[266] The first of these is the city of Cain, followed, after the Flood, by the men of Babel and of Ur. *Every* earthly city is included under this designation [1 Jn 5.19], with the significant exception of Jerusalem when God resided there in the Tabernacle and the Temple. *Your* city is no exception, nor is your nation.

The *earthly* city is entered by natural birth, like Enoch the son of

Cain, and its hope ends with the grave like Ur, the burial city. The *spiritual* city is apprehended through the faith of believers of every age. The spiritual city is inherited by a supernatural birth, of which the birth of Isaac is a type, and is entered via resurrection.

One aspect of terrestrial or geographic Babylon the Great is the consecutive generations of earthly cities, the cities of the Gentiles that are built in the same spirit by every empire in every geography, by every ethnicity in every historical era.

They are the capitals of every Gentile empire, but they are also the great industrial centers and religious cities such as Ur, Thebes, Nineveh, Babylon, Athens, Rome, Washington D.C., New York, Moscow, Beijing, et. cetera.

Babylon the Great as the Capital of the New World Order

The name *Mystery* Babylon the Great is a symbolic name. It implies that whatever the ancient Babylon was will become the essence of something else that follows it in time. It has been argued that in one sense, this is the spirit that animates the cities of this world, the cities of men, where "the Great" refers to the geographic and temporal extent of Mystery Babylon as a spiritual influence.

On the other hand, "that great city, which reigneth over the kings of the earth" may also refer to a literal city, which although not the ancient Babylon, possesses the character and function of the original city *during the reign of the Antichrist*. Such a city could be considered the headquarters of the Antichrist and the capital of the New World Order.

Babylon Was Destroyed, But Will Live Again

The Babylon of old was destroyed and God vowed that it would never be rebuilt. Ancient Babylon, even if the correct location has been identified, is in ruins. Whatever Babylon the Great is in the future, it will not be the geographical Babylon of history. [267]

The prediction of the destruction of Babylon is one of the prominent themes in the Old Testament [Isa 13; Jer 50-51]. Its destruction is compared to that of Sodom and Gomorrah.

> Isaiah 13:19–20 (KJV 1900)
> 19 And Babylon, the glory of kingdoms, The beauty of the Chaldees' excellency, Shall be as when God overthrew Sodom and Gomorrah. 20 It shall never be inhabited, Neither shall it be dwelt

in from generation to generation: Neither shall the Arabian pitch tent there; Neither shall the shepherds make their fold there. Babylon was made a desolation [Jer 51.26] and a wilderness.

Jeremiah 50:13 (KJV 1900)
13 Because of the wrath of the LORD it shall not be inhabited, But it shall be wholly desolate: every one that goeth by Babylon shall be astonished, And hiss at all her plagues.

In view of this, how does Babylon reappear to rule the kings of the earth in the Apocalypse? Is it because Babylon is now Papal Rome? Papal Rome is not as ancient as Mystery Babylon. It has not even existed since the beginning of Rome. Although Papal Rome is undoubtedly an historical and contemporary manifestation of Mystery Babylon, it is not synonymous with it.

Lucifer is identified in scripture with Babylon.[268] Although Babylon was destroyed, Satan remains and his plan remains in operation through the empires since Babylon, as Daniel reveals [Dan 2, 7]. Mystery Babylon is described in Revelation 17 as a harlot riding a beast in a desolate wilderness [Rev 17]. Mystery Babylon, in one sense, is the greatest Urban Renewal operation ever achieved. A single empire [Babylon] is destroyed yet reanimated into one that encompasses the entire world for the remainder of history. In another sense, it is Lucifer portraying what is a desolate moral and philosophical wilderness [Rev 17.3] as a utopian World Order.

If Babylon is destroyed, never to be rebuilt, what then is destroyed in Rev 14.8; 16.19; 18.10, 18-19, 21?

Capitals

Daniel 6:1–2 (KJV 1900)
1 It pleased Darius to set over the kingdom an hundred and twenty princes, which should be over the whole kingdom; 2 And over these three presidents; of whom Daniel was first: that the princes might give accounts unto them, and the king should have no damage.

These verses relate the organization of the Medo-Persian empire during the reign of Darius the Mede. The kingdom included the territory of the vanquished Babylonians. The administrative organization of this kingdom was not dissimilar to that of Babylon.

Daniel 3:1–2 (KJV 1900)
1 Nebuchadnezzar the king made an image of gold, whose height was threescore cubits, and the breadth thereof six cubits: he set it up in the plain of Dura, in the province of Babylon. 2 <u>Then Nebuchadnezzar the king sent to gather together the princes, the governors, and the captains, the judges, the treasurers, the counsellers, the sheriffs, and all the rulers of the provinces</u>, to come to the dedication of the image which Nebuchadnezzar the king had set up.

In the Medo-Persian empire the kings held court in Susa or in Achmetha [Ecbatana]. Nebuchadnezzar reigned in Babylon. In either case the kingdom was divided into provinces and management of these provinces funneled up to the capital city. In the days of the fourth kingdom, the kingdom of the Beast, there will be at least ten kingdoms through which the Antichrist will rule the world. There is no good reason to believe that there will not be a capital, as there had been in the case of Babylon, Medo Persia, Greece and Rome.

The Great City

The term *"the/that great city"* is used in the book of Revelation in a mysterious way. It appears ten times in the book of Revelation. Two of the references are to Jerusalem. One of these is a reference to the New Jerusalem, which shall descend out of heaven in Rev 21.10. The other is the place where the two great end time prophets are killed [Rev 11.8]. In 11.8, *the great city* is equated with Sodom and Egypt. The other eight references in the book of Revelation are references to "Babylon." Revelation conflates or merges the city of Jerusalem and "Babylon."

Jerusalem

The book of Revelation makes use of the name *Jerusalem* in an unusual way. In the three occasions where the name Jerusalem is specifically used, all three are references to the new Jerusalem which descends from heaven [Rev 3.12; 21.2, 10]. None of these references occur in the chapters which pertain to Daniel's 70th week or Rev 6.1-20.4. The name of Jerusalem is not specifically mentioned during God's judgment of the earth during the Day of the Lord.

Revelation 11:1–2 (KJV 1900)
1 And there was given me a reed like unto a rod: and the angel stood, saying, Rise, and measure the temple of God, and the altar, and them that worship therein. 2 But the court which is without the temple leave out, and measure it not; <u>for it is given unto the Gentiles: and the holy city shall they tread under foot forty and two months.</u>

Here an indirect mention of Jerusalem indicates that the "holy city[269]" will be put to unholy use by the Gentiles for 42 months or three- and one-half years. Of course, this period corresponds to the beginning of reign of Antichrist as the head of the New World Order, inaugurated by the abomination of desolation in the temple of Jerusalem [Mt 24.15].

2 Thessalonians 2:3–4 (KJV 1900)
3 Let no man deceive you by any means: for that day shall not come, except there come a falling away first, and that man of sin be revealed, the son of perdition; 4 Who opposeth and exalteth himself above all that is called God, or that is worshipped; <u>so that he as God sitteth in the temple of God</u>, shewing himself that he is God.

Sodom and Gomorrah

Jerusalem *and* Babylon are connected to the sins and the judgments visited upon Sodom.

Isaiah 13:19 (KJV 1900)
19 And Babylon, the glory of kingdoms, The beauty of the Chaldees' excellency, Shall be as when God overthrew Sodom and Gomorrah. [Jer 50.40]

Revelation 11:8 (KJV 1900)
8 And their dead bodies shall lie in the street of <u>the great city</u>, which spiritually is called <u>Sodom</u> and Egypt, <u>where also our Lord was crucified</u>. [Isa 1.10]

By now it is clear that Jerusalem may possibly be the future capital of the New World Order, and the geographic center of Mystery

Babylon the Great.

Babylon the First and Last Desolator of Jerusalem

Babylon represents the first as well as the final desolation to be brought upon Jerusalem. Under Nebuchadnezzar, king of Babylon, the Times of the Gentiles began with the destruction of the city and the Temple in Jerusalem. At the end of the Times of the Gentiles, Mystery Babylon the Great will find its geographic center in Jerusalem, and the Temple will be ground zero where the Antichrist will proclaim his identity via the Abomination of Desolation.

Jerusalem Trodden Under Foot-The Times of the Gentiles Begin

> 2 Kings 25:8–11 (KJV 1900)
> 8 And in the fifth month, on the seventh day of the month, which is the nineteenth year of king Nebuchadnezzar king of Babylon, came Nebuzar-adan, captain of the guard, a servant of the king of Babylon, unto Jerusalem: 9 And he burnt the house of the LORD, and the king's house, and all the houses of Jerusalem, and every great man's house burnt he with fire. 10 And all the army of the Chaldees, that were with the captain of the guard, brake down the walls of Jerusalem round about. 11 Now the rest of the people that were left in the city, and the fugitives that fell away to the king of Babylon, with the remnant of the multitude, did Nebuzar-adan the captain of the guard carry away.

Jerusalem as the Headquarters of Antichrist: When the Times of the Gentiles are Completed

> Revelation 17:1-3, 5, 18 (KJV 1900)
> 1 And there came one of the seven angels which had the seven vials, and talked with me, saying unto me, Come hither; I will shew unto thee the judgment of the great whore that sitteth upon many waters: 3 So he carried me away in the spirit into the wilderness: and I saw a woman sit upon a scarlet coloured beast, full of names of blasphemy, having seven heads and ten horns. 5 And upon her forehead was a name written, MYSTERY, BABYLON THE GREAT, THE MOTHER OF HARLOTS AND ABOMINATIONS OF THE EARTH.18 And the woman

which thou sawest **is that great city, which reigneth over the kings of the earth**.

2 Thessalonians 2:3–4 (KJV 1900)
3 Let no man deceive you by any means: for that day shall not come, except there come a falling away first, and that man of sin be revealed, the son of perdition; 4 Who opposeth and exalteth himself above all that is called God, or that is worshipped; so that he as God sitteth in the temple of God, shewing himself that he is God.

Prophetic Typology Makes Jerusalem Headquarters of Antichrist

Daniel 11 provides a detailed prophecy regarding the conflict between two kingdoms which were formed after the death of Alexander of Greece. The Bible accurately predicts the conflict between the Seleucids, rulers of Syria and the Ptolemies, rulers of Egypt many years before it occurred. Daniel 11.21 announces the coming of a Seleucid king, whom history identifies as Antiochus IV [Epiphanes]. In many respects this man is a type of the coming Antichrist. He is vile [v21], he comes to power peaceably [v21], he will make a deceitful covenant with Israel [v23]. He will oppose the religious practice of the Jews, kill the faithful, and commit his own "abomination of desolation" in the temple [v31-33].

In Daniel 11.36, this narrative begins to describe events concerning a time yet future even to Antiochus Epiphanes.[270] None of the following events can be determined to have occurred in history, they point to a time that has yet to come.

In these events, this character called by some "the willful King" also behaves like the Antichrist. In Daniel 11.36 he closely resembles the man of sin of 2 Thessalonians 2. The rest of the chapter describes his character, practices, and wars. His headquarters appears to be the "Holy Mountain[271]" or Jerusalem.

Daniel 11:45 (KJV 1900)
45 And he shall plant the tabernacles of his palace between the seas in the glorious holy mountain; yet he shall come to his end, and none shall help him.
The events of Dan 11.35-45 have not appeared in the time of

Antiochus or in history since his times. It is likely that they will not occur until the second half of Daniel's seventieth week. The unstable political nature of the Antichrist's kingdom has been noted. Not only is rule initially distributed between ten rulers, the prophecy in Daniel 2.41-43 also describes that confederacy as consisting of the "union" of iron and clay, which mix, mingle, but do not adhere [cleave] to one another. Therefore, it is not surprising to find the wars that characterized the beginning of Danial's final prophetic week [the first four seal judgments] to spill over into the second three and one-half years, especially after the declarations of the Man of Sin at the Abomination of Desolation.

In the very next verse, the invisible spiritual influences which precipitate the rash action of the Beast are unveiled.

> Daniel 12:1 (KJV 1900)
> 1 And at that time <u>shall Michael stand up</u>, the great prince which standeth for the children of thy people: and there shall be <u>a time of trouble,</u> such as never was since there was a nation even to that same time: and at that time <u>thy people shall be delivered, every one that shall be found written in the book.</u>

This verse corresponds to the events of Revelation 12.7, until the final deliverance of redeemed Israel. The war in heaven, the expulsion of Lucifer and his angels from heaven, the appearance of the Beast upon the earth in Rev 13.1. Following this, the worldwide persecution of believing Jews and Christians and the setting up of his New World Order. Throughout this time, God will supernaturally protect and defend redeemed Israel.

The establishment of the *military* headquarters in the "glorious land" and the "glorious holy mountain" [Dan 11.41, 45] sets the stage for his final confrontation with the nations at the very moment when Christ returns to the earth [Chapter 29-The End of the Antichrist]. Daniel 11.41 identifies the "glorious land" by its proximity to Edom, Moab, and Ammon. Jerusalem is already the *administrative* center of the New World Order, led by the Prime Minister/False Prophet and the *spiritual* capital by virtue of the Antichrist's takeover of the Temple.

The Testimony of Jesus

Revelation 18:24 (KJV 1900)
24 And in her [Babylon the Great-Rev 18.2] was found <u>the blood of prophets</u>, and of saints, And of <u>all</u> that were slain upon the earth.

Matthew 23:34–37 (KJV 1900)
34 Wherefore, behold, I send unto you prophets, and wise men, and scribes: and some of them ye shall kill and crucify; and some of them shall ye scourge in your synagogues, and persecute them from city to city: 35 <u>That upon you [Jerusalem-v37]</u> may come <u>all the righteous blood shed upon the earth,</u> from the blood of righteous Abel unto the blood of Zacharias son of Barachias, whom ye slew between the temple and the altar. 36 Verily I say unto you, All these things shall come upon this generation. 37 <u>O Jerusalem, Jerusalem, thou that killest the prophets, and stonest them which are sent unto thee,</u> how often would I have gathered thy children together, even as a hen gathereth her chickens under her wings, and ye would not!

The statement in Revelation 18 is spoken regarding the great city Babylon.[272] The statement in Matthew 23 is spoken by Jesus against Jerusalem. Again, the two cities are merged in this condemnation that is connected to Mystery Babylon and the Antichrist.

Revelation 17:6 (KJV 1900)
6 And I saw the woman <u>drunken with the blood of the saints, and with the blood of the martyrs of Jesus</u>: and when I saw her, I wondered with great admiration. [Dan 7:21, 25]

It appears that the "great city" of Revelation 17.18 is ***Jerusalem***, under the authority of the Antichrist in the days of the Beast kingdom. This fact is a significant aspect of the "mystery" that is Babylon the Great. In Lucifer's quest to be as the Most High, he desecrates that which God has made holy: *marriage*, in the garden of Eden; *family*, in the death of Abel; *government*, at Babel; and Israel, in the last days when Jerusalem becomes synonymous with the devil's kingdom as the capital of the New World Order.

The Destruction of the Babylon the Great

> Revelation 16:17–19 (KJV 1900)
> ¹⁷ And the seventh angel poured out his vial into the air; and there came a great voice out of the temple of heaven, from the throne, saying, It is done. ¹⁸ And there were voices, and thunders, and lightnings; and there was a great earthquake, such as was not since men were upon the earth, so mighty an earthquake, *and* so great. ¹⁹ And <u>the great city was divided into three parts, and the cities of the nations fell</u>: and <u>great Babylon came in remembrance before God</u>, to give unto her the cup of the wine of the fierceness of his wrath.

Today, the great enabler of globalism is the rapid development of microprocessor based digital technologies. International information networks make instantaneous communications, commerce, travel, and military operations possible. These capabilities will be even more efficient in the future.

> "Kurzweil's Law (aka "the law of accelerating returns")
> *In an evolutionary process, positive feedback increases order exponentially. A correlate is that the "returns" of an evolutionary process (such as the speed, cost-effectiveness, or overall "power" of a process) increase exponentially over time — both for biology and technology."*[273]

> Daniel 12:4 (KJV 1900)
> 4 But thou, O Daniel, shut up the words, and seal the book, even to the time of the end: many shall run to and fro, and knowledge shall be increased.

In the time of the New World Order, the ability to organize worldwide control of all commerce and to project military power will be no less than it is today and probably much greater. Compared to the times of the apostle John it will be child's play for the False Prophet to manage a one world government, religion, and economy from Jerusalem. He will manage the ability of the world population to buy and sell from the headquarters of the Antichrist's kingdom with technology that is already available today. Big data: enriched data profiles of every person on earth, containing real time details about family [genealogy], social networks, finances, medical history, personal preferences, and location will maximize that control. These profiles are already in existence for a very high percentage of the world's population.

The earthquake and hail that occurs in the final plague of Revelation 16 will deal a catastrophic blow to these networks, ending the reign of terrestrial Babylon, just as the ten kings will have brought a recent end to ecclesiastical Babylon [Rev 17.16-18]. The judgment of the earthquake and hail do not come from the political leadership of the world, authorized by the Beast, but from God himself.

In Revelation 16.17-19, the result of this judgment is described as "great Babylon came into remembrance before God, to give unto her the cup of the wine of the fierceness of his wrath." The clauses pertaining to the "city" and the "cities" [Rev 16.19] are separated by a colon[274] from the descriptor "great Babylon" in the KJV. In the description of the devastation caused by the plague, both the "great city" as well as the "cities of the nations" were severely damaged or "fell." Both are called parts of "great Babylon."

As earlier postulated, it appears that "great Babylon" will include both the "cities of the nations" as well as "that great city," Jerusalem. It appears that the destruction of the "great city" may have been triggered by the murder and resurrection of the two witnesses of Revelation 11. These witnesses begin their ministry in sackcloth at the beginning of the desolation of Jerusalem by Antichrist [2 Th 2.3-4; Rev 11.1-3]. They are killed at the end of the designated 1260 [Rev 11.2-3] days which would correspond to the end of the forty-two months of the second half of Daniel's 70th week.

> Revelation 11:7–8, 12-13 (KJV 1900)
> 7 <u>And when they shall have finished their testimony,</u> [at the end of the 1260 days or 42 months] the beast that ascendeth out of the bottomless pit shall make war against them, and shall overcome them, and kill them. 8 And their dead bodies *shall lie* in the street of the great city, which spiritually is called Sodom and Egypt, where also our Lord was crucified. 12 And they heard a great voice from heaven saying unto them, Come up hither. And they ascended up to heaven in a cloud; and their enemies beheld them. 13 <u>And the same hour was there a great earthquake,</u> and the tenth part of the city fell, and in the earthquake were slain of men seven thousand: and the remnant were affrighted, and gave glory to the God of heaven.

Revelation 16 recounts this earthquake with more details.

Revelation 16:18–21 (KJV 1900)
[18] And there were voices, and thunders, and lightnings; and <u>there was a great earthquake</u>, such as was not since men were upon the earth, so mighty an earthquake, *and* so great. [19] And the great city was divided into three parts, and the cities of the nations fell: and great Babylon came in remembrance before God, to give unto her the cup of the wine of the fierceness of his wrath. [20] And every island fled away, and the mountains were not found. [21] And there fell upon men a great hail out of heaven, *every stone* about the weight of a talent: and men blasphemed God because of the plague of the hail; for the plague thereof was exceeding great.

The consequence of this final earthquake of history is the geological disruption of the planet itself. It will result in the fall of terrestrial Babylon: its information-based power of world control and the subsequent failure of markets and financial systems. This is why the kings of the earth will wail [Rev 18.9]. The city will be divided into three parts by the earthquake with significant loss of life. What the earthquake did not destroy, the plague of hail will, undoubtedly killing many more in Jerusalem. The combination of these events with the military action against Israel and Jerusalem described in Zechariah 12.1-3, the Armageddon Campaign, will reduce the population to the remnant that will be rescued by the returning Christ.[275]

In or just prior to the Millennium, the entire city of Jerusalem will be rebuilt within an enlarged Israel that is reapportioned to the tribes of Jacob [Eze 40 sq.].

22
Two Aspects of Babylon-The Woman and the Beast: Revelation 17

Revelation 17:1–5 (KJV 1900) 1 And there came one of the seven angels which had the seven vials, and talked with me, saying unto me, Come hither; I will shew unto thee the judgment of the great whore that sitteth upon many waters: 2 With whom the kings of the earth have committed fornication, and the inhabitants of the earth have been made drunk with the wine of her fornication. 3 So he carried me away in the spirit into the wilderness: and I saw a woman sit upon a scarlet coloured beast, full of names of blasphemy, having seven heads and ten horns. 4 And the woman was arrayed in purple and scarlet colour, and decked with gold and precious stones and pearls, having a golden cup in her hand full of abominations and filthiness of her fornication: 5 And upon her forehead was a name written, MYSTERY, BABYLON THE GREAT, THE MOTHER OF HARLOTS AND ABOMINATIONS OF THE EARTH.

We have discussed the spirit of antichrist as a spiritual agenda [the Mystery of Iniquity] which has political implications for the world. These spiritual and political agendas are moving towards an end game that culminates in the world system dominated by the son of Lucifer, the Man of Sin, the Antichrist.

Under the Antichrist, the global organization imagined in the Satanic rebellion of eternity past takes concrete form. Leadership by deception evolves into open blasphemy. Although there is nothing mysterious about iniquity in itself; the mystery lies in the fact that Iniquity or Lawlessness is an *organized system* with specific short and long-term objectives. Chiefly, the Mystery of Iniquity opposes the Mystery of Godliness [1 Tim 3.16] by working to advance the doctrine that Jesus is not the Christ. We have also demonstrated that since the incarnation, the Mystery of Iniquity coincides with the spirit of Antichrist [1 Jn 2.16-23; 4.3].

The Beast Revisited[276]

In Revelation 17 there is a woman riding the beast. This beast with whom we have become familiar in the Book of Daniel and Revelation 13, now appears with another personality in close association.

> "Revelation 17 represents one of several pictures of the Mystery of Iniquity in the scriptures. Each element of this conspiracy is represented in this picture: the demonic character of the Mystery of Iniquity [the beast itself], the procession of empires [the heads], the future political system under the fourth kingdom [the horns], the Antichrist [one of the horns] and Mystery Babylon, the spiritual and ecclesiastical leadership of the movement [the woman]." p. 119

The beast is scarlet as is the clothing of the Harlot, Mystery Babylon. Scarlet is identified with religious authority [blood, sacrifice, covenant, remission of sin]. In the New Testament it was the color of the robe placed upon the beaten and disfigured Jesus [Mt 27.28]. The color represents both sin as well as that which covers or removes sin. The beast here, as the Dragon in Revelation 12, is red, symbolic of his association with Lucifer. Hence, red or scarlet identify the beast and the Dragon with sin, transgression and with religious authority, illegitimately assumed. The beast is not the devil himself. The beast [and harlot] are Satan's means by which the world is subjected to his rule and his worship. Thus, these symbols [the scarlet beast, the Harlot's royal purple, and scarlet clothing] signify the character and the scope of his rule over the world system that has yet to fully recognize him as God.

Consistent with Lucifer's claim to godhood [Isa 14.14], the beast is covered with names of blasphemy. These are likely titles of exaltation and divine privilege but are only names of blasphemy from the viewpoint of the Lord [Mark 2.7].

As seen in chapter 13 of Revelation, the beast from the sea has seven heads which identify this final kingdom with the Gentile world kingdoms which preceded it in history, [Egypt/Cush, Assyria, Babylon, Medo-Persia, Greece, Rome and the seventh kingdom represented by the ten horns].

The Harlot-Spiritual Babylon: The Key to Gentile History

Here in Revelation 17, there is a woman who, as we have already seen, has spiritual and geographic interpretations. The harlot represents a system which commits abominations but purports to be the solution to sin. Lucifer claims a spiritual legitimacy that is, in his own mind, superior to that of the Lord. Although his rebellion is an abomination, he represents himself as a moral improvement over Jehovah, whom he implies is a hypocrite.

This woman is supported and is conveyed by the beast. It is likely that she is also directing the beast. They are at work together and for a long time share the same interests. Before we begin a more detailed investigation of the activities of this woman, here is a description of Mystery Babylon from an earlier chapter.

> "Like the Mystery of Iniquity, Mystery Babylon is a *spiritual construct*, but it is primarily concerned with the *management of the procession of Gentile empires* which follow the Flood. Mystery Babylon is characterized by the symbiosis of Church and State, it is *the religious state* [Rev 17.1-3]. It is *ecumenical*, acknowledging the validity of every false religious concept while denying and persecuting the one true Church of Jesus Christ revealed in scripture. It is *demonic*, its ritual and power based upon the invoking and evoking of fallen spirits. The *Mystery Religions* are the repositories of its spiritual heritage and science. *Mystery Babylon is the thinking of Satan applied to religion, government, economics, and social organization.*" p. 56

FUNCTIONS OF MYSTERY BABYLON	
She [Mystery Babylon] is a religious force, the mother or source of false religion	Rev 14.8; 17.5;18.3, 9, 23; 19.2
She is global in her operations and influence:	Rev 17.1,2,15; 18:3, 9,11,23
She influences world politics:	Rev 17.2, 15; 18.3, 9
She is critical to international commerce:	Rev 17:1-2, 15; 18: 3, 9, 11-19
She is a key actor in genocides, especially of believers	Rev 16.6; 17.6; 18:20, 24; 19.2

Figure 10: Functions of Mystery Babylon

Women as Symbols of Doctrinal Systems

In scripture, Babylon is sometimes referred to as a woman.[277] Women in the New Testament sometimes symbolize systems of doctrine or an entire spiritual class of individuals.

WOMAN/SYMBOL	MEANING	REFERENCE
The Bride/Wife	The Church	2 Cor 11.2; Eph 5.25-32
Woman Hiding Leaven	The Kingdom of Heaven	Mt 13.13
The Widow	Jews dead to the Law [their husband] and married to Christ.	Rom 7.1-4
The Bondwoman and the Freewoman	The Bondwoman: Hagar, Mt Sinai, the Law, Jerusalem below. The Freewoman: Sarah, the Promise, Jerusalem above.	Gal 4.22-26
Jezebel	A system of false doctrine	Rev 2.20-24
The Pregnant Woman	Israel	Rev 12
The Whore	Mystery Babylon	Rev 17

Figure 11: Women as Doctrinal Systems

Mystery Babylon represents a system of false worship which opposes God according to the spirit of antichrist. This religion is the secret factor that unites and enables the components of Satan's world system.

WOMAN OF REVELATION 12	WOMAN OF REVELATION 17	NOTES
Hides in the wilderness	Thrives in the wilderness	Relation to this world
Persecuted by Dragon	Supported by Beast	Relation to Lucifer
Clothed in the sun, moon	Clothed with purple, scarlet, pearls and jewels	Celestial as opposed to earthly honor
Carrying a child	The mother of harlots	Relation to truth
A garland of stars on her head	Blasphemy on her forehead	Relation to the plan of God

Figure 12: Women of Revelation 12 and 17

[Concept adapted from Pink: "The Antichrist"[278]]

The Great Harlot, Mystery Babylon, is critical to understanding Gentile history. Revelation 17, 18 reveals that this woman is intertwined with every aspect of the Satan's earthly operations.

She [Mystery Babylon] is a religious force, the mother or source of false religion: Rev 14.8; 17.5;18.3, 9, 23; 19.2

Revelation 17:4–5 (KJV 1900)
4 And the woman was arrayed in purple and scarlet colour, and decked with gold and precious stones and pearls, having a golden cup in her hand full of abominations and filthiness of her fornication: 5 And upon her forehead was a name written, MYSTERY, BABYLON THE GREAT, THE MOTHER OF HARLOTS AND ABOMINATIONS OF THE EARTH.

This woman is identified with the beast, identified with the earth. She is wearing the wardrobe of political [royal] and religious power and influence [purple and scarlet]. She is not a politician, but she wields political influence. She is a religious force, but her domain is not heavenly but earthly [James 3.15]. Note that although she appears a primarily a religious influence, she is *not* associated with the False Prophet.

The Name Mystery Babylon

The title Mystery Babylon conveys that this woman is a symbol of a spiritual power.

Spiritual Babylon, the Harlot, is the religious aspect of the Satan's post flood world system including its doctrine, ecclesiastical structure, and strategies of world control through these means. The harlot entices both kings and kingdoms into God-rejecting idolatry in service to Satan [Jer 51.7; Rev 17.2, 4]. Mystery Babylon in this sense is the Greater and Lesser Mystery religions[279] which represent the distilled essence of Lucifer's thinking and plan.

As we have already seen, Mystery Babylon has always sought to consolidate spiritual authority. Outside of the true faith revealed in the scriptures, there is only one other religion, [280] expressed under various philosophical concepts and cultural motifs. These world religions might correspond to the Lesser Mysteries that are reserved for the consumption of the masses [symbolically identified as "the wine of her fornication" Rev 17.2].[281] The New World Order will be defined by the general revelation of the Greater Mystery [symbolically described as fornication (Rev 17.2)], whose center will be the Antichrist, the Son of Perdition. Satan tolerates "religious diversity" because, apart from Christ, there is no actual religious diversity, only one Christ rejecting faith, with a few who worship according to knowledge and a great many who worship in ignorant darkness.

The *ecumenical spirit is the end of the Lesser Mysteries*: an organizational unity under which is assembled the Babel of the religions of the world. The distillation of the doctrine of all these faiths are the doctrines of demons [1 Tim 4.1]. This is the only logically possible reduction since all competing theologies to the Mystery of Godliness [1 Tim 3.16] exist under the auspices of Satan.

Spiritual Babylon created terrestrial Babylon, which is the schema for every post flood empire. It is through these earthly empires that spiritual Babylon controls world affairs by both secular and supernatural means, chief of which is through the control of religion.

> ➤ The Babylon *of Genesis 11* represents the unification of all people under a single social, religious, and political organization that is opposed to the commands of God. Even today, agreement among a group of people is expressed by saying that they all "speak the same language."
> ➤ The Babylon *of Nebuchadnezzar* required that every faith submit itself to the state religion of Babylon and the Image that represented this system of belief, under the pain of death. What

put the three Hebrews into the furnace of fire was not that they practiced the Law of Moses, but that they refused to subsume Jehovah under the Babylonian pantheon.

- ➤ Mystery Babylon *of tomorrow* will give way to the New World Order in its final form. Mystery Babylon will be destroyed in conjunction with the movement which will eliminate all faiths except that of the pure worship of Lucifer. The secret faith of the mystery religions and secret societies will no longer be a mystery and competing as well as complementary religious systems will be eliminated for the exclusive worship of Lucifer to be realized [Revelation 17.16-18].
- ➤ Mystery Babylon *of today* is the organizing principle of *ecumenical* religion. The purpose of the Lesser Mysteries is purification. The purification to which the world is currently being subjected is the removal of belief in the scriptures and the moral order that they establish.

Ecumenism seeks to subject all to the idolatry of spiritual unity for the apparent purpose of service to humanity. This unity is *artificial*, because the Mystery of Godliness will not be reconciled to the Mystery of Lawlessness. This unity is *powerless*, because it preserves all the prejudices and oppressions that have always existed among men. It could not do otherwise. This unity is *perilous*, because it promotes that there is a good that exists outside of God's Word and that God's Plan may be achieved by the violation of His Word. In this, the ecumenical Church becomes the formal vehicle of the lies of the serpent in Eden and the victory of the creed of Babel.

> Proverbs 16:25 (KJV 1900)
> 25 There is a way that seemeth right unto a man, But the end thereof are the ways of death.

Mystery Babylon is the Mother of Harlots:

Harlotry or spiritual adultery is the name that the Bible gives to one who claims allegiance to God, but serves other, false gods.

Judges 2:16–17 (KJV 1900)
16 Nevertheless the LORD raised up judges, which delivered

them out of the hand of those that spoiled them. 17 And yet they would not hearken unto their judges, <u>but they went a whoring after other gods</u>, and bowed themselves unto them: they turned quickly out of the way which their fathers walked in, obeying the commandments of the LORD; but they did not so.

The theology of Mystery Babylon is the source code for all systems of thought by which Satan administers this world system. Spiritual harlotry is related to deception and betrayal just as its marital counterpart.

Marital adultery is a married person partaking of the love of another to whom he is not married. The theology of Mystery Babylon teaches that you can have Jesus and idols, Jesus and false doctrine, Jesus and pagan religion, Jesus and the Lodge, Jesus and sin, Jesus, and the ecumenical association. This is harlotry, spiritual adultery. Spiritual adultery weakens the spiritual influence of God's people, resulting in the loss of the witness which calibrates the conscience of the unbelieving world [Mt 5.13-16; 1 Pet 2.12]. The believer has two gospel witnesses: the witness of his *lips*; and that of his Christian *life*. It is the dual witness of the believer that is the invisible influence that stabilizes society.

The immediate effect of spiritual adultery [harlotry, whoredom] is the weakening and destruction of the human institutions which support civilization. Human free will is decayed by various categories of addiction; marriage and family are destroyed by fornication, adultery, divorce, and gender confusion. With the loss of the family, it is inevitable that government is undermined. Government cannot be stronger than the families which comprise the nation.

Isaiah 14:12 (KJV 1900)
12 How art thou fallen from heaven, O Lucifer, son of the morning! How art thou cut down to the ground, which didst <u>weaken the nations</u>!

The longer-term effect of spiritual adultery is the judgment of God. This judgment comes in gradually increasing levels of intensity until, if there is no repentance, the offending communities or nation are excised from the midst of the nations by terminal judgment.[282]

Mystery Babylon promotes a breakdown of the systems designed by God for the reasonably healthy function of civilization ["*the inhabitants of the earth have been made drunk with the wine of her fornication*"

Rev 17.2b]. For example, Mystery Babylon causes the malfunction of God's systems of morality and conscience for unbelievers. Massive degeneracy results from this failure resulting in social and political disaster. *Current geopolitical circumstances result from prior spiritual conditions.*

The presence of the Church, the Body of Christ, exercises a restraining effect upon this destructive tendency in society. However, as history has demonstrated, the Church itself is not immune to "the wine of her fornication." The ultimate victory of the Church does not mean that *your* local church will not apostatize [Rev 2.4-5], nor does it mean that your nation will endure forever. When believers, weakened by false teaching and ecumenism, are unwilling to stand for biblical truth and against evil, then the days of a nation are numbered.[283] It is the spiritual function of the Church, in its witness to the gospel and of personal righteousness that serves as a secondary source[284] of calibration for the consciences of the unbelievers. The failure of any generation of believers to achieve and maintain spiritual maturity places a nation, and many of its Churches, in a dire situation.

Symbol of Harlotry: The Gold Cup

The gold cup was used in the Babylonian Mysteries to provide the candidate for initiation with an intoxicating and stupefying beverage that prepared the initiate for the depravities and desecrations to follow.[285] The outcome of these initiations was demon possession and the ultimate acknowledgement, under various cultural forms and symbols, of Lucifer as the true God. This same golden cup is here present in the same significance. The Harlot is a representative, an employee of the devil. Fornication with her is to engage in a worship[286] that unlocks the riches and privileges that Satan can provide.

> Luke 4:5–7 (KJV 1900)
> 5 And the devil, taking him up into an high mountain, shewed unto him all the kingdoms of the world in a moment of time. 6 And the devil said unto him, All this power will I give thee, and the glory of them: <u>for that is delivered unto me; and to whomsoever I will I give it. 7 If thou therefore wilt worship me, all shall be thine.</u>

The Bible recognizes the existence of the Babylonian Mysteries.

Jeremiah 51:7 (KJV 1900)

7 Babylon hath been a golden cup in the LORD's hand, That made all the earth drunken: The nations have drunken of her wine; Therefore the nations are mad.

In Jeremiah, within the context of a prediction of judgment against Babylon, God uses the symbolism of the golden cup to remind the world of His use of Babylon as a golden cup of judgment to Israel and the nations of the world during the 6th century B.C. Rather than "enlightenment" and privilege, that cup brought trembling and violent destruction to the nations and to Israel in the time of Nebuchadnezzar. The idolatry represented by that cup was a chief reason for the implementation of that judgment [Jer 50.38].

Babylon is associated with gold. The kingdom of Babylon under Nebuchadnezzar was prophetically called the "head of gold" [Dan 2.38]. Babylon was the "golden city" [Isa 14.4]. It was golden not only in its prolific use of gold in construction, but that it is the prototype Gentile kingdom upon which future kingdoms would be built. Babylon is the spiritual name of the overarching mechanism [Mystery Babylon] by which history has been directed by Satan. Gold is also connected to the riches of Babylon. These riches were a means of seducing the kings of the earth [politics] as well as their merchants [commerce]. Then as now, gold facilitated the seduction of some and the oppression of many others:

Isaiah 14:4 (KJV 1900)
4 That thou shalt take up this proverb against the king of Babylon, and say, How hath the oppressor ceased! the golden city ceased!

Revelation 18:15–16 (KJV 1900)
15 The merchants of these things, which were made rich by her, Shall stand afar off for the fear of her torment, Weeping and wailing, 16 And saying, Alas, alas, that great city, That was clothed in fine linen, and purple, and scarlet, And decked with gold, and precious stones, and pearls!

Revelation 18:23 (KJV 1900)
23b ... For thy merchants were the great men of the earth; For by thy sorceries were all nations deceived.

The enticements of Mystery Babylon to the kings of the earth and to their subjects, to which the cup and its contents pertain, are not random invitations to sin, but elements of a complete system of fallen, demonic religion [Eze 8]. The *kings of the earth* have for millennia been initiated into culturally distinct versions of the Mysteries. They are said to have *committed fornication* with Mystery Babylon [Rev18.3, 9]. This is the conscious and intimate association with the worship of Lucifer. Fornication is, by definition, conscious, intimate, and illicit. The kings of the earth are generally involved in this worship through secret societies and the various forms of the mystery religions. It is not necessary that every single sovereign be initiated, but that the intergenerational heritage of the kingdoms of this world be so engaged. An examination of these kingdoms will reveal this involvement. This reality is difficult for many to accept, but the fact of Satan's spiritual rule of this world and its compatibility with the indwelling sin nature of man makes this reality not only possible, but necessary.[287] Furthermore, the Revelation is plainly saying that the "kings of the earth" are engaged in spiritual adultery with the Harlot.

The people of these nations, on the other hand, have been intoxicated by "the wine of her fornication."[288] The public is typically not in conscious cooperation with Satan. The public *is* necessarily engaged with his demonic world system which provides many pleasures and rewards that appeal to the fallen natures of men [1 Jn 2.15-16]. Thus indirectly, the public supports and ratifies this God dishonoring system while at varying degrees of consciousness regarding the existence of the system itself.

If the spiritual fornication of the kings of the earth means that they are engaged in the secret worship of Lucifer and seek to advance his program in the world, then the wine of this fornication is the intoxication of everyone else with the philosophies, promises and pleasures that will lead to the demolishing of the current order and the creation of a new kind of sinner for the coming new world. This wine of fornication is the existing world system that has been constructed to manufacture the kind of society and people that will eventually assimilate into the New World Order.

There is a religious idea that is hidden in the pursuits and priorities promoted by Mystery Babylon. On its surface it appears to be the promotion of human freedom under the rubric of "do as thou wilt." People can easily believe that what they are doing with their lives is their own choice and that they are the masters of their fate. To an extent this is true. However, just as in the case of Eve, humanity's rejection of God and His wisdom has perverted their understanding so that *they cannot see the logical consequences* of the spiritual drunkenness to which they have succumbed. Every temptation and indulgence of the world is designed to pervert the judgment and to win allegiance to that mode of thinking which will be used to introduce and achieve the worship of Satan's man, the Antichrist. An example of how this process of intoxication operates will be demonstrated in the coming pages.

Thus, the golden cup represents the initiation and matriculation of the kings of the earth to the greater mysteries, whereby conscious participation in the deep things of Satan [Rev 2.24] is obtained. This secret religion is a chief means by which the leadership of the nations by Mystery Babylon is maintained. At the same time, this secret religion is the fount of harlotries and abominations whereby the common people are spiritually seduced and intoxicated. All in all, this spiritual influence is the invisible fabric of the nations. The Bible refers to this spiritual structure as "the world" in Romans 12.2

> Romans 12:2 (KJV 1900)
> 2 And be not conformed to this world: but be ye transformed by the renewing of your mind, that ye may prove what is that good, and acceptable, and perfect, will of God.

"The word "world" is aiōn (αἰων), which Trench defines as follows:

> "All that floating mass of thoughts, opinions, maxims, speculations, hopes, impulses, aims, aspirations, at any time current in the world, which it may be impossible to seize and accurately define, but which constitute a most real and effective power, being the moral, or immoral atmosphere which at every moment of our lives we inhale, again inevitably to exhale,— all this is included in the aiōn (αἰων) (age), which is, as Bengel has expressed it, the subtle informing spirit of the kosmos (κοσμος) or world of men who are living alienated and apart from God."[289]

Abominations

> Revelation 17:4 (KJV 1900)
> 4 And the woman was arrayed in purple and scarlet colour, and decked with gold and precious stones and pearls, having a golden cup in her hand full of abominations and filthiness of her fornication:

Because of this loss of moral direction in the masses, and the hidden Luciferianism of the ruling class, spiritual harlotry leads to *abominations*. An abomination is [NT: 946] "a loathsome thing because of its stench." The word is often associated with idolatry. The person who is unrestrained by the law of God will engage in the most extreme forms of debauchery and violence without regard for moral standards or the dictates of conscience [Rom 1]. Thus, not only is Mystery Babylon *itself* an abomination because of its promotion of idolatry through direct appeals to the worship of Lucifer [Mt 4.9; Rev 2.24], it produces abominable acts in its devotees by seducing them away from the moral dictates of conscience and the scriptures. She is truly the mother of harlots and of abominations.

> Ezekiel 16:20–21 (KJV 1900)
> 20 Moreover thou hast taken thy sons and thy daughters, whom thou hast borne unto me, and these hast thou sacrificed unto them to be devoured. Is this of thy harlotdoms a small matter, 21 That thou hast slain my children, and delivered them to cause them to pass through the fire for them?

> 2 Kings 17:16–17 (KJV 1900)
> 16 And they left all the commandments of the LORD their God, and made them molten images, even two calves, and made a grove, and worshipped all the host of heaven, and served Baal. 17 And they caused their sons and their daughters to pass through the fire, and used divination and enchantments, and sold themselves to do evil in the sight of the LORD, to provoke him to anger.

The Law of Moses prescribed what constituted an abomination before the Lord. Some of these things were ceremonial and are no longer applicable under the dispensation of the Church. Others remain abominations, transcending the advancing ages of divine administration. Still others remain abominations, but the civil penalties have been discontinued during subsequent ages [e.g., Idolatry]

Abomination Cited in Old Testament	Limited to Law of Israel [Or, subject to legal penalty then]	Transcending Age of Israel
Improper treatment or consumption of Animal Sacrifices	Lev 7.18; 19.7; 20.25; Dt 17.1	NO
Touching or eating unclean animals or things	Lev 7.21; 11; Dt 14.3; Isa 65.4; 66.17; Eze 4.14; Zech 9.7;	NO
Homosexuality	Lev 18.22; 20.13; Dt 22.5; 1Kings 14.24	Mt 19.4; Rom 1.26,27; 1 Cor 6.9; 1 Tim 1.10; Jude 7
Idolatrous images	Ex 20.4-5; Dt 7.25, 26; 27.15 [secret worship]; 29.17; 32.16; 1Kings 21.26; 2Kings 21.11 [Manasseh]; 2Ch 15.8; Isa 44.19; Eze 6.9; 7.20; Eze 14.6; 20.7-8;	Acts 19.26; Rom 1.23; Rev 9.20
Human sacrifice	Dt 12.31; 2Ch 28.3; Jer 32.35	The substitutionary death of Christ obviates the need for men to be sacrificed for their sins or the sins of others Rom 5.6-8; 1 Cor 15.3; 1 Pet 3.18
Idolatry/False Gods/False Religion	Dt 13.13-17; 17.2-7; Mal 2.11; 1Kings 11.5-7 [Solomon]; Eze 8;	Gal.5.20; Col 3.5; 1 Cor 10.14; 1 Pet 4.3
Offerings from proceeds of prostitution	Dt 23.18	1 Cor 6.15-18
Divorce and remarriage of former wife after she married a 2nd time	Dt 24.4	This prohibition is made stricter by Christ. Mt 5.32; 19.9; 1 Cor 7.10-11
Dishonesty in business [terms of trade, weights and measures]	Dt 25.13-16; Prov 11.1; 20.10, 23	1 Cor 10.24, 31
Witchcraft	2 Kings 23.24	Gal 5.20; Rev 9.21
Lists of Abominations		Proverbs 6:16–19 [Proud look [Prov 16.15] lying tongue, feet that run to do mischief, hands shedding innocent blood, hearts that devise wicked thoughts [Prov 15.26], lips that spread discord among brethren.]
Wickedness in Government	Prov 16.12; 17.15	Ps 94.20; Isa 10.1; Rev 13.15-17
Usury	Eze 18.13; Dt 23.20	NO
Adultery, Incest	Eze 22.11; 33.26;	Mt 5.27-28; Gal 5.19

Figure 13: Abominations in Scripture[290]

Understanding Abominations

The first principle in understanding the concept of abomination is that it is the Word of God that defines what constitutes it. Society does not determine what is abominable, God does. Because Lucifer denies the right of God to rule the universe, he is utterly opposed to divine standards and exalts that which is abominable. Therefore, Satan seeks to progressively overturn divine standards in society [he "weakens the nations" Isa 14.12]. The mystery initiations introduce the follower of the mystery cults into the "deep things of Satan" which constitute even greater abominations, some of which are too abominable to admit to the public due to their great wickedness, illegality, and their express association with the devil in the minds of the public.

Much of the extremes of cruelty and atrocity upon the earth today have been committed in service to the current manifestation of Mystery Babylon in the world. A surprising amount of crime in the drug trade and human trafficking are in direct service to the Initiates of Mystery Babylon. The existence of perpetual warfare is motivated by service to the geopolitical aims of Mystery Babylon but blamed upon the God of the Bible.

Abomination, or desecration is the spiritual center of Luciferian religion. Abomination perfectly represents the attitude and objectives of the devil in the Fall of both angels and men. It puts to the lie the concept that Satan is concerned about the needs and aspirations of any of God's creation in heaven or upon the earth.

> John 8:44 (KJV 1900)
> Ye are of your father the devil, and the lusts of your father ye will do. He was a murderer from the beginning, and abode not in the truth, because there is no truth in him. When he speaketh a lie, he speaketh of his own: for he is a liar, and the father of it.

> John 10:10 (KJV 1900)
> The thief cometh not, but for to steal, and to kill, and to destroy: I am come that they might have life, and that they might have it more abundantly.

Abomination is depicted in the image of Mystery Babylon of Revelation 17. She is, among other things, a system of doctrine predicated upon The Lie that Jesus is not God. Her kingdom is of this world. She is the ancient servant of the evil one, who rules the world as his proxy until her time has come to an end.

As the source of ***all*** false religion in the world, Mystery Babylon is the expression of the mind of Lucifer who told Eve that God could not be trusted, that he [the devil] was the source of both secret wisdom and spiritual evolution into godhood. Mystery Babylon sponsors every system of religion that seeks to divert men and women away from the Word of God by both near-truths and outright falsehoods. Regardless of the outward trappings and pronouncements of false religions, at their center, they *must* conceal abominations, for this is the foundational truth and reality of the character of their Mother. In view of this, the unwillingness of believers to confront and expose false religion, especially false religion labeled as Christian, is capitulation to Mystery Babylon and spiritual defeat.

Revelation 17:5 (KJV 1900)
5 And upon her forehead was a name written, MYSTERY, BABYLON THE GREAT, THE <u>MOTHER</u> OF HARLOTS <u>AND ABOMINATIONS</u> OF THE EARTH.

Richard G. Walker

23
The Woman and the Beast: The World Church

An Example of Religious Babylon: The Ecumenical Movement

Satan's objective in his war against God is the establishment of his own rule over the heavens and the earth [Isa 14.13-14; 2 Th 2.4]. An important element of his multifaceted strategy to accomplish this end is the creation of a single World Order, let's call it the World Order Phase One, which will require the membership and cooperation of all earthly secular as well as spiritual organizations, regardless of their systems of belief. World Order Phase One will be united upon the basis of an ecumenical amalgamation of nations and peoples. Its true role, however, will be to gather the unbelieving yet religious world as the first cohort of converts when Lucifer will be revealed to them as the true god they must worship. Mystery Babylon has always influenced society towards such an end, which will not be entirely successful until the Body of Christ is removed from the earth.

Ecumenical

"Ecumenical," according to Webster's dictionary, means "pertaining to the entire inhabited earth; universal in extent." The "ecumenical movement" began within Protestant Christianity, expanded through organizations like the Federal and then World Council of Churches, and now, through grassroots clergy associations, is understood as a complete interfaith dialogue.[291]

Ecumenism

"The word ecumenism is derived from the Greek words oikoumenē ("the inhabited world") and oikos ("house") and can be traced from the commands, promises, and prayers of Jesus. After the International Missionary Conference held at Edinburgh in 1910, Protestants began to use the term ecumenism to describe the gathering of missionary, evangelistic, service, and unitive forces. During and after the second Vatican Council (1962–65), Roman Catholics used ecumenism to refer to the renewal of the whole life of the Church, undertaken to make it more responsive to "separated Churches" and to the needs of the world."[292]

The modern version of ecumenism began in the early 20th century and was influenced by a practical ecumenism in the mission fields where missionaries of different Christian backgrounds cooperated for the sake of efficiency and the perception of unity before the objects of their evangelistic efforts. The 20th century movement was helped by the success of older, worldwide ministries like the YMCA, missions' societies, and temperance organizations, which were ecumenical in their emphasis.

The dominant idea was that Christian *service to society* was a better gospel witness than uniformity of Christian doctrine. Consequently, there was a focus upon the implementation of the Social Gospel via the early ecumenical groups, which emphasis continues to this very day.[293]

The Social Gospel:

"The Social Gospel, a liberal movement within American Protestantism that attempted to apply biblical teachings to problems associated with industrialization. It took form during the latter half of the 19th cent. under the leadership of Washington Gladden and Walter Rauschenbusch, who feared the isolation of religion from the working class. They believed in social progress and the essential goodness of humanity. The views of the Social Gospel movement were given formal expression in 1908 when the Federal Council of the Churches of Christ in America adopted what was later called "the social creed of the Churches." Advocated in the creed were the abolition of child labor, better working conditions for women, one day off during the week, and the right of every worker to a living wage."[294]

The ecumenical movement has also been influenced by an incorrect interpretation of Jn 17.11, 21-23.

John 17:11 (KJV 1900)
11 And now I am no more in the world, but these are in the world, and I come to thee. Holy Father, keep through thine own name those whom thou hast given me, <u>that they may be one</u>, as we are.

John 17:21–23 (KJV 1900)
21 <u>That they all may be one</u>; as thou, Father, art in me, and I in thee, that they also may be one in us: <u>that the world may believe</u> that thou hast sent me. 22 And the glory which thou gavest me I have given them; that they may be one, even as we are one: 23 I in them, and thou in me, that they may be made perfect in one; and that the world may know that thou hast sent me, and hast loved them, as thou hast loved me.

The faulty interpretation of these verses *as a call for visible, organizational unity* is given as a reason for the effort to establish a worldwide visible Christian Church.[295] The prayer of John 17 is addressed by Jesus to the Father and can only be accomplished by the Father, who by the Spirit calls men to be saved. The actual basis for Christian unity is the new birth, which is a consequence of faith in an accurate gospel.

John 17:1–3 (KJV 1900)
1 These words spake Jesus, and lifted up his eyes to heaven, and said, Father, the hour is come; glorify thy Son, that thy Son also may glorify thee: 2 As thou hast given him power over all flesh, <u>that he should give eternal life to as many as thou hast given him</u>. 3 <u>And this is life eternal, that they might know thee the only true God, and Jesus Christ</u>, whom thou hast sent.

John 3:3, 7 (KJV 1900)
3 Jesus answered and said unto him, Verily, verily, I say unto thee, Except a man be born again, he cannot see the kingdom of God…7 Marvel not that I said unto thee, Ye must be born again.

There is no biblical justification for the organizational unity of all of Christendom based upon John 17. Christendom is the visible collection of believers and unbelievers who profess Christian belief. Christendom *contains* the true Church, but it is not the true Church. Neither is the Social Gospel a justification for the unification of Christendom. Biblical Christianity requires the new birth. Only individuals can be born again, Society cannot be born again. Society can receive the benefits of the Christian discipleship of its citizens, but society cannot respond to the gospel. Furthermore, salvation is obtained by faith in the sacrifice of Jesus Christ upon the cross as our substitute. There is no salvation in the efforts of men, be those efforts moral or immoral, unified or in conflict to one another.

1 Peter 3:18 (KJV 1900)
18 For Christ also hath once suffered for sins, the just for the unjust, that he might bring us to God, being put to death in the flesh, but quickened by the Spirit:

Titus 3:5 (KJV 1900)
Not by works of righteousness which we have done, but according to his mercy he saved us, by the washing of regeneration, and renewing of the Holy Ghost;

A Christian unity that sacrifices the truth of the gospel for the sake of the appearance of unanimity is a betrayal of God, who commands the Church to remain faithful to the teachings of Christ, foremost among them being man's need for redemption [John 3].

John 17:8, 17 (KJV 1900)
8 <u>For I have given unto them the words which thou gavest me;</u> and they have received them, and have known surely that I came out from thee, and they have believed that thou didst send me…17 Sanctify them through thy truth: thy word is truth.

Matthew 28:19–20 (KJV 1900)
19 Go ye therefore, and teach all nations, baptizing them in the name of the Father, and of the Son, and of the Holy Ghost: 20 <u>Teaching them to observe all things whatsoever I have commanded you:</u> and, lo, I am with you alway, even unto the end of the world. Amen.

Jude 3–4 (KJV 1900)
3 Beloved, when I gave all diligence to write unto you of the common salvation, it was needful for me to write unto you, and exhort you that <u>ye should earnestly contend for the faith which was once delivered unto the saints</u>. 4 For there are certain men crept in unawares, who were before of old ordained to this condemnation, ungodly men, turning the grace of our God into lasciviousness, and denying the only Lord God, and our Lord Jesus Christ.

It shall be shown that it is precisely the gospel of Jesus Christ and sound biblical teaching that are the first casualties of the Ecumenical Movement. In John 17, Jesus is praying for a unity that is between redeemed people who are indwelt by God. He is not praying for a social unity between believers and unbelievers, some who love God and the rest who reject His testimony in the scriptures.

Under ecumenism, it is believed that the unification of Christendom will bring about the greatest evangelistic witness to the world. From its beginnings in Europe in the early 20th century, the ecumenical movement has out-grown this strictly Christian conception of religious unity. Both the Catholic Church and the World Council of Churches promote a single spiritual organization that includes the non-Christian religions as well.[296] This development cannot possibly align with even the incorrect understanding of John 17 that "oneness" speaks to a visible Christian organization.

Although at their inception, the Roman Catholic Church was not a formal part of the ecumenical meetings and conferences, today it is a driving force in the movement, perhaps the leading force. What began as an effort of liberal leaning Protestant Churches has become identified with the Pope and the Roman Catholics.[297]

The charismatic movement has also become a premier catalyzing element for the growth of the ecumenical movement [the "Fourth Ecumenism"].[298] What in the past were a hodge-podge of Christian organizations that could not agree on the sacraments, the gospel, or the identity of the Person of Christ, are now largely united, not by their theology, but by the common experience of speaking in tongues and the other sign gifts. The recognition of these gifts by the Vatican has accelerated the amalgamation of the evangelicals with the Catholic Church in ecumenical association.

"As experienced in the Catholic Charismatic Renewal baptism in the Holy Spirit makes Jesus Christ known and loved as Lord and Savior, establishes or reestablishes an immediacy of relationship with all those persons on the Trinity, and through inner transformation affects the whole of the Christian's life. There is new life and a new conscious awareness of God's power and presence. It is a grace experience which touches every dimension of the Church's life: worship, preaching, teaching, ministry, evangelism, prayer and spirituality, service and community. Because of this, it is our conviction that baptism in the Holy Spirit, understood as the reawakening in Christian experience of the presence and action of the Holy Spirit given in Christian initiation, and manifested in a broad range of charisms, including those closely associated with the Catholic Charismatic Renewal, is part of the normal Christian life." U.S. (Catholic) Bishops Ad Hoc Committee[299]

"Neo-Pentecostalism is not an island; it is a part of the mainstream of the ecumenical movement."[300]

What are the fundamental principles of the ecumenical movement? The information that follows was adapted from the author Rene Pache in a paper presented in the 1950 Griffith Thomas Lectures of Dallas Seminary and printed in the journal Bibliotheca Sacra.[301] This paper was presented prior to the entrance of the Catholic Church as a primary [visible] actor in the movement and before the explosion of the Charismatic Movement in the 1960's and 1970's. It provided a clear representation of the founding actions and principles of the movement by one who was contemporaneous with their development. Each of these principles can be shown to be in operation in today's ecumenical effort.

Principles of the Ecumenical Movement

Liberty in Doctrinal Interpretation:

The participants in the ecumenical movement were originally committed to organizational unity without regard to their biblical beliefs, or lack of them. Neither a Christian body nor individual had to have specific beliefs about the Bible, Christ, or salvation to become a member of the ecumenical associations. In fact, it was not necessary for a body or individual to have any stated Christian beliefs at all except a belief in God and Jesus, which we will see could be *understood* in any way that they pleased.

The fruit of this principle may be seen in the character of the modern ecumenical movement. Not only is every theological shade of Protestantism included under its umbrella, but also the several Catholic traditions and the non-Christian religions as well.[302] The World Council of Churches actively works with the United Nations to ensure that the ecumenical agenda is considered in the decisions of that body.[303] The basis of ecumenical unity is not Christ, evangelism, or the Word of God, but *unity itself.* Because of this it does not matter what any participant believes theologically.[304] Some ecumenical denominations believe in the biblical Christ, while others see Him as merely a human being who died and remains dead, while yet others see him as a consciousness that descends upon any human being who is properly prepared. Inasmuch as every intelligent Evangelical participant in the movement must realize this fact, their participation stands as a blatant disregard of the authority of the Word of God which speaks clearly to this kind of association.[305]

Distinction Between Doctrine And Faith:

There was a distinction made between "practical theology" and "faith" explained as a distinction between faith *as lived out* and "abstract theology."[306] Thus the true expression of the ecumenical spirit was found in the *works performed* rather than the theological reason for their performance or the true relation of the worker to God.[307] According to ecumenism, it is not the workers relation to God [as evidenced by his obedience to the Word of God, the Bible] that validates his work, but the work itself validates the believer as a child of God. We hear this concept today in the statement that "People would rather see a sermon than hear one." Essentially, this is the old liberalism.[308]

This severing of doctrine and faith was also expressed in the early 20th century ecumenical movement as the difference between "personal experience" and "creeds." This distinction is not surprising among religious groups that do not hold to the inerrancy or authority of scripture. The belief that the scriptures were not inerrant resulted in the literary analysis of the Bible as one would evaluate any other book. The devaluation of the scriptures through "higher criticism" resulted in the critical Hebrew and Greek texts, which in turn gave rise to the proliferation of modern Bible translations. Why then, some argued, should theology [creeds] drawn from a *flawed revelation* [this, of course, is an oxymoron] prevent the unity of the world's Christians in the performance of God's work?

"Personal Experience" sets the stage for a development that would gain momentum in the 1960's. The Charismatic Movement is a conveyor belt to ecumenical progress among the various Christian denominations.[309] Evangelical charismatic groups often considered the "gift of tongues" the evidence that Catholics and others were in fact born again.

This contrast between one's deeds and one's doctrine call to mind the Social Gospel. However, our works do not certify divine acceptance if there is no corresponding assent to the truth of the scriptures. Works that do not align with what the Bible teaches cannot possibly be God's plan for the Church. If one's works are not biblically motivated or in alignment with God's Word, upon what basis are the works spiritually valid?[310]

The division of faith from theology enables the version of "good" experienced by Adam and Eve when they partook of the Tree of the Knowledge of *Good* and Evil. Satan convinced Eve that there was a "good" which had been denied them by God, a "good" which could only be experienced once one rejected God's authority. This "good" then would serve their highest interests by providing them with spiritual enlightenment and godhood. Is this not the intrinsic promise of the Ecumenical Movement: the attainment of the Kingdom[311] upon the earth that God has heretofore appeared unable to deliver?

Finally, the faith and theology distinction seem to be based upon the equally faulty "head and heart" dichotomy,[312] the popular idea that only that which originates from or includes the affective faculty reflects what is really believed. In fact, the Bible makes a direct appeal to man's rational faculty, which can receive and process spiritual information with the aid of the Holy Spirit.[313] Christians will be held responsible for what they thought of as well as what they did with the teachings of the scriptures [Rom 14.12].

Unity Taken by Faith:

There was no unity in fact among the ecumenical participants:[314] They would not take the Eucharist together due to different doctrines, disagreed on who Christ was and much more. The Churches agreed to believe that true unity was a miracle that God would eventually perform if they showed sufficient faith by becoming one and doing good works together. The following is a statement that has proved to be prophetic, made in 1950:

> "Meanwhile the principle of performing an act of faith plays a most important role in the ecumenical movement. It has helped a large number of evangelical believers to justify their presence in the movement, [again, in 1950 rw] while closing their eyes to the compromise thereby involved. One reasons as follows: "It is true that our positions differ and that the true unity is still future; but that unity is something so important in the divine will that, from this point on, we must take it by faith. Those who hesitate to join the movement do so only because they lack the necessary faith.""315

In other words, they recognize that there is no rational way that persons with radically differing beliefs about God, Christ, salvation, and the scriptures, can come together in agreement based on a common revelation or doctrine to serve God. However, despite this, the lot of them did know for a fact that their unity was according to the Divine Will [???]. They all decided to move towards ecumenical unity and action BY FAITH, without an agreed upon biblical referent. This appears to be *a new kind of faith*, one that is common in today's Charismatic Movement, which likewise does not require sound biblical basis for its "faith" pronouncements.

The ecumenists *are* hearing the call of a god to unite, and he will indeed enable that unity, but that god is not Christ.

2 Thessalonians 2:3–4, 9-12 (KJV 1900)
3 Let no man deceive you by any means: for that day shall not come, except there come a falling away first, and that man of sin be revealed, the son of perdition; 4 Who opposeth and exalteth himself above all that is called God, or that is worshipped; so that he as God sitteth in the temple of God, shewing himself that he is God.

9 Even him, whose coming is after the working of Satan with all power and signs and lying wonders, 10 And with all deceivableness of unrighteousness in them that perish; because they received not the love of the truth, that they might be saved. 11 And for this cause God shall send them strong delusion, that

they should believe a lie: 12 That they all might be damned who believed not the truth, but had pleasure in unrighteousness.

The Bible indicates that there will be catalyzing events that will precipitate this union under apostasy. Today we see events and movements that are working to the same end of ecumenical unity.

Events in progress:

- A global Charismatic Movement and the commitment of the Catholic Church to it as a catalyst for ecumenical unity.[316]
- A rapidly growing, neoliberal Emerging Church,[317] that has little regard for the authority of the scriptures and is comfortable with ecumenical principles.
- The theological trend towards debasing the authority of the scriptures[318] reducing the importance of doctrinal distinctives, reducing the friction that hampered the ecumenical movement in its early days.
- The weakening of doctrinally sound Churches, such as the Southern Baptist Convention, that have succumbed to both the charismatic[319] and ecumenical movements,[320] along with many independent evangelical Churches and organizations.

These trends have accelerated due to the evangelical apostasy,[321] which while evident today, has been gaining momentum since the Second World War.[322]

Predicted events:

- The Rapture or translation of the Church will occur [1 Th 4.14-18], removing the special restraint of the Holy Spirit [through the Church][323] upon the Mystery of Iniquity, making it much easier for the public to accept the Lie that Jesus is not the Christ.
- God himself will send a spirit of delusion[324] [2 Th 2.6-12] which will hasten the headlong, worldwide rush into error.
- After the disappearance of the Church, there will appear a world leader, the Antichrist, the Man of Sin [Dan 9.27; 2 Th

2.3; Rev 6.1-2], who will *temporarily* promote the ecumenical movement.

Free Interpretation:

Early ecumenical organizations felt the need to provide some doctrinal framework for their activity and thus constructed the vaguest, most watered-down doctrinal pronouncements. Despite this, even the statement "Lord Jesus Christ as God and Savior" in the World Council of Churches doctrinal statement drew many protests from member organizations who stated that they would simply interpret the statement as they saw fit. Therefore, *ecumenical statements regarding theology are meaningless*, as every individual is entitled to freely interpret them as they please. In other words, a statement as straightforward as "Jesus Son of God," can be taken in completely opposite ways by two different member organizations or by two individuals within the Council.[325]

This principle shines a great deal of light upon the many evangelicals that have signed the various ecumenical documents of the last few decades.[326] Most of these men understand the ecumenical movement and the Roman Catholic Church, which has become the vanguard for ecumenism. However, they pretend that this principle of free interpretation does not exist, they pretend that statements like Evangelicals and Catholics Together can be interpreted based on the evangelical meaning of the words used in the document, and they pretend that they never heard of the anathemas of the Council of Trent,[327] which have not been rescinded. The doctrine of the Roman Catholic Church has not changed[328] and most of these evangelical signers are educated enough to know it.

The meaning of this is clear: these documents, such as Evangelicals and Catholics Together, the Manhattan Declaration and The Joint Declaration on the Doctrine of Justification are for the *public*: for the deception of the *congregations* back home that do not understand the ecumenical principle of Free Interpretation, nor do they understand the concept of "*equivocation*."[329] Their pastors and scholars know full well about both concepts, many of them have terminal degrees in theology, apologetics and philosophy. *They know that the doctrinal statements are meaningless but that the commitments to unity are quite real.*

"**Equivocation**

("to call by the same name") is an informal logical fallacy. It is the misleading use of a term with more than one meaning or sense (by glossing over which meaning is intended at a particular time). It generally occurs with polysemic words (words with multiple meanings).

"Albeit in common parlance it is used in a variety of contexts, when discussed as a fallacy, equivocation only occurs when the arguer makes a word or phrase employed in two (or more) different senses in an argument appear to have the same meaning throughout."[330]

Abstention from Proselytizing[331]:

This is a deadly characteristic of the ecumenical movement.[332] In declaring Christian disunity to be the cardinal sin of the age, in that it works against the "divine" command for Christian oneness, the act of evangelizing other members of the ecumenical movement becomes a sin as well.[333] Thus the evangelization of a Catholic or an Orthodox believer by a Baptist becomes a sin and is forbidden.[334] All of South America becomes off limits to Protestant evangelicals if they participate in ecumenical associations with Roman Catholics. *The larger the sphere of ecumenical cooperation the greater the absence of evangelism.* It is not hard to imagine a time when evangelism will bring persecution upon those who insist upon obeying the Great Commission. In fact, it has already begun.[335]

The ecumenical movement is a clear representation of both the values and priorities of Mystery Babylon as a religious force. Mystery Babylon is fundamentally a spiritual entity, its influence begins in the religious realm and extends its control into the other aspects of civilization such as finance, government, and culture. Seen from the esoteric perspective, Mystery Babylon is the religion of the power elite. It is also Satan's delegated authority supervising this world. As a religious force Mystery Babylon seeks to accomplish, in the present age, the following:

1. Covertly establish the lie that Jesus is not the Christ
2. Weaken the true Church through martyrdom and by the undermining of accurate Bible teaching
3. Operate as an invisible hand guiding finance, media, education, religion, and government towards the realization of the New World Order to be achieved in the last days.
4. Organize apostate Christianity and the non-Christian religions under the umbrella of a single Christ-rejecting organization

which may be eventually led into the worship of Lucifer as God. This ecumenical unity is a short-term objective critical to the ultimate establishment of the New World Order.

In the last days, the Mother of Harlots will be replaced by the False Prophet, who will be the Prime Minister of the New World Order. The then-redundant Mystery Babylon, along with all who continue to cling to her suddenly obsolete worldview, will be destroyed by the very persons she once ruled on Lucifer's behalf [Rev 17.16-18].

24
The Woman and the Beast: World Government

She [Mystery Babylon] is global in her operations and influence: Rev 17.1,2,15; 18:3, 9,11,23

Revelation 17:1 (KJV 1900)
¹ And there came one of the seven angels which had the seven vials, and talked with me, saying unto me, Come hither; I will shew unto thee the judgment of the great whore <u>that sitteth</u> upon many waters:

To "sit" is to hold session or a measure of control. To comprehend the extent of the control of Mystery Babylon, one must recalibrate their concept of Good and Evil to a biblical standard. It would be natural for a person to assume that Mystery Babylon could not possibly be in control everywhere because of "all of the good" in the world at any given time.

Understanding Good and Evil

Since the Mystery of Iniquity does not and cannot control the Body of Christ, any works initiated by the power of the Spirit operating through the true and invisible Church are not products of Mystery Babylon.[336] Christ rejecting humanity, residing under the sway of the Mystery of Iniquity, outside of the precincts of eternal life, is incapable of intrinsic good because it rejects the source of all true goodness which is God through Jesus Christ. Any "good" produced by the world is done entirely within the context of this estrangement from God. The tree of the Knowledge of *Good* and Evil was a tree whose influences were not experienced until Adam and Eve had *disobeyed* God. Outside of the works of the true Church, one must recognize the existence of a category of good which can only be achieved once one has rejected God. It was after the devil succeeded in tempting the man and the woman that they became aware of this new category of good, a knowledge that they demonstrated by hiding their nakedness. Until then, good was synonymous with the will of God. Ever since the day of the fall, all the human good, produced outside of relationship with God, is of this new God-rejecting character. In this sense, there is no genuine good produced outside the true Church because this good excludes God and His will.

Once this is understood, the scope, both geographical and historical, of Mystery Babylon can begin to be imagined.

International Spiritual Adultery

> Revelation 17:2 (KJV 1900)
> 2 With whom the kings of the earth have committed fornication, and the inhabitants of the earth have been made drunk with the wine of her fornication.

The Bible associates the whore with the entire world, her influence is seen above to be global, intimate, and encompassing all levels of society.

All the nations or kingdoms of the earth are involved in illicit relations with a system that has been spawned by Satan. The golden cup held by the woman is an allusion to the Mysteries, where the communicant was drugged before his participation in the debaucheries [Rev 17.4-abominations, filthiness] to follow in his initiation. The Bible repeatedly refers to involvement with false religion in sexual terms: as adultery or fornication.[337] Thus, the relationship between the nations and the harlot involves a spiritual intercourse, she represents the religious emphasis of the kingdoms of this world. They are in revolt against God and His revelation both general [in creation and the divine institutions] and special [in the scriptures]. Because of this they are intimate with His enemy, Lucifer, performing his worship and pursuing his program.

Psalm 2:1–3 (KJV 1900)
1 Why do the heathen rage, And the people imagine a vain thing? 2 The <u>kings of the earth</u> set themselves, And <u>the rulers</u> take counsel together, Against the LORD, and against his anointed, saying, 3 Let us break their bands asunder, And cast away their cords from us.

The nations [the kings of the earth [Rev 17.2], the rulers] have joined the devil in conspiracy to overthrow the authority of the Lord, and His Anointed. It should not be surprising that Satan exercises significant influence and control over the nations of this world. They are his domain yet simultaneously objects of his scorn:

Isaiah 14:12 (KJV 1900)
12 How art thou fallen from heaven, O Lucifer, son of the morning! How art thou cut down to the ground, which didst weaken the nations!

1 John 5:19 (NKJV)
19 We know that we are of God, and the whole world lies under the sway of the wicked one.

2 Corinthians 4:4 (KJV 1900)
4 In whom <u>the god of this world</u> hath blinded the minds of them which believe not, lest the light of the glorious gospel of Christ, who is the image of God, should shine unto them. [Dan 10; Rev 16.13].

The Control of Ideas

Revelation 18:23–24 (KJV 1900)
23 And the light of a candle shall shine no more at all in thee; And the voice of the bridegroom and of the bride shall be heard no more at all in thee: <u>For thy merchants</u> were the great men of the earth; For by thy sorceries were all nations deceived. 24 And in her was found the blood of prophets, and of saints, And of all that were slain upon the earth.

Mystery Babylon is not just involved with the power elite but with all classes of people everywhere. Kings, merchants, and the common folk are all engaged in some way with the harlot. The spiritual influence behind the New World Order affects the function of finance and government, but Mystery Babylon generates even greater world changing power from its activities in the realm of ideas. All actions are preceded by an idea. It is through ideas, philosophies, and doctrines that this system influences and guides civilization.

Satan will seek to change times and laws. He is attempting to create a new kind of sinner in a new kind of world. The kind of thinking that the devil sponsors in this world system is synchronized with the lusts inherent in fallen mankind to inexorably guide the world to the eschatological resolution that he desires.

Satan used a series of *ideas* to engineer the fall of mankind. He produced *arguments* that convinced a portion of the angels to do the same.[338] Ever since that time he has used philosophy and false doctrines to weaken the nations [Col 2.8; 1 Tim 6.20]. Ideas enable the age-encompassing control that spans cultures and generations. Due to their compatibility with the fallen natures of mankind, ideas spread via Lucifer's demonic organization are impervious to armies, cultures, or economies. The only weapon against this ideological assault is the Word of God, a superior doctrine, activated by a superior Power, the Holy Spirit.

The Substructure of Luciferian Doctrine

Principle of Deception: Genesis 3.1 If you ever encounter Lucifer, you will not recognize him. Lucifer modifies his appearance and manner to deceive men.

Principle of The Lie: Genesis 3.4-5 Matthew 4.3a Lucifer denies that Jehovah is who He claims to be in scripture. He denies that Jesus is Christ. He claims that God lied to Adam and Eve to prevent their spiritual progress.

Principle of Occult Religion: Genesis 3.4-5 Lucifer represents himself as the benefactor of man, the champion of freedom and the conductor of souls to spiritual evolution and godhood.

Principle of Human Non-Culpability: Genesis 3.4 Lucifer claims that disobedience to God leads not to death but to spiritual evolution.

Principle of Scriptural Misuse: Gen 3.1 Matthew 4.1-10 Satan uses his mastery of the scriptures to deceive man by their misuse. Satan attempted to use God's own words to control Him.

Principle of the Superhero: Matt 4.3-10 Lucifer represents spiritual power, spiritual gifts and spiritual ministry as ours to use as we please.

Principle of Prosperity: Job 1.1-11; 2.3-7 Lucifer argues to God that man serves Him because it is in his best interests to do so. Man serves God to receive blessings and protection alone. The inverse of this argument is that man is entitled to prosperity [health, wealth, and protection] at all times as a servant of God. [Job 2.7-10].

Principle of Pragmatism: Genesis 3.4-5 Matthew 4.8-10 Satan deceives men by the claim that God's plan can be advanced by the violation of His Word. Man is the judge of scripture. His ends justify his means.

Figure 14: Satanic Doctrines in Eden

There are only two systems of philosophy in the world, one derives itself from God and His revelation to mankind and the other originates in the thinking of Lucifer [1 Jn 2.15-16 c.f. 2 Cor 10.4-5]. Since Lucifer's ideas and philosophies stand in opposition to the Word of God, they must also be contrary to *reality* in some way and therefore logically flawed. It is therefore necessary that a measure of deception be used to disguise the fundamental flaws in Satanic thinking.

2 Corinthians 10:4–5 (KJV 1900)
4 (For the weapons of our warfare are not carnal, but mighty through God to the pulling down of strong holds;) 5 Casting down <u>imaginations</u>, and every high thing that exalteth itself against <u>the knowledge</u> of God, and bringing into captivity <u>every thought</u> to the obedience of Christ;

Even in the context of a fallen world, Satan must rely upon deceptions to advance his objectives. Regarding the word *sorceries* found in Rev 18.23:

"sorceries" 53.100 φαρμακεία, ας f; φάρμακον, ου n: [pharmakeia-rw] the use of magic, often involving drugs and the casting of spells upon people..."[339]

The ideas and doctrines by which Lucifer intoxicates the world are transmitted via his control of its secular and religious institutions. Education, media, and Christendom[340] are dominated by the devil and his representatives who commit themselves to conveying doctrines of demons into the thinking of men and women. The true Church has also been influenced by the successful efforts of the devil to infiltrate false teachers and ecumenical associations that weaken the doctrinal emphasis that contributes to the restraint of evil in the world.

The New World Order is not merely a system of economics or of geopolitics. The New World Order, is a *global spiritual initiative*. Concepts such as *ecumenical unity, world government, sustainability* and many others are means by which ideas are controlled on a global scale. Satan is a master at taking legitimate human concerns, such as a desire for peace, economic stability or a sustainable planet and using these desires to advance plans which will fulfill his own spiritual agenda. Beneath the intellectual strategy, behind the marketing of the New World Order, is genuine spiritual power exercised by Satan and the demonic hierarchy. Without the active restraint of God via the ministry of the Body of Christ, the true Church, the plans of Lucifer would already be fully implemented. Even if it were so inclined, the world is no match for Lucifer.

Ephesians 6:12 (KJV 1900)
12 For we wrestle not against flesh and blood, but against principalities, against powers, against the rulers of the darkness of this world, against spiritual wickedness in high places.

There is *no* intellectual, political, economic, or military solution to Mystery Babylon. There is no combination of nations capable of stopping this spiritual movement. The only power sufficient to defeat the New World Order is Jesus Christ. It is truly a spiritual conflict, *marketed* by the devil as the coming of a utopian new age, but is in fact a coming age of global demonic despotism.

She [Mystery Babylon] influences world politics: Rev 17.2, 15; 18.3, 9

The first two verses of Revelation 17 also provide insight into the *political* influence of Mystery Babylon. Fornication is the term used to describe the relationship between the world political leaders and Mystery Babylon. Fornication[341] is immoral sexual conduct, including the concept of prostitution and is an appropriate description of the activities of a harlot. As prostitution, it implies a transaction where one thing is exchanged for another. The kings of the earth engage in false worship [fornication] to obtain, maintain and increase their power and wealth. If you will recall, the empires represented by the heads of the beast are depicted in Daniel 7 as violent super predators, each seeking world domination at the expense of its predecessor. The whore enables the achievement and maintenance of these political aspirations.

Luke 4:5–7 (KJV 1900)
5 And the devil, taking him up into an high mountain, shewed unto him all the kingdoms of the world in a moment of time. 6 And the devil said unto him, All this power will I give thee, and the glory of them: <u>for that is delivered unto me; and to whomsoever I will I give it</u>. 7 If thou therefore <u>wilt worship me, all shall be thine</u>.

The religion of Mystery Babylon requires the disavowal of God [Ps 2] and a commitment, sealed by an initiation that is symbolized by the *cup* and the *wine [Rev 17.2, 4]*, to another God who promises benefits to the one so initiated. According to Revelation 17, the secret, demonic religion of Mystery Babylon is a source of spiritual and worldly power, it is an initiation into a fellowship of like-minded persons who oppose God, a fellowship which invisibly promotes the function of Satan's kingdom in the world. It is secret, [*Mystery*][342] not public. It is conscious and willful. It is illicit and unholy.

This fornication is committed with *all* the kings [or kingdoms] of the earth, not a few. Mystery Babylon is a system of spiritual doctrine, one in which all the kingdoms of the world have intimately and secretly tasted.

> Revelation 17:1–2 (KJV 1900)
> 1 And there came one of the seven angels which had the seven vials, and talked with me, saying unto me, Come hither; I will shew unto thee the judgment of the great whore that sitteth upon many waters: 2 With whom the kings of the earth have committed fornication, and the inhabitants of the earth have been made drunk with the wine of her fornication.

This means that the organized system of the Mysteries exists in one form or another in every nation of the world and that the high-ranking members of the governments of these nations have experienced initiation into these mysteries and identify with their aims and discipline.

This does *not* mean that every single leader of every single nation in history was or is a worshipper of the devil. What it means is that every *kingdom* enjoys an intergenerational connection to this worship [or fornication] and are under the virtual control of the devil via Mystery Babylon. This is because this world is Satan's kingdom.

> John 14:30 (KJV 1900)
> 30 Hereafter I will not talk much with you: <u>for the prince of this world cometh</u>, and hath nothing in me.

Because of this rulership, the character of every institution is heavily influenced by the devil's thinking. There is a cohesive correspondence between the indwelling sin nature in men and the disposition of the world system that is created and maintained by Lucifer.

1 John 2:16 (KJV 1900)
16 For <u>all</u> that is in the world, the lust of the flesh, and the lust of the eyes, and the pride of life, is not of the Father, but is of the world.

As an illustration, for a brief period, Babylon was ruled by a regenerate king, Nebuchadnezzar, [Dan 4; 7.1-4] and the prophet Daniel. This fact did not change the underlying character of the Babylonian Empire. This principle is a reason that government cannot be relied upon to pursue a biblical spiritual agenda. Not only is government *not* entrusted with such a mandate from God, the relationship of fallen mankind and therefore government, to Satan forbids such a role. The domain of government, at its best, is the *restraint* of evil.[343] The domain of the Church is the *elimination* of evil via the Mystery of Godliness [1 Tim 3.16].

Inasmuch as the objective of Mystery Babylon is to create a world situation suitable for the revelation of Antichrist, then this becomes the joint objective of these kingdoms described in chapter 17 of Revelation. They are richly rewarded with the things of this world and the prerogatives of power for their commitment and thus their aim, whether by coercion or loyalty, is to advance the agenda of Mystery Babylon.

Naturally, these aims often run counter to the best interests of their individual nations. Therefore, the populations of these nations must be intoxicated with the wine of the harlot as well. Their aims, aspirations and sense of well-being must be manipulated [via the control of *ideas*] so that they also serve the interests of the harlot. An intoxicated person firmly believes that he is serving his own interests while inebriated, but in fact he is usually doing the very opposite.

Meanwhile, for the sober thinkers, there is difficulty in aligning the *public* expressions of the aims of government with its actual practice once these practices can be discovered. The political, economic, and social proclamations of the leadership of the nation do not align with the actions ultimately taken in these same areas. This is because these leaders cannot publicly acknowledge that their true aim is to implement Mystery Babylon and its doctrines of demons in preparation for a world ruler who will represent Satan. Increasingly however, world leaders are willing to speak about their commitment to the establishment of a New World Order, an ideal to some and a code word to others.

"Hitler has often protested that his plans for conquest do not extend across the Atlantic Ocean. His submarines and raiders prove otherwise. So does the entire design of his new World Order."[344]

In view of the role of abomination in the theology of Mystery Babylon, we should understand that there is no limit to the actions that she will take to implement her global strategy. The violation of treaties, deliberate lies to allies, using crime to facilitate illegal wars, torture, the support of terrorism to achieve political aims, ethnic cleansing [racial genocide], the creation of new religions for the purpose of forming the New World Order, and much more, are all within the scope of Mystery Babylon's political operations.

An Example of Political Babylon: World Government

The Bible predicts that Jesus Christ will rule the entire world[345] from his throne in Jerusalem. This outcome is in direct conflict with the objectives of Lucifer, who not only desires to usurp Christ's place of leadership [Isa 14] but also exercises supervisory authority over the earth at this present hour. Dominion over the earth was first delegated to Adam and Eve by God [Gen 1.26-28]. This dominion was forfeited to the devil at the fall who then became the prince/god of this world [Jn 12.31; 1 Cor 4.4]. Satan now delegates this dominion to the world powers [Lk 4.5-7; Dan 2; 7] via Mystery Babylon, the spiritual aegis by which he rules the earth [Rev 17.1-2, 5, 15].

It is therefore not surprising to see repeated efforts to consolidate the nations of the earth under world government [Dan 2.36-40]. World government involves centralized authority working out a single vision via one agenda. A world consisting of sovereign nations is inimical to the concept of a single World Order. The extraordinary violence of the fourth beast or kingdom of Daniel 7 is directed towards two objects: those who resist world government and those who do not accept a one world religion.

God defeated the two early attempts at world government: in the Garden of Eden and at Babel.

Genesis 3:22–24 (KJV 1900)
22 And the LORD God said, Behold, the man is become as one of us, to know good and evil: and now, lest he put forth his hand, and take also of the tree of life, and eat, and live for ever: 23 Therefore the LORD God sent him forth from the garden of Eden, to till the ground from whence he was taken. 24 <u>So he</u>

drove out the man; and he placed at the east of the garden of Eden Cherubims, and a flaming sword which turned every way, to keep the way of the tree of life.

Genesis 11:6–8 (KJV 1900)
6 And the LORD said, Behold, the people is one, and they have all one language; and this they begin to do: and now nothing will be restrained from them, which they have imagined to do. 7 Go to, let us go down, and there confound their language, that they may not understand one another's speech. 8 So the LORD scattered them abroad from thence upon the face of all the earth: and they left off to build the city.

Genesis 3.22 shows that God did not withhold self-realization from Adam and the woman by His prohibitions, as Lucifer claimed. Whatever man was to become, he was to become it through the auspices of God, his sovereign. What the serpent sought was that mankind join his own revolt against God, through disobedience.

God determined that humanity after the flood should realize its destiny via distribution across the entire earth.[346] The relation of each person to God would secure their collective oneness in Him, whatever their physical location on earth. Mystery Babylon sought instead a localized, visible one world government and religion in opposition to God. They sought to be one by the corporate act of rejecting God. The tendency to world government based upon false spiritual principles has continued throughout history.

The organizational structure of Gentile governments in scripture has varied; from Babylon of Nebuchadnezzar's time until today there have existed a variety of governmental types, all attempting to exercise the dominion mandate that was lost. In the empires represented by the image in the dream of Nebuchadnezzar [Dan 2], a variety of governmental types are represented: despotism, monarchies, republics, democracies, appear and fade from the scene. Because of changing historical circumstances, every form of government is not equally efficient in achieving and maintaining dominion. In fact, the vision given to the king of Babylon demonstrates the loss in the efficiency of power over time.

It was the success of Nebuchadnezzar [the "head of gold" in Daniel 2.38] of Babylon which established the template for all future efforts of world government. Babylon is the prototype world government.

Nebuchadnezzar, King of Babylon was given a dream regarding the future that is recorded in the Book of Daniel. It will be profitable to take a closer look at Daniel 2, where God reveals the reality of the existence of a conspiracy to establish world government as well as His perspective on it.

The Reason for the Dream: "What shall be in the latter days"

> Daniel 2:28 (KJV) But there is a God in heaven that revealeth secrets, and maketh known to the king Nebuchadnezzar what shall be in the latter days. Thy dream, and the visions of thy head upon thy bed, are these; 29 As for thee, O king, thy thoughts came into thy mind upon thy bed, what should come to pass hereafter: and he that revealeth secrets maketh known to thee what shall come to pass.

The dream experienced by king Nebuchadnezzar was given by God. It revealed the political course of the Gentile world from Nebuchadnezzar's time until the second coming of Christ. It is a revelation to the king, to Daniel and through the prophet, to us also.

The purpose of Nebuchadnezzar's dream was multifaceted. The revelation was enlightening, showing the king to the true character of world events and the existence of the cosmic conflict. The revelation was evangelistic, unveiling the God of the Jews as the true God, providing him the opportunity to believe in Him. The revelation was enabling, giving Nebuchadnezzar a unique understanding of world events that could make him the wisest ruler of his time.

The Dream: One World

> Daniel 2:31–35 (KJV 1900)
> 31 Thou, O king, sawest, and behold a great image. This great image, whose brightness was excellent, stood before thee; and the form thereof was terrible. 32 This image's head was of fine gold, his breast and his arms of silver, his belly and his thighs of brass, 33 His legs of iron, his feet part of iron and part of clay. 34 Thou sawest till that a stone was cut out without hands, which smote the image upon his feet that were of iron and clay, and brake them

to pieces. 35 Then was the iron, the clay, the brass, the silver, and the gold, broken to pieces together, and became like the chaff of the summer threshingfloors; and the wind carried them away, that no place was found for them: and the stone that smote the image became a great mountain, and filled the whole earth.

The image represents One World. Daniel would inform the king that this vision, a single image, explained a vast expanse of centuries. The image pertained to government or political organization, specifically, a succession of Gentile kingdoms that would exist from the time of Nebuchadnezzar: the one to whom God gave the dream, the one chosen to initiate the Times of the Gentiles, until the return of Christ. The image excluded the world empires prior to Babylon and those kingdoms which were not essential to the unfolding of God's plan for the world through Israel.

When God frustrated the efforts for world government at Babel, he scattered the people by the confusion of their languages. These families settled around the world, creating ethnic and national identities which were the precursors of the countries which exist in the biblical record [Gen 10.20]. God originated the sovereign state. God has not authorized a single world state, except the one which will be ruled by Christ in the Millennium [Rev 20.4].[347]

Satan in his efforts to manipulate human history to his own ends, has made a major contribution to the world conditions depicted in the image that appeared in Nebuchadnezzar's dream. Satan seeks to implement world government [One World] to establish his worship upon the earth and pre-empt the prophesied kingdom of God. Human history is, from this perspective, the repetitive pattern of efforts to establish world government and the generational misery and anguish that attend these attempts. For the student of the New Testament, this vision is part of a larger revelation that proves that world government is an historical imperative inspired by spiritual forces that are hostile to the Mystery of Godliness.

From God's standpoint the earth is, in one sense, already One World: it is one in its aims, its policies and its authority [Jn 12.31]. However, when we speak of a New World Order, or the worldwide religion which will be one of its chief attributes, we are viewing the end times from the perspective of the creature. The inchoate grumbling against God will become progressively more articulate and popular as the end of history approaches. Even as the best qualities of man are in decline, he will become more consciously acrimonious towards God and His clearly revealed plan for mankind found in the scriptures.

Psalm 2:1–3 (KJV 1900)
1 <u>Why do the heathen rage,</u> And the people imagine a vain thing?
2 The kings of the earth set themselves, And the rulers take counsel together, Against the LORD, and against his anointed, saying, 3 Let us break their bands asunder, And cast away their cords from us.

The Dream: One Man

Daniel 2:31–33 (KJV 1900)
31 Thou, O king, sawest, and behold a great image. This great image, whose brightness was excellent, stood before thee; and the form thereof was terrible. 32 This image's head was of fine gold, his breast and his arms of silver, his belly and his thighs of brass, 33 His legs of iron, his feet part of iron and part of clay.

Nebuchadnezzar saw an image that was at once beautiful, awesome yet terrifying.[348] It was the image of a man, immense in stature, consisting mostly of metal, different metals comprising different parts of the body.

First, *it was the image of a man*. God is communicating information regarding future kingdoms led by men. This is verified by Daniel later in the chapter [*kingdom*-Dan 2.37-39] Therefore the vision represents a succession of governments, kingdoms which vary in their geography, ethnicity, and duration, but governments consisting of human leadership.

The fact that these kingdoms will eventually be destroyed by God [v44] means that these are *not* governments that serve God, share his agenda, or submit to his authority. The image is man living by what he believes to be his own guidance, his own counsel.[349] This is the World System, or the devil's world which consists of the knowledge, culture, organization, and power that can be wielded by man in a state of independence from God. This image is the consequence of the Tree of the Knowledge of Good and Evil: *the function of good [and evil] that can only be exercised after one has rejected God*, a system of organization that deliberately excludes God, progress without moral advance; the divine institutions of marriage, family and government resting upon a foundation of the rejection of divine truth.

Not only is the statue that of a man, but *the image was made of metal,* not of stone or of earth. The image is made of materials that are taken from the earth but must be manufactured to their present state, *the image is man-made*. The image is man-made, but it is revealed by God to Nebuchadnezzar. This "future history" will be created by the decisions and actions of men, yet God sees and uses these decisions and actions to create an end of his own making. The vision represents the activity of man based upon the will of man. It is important to understand that although the content of the vision is allowed by God to transpire, this was not God's original intent for mankind [Gen 1.26-28]. This vision reveals God working within the context of the free will decisions of men.

The Dream: One Agenda

On another level of understanding, the future of humanity can be seen as a single community of human leadership, one system under one idea[350] spanning the generations- One World Order.

Nebuchadnezzar did not receive a vision of four statues, one of gold, another of silver and so on. There was *one* image representing four separate kingdoms which, because they are one, share the same objectives, the same character, the same authority and as Daniel reveals, the same destiny.

Therefore, although we are seeing four kingdoms, four governments, we are seeing one man, we are being shown that these kingdoms possess:

- One pair of eyes-they share the same vision,
- One pair of hands-they do the same deeds and
- One pair of legs-they are going in the same direction,
- One mouth-they are saying the same things

What is the unifying concept and doctrine which unites the Gentile kingdoms from the time of Nebuchadnezzar until the return of Christ? What agenda unites these kingdoms or governments of different cultures and different ages?

It is possible that the answer to this question is the thing that troubled Nebuchadnezzar when he originally received the dream.

Daniel 2:1–3 (KJV 1900)
1 And in the second year of the reign of Nebuchadnezzar

Nebuchadnezzar dreamed dreams, <u>wherewith his spirit was troubled,</u>[351] <u>and his sleep brake from him</u>. 2 Then the king commanded to call the magicians, and the astrologers, and the sorcerers, and the Chaldeans, for to shew the king his dreams. So they came and stood before the king. 3 And the king said unto them, I have dreamed a dream, <u>and my spirit was troubled to know the dream</u>.

The *reality* of the world is not identical to its perception by fallen humanity. Something in the countenance and the orientation [Dan 2.31 in original] of the statue conveyed a sense of magnificence and something else that provoked terror. The realization did not remain with the king but was lost when he awakened from the dream. However, Daniel's description of the image and its end provided the information necessary for Nebuchadnezzar to see that this image, or what it represented, was abhorred by God. It was smitten, obliterated, and replaced with another, eternal kingdom compatible with His own holiness and glory.

Daniel 2:33–35 (KJV 1900)
33 His legs of iron, his feet part of iron and part of clay. 34 Thou sawest till that a stone was cut out without hands, which smote the image upon his feet that were of iron and clay, and <u>brake them to pieces</u>.[352] 35 Then was the iron, the clay, the brass, the silver, and the gold, broken to pieces together, and became like the chaff of the summer threshingfloors; and the wind carried them away, that no place was found for them: and the stone that smote the image became a great mountain, and filled the whole earth.

Nebuchadnezzar was meant to understand the opposition of the kingdoms of this world to God, including his own kingdom. No person can be saved until they are first convinced that they are a sinner. The kingdoms of this world are empowered and led by Lucifer. The king needed to know that, because of the fall of Adam, the leadership of the human realm has fallen to the adversary of God.

By his interpretation of the dream, Daniel the prophet becomes an evangelist. In the future, this king would acknowledge Jehovah as the true God, above all who claim to be god [Dan 4.34-37 c.f. Dan 7.4].

This image was a three-dimensional characterization of the world as it truly is. *The future depicted as a man animated by and sharing the attitude and thinking of the devil.* After the interpretation by Daniel, the king would know that his kingdom was the best that the Satan had to offer the world, but it should have been small comfort. The countenance and posture of the image explained the kingdoms of the world as anti-God and perhaps even anti-man. The vision also disclosed the divine attitude towards his kingdom and the others: they would all be completely destroyed. This is why Nebuchadnezzar's dream and the visions of Daniel [Daniel 2.1, 3, 31; 7:15] were so disturbing to them both.

The Myth of Human Progress

Daniel 2:32–33 (KJV 1900)
32 This image's head was of fine gold, his breast and his arms of silver, his belly and his thighs of brass, 33 His legs of iron, his feet part of iron and part of clay.

The image declines in the value and beauty of its construction materials. Also, the image stands upon the most unstable part of its construction.

The declining value of the metals comprising the statue demonstrate that civilization is getting worse and not better. The four metals: gold, silver, brass, and iron have declining atomic weight,[353] declining specific gravity[354] and declining commercial value. Man, and society are degenerating, we are not evolving biologically, cognitively, or spiritually.

> - Gold is worth 90 times as much as silver
> - Silver is worth 90 times as much as brass (copper)[355]
> - Brass/Copper is worth 84 times as much as iron[356]

Even after the Fall, from the standpoint of creation, Adam and Eve were far better a man and woman than we today, in every way. Man is de-evolving and these insights regarding man from God's point of view in the Book of Daniel make this point emphatically.

We can also see that the metals decline in value and beauty while increasing in strength. This leads to the conclusion that physical strength, though important in a world dominated by conflict, is not positively correlated with overall civilization. To relate this more specifically to our times: *technology is not civilization*. The metals represent kingdoms and according to the vision, the kingdoms are declining in quality as God sees quality. God is breaking the paradigms of Nebuchadnezzar, and this is another reason that he is troubled. We should be troubled with him.

We believe today that technology is progress and conveniences constitute civilization. Therefore, the more technology a nation possesses the more civilized it is. Inside plumbing, motorized travel, modern healthcare, integrated circuits, mapping the genome,[357] Big Data, artificial intelligence all provide conveniences that improve everything about daily life except the behavior of man. As technology improves over time, man is simultaneously becoming more degraded. At the time of man's greatest technological achievement, a good portion of the world is starving, war ravages the planet, unborn children are routinely killed, the ecological balance has been endangered and disease systems are multiplying. The scriptures attest to this.

2 Timothy 3:13 (KJV 1900)
13 But evil men and seducers shall wax worse and worse, deceiving, and being deceived.

2 Peter 3:3–4 (KJV 1900)
3 Knowing this first, that there shall come in the last days scoffers, walking after their own lusts, 4 And saying, Where is the promise of his coming? for since the fathers fell asleep, all things continue as they were from the beginning of the creation.

Daniel 12:4 (KJV 1900)
4 But thou, O Daniel, shut up the words, and seal the book, even to the time of the end: many shall run to and fro, and knowledge shall be increased.

At the same time, man cannot [and will not] resolve the ethical issues associated with the technology he has created. This is primarily because much of this technology was developed to control and to extract profit from ever larger portions of humanity. Look ahead to Daniel chapter seven to see the fourth beast of Daniels vision.

Daniel 7:7 (KJV 1900)
7 After this I saw in the night visions, and behold a fourth beast, dreadful and terrible, and strong exceedingly; and it had great iron teeth: it devoured and brake in pieces, and stamped the residue

with the feet of it: and it was diverse from all the beasts that were before it; and it had ten horns.

The final empire of Gentile history is characterized as exceedingly strong. It uses that strength for the purpose of destroying and devouring, which appear to correspond to the mechanisms of *warfare* [brake in pieces...stamped the residue] and *commercial exploitation* [devouring]. Technology is not necessarily related to an increase in cultural sophistication or in moral excellence. While technology has dramatically advanced in our society it has also made us more effective in the exploitation of others and sophisticated in shielding our own eyes and minds from the reality of that exploitation.

Daniel 2:32–33 (KJV 1900)
32 This image's head was of fine gold, his breast and his arms of silver, his belly and his thighs of brass, 33 His legs of iron, <u>his feet part of iron and part of clay</u>.

The image stands upon the most unstable part of its construction. The feet are made of both iron and clay, which do not naturally adhere to one another. The one is strong and the other brittle. The Fall of mankind and the rise of demonic hegemony has not only affected the character of the earth and mankind, but by necessity, its institutions as well. It is impossible that any World Order based upon the Fall could persevere and produce genuine well-being for the earth or its inhabitants. To believe otherwise, to accept the concept of the evolution of humanity or its institutions is a lie of Satan. The procession of Gentile kingdoms will come to an end in the days of the instability of the Fourth Kingdom. God will establish at that time an immortal kingdom, designed for immortal people rightly related to Himself.

The End of Human Government

Daniel 2:34–35 (KJV 1900)
34 Thou sawest till that a stone was cut out without hands, which smote the image upon his feet that were of iron and clay, and brake them to pieces. 35 Then was the iron, the clay, the brass, the silver, and the gold, broken to pieces together, and became like the chaff of the summer threshingfloors; and the wind carried them away, that no place was found for them: and the stone that smote the image became a great mountain, and filled the whole

earth.

The natureof these four kingdoms can be discerned by the manner of their end. In the day of the ten toes of the Iron Kingdom, supernatural action will destroy the entire structure. The entire system of political rule: its doctrines and policies, its objectives and its system of authority will be crushed by a new system, a new government represented by a stone and a mountain which are unmanufactured and deployed by supernatural power. This combination of the natural and the supernatural is an apt picture of Christ.

Had these governments been righteous, in line with God's law, then they would have persevered. They were destroyed because they opposed the rule of God.

The Times of the Gentiles will not simply fade away, nor will they merge into the Millennial Age, but will be violently terminated by divine action. In fact, the Gentile kingdoms will be obliterated so that no trace of them may be found.

Although the stone will smite the image in the feet, the entire image will be destroyed. In other words, it is not merely the fourth kingdom that will be pulverized by the stone, but the entire system that united the four kingdoms into one body.

The stone/mountain will be revealed to be the kingdom of the Messiah in Daniel 2.44 [*kingdom*]. The coming of this new kingdom will demolish the political structure of the fourth kingdom, but it will also destroy the system of Lucifer which energized and sustained the four kingdoms. The author of the Mystery of Iniquity, Lucifer and his earthly regents, the Antichrist and False Prophet will be incarcerated in the Lake of Fire [Rev 19.19-20.2].[358]

Psalm 1:4 (KJV 1900) 4 The ungodly *are* not so: But *are* like the chaff which the wind driveth away.

The stone is [v. 34] the one that "the builders rejected" (Ps 118.22) which has become the head cornerstone. Scripture refers to this rock many times. It is the rock that followed Israel in the wilderness [1 Cor 10.4], the rock in whose cleft Moses [Ex 33.22] hid. Moses also sang of this Rock [Dt 32.4], as did David [2 Sam 22.2] as did Hannah [1 Sam 2.2]. Isaiah called it the "stone of stumbling and a Rock of offense" [Isa 8.14]. He also called it the "Rock of thy strength" [Isa 17.10]. Jesus warns all to build upon the Rock if you want to be secure [Luke 8.13].

> 1 Corinthians 10:1–4 (KJV 1900)
> 1 Moreover, brethren, I would not that ye should be ignorant, how that all our fathers were under the cloud, and all passed through the sea; 2 And were all baptized unto Moses in the cloud and in the sea; 3 And did all eat the same spiritual meat; 4 And did all drink the same spiritual drink: for they drank of that spiritual Rock that followed them: <u>and that Rock was Christ.</u>

This Rock represents a king and a kingdom. That King is Christ. It is anticipated in the Abrahamic Covenant[359] which promised an everlasting King and Kingdom which could only be inherited by an everlasting people, a regenerated and resurrected people [Heb 11.12-19]. This kingdom is founded upon better promises, better sacrifices, and a better high priest. It is a city which has foundations, whose builder and maker is God. It is a kingdom in which true Israel [Rom 9.6-13] is vindicated and the Church is victorious [Rev 19.6-9].

God and World Government

It is not entirely accurate that God opposes world government. He opposes world government animated by Luciferian principles. Any government outside the sovereign reign of Christ will be ruled by sinful men who are spiritually connected to Satan and seek to do his will [Eph 2.1-3 c.f. Jn 8.44]. During the Millennium, God will establish His own world government in the midst of such fallen individuals.[360] The Millennium is referred to in the Old Testament as the time of the fulfillment of God's promises to redeemed [born again] Israel, in the Gospels as simply "the kingdom" and in the Book of Revelation, as the 1000-year reign of Christ [Rev 20.4-10]. The rock which is cut out without hands symbolizes this kingdom.

> Revelation 20:1–10 (KJV 1900)
> 1 And I saw an angel come down from heaven, having the key of the bottomless pit and a great chain in his hand. 2 And he laid hold on the dragon, that old serpent, which is the devil, and Satan, <u>and bound him a thousand years,</u> 3 And cast him into the bottomless pit, and shut him up, and set a seal upon him, that he should deceive the nations no more, <u>till the thousand years should be fulfilled: and after that he must be loosed a little season.</u> 4 And I saw thrones, and they sat upon them, and judgment was given

unto them: and I saw the souls of them that were beheaded for the witness of Jesus, and for the word of God, and which had not worshipped the beast, neither his image, neither had received his mark upon their foreheads, or in their hands; <u>and they lived and reigned with Christ a thousand years</u>. 5 <u>But the rest of the dead lived not again until the thousand years were finished</u>. This is the first resurrection.[361] 6 Blessed and holy is he that hath part in the first resurrection: on such the second death hath no power, but they shall be priests of God and of Christ, and shall reign with him a thousand years. 7 <u>And when the thousand years are expired</u>, Satan shall be loosed out of his prison, 8 And shall go out to deceive the nations which are in the four quarters of the earth, Gog and Magog, to gather them together to battle: the number of whom is as the sand of the sea. 9 And they went up on the breadth of the earth, and compassed the camp of the saints about, and the beloved city: and fire came down from God out of heaven, and devoured them. 10 And the devil that deceived them was cast into the lake of fire and brimstone, where the beast and the false prophet are, and shall be tormented day and night for ever and ever.

25
The Woman And The Beast: World Economics

She [Mystery Babylon] is critical to international commerce: Rev 17:1-2, 15; 18: 3, 9, 11-19

Revelation 18:3 (KJV 1900)
3 For all nations have drunk of the wine of the wrath of her fornication, And the kings of the earth have committed fornication with her, And <u>the merchants of the earth are waxed rich through the abundance of her delicacies</u>.

Revelation 18:23 (KJV 1900)
23 And the light of a candle shall shine no more at all in thee; And the voice of the bridegroom and of the bride shall be heard no more at all in thee: <u>For thy merchants were the great men of the earth; For by thy sorceries were all nations deceived</u>.

In an unpublished manuscript "The Christian and Government," I explained the relationship between Mystery Babylon and commerce as follows:

> "Mystery Babylon and the political and religious constructs through which it operates are responsible for the <u>spiritual deception</u> of the public <u>through</u> worldwide commercial enterprise designed to produce wealth *by* the corruption of the ethics and morality of

common people.

> "The commercial mechanisms of Mystery Babylon are called *sorceries* because they do not merely pertain to marketing, but to the indoctrination of a philosophy that promotes demonism, and opposition to the rule of God. You cannot buy a product today [and especially any entertainment product] without in some way ratifying a God dishonoring system and enriching those who believe in that system. This situation will be formalized with the "mark" which will [completely] merge your religion with your finances."

In television and movies, blasphemy against God and Christ appear to be *requirements* for distribution. While God is cursed, Lucifer himself had a television show[362] where he received favorable treatment as a friend to man. Themes of serial and ritual murder, demonism, and witchcraft dominate entertainment products today. The same applies to the music industry. Many entertainers incorporate into their art lyrics, symbols, and gestures that suggest satanic involvement.

The debasing of each divine institution is another mandatory aspect of every media product: the undermining of conscience, the confusion of gender, the repudiation of marriage, and negation of the concept of justice in government are all conscientiously taught to the public via media.

There is an evil intersection of finance/commerce, politics, and religion in the world. This situation has existed for centuries and millennia. Ezekiel wrote in detail about this system six centuries before Christ. A description of a commercial enterprise of this same character is identified with the nation of Tyre in Ezekiel 27-28. In Isaiah the following is said about its merchants:

Isaiah 23:8 (KJV 1900)
8 Who hath taken this counsel against Tyre, the crowning city,
Whose merchants are princes, whose traffickers are the
honourable of the earth?

Ezekiel prophesies about the prince [Eze 28.1-11] and king [Eze 28.12-19] of Tyre. These same prophecies are believed to also pertain to the Antichrist and to Lucifer.

The rebellion against God and Christ can be observed in the religious function of Mystery Babylon but also in the operation of its politics and commerce. Its system of religion is so seamlessly interwoven into the function of the world that the inhabitants of the earth are corrupted even by interaction with its apparently secular elements.

It is an objective of this system to make buying and selling a religious act [Rev 13.16-17].

An Example of Economic Babylon: The Hip Hop Industry

We have described the biblical background of Mystery Babylon and traced out it's character and program from the scriptures. It's time to see an example of Mystery Babylon in action.

The Four Characteristics of Economic Babylon

Since Mystery Babylon is of this present world, we can naturally expect to see her operations in the world of finance and commerce. Mystery Babylon as a doctrinal idea penetrates every institution of the world. Doctrine and philosophy matter and this axiom is as true in marketing and finance as it is in theology.

When we see the commercial behavior of Mystery Babylon described in scripture, we can discern the following characteristics:

- **Wealth Transfer** [from the Public to Mystery Babylon][363]
- **Corruption of Values** of Common People [Intoxication with 'the wine of her fornication']
- **Promotion of Luciferian Religion** [Infiltration of "the Lie"]
- **Political End Game** [to Enable the Appearing of the Antichrist and his New World Order]

The Hip Hop music industry is an excellent example of the methods and objectives of Mystery Babylon.

Hip Hop is a formula which focuses the energy of youth and the creativity of the black musical heritage through the prism of the cruel urban reality that is reserved for the majority of black young people. Add to the mix intense sexuality, false prosperity concepts and a poisoned value system that is anti-life and you have hip hop culture. Hip Hop culture is an important element of a new, Black, do-it-yourself genocide.

Wealth Transfer

Genre	Percent of Total Volume [selected genres]
RB/Hip-Hop	26.5
Rock	19.4
Pop	13.1
Country	7.2
Latin	4.7
Christian	2.3
Jazz	1.0
Classical	1.0

Figure 15: Share of Total Volume by Format and Genre: Total Volume Mid-Year 2019[selected top genres]

"Listeners sought out more rap singles and more rap albums last year. Hip-hop tracks were already more popular than any other kind in 2017, accounting for 20.9 percent of songs consumption. That number jumped to a stunning 24.7 percent in 2018, meaning that nearly a quarter of all tracks listened to in the U.S. came from rap."[364]

"Streaming platforms take center stage in Goldman Sachs latested [sic] forecast that music revenue is going to more than double to about $131 billion by 2030. Currently music streaming sales are dominated by top R&B and hip-hop artists such as Drake, Kendrick Lamar, The Weeknd, Migos and Cardi B. Music publishers and labels also stand to profit greatly from the rise of streaming, led by black listeners who are the largest user group.

"The Breakdown You Need to Know

"R&B and hip-hop are music's most consumed genre and leading the industry's revival. In 2017, Goldman found live music, publishing and recorded songs made $26 billion, $6 billion and $30 billion respectively. The firm estimates by 2030 these categories are going to reach $38 billion for live music, $12.5 billion for publishing, and the biggest gain will be seen in recorded songs at $80 billion."[365] [emphasis added]

Despite the revenue generation of hip hop music, videos and performances, black folks are not the beneficiaries of this wealth.

Blacks may provide the creative input and performance excellence, but beyond the star performers, well paid employees and front men and women, the bulk of the wealth is directed away from the artistic creators and black consumers of rap music.

> "African Americans spend 38 hours each week listening to music and $173 each year on purchased music, exceeding the total population, which averages 32 hours weekly and $156 annually. Additionally, in a typical week, African American music listeners listen to music on an average of four devices, versus 3.4 devices for the total population. African Americans spend 39% more than the total population on satellite radio (which is 11% of their total music spend), 57% more on physical music such as CDs and vinyl (22% of total spend) and 80% more on digital tracks and albums (13% of total spend)." *366

The real beneficiaries of the rap music industry are essentially *three* multinational corporations and the industries which support them. The capital, marketing, creative direction, and distribution of hip-hop music is controlled by these organizations. What you see and what you hear is approved by them or you do not see it or hear it.[367]

The economic function inherent in the hip hop industry is a *wealth transfer mechanism*. The least affluent pour their earnings and their talent into hip hop and this wealth and talent is used to create opportunity for others who not only are *not* a part of the black community, but who provide that community with a destructive product. This is an essential facet of Mystery Babylon: *Wealth Transfer through commerce which promotes Mystery Babylon and enslaves and degrades the consumer*. This mechanism has been going on around the world for multiplied centuries.

These large companies generated almost ten billion dollars in overall *recording* revenues in fiscal 2018, a quarter of which was attributable to hip-hop and R&B music recordings. The artists come and go, sometimes to other labels, often into obscurity or, more often than one might imagine, to untimely deaths. The black community provides the talent, pays for the product of the artists, but the wealth is transferred elsewhere.

Institutional Corruption of Values

The cultural message of Hip Hop illustrates how Mystery Babylon manipulates races and cultures to achieve her spiritual and temporal objectives. The Harlot has scripted a role for each nation and people group to play in the unfolding of her revolt against God. The role set aside for black Americans is to be used, among other things, as an artificial justification for continuing domestic policy encroachments upon freedom.[368] By a similar process, young black people are encouraged to be the *carriers* of a world view [Hip-Hop, Thug culture, etc.] that destroys communities and cultures. In this sense, the Hip Hop movement, which is capitalized and directed by international business concerns, is a massive psychological operation[369] against both blacks and whites in America and abroad.

When one considers the performers of the hip-hop movement and their artistic production, the cultural impact of hip-hop is easily deduced. The lyrics of any hip-hop star are available for free on the Internet.[370] Hip-hop videos are available online as well as on television. The following is a list of the cultural aims of the hip-hop phenomenon:

- Create and implant *a cultural concept of blackness* as a negation of value and virtue. Identify blackness within a context where options are limited to futility and moral failure. The black reality so constructed will exclude [outside of a narrow range of expression including entertainment and crime] achievement, genius, professional skill, or the protective instinct towards family and community. Hip hop culture is an efficient factory, mass-producing the stereotypes that generations fought to expunge from American art and culture.

- Promote *a prosperity doctrine* entirely focused upon currency accumulation. Celebrate money as a means to individual prosperity of the lowest denomination: personal pleasure, rather than family, community, or nation building.

- *Degrade the image of black women*, by degrading names, violence towards women, using women [or women portraying themselves] as sexual objects, denying support and protection to women.

- *Promote black self-hatred.* Continue the historic strategy of directing the rage produced by systematic racism inwards towards oneself and outward towards other blacks. Hip-hop promotes the killing of other black males with words, called, "lyrically" assassinating other black men by describing how you would like to kill them. Perpetuate demeaning nomenclature directed at every black man, woman, and child.

- *Degrade the value of the relationship between black men and women* by the rejection of marriage, and the rejection of the responsibilities of fatherhood and motherhood. Feminize the black male through gender confusion.
- *Promote the drug culture* by which the soul is destroyed and thereby subvert the institutions that rely upon the healthy function of the mature soul: marriage, family, and citizenship. hip hop artists faithfully celebrate the drug sales and distribution culture as financially rewarding, amoral and socially affirming.

Institutional corruption begins with the corruption of the individual soul. Mystery Babylon, despite its claims, is anti-man. The clearest expression of this fact is seen in how it marginalizes African Americans. This marginalization results in the destruction of the institutions devised by God for the healthy function of human civilization. What is not understood by most people is that you cannot destroy these foundations in *one* people without concomitantly undermining one's own culture. You cannot commit to the agenda of Mystery Babylon when it comes to one oppressed group without accepting the authority of that agenda for your own soul as well.

Promote Luciferian Religion

A survey of hip-hop videos and lyrics will confirm that, beyond its characteristic amorality, there is an anti-Christian spiritual emphasis to the genre. The primary function of hip hop is the corruption of the thinking of youth, particularly black youth, through the insinuation of culturally corrosive messages. There is, however, a deeper spiritual component which connects hip hop to all the other departments of the Mystery of Iniquity. It is the lie that Jesus is not the Christ. The lie is advanced via the desecration of Christ and by the promotion of Lucifer: satanic symbolism, Freemasonry [the Mysteries], and Luciferian eschatology included not only in the music but in live performances and the personal style of the artists.

At least since the time of Babel, there has been a covert system of religious expression with Lucifer as its deity. The existence of such a system is consistent with the reality of the devil as the temporary ruler of this world. The conscious followers of this doctrine count themselves enlightened. The mass of unconscious, unredeemed individuals with religious inclinations worship under liberal systems that veil this occult truth while embracing its values. This world is headed somewhere. Satan and his followers, conscious or otherwise, are pursuing an agenda which will result in the prophesied New World Order, headed by the Antichrist. This agenda includes the progressive externalization of the doctrine and worship which has for centuries, and millennia remained occult or hidden. The hip-hop movement, beneath its culture crushing catechism has an undercurrent that glorifies Satan's spiritual message, despising Christ, and His Church.

References to Christianity in hip hop are overwhelmingly negative; the name of Jesus and the name of Jehovah are regularly desecrated. The wearing of crosses appears to be for the purpose of defaming the work of Christ on behalf of sinners. When a symbol which represents one thing is worn by an individual who stands for the exact opposite, what message is being sent [Acts 16.16-18]? At best, hip hop's representation of Jesus is one who is well-meaning but impotent to solve the problems of poverty and injustice. On the other hand, allusions to Lucifer, to secret societies, occult hand signs, choreographed mystical dance, references to secret knowledge, the proliferation of references to 666, the Illuminati, demonic alter egos, etc. find an honored place in the lifestyles and the artistic expression of the hip hop performers. Apparently, according to these artists, Satan delivers [Lk 4.5-6].

The music that began as a form of expression designed to enhance consciousness and promote personal responsibility now hardly refers at all to the causes, movements and individual heroes who characterize the strength, bravery, achievement, and genius of black people. *It should be emphasized and reiterated that the people who capitalize this music and who reap its financial benefits are the ones who control its content.*

What *was* consciousness raising music has become a recruitment vehicle for the Lake of Fire. Hip-Hop has taken to a new level the demonic sub-culture which has become mainstream in movies, television, fashion and even education.

Political End Game

When one looks at the intersection of hip hop artists, professional athletes, Hollywood, a segment of black professional people and a small circle of white billionaires, we are seeing the tip of a political nexus that has yet to take visible form, but probably has an invisible antecedent. Enough is being made visible to offer the false hope that you too can join forces with the superstars if you forsake the Lord and support the genocidal cultural messages of Hip Hop. There is a *reverse evangelism* going on which is in preparation for the end time manifestation of the Antichrist.

Black Americans are also being used as a symbol for the forces that America must prepare to resist, even at the cost of their liberties. The images and messages of Hip-Hop are driving political reaction in the centers of power both within the government and the voting public. Hip-Hop is a part of the long-standing psychological operation which is polarizing America based on race. For decades, demonic despotism has been beta-tested piecemeal upon black Americans.[371] Race as the lowest common denominator of domestic and international policy is now accepted by many in America and abroad. Hip hop is a tool that maintains and freshens the stereotypes which form the foundation of racial consciousness globally. The corrupted political values that result from this manufactured consciousness drive the making of repressive new laws and the repeal of those laws which preserved freedom for everyone. A few blacks are being offered safe passage through a coming racial cataclysm, for a price. The coming storm will *appear* to be racial, and it will have real consequences for black America and people of color around the world, but it will spell the end of freedom for *all* of America, which will find itself trapped and ensnared by Mystery Babylon by means of its own racial bigotry.

Another consequence of this cultural, economic, political, and theological conspiracy called Mystery Babylon is a generation of *Christian* youth who are addicted to hip hop and the culture which accompanies it. Christian hip-hop today appears to maintain contact with the same worldly spirit, appeals to the same emotions and maintains the same associations as its secular counterpart. [372]

Christian young people live in a time where much of the biblical preaching which is an antidote to the cultural influence of hip-hop is gone. Churches are preoccupied with membership growth and will tolerate a great deal to gain and to keep members. In an environment where sound Bible teaching is atypical, Christian hip-hop will act as a retrovirus, spiritually incapacitating the next generation. Hip-hop is certainly not the only vehicle in use by Mystery Babylon against black America, but it is an effective weapon to prevent a counter offensive against the devil in the next generation. *The Church will ultimately be victorious, but that does not mean that it must be victorious here in America.* We can suffer the effects of divine judgment just like others before us.

The baby boomer generation [born 1946 to 1964] embraced secular music which promoted promiscuity and two generations of broken marriages and illegitimacy have resulted. The cultural impact of hip-hop is no less than what paleontologists call an *extinction level event* for black culture and black people. This is Mystery Babylon at work, and it has many, many other projects working throughout the world.

Isaiah 14:12 (KJV 1900)
12 How art thou fallen from heaven, O Lucifer, son of the morning! How art thou cut down to the ground, <u>which didst weaken the nations</u>!

26
The Woman And The Beast: World Oppression

She [Mystery Babylon] is a key actor in genocides, especially of believers Rev 16.6; 17.6; 18:20, 24; 19.2

Revelation 17:6 (KJV 1900)
And I saw the woman drunken with the blood of the saints, and with the blood of the martyrs of Jesus: and when I saw her, I wondered with great admiration.

This addiction to the blood of the saints, her specific interest in the genocide of believers clearly identifies this Whore as a religious system. The will to destroy that single system standing against the religions of this world i.e., biblical Christianity, plainly reveals that the character of Mystery Babylon is in alignment with the spirit of Antichrist and the Mystery of Iniquity.

> Revelation 18:24 (KJV 1900)
> And in her was found the blood of prophets, and of saints, And of all that were slain upon the earth.

> Matthew 23:34–35 (KJV 1900)
> 34 Wherefore, behold, I send unto you prophets, and wise men, and scribes: and some of them ye shall kill and crucify; and some of them shall ye scourge in your synagogues, and persecute them

from city to city: 35 That upon you may come all the righteous blood shed upon the earth, from the blood of righteous Abel unto the blood of Zacharias son of Barachias, whom ye slew between the temple and the altar.

Mystery Babylon is responsible for *all* the deaths of the righteous upon the earth in its role as the opponent to the advancement of the Mystery of Godliness. Mystery Babylon includes the false religion of all generations, which she sponsors. Mystery Babylon cannot be limited to the Roman Catholic Church, which it certainly includes, but it is a concept that encompasses all organized spiritual opposition to the plan of God, including even apostate Israel of the past and present.[373] This is because the coordinated functions of false religion are administered by Satan to accomplish his objective of the overthrow of God and Christ.

Isaiah 14:12–17 (KJV 1900)
12 How art thou fallen from heaven, O Lucifer, son of the morning! How art thou cut down to the ground, which didst weaken the nations! 13 For thou hast said in thine heart, I will ascend into heaven, I will exalt my throne above the stars of God: I will sit also upon the mount of the congregation, in the sides of the north: 14 I will ascend above the heights of the clouds; I will be like the most High. 15 Yet thou shalt be brought down to hell, to the sides of the pit. 16 They that see thee shall narrowly look upon thee, and consider thee, saying, <u>Is this the man that made the earth to tremble, that did shake kingdoms; 17 That made the world as a wilderness, and destroyed the cities thereof; That opened not the house of his prisoners</u>?

Why is Mystery Babylon committed to the eradication of the saints and the prophets?

> ➢ Because Mystery Babylon is <u>opposed to the Mystery of Godliness</u>: [1 Tim 3.16] the revelation of Jesus Christ as God's Champion for the rescue of mankind and the resolution of the angelic rebellion. The incarnation and

ministry of Christ repudiates every claim of the devil against God's character and plan.
- Because the prophets and the saints of God <u>expose</u> through teaching and preaching <u>the true character of Mystery Babylon</u> as a demonically inspired system behind the world's institutions that rests upon the central untruth that Jesus is not God.
- Because Satan is specifically interested in <u>preventing the fulfillment of the covenant promises</u> to Abraham via regenerate [elect] Israel. God's failure to fulfill these promises would mean victory for Lucifer. Therefore, the elimination of Israel by genocide is a cornerstone of the devil's earthly strategy.

Because Mystery Babylon is opposed to the advance of the Mystery of Godliness

Mystery Babylon is not opposed to Churches or to Church going people. She is not opposed to politically focused Churches since she controls both sides of every political system and philosophy on earth [binary traps[374]]. In fact, Mystery Babylon is sponsoring the growth of the visible Church to unprecedented levels around the world based on false gospels and destructive systems of discipleship.

What she cannot allow is Bible teaching Churches that proclaim the full counsel of God. This includes a gospel of justification by faith *alone* and a commitment to the instruction of believers in *all* that the Bible has to say.

Matthew 28:19–20 (KJV 1900)
19 Go ye therefore, and teach all nations, baptizing them in the name of the Father, and of the Son, and of the Holy Ghost: 20 Teaching them to observe <u>all things</u> whatsoever I have commanded you: and, lo, I am with you alway, even unto the end of the world. Amen.

Christ's ministry through the Church operates as a restraining force upon the Mystery of Iniquity through the constant infusion of biblically trained disciples into the world which produce a cleansing and uplifting effect upon communities and nations. When the Church is operating as it should, the darkest aspects of the sin natures of men are restrained, civilization advances, culture is purified, and institutions are strengthened. The Church is truly a source of blessing to the world, not only through its proclamation of the life-giving gospel of Christ, but also because of its felicitous effects upon the nations in which it is fully proclaimed.

This is the exact opposite of the aims of Mystery Babylon. She is committed to the smothering of the Word of God and the local churches that guard it and has not hesitated to kill millions to accomplish this aim.[375][376][377][378]

Mystery Babylon has used the bigotry of the public, the law making and war making powers of the state and even Christendom itself to commit these genocides. Nor did the atrocities begin with the New Testament age. Satan has continually attempted to destroy Israel though spiritual apostasy, inciting God to destroy them due to their breaking of His covenant. The Old Testament is largely the record of the efforts of the nation's [Gentiles] to corrupt or destroy the nation of Israel, counterpoised by the efforts of the faithful prophets and priests to resist them by building the spiritual resources of the people. *The genocide of the Jews defeats the Mystery of Godliness [Rev 12.3-6].* Israel today does not receive Christ as her Messiah; nevertheless, the devil will leave nothing to chance and will kill millions of Jews in a vain attempt to prevent Christ's victorious return.

Because the prophets and the saints expose through teaching and preaching the true nature of Mystery Babylon as a demonically inspired system.

Satan is committed to the genocide of God's prophets and saints because Bible believing and proclaiming Churches can identify the operations of Mystery Babylon on sight and are conscientious proclaimers of her deceptions. Furthermore, the Bible proclaiming Church holds the only true solution to the problem of sin and evil in the gospel of salvation through faith in Jesus Christ. The true Church is the only effective earthly opponent of Mystery Babylon.

For example, a key end time objective of Mystery Babylon is the temporary creation of a false Church via the Ecumenical Movement. The Ecumenical Movement is the product of an *apparently* spiritual alliance of believers, false teachers and unbelievers focused upon the improvement of mankind and this world. Bible believing Churches realize that no combination of Christians and unbelievers will accomplish God's purposes. Biblically sound Churches reject the use of the concept of *culture war* to cause believers to sacrifice sound teaching for the sake of the improvement of the devil's world. Consequently, they also reject the use of hot button issues such as abortion to drive ecumenical unity. Because they reject the concept of culture war as the mission of the Church, they cannot be drawn into secular political alliances which always result in the compromise of the principles of scripture. Bible teaching Churches do not trust that the Kingdom of God will be established by government.

For these reasons, the local churches that exalt the authority of the scriptures, following and teaching them, are the Churches that Mystery Babylon cannot tolerate. When the political conditions are right, she will not hesitate to kill these believers, as history has shown. Until then, she attempts to assimilate, harass, and intimidate them, increasingly using the government to do so.

Mystery Babylon's ecumenical initiative advertises itself as the thinking person's approach to reaching the world. However, you cannot fulfill the will of God by violating the Word of God. Satan will use reason to sway his opponents when he can. Lucifer used faulty reasoning to deceive Eve; he offered apparently logical challenges to Jesus to tempt Him to operate outside of the will of God. The philosophies and speculations of false religion appeal to culture, to intellectual inquiry and religious feeling, but are great deceptions designed to blind and obscure minds to the clear truth of their actual spiritual condition and the way out of it [Rom 16.17-18]. The same can be said about the utopian, New World pretensions of Mystery Babylon, these also are deceptions. However, to spiritually mature, biblically literate believers, Mystery Babylon appears as it actually is. Therefore, when circumstances permit, genocide is perpetrated upon the Church. *Stripped to its bare reality, political philosophy of Mystery Babylon and the New World Order is demonic despotism, a violent and sadistic form of totalitarianism.*[379] Its sensuality and promises of godhood are partially true, but in the way that the bait at the end of a hook is real and true. It is the commitment of Mystery Babylon to extreme violence and genocide that reveals her true nature and the end of her theology.

Because Satan is specifically interested in preventing the fulfillment of the covenant promises to Abraham via regenerate Israel. God's failure to fulfill these promises would mean victory for Lucifer.

Once Satan has been thrust out of heaven in Revelation 12 and he sees that his attempt at a direct attack upon heaven has failed, his last resort will be to attempt yet again to annihilate the Jews to preclude God's fulfillment of the covenant to Abraham [Mt 24.15-22].

> Genesis 17:4–8 (KJV 1900)
> 4 As for me, behold, my covenant is with thee, and thou shalt be a father of many nations. 5 Neither shall thy name any more be called Abram, but thy name shall be Abraham; for a father of many nations have I made thee. 6 And I will make thee exceeding fruitful, and I will make nations of thee, and kings shall come out of thee. 7 And I will establish my covenant between me and thee <u>and thy seed after thee in their generations for an everlasting covenant</u>, to be a God unto thee, and to thy seed after thee. 8 And I will give unto thee, and to thy seed after thee, the land wherein thou art a stranger, <u>all the land of Canaan, for an everlasting possession; and I will be their God</u>.

It is critical to note that the unconditional covenants, including the possession of the land of Israel, are not promised to *unbelieving* Israel. The promises apply to *believing* Israel, those who have acknowledged Jesus Christ as their Messiah.

> Galatians 3:6–9 (KJV 1900)
> 6 Even as Abraham believed God, and it was accounted to him for righteousness. 7 Know ye therefore that they which are of faith, the same are the children of Abraham. 8 And the scripture, foreseeing that God would justify the heathen through faith, preached before the gospel unto Abraham, *saying*, In thee shall all nations be blessed. 9 <u>So then they which be of faith</u> are blessed with faithful Abraham.

> Romans 9:6–8 (KJV 1900)
> 6 Not as though the word of God hath taken none effect. For

they are not all Israel, which are of Israel: 7 Neither, because they are the seed of Abraham, are they all children: but, In Isaac shall thy seed be called. 8 That is, They which are the children of the flesh, these are not the children of God: but the children of the promise are counted for the seed.

The Jews today largely deny that Christ is their Messiah, but the devil knows better. If Jesus succeeds in establishing the Kingdom in Jerusalem, a doctrine that is popularly ridiculed today, then Satan's attempt to prove his case against God in human history will have finally failed.

The establishing of His kingdom will yet again demonstrate the magnificent *grace* and *love* of God for His fallen creation, which having fallen at Satan's instigation, was unable to save itself. God has already demonstrated his unchanging *righteousness*, in pouring His wrath upon His own Son in payment for the sins of mankind [Jn 3.16-18]. He will demonstrate His own *wisdom* and *power*, by accomplishing His salvation in the face of the free will choices of both angels and men to oppose Him.

It is this victory which will result in the eternal praise of elect men and angels and the eternal doom of those who reject and oppose Christ. Therefore, to prevent the Kingdom, Lucifer will mount a multifaceted attack involving both human and demonic forces to eradicate every Jew on earth.

Revelation 16:13–14 (KJV 1900)
13 And I saw three unclean spirits like frogs come out of the mouth of the dragon, and out of the mouth of the beast, and out of the mouth of the false prophet. 14 For they are the spirits of devils, working miracles, which go forth unto the kings of the earth and of the whole world, to gather them to the battle of that great day of God Almighty.

Zechariah 14:1–3 (KJV 1900)
1 Behold, the day of the LORD cometh, And thy spoil shall be divided in the midst of thee. 2 For I will gather all nations against Jerusalem to battle; And the city shall be taken, and the houses rifled, and the women ravished; And half of the city shall go forth into captivity, And the residue of the people shall not be cut off from the city. 3 Then shall the LORD go forth, and fight against those nations, As when he fought in the day of battle.

Although the devil will kill many Jews, this effort will be futile as God has promised to preserve His remnant against any satanic initiative [Rom 9.27; 11.5]. The character of God is the ultimate protection of every believer. Protection, however, does not mean that the believer is exempted from the trials and suffering of the spiritual warfare, but that spiritual victory under suffering serves an eternal purpose and will be rewarded.

A principle here is that although God allows believers to suffer and to die, that suffering cannot overthrow God's intentions. Hebrews 11 illustrates that the suffering of believers will result in an "eternal weight of glory" [2 Cor 4.17] in the life to come and for this reason some saints did not accept release from torture, that they might receive "a better resurrection" [Heb 11.25].

Neither the philosophy or theology of Mystery Babylon are rational systems and are unable to deliver the historical or personal outcomes that she promises. Compensation for these deficits requires mass violence of the worse possible denomination. Truly, the thief cometh only to "kill, and to steal and to destroy."

27
Collecting Our Thoughts Regarding Mystery Babylon

Revelation 17:1–5 (KJV 1900)
1 And there came one of the seven angels which had the seven vials, and talked with me, saying unto me, Come hither; I will shew unto thee the judgment of the great whore that sitteth upon many waters: 2 With whom the kings of the earth have committed fornication, and the inhabitants of the earth have been made drunk with the wine of her fornication. 3 So he carried me away in the spirit into the wilderness: and I saw a woman sit upon a scarlet coloured beast, full of names of blasphemy, having seven heads and ten horns. 4 And the woman was arrayed in purple and scarlet colour, and decked with gold and precious stones and pearls, having a golden cup in her hand full of abominations and filthiness of her fornication: 5 And upon her forehead was a name written, MYSTERY, BABYLON THE GREAT, THE MOTHER OF HARLOTS AND ABOMINATIONS OF THE EARTH.

The Accurate Interpretation of History

Human history cannot be properly understood apart from knowledge of the existence and function of Mystery Babylon.

Mystery Babylon explains a great deal that is in the newspaper today, as well as many things that will never make the daily news broadcasts.

Many Bible students will acknowledge that the devil is the temporary ruler of this world, *but they will not follow that thought to its logical conclusion*. If the devil is the ruler of this world, as Jesus and Paul openly acknowledged, then the Satan's aims are being pursued and his methods are being utilized in his administration of the earth.

Ephesians 2:1–2 (KJV 1900)
1 And you hath he quickened, who were dead in trespasses and sins; 2 Wherein in time past ye walked according to the course of this world, <u>according to the prince of the power of the air, the spirit that now worketh in the children of disobedience</u>:

Ephesians 6:12 (KJV 1900)
12 For we wrestle not against flesh and blood, but against principalities, against powers, against <u>the rulers of the darkness of this world</u>, against spiritual wickedness in high places.

Satan is guiding this world, through its leaders and its institutions, to a destination. That destination is the vision that John described in Revelation chapters 13 and 17. It is the consolidation of every facet of civilization: religious, political, economic, and social under the control of Luciferian religion in opposition to God, the Bible and believers, the end of which is a New World Order.

The illicit, secret cooperation between Satan and men is currently in operation in the highest circles of world leadership and has been for millennia. In the days of the Old Testament, world empires exchanged capitals, but the religion stayed essentially the same. Whether the capital was Thebes, Babylon, Nineveh, Athens or Rome, there were the same mysteries, the same initiations, the same collaboration with the devil under the secrecy of symbols, the same lack of alignment between public policy statements and actual policy objectives.

Our willingness to accept the testimony of the scriptures regarding Mystery Babylon, to know and affirm God's verdict against Egypt, Babylon, and their heirs the Persians, Greeks and Romans will inevitably lead us to the proper assessment of our world today.

The Accurate Understanding of Spiritual Warfare

When Christians see this world for what it truly is, we will adjust our strategies from the secular to the spiritual. Only God's personal intervention at the end of the age will permanently defeat the Mystery of Iniquity. Only a daily commitment to personal to spiritual growth in discipleship will allow you to play a useful role in God's eternal program today [2 Pet 3.18]. We cannot put Mystery Babylon into service for us, many have tried and failed. You cannot defeat a spiritual enemy with secular weapons. Our enemy is spiritual, and his primary weapons are spiritual as well. You cannot defeat Satan with a vote any more than you can kill him with a gun.[380]

> 2 Corinthians 10:3–5 (KJV 1900)
> 3 For though we walk in the flesh, we do not war after the flesh: 4 (For the weapons of our warfare are not carnal, but mighty through God to the pulling down of strong holds;) 5 Casting down imaginations, and every high thing that exalteth itself against the knowledge of God, and bringing into captivity every thought to the obedience of Christ;

Secular actions can only prosper when the spiritual victory has already been attained. We cannot reverse Satan's hold upon our families and communities until we have laid the groundwork of personal revival, evangelism and disciple making. Believers must begin to obey and serve God before any effective movement on the secular level can succeed. Why would we expect God to bless the civic efforts of those who are opposed to His rule in their lives? We wish to retain our lusts and prejudices and still receive God's blessing under the concept of our "heritage as a Christian nation." This is self-deception and another psychological operation of the devil.

> Ephesians 6:13 (KJV 1900)
> Wherefore take unto you the whole armour of God, that ye may be able to withstand in the evil day, and having done all, to stand.

The Christian is involved in a spiritual warfare where he is either a victor or a victim. This spiritual warfare turns upon whether the individual believer obeys the scriptures and advances to spiritual maturity. It is in spiritual maturity where he can have maximum historical impact and usefulness to God. Spiritual warfare is all about the believer's function in marriage, in the family, in the community and in ministry.

What is Spiritual Warfare?

- Fighting to control our bodies is spiritual warfare
- Fighting for a good marriage is spiritual warfare [the Fall began with the failure of a marriage]
- Fighting to properly raise our children is spiritual warfare
- Caring for our extended families is spiritual warfare
- Having a good Christian reputation is spiritual warfare
- Evangelism is spiritual warfare.
- Prayer is spiritual warfare.
- Effective utilization of your spiritual gift is spiritual warfare
- Support of your <u>Bible-believing</u> local church is spiritual warfare [Christians will give an account for subsidizing false teaching]
- Ministry to fellow believers is spiritual warfare
- Good citizenship is spiritual warfare

Spiritual warfare is not what we think it is. Spiritual warfare is living in obedience to the Word of God by the power of the Holy Spirit *to the glory of God*.[381] The cumulative effect of believers living in spiritual victory is, first, maximum evangelistic impact upon that generation and second, the temporal blessing of that nation's institutions. You have the spiritual power in your small local church to create the spiritual environment that can change your community, but before your community is changed, you yourself must be changed [Gal 2.20].

28
The End Of Mystery Babylon

Revelation 17:15–18:2 (KJV 1900)
15 And he saith unto me, The waters which thou sawest, where the whore sitteth, are peoples, and multitudes, and nations, and tongues. 16 And the ten horns which thou sawest upon the beast, these shall hate the whore, and shall make her desolate and naked, and shall eat her flesh, and burn her with fire. 17 For God hath put in their hearts to fulfil his will, and to agree, and give their kingdom unto the beast, until the words of God shall be fulfilled. 18 And the woman which thou sawest is that great city, which reigneth over the kings of the earth. 1 And after these things I saw another angel come down from heaven, having great power; and the earth was lightened with his glory. 2 And he cried mightily with a strong voice, saying, Babylon the great is fallen, is fallen, And is become the habitation of devils, And the hold of every foul spirit, And a cage of every unclean and hateful bird.

Reasons for the Demise of the Harlot

Eventually, Satan will transition the world from following the deceptions of Mystery Babylon to the pure worship of himself. This has been his objective since the beginning of his rebellion [Isa 14.12-14] and is the secret end of all his appeals to men [Mt 4.8-10]. Eventually, Mystery Babylon will have served its purpose and he will use the federation of nations under his influence to destroy her.

It has been noted that Mystery Babylon is spiritual power that *influences* politics and economics. This is the same function that the False Prophet,[382] the beast from the earth, performs. But the false prophet also directs worship to the first beast, or the Antichrist. We do not see this same feature in Mystery Babylon, who is using the beast as a means of locomotion, even directing the beast, rather than simply serving the beast. There is a saying that you can advance as far as you wish in an organization, if you don't care who gets the credit. The False Prophet directs worship to the beast; Mystery Babylon uses the beast as transportation, serving its interests, while serving her own interests as well.

Mystery Babylon advanced the interests of the devil throughout the ages by means of a bewildering system of Luciferian worship that was hidden behind many front religions which varied nation by nation. The front religions either openly deny Jesus Christ, or tacitly deny him by adding works to salvation, or diminishing his deity, or his sacrifice on the cross for sin. Behind these front religions [exoteric] is the actual [esoteric] religion of Lucifer, disguised by symbols and allegorical language and systems of degrees where the candidate passes through a series of initiations where the partially correct information that he initially receives is replaced with more accurate information regarding the true nature of the secret faith. This is especially necessary in cultures where it would be inappropriate to publicly name Satan as lord. This same system exists, in these different forms, all over the world and has existed almost since the Fall of man.

This system, by its very age and scope has resulted in a great deal of accumulated wealth and power. The ability to trade and engage in high level finance requires sanction by initiation into this system, political power requires an introduction into this system [Rev 17.2, 15; 18.3, 9]. Protections, privileges, and access unavailable to common men and women are provided through membership in this system and can be taken away by the action of this same system. This matrix of influence and control has grown exponentially over the centuries. And by the time of the events in our passage, the system designed to serve Satan is now a load upon the back [Rev 17.3] of his son, the Antichrist.

The kings and kingdoms represented by the ten horns received benefits from their illicit association with Mystery Babylon, called "fornication" in Rev 17. But, as with fornication in the literal sense, there is always a steep cost.

Proverbs 6:26 (KJV 1900)
26 For by means of a whorish woman a man is brought to a piece

of bread: And the adulteress will hunt for the precious life…32
But whoso committeth adultery with a woman lacketh
understanding: He that doeth it destroyeth his own soul.

This fornication with Mystery Babylon has cost these rulers in authority and in freedom of action. By virtue of their sin, they have compromised the security of nations and made themselves subject to blackmail. Recall that the ten horns are a part of the beast, so the harlot is riding the backs of these kings as well.

Therefore, these kings are motivated by two factors: their own resentment of Mystery Babylon and the decision of their lord, the Antichrist to terminate the existence of the Harlot.

Revelation 17:16–17 (KJV 1900)
16 And the ten horns which thou sawest upon the beast, these shall hate the whore, and shall make her desolate and naked, and shall eat her flesh, and burn her with fire. 17 For God hath put in their hearts to fulfil his will, and to agree, and give their kingdom unto the beast, until the words of God shall be fulfilled.

The disposal of the Harlot is not in the way one would treat an ally, but a hated and despised enemy. Clearly the relationship between the Beast/Antichrist and Mystery Babylon was an unstable one for some time. This should serve as a warning to all Christians who would seek out the Ecumenical Movement as a solution to the world's problems. Satan will ultimately turn upon this system, requiring compulsory, direct worship, via the imposition of the Mark, without the deceptions conceded in the nascent one world Church [Rev 13.11-18].

This judgment of the Harlot is also an illustration of how God can use his enemies to accomplish His purpose. God can use our own sin to punish us; He can use our own allies to discipline us. God is not the author of evil, but he can and does allow and assist in the destruction of people via their own wickedness [Jas 1.13-15].

Revelation 17:18–18:2 (KJV 1900)
18 And the woman which thou sawest is that great city, which reigneth over the kings of the earth. 1 And after these things I saw another angel come down from heaven, having great power; and the earth was lightened with his glory. 2 And he cried mightily with a strong voice, saying, Babylon the great is fallen, is fallen,

And is become the habitation of devils, And the hold of every foul spirit, And a cage of every unclean and hateful bird.

In the Bible, Babylon is a city, a country, an empire, and a concept. Babylon the Great is a Mystery; it both includes and supersedes mere geography. It is a worldview, a religious/commercial system, and a synonym for Satan's ambition. It is also Jerusalem, the last headquarters for Mystery Babylon the Great, at the end of history. [383]

The ultimate end of Babylon the Great will be decisive and total annihilation. It will retain its demonic character however, even in death. It will literally be an unclean place. The system that was disguised by wealth, culture, power, and religious pretense will have its true character revealed.

Repercussions of the Demise of the Harlot

Revelation 18:9–11 (KJV 1900)
9 And <u>the kings of the earth</u>, who have committed fornication and lived deliciously with her, Shall bewail her, and lament for her, When they shall see the smoke of her burning, 10 Standing afar off for the fear of her torment, Saying, Alas, alas, that great city Babylon, that mighty city! For in one hour is thy judgment come. 11 And the merchants of the earth shall weep and mourn over her; For no man buyeth their merchandise any more:

The attitude of the ten super kings [horns] directly connected to the beast will not be shared by the other *lower kings of the earth*. These kings will feel the loss of power and revenue far more than they will benefit from the destruction of Babylon. They are not directly associated with the beast and have grown accustomed to the relationship with Mystery Babylon, however abusive it might have occasionally been.

The *merchants* of the earth had become *kings* by association with Mystery Babylon,

Revelation 18:23 (KJV 1900)
23 And the light of a candle shall shine no more at all in thee; And the voice of the bridegroom and of the bride shall be heard no more at all in thee: <u>For thy merchants were the great men of the earth</u>; For by thy sorceries were all nations deceived.

The merchants will sorely miss the coordination and power afforded by the existence of Mystery Babylon. For example, the ability to manipulate markets through the control of populations via false religion. Religion has been used to initiate the *wealth transfer mechanism*[384] through wars.

War is the most profitable of all businesses:[385] financing loans, selling weapons, burning fuel, obtaining land, natural resources, markets, workforces, and then pocketing profits for rebuilding the defeated country [or the countries of our allies] for the benefit of the new owners, at taxpayer expense.

These wars generate vast profits for the use of Mystery Babylon. The current use of *Islam* to prime the wealth transfer machine is a perfect example of this. The manipulation of the concept of "Islamic terrorism"[386] is used in this manner to:

➤ Effect regime change in otherwise independent countries[387]
➤ Extort funds from citizens via taxation for the "national defense" [388]
➤ Eliminate freedoms due to the threat of "terrorism"[389]
➤ Provide arms-length management of the drug trade and other illegal but massively profitable activities[390]

These religion-based movements have been manufactured largely to serve the purposes of Mystery Babylon.[391]

The power of religion is used to justify the exploitation of subject peoples for financial gain and for the purpose of social engineering. For example, *versions* of Christianity have been created that justify and support imperialism, genocide, slavery, and *de-jure* discrimination. Both Europe and America developed and continue maintain a version of Christianity that can coexist with both de-jure and de-facto segregation and institutionalized discrimination based upon race. Such systems aid in ensuring that wealth transfers flow in one direction only, from common people, prioritized by ethnicity, to the "kings of the earth."

In this brief discussion we can see that Mystery Babylon is the administrative authority behind oppression in the world. Although the drive to oppress is a product of the individual sin nature, Mystery Babylon specializes in the *science* of oppression to the end of maintaining control of the unbelieving population and creating the conditions that will lead to the emergence of the New World Order. The Antichrist will, at the midpoint of the seven-year period described in Daniel 9, reveal oppression to be the true character of his kingdom as well. The destruction of Mystery Babylon by the servants of the Antichrist is not based upon philosophical differences, but upon the necessity of the evolution of his movement to the singular worship of himself and Satan.

> Isaiah 14:15–17 (KJV 1900)
> [15] Yet thou shalt be brought down to hell, to the sides of the pit. [16] They that see thee shall narrowly look upon thee, *and* consider thee, *saying, Is* this the man that made the earth to tremble, that did shake kingdoms; [17] *That* made the world as a wilderness, and destroyed the cities thereof; *That* <u>opened not the house of his prisoners</u>?

With the death of Mystery Babylon, all these advantages are now gone for the smaller players, the "kings of the earth," many of whom will experience downward mobility from privilege to the status of common men. Thus, there will be weeping and lamentation, due to the loss of the power to easily gain wealth and privilege through exploitation.

29
The End Of The Antichrist

Revelation 16:12–16 (KJV 1900) 12 And the sixth angel poured out his vial upon the great river Euphrates; and the water thereof was dried up, that the way of the kings of the east might be prepared. 13 And I saw three unclean spirits like frogs come out of the mouth of the dragon, and out of the mouth of the beast, and out of the mouth of the false prophet. 14 For they are the spirits of devils, working miracles, which go forth unto the kings of the earth and of the whole world, to gather them to the battle of that great day of God Almighty. 15 Behold, I come as a thief. Blessed is he that watcheth, and keepeth his garments, lest he walk naked, and they see his shame. 16 And he gathered them together into a place called in the Hebrew tongue Armageddon.

Demonic Control of World Affairs

The final chapter of Gentile history repeats the theme of angelic and human cooperation against God that has characterized the ages since the fall of humanity. The nations are led by Lucifer, who is the temporary prince of this world [Jn 12.31; 1 Jn 5.19]. He administers his kingdom through the agency of many demons, three of which are mentioned in Revelation 16.13-14. The unbeliever and the Christian who is ignorant of the Bible do not realize that the visible world is powerfully influenced by invisible spiritual factors. Consequently, man harbors a completely unrealistic perception of reality, and an overestimation of his own power and knowledge.

Psalm 127:1–2 (KJV 1900)
1 Except the Lord build the house, they labour in vain that build it: Except the Lord keep the city, the watchman waketh *but* in vain. 2 *It is* vain for you to rise up early, to sit up late, To eat the bread of sorrows: *For* so he giveth his beloved sleep.

The role of angels and demons in the spiritual influence of this world is illustrated in the book of Daniel where the prayer of the prophet was answered by an angel who had been delayed by conflict with a demon prince who sought to prevent his errand to the prophet. This angel conveyed the reality of the spiritual rulership of the nations in clear language:

Daniel 10:12–13 (KJV 1900)
12 Then said he unto me, Fear not, Daniel: for from the first day that thou didst set thine heart to understand, and to chasten thyself before thy God, thy words were heard, and I am come for thy words. 13 But the prince of the kingdom of Persia withstood me one and twenty days: but, lo, Michael, one of the chief princes, came to help me; and I remained there with the kings of Persia.

Daniel 10:20–21 (KJV 1900)
20 Then said he, Knowest thou wherefore I come unto thee? and now will I return to fight with the prince of Persia: and when I am gone forth, lo, the prince of Grecia shall come. 21 But I will shew thee that which is noted in the scripture of truth: and there is none that holdeth with me in these things, but Michael your prince.

Every nation is assigned a fallen angel from the demonic hierarchy. There are no exceptions. Although God is free to overrule their will, as in the case above, they exercise significant power and influence over their dominions. This power is demonstrated by the demonic guidance which will bring about the greatest war in world history. Yet again the following verse is impressed upon the mind of the reader:

Ephesians 6:11–12 (KJV 1900)
11 Put on the whole armour of God, that ye may be able to stand against the wiles of the devil. 12 For we wrestle not against flesh and blood, but against principalities, against powers, <u>against the rulers of the darkness of this world</u>, against spiritual wickedness in high places.

World System Created, Empowered and Administered by Satan [392]

The unbeliever, and unfortunately many believers, fail to understand that Satan's world system is *entirely* evil [1 Jn 2.15-17; 5.19].[393] The presence of apparent good within his system must be counterbalanced with the understanding that such good is accomplished in total defiance towards God. Instead, Satan rejects God's right to rule the universe and the heavens and seeks to unseat Him. There exists a category of good that can only be pursued *after* one has rejected God. This is one lesson of the Garden of Eden.

Every unbeliever is ensconced within a spiritual system of slavery which promotes spiritual blindness [Rom 3.11; 1 Cor 2.14, 15]. It encourages incorrect views about God *and* the devil. From this labyrinth of ignorance and hostility towards the God of the Bible the unsaved individual habitually pursues the agenda of the god of this world. Regardless of intelligence or privilege, spiritual death within the human heart finds itself at home within this world system.[394]

The sympathetic relationship between the Satan, his world system and the unbeliever are energized by an animating spirit which finds its source in Satan.

> Ephesians 2:1–2 (KJV 1900)
> ¹ And you *hath he quickened*, who were dead in trespasses and sins; ² Wherein in time past ye walked according to the course of this world, according to the prince of the power of the air, *the spirit that now worketh* in the children of disobedience:

Consequently, all the controversies of the world's social, political, and philosophical paradigms serve the interest of Satan.[395] Other than within the lives and assemblies of Bible-following Christians, there is no ground upon earth where his purposes are not served. Only in heaven and in that Word which originates from heaven, the Scriptures, may be found the key to reality and to truth. Only in heaven may be found the means of the defeat of Satan and his plans. Only by faith in the blood of Jesus Christ is found escape from Satan's dominion of spiritual and ethical darkness [Col 1.13], access to God [1 Jn 1.7] and fellowship with the saints of light.

> Hebrews 4:15–16 (KJV 1900)
> 15 For we have not an high priest which cannot be touched with the feeling of our infirmities; but was in all points tempted like as we are, yet without sin. 16 Let us therefore come boldly unto the throne of grace, that we may obtain mercy, and find grace to help in time of need.

The Armageddon Campaign

> Revelation 16:12–16 (KJV 1900)
> 12 And the sixth angel poured out his vial upon the great river Euphrates; and the water thereof was dried up, that the way of the kings of the east might be prepared. 13 And I saw three unclean spirits like frogs come out of the mouth of the dragon, and out of the mouth of the beast, and out of the mouth of the false prophet. 14 For they are the spirits of devils, working miracles, which go forth unto the kings of the earth and of the whole world, to gather them to the battle of that great day of God Almighty. 15 Behold, I come as a thief. Blessed is he that watcheth, and keepeth his garments, lest he walk naked, and they see his shame. 16 And he gathered them together into a place called in the Hebrew tongue Armageddon.

Two Different Motivations for Armageddon

Verses twelve and thirteen above are connected. God Himself prepares the way for the kings of the east to move west to serve His purpose of gathering the nations to meet their end in Israel. Lucifer has also read the scriptures and executes his own plan. He sends demonic messengers to supernaturally persuade the kings of the earth to converge upon the strategic center of the kingdom of Antichrist.

Recall that in Chapter 12 of Revelation, Satan and his angels are defeated in heaven and cast out. We determined that this occurred at about the midpoint of Daniel's seventieth week. Immediately after this event, the Antichrist is revealed by the Abomination of Desolation, where he claims to be Messiah [Christ] and God. The life of every individual who is unwilling to acknowledge the Beast as Christ is forfeit.

Through the power of the Dragon, the system of the Antichrist and the False Prophet holds together [Rev 13.2-8]. Many disobedient Jews continue to occupy Israel and the world worships the Beast and the Dragon [Rev 13.11-12].

However, once it appears that the way is open for attack upon the kingdom of the Antichrist, Lucifer doubles down on the Lord's preparations by encouraging *all* the kings of the earth to attack the kingdom that he supports. Why is this?

After his decisive defeat in heaven, the only way that Lucifer has any chance of overcoming the Lord is through the elimination of the Jews. God has made a series of promises to redeemed Israel which have not yet been fulfilled. Although the amillennialist Roman Catholic Church and a host of Protestant scholars have awarded these promises to themselves,[396] the scriptures clearly teach that these promises are yet to be fulfilled [Dt 30.1-10; Isa 59.20-21; 61.8-9; Jer 31.31-31; Eze 11.19-20; 36:24–32; Joel 2.28-32; Zech 12.10; Heb 8.1-13] also [2 Sam 7.11-17].

Should God be unable to keep these promises because of the genocide of the Jews, then Satan will have his point against God. Satan denied to Eve that the wages of sin are death [Gen 3.1-5]. Perhaps he actually meant it. Evidence that God is unable to keep His promises would make Him a liar and thus unholy, as Satan implied to Eve. Therefore, the devil must precipitate the attack of his own kingdom, realizing that its strategic geographical center is Israel. By amassing the world's armies at this single point, the likelihood of the destruction of the Jews is high, particularly if aided by demonically implanted suggestions that the Jews are a part of their problem. Such a suggestion has worked in the past.[397]

In fact, during the Siege of Jerusalem, a very large number of Jews will be killed [Micah 4.11-5.1; Zech 12-14].

Zechariah 13:7–9 (KJV 1900)
7 Awake, O sword, against my shepherd, and against the man that is my fellow, Saith the LORD of hosts: Smite the shepherd, and the sheep shall be scattered: And I will turn mine hand upon the little ones. 8 And it shall come to pass, that in all the land, saith the LORD, Two parts therein shall be cut off and die; But the third shall be left therein. 9 And I will bring the third part through the fire, And will refine them as silver is refined, And will try them as gold is tried: They shall call on my name, and I will hear them: I will say, It is my people: And they shall say, The LORD is my God.

Daniel 11 and the Prophecy of the Armageddon Campaign

Daniel 11.1-35 commences the final vision to Daniel during the third year of Cyrus of Persia. Daniel is given the future of the world from his time until the end of the reign of Antiochus IV [Epiphanes] 164 BC. This Syrian king is a precursor of the Antichrist, performing an early version of many of the actions of the future Antichrist. This prophecy to Daniel covers:

- The four last kings of Persia
- The emergence of Greece
- The demise of Alexander and the rise of the four generals/kings who divide Alexander's kingdom.
- The wars between two of these dynasties: the Seleucids of Syria and the Ptolemy's of Egypt
- The rise of the Seleucid Antiochus IV, a type of the Antichrist

In verse thirty-five of chapter 11, the information concerning Antiochus ends and in verse 36, the Willful King[398] is introduced. This individual is yet future: we know this because the events of verses 36 through 54 have not yet occurred. Thus Daniel 11, like Daniel 8, combines the prophecy of Antiochus with the revelation of another ruler in the far distant future.

Daniel 11.36 begins a description of the activities of the Antichrist in the last days[399]

> Daniel 11:36–38 (KJV 1900)
> 36 And the king shall do according to his will; and he shall exalt himself, and magnify himself above every god, and shall speak marvellous things against the God of gods, and shall prosper till the indignation be accomplished: for that that is determined shall be done. 37 Neither shall he regard the God of his fathers, nor the desire of women, nor regard any god: for he shall magnify himself above all. 38 But in his estate shall he honour the God of forces: and a god whom his fathers knew not shall he honour with gold, and silver, and with precious stones, and pleasant things.

The strategy of the *Antichrist* involves the consolidation of operational control over the earth, the destruction of Mystery Babylon, and the maintenance of the worldwide worship of himself as god and Messiah. On the other hand, *Lucifer* hopes to prevent God from fulfilling His unconditional covenants to Israel and invalidating His rule of the universe by demonstrating His inability to keep His promises to redeemed Israel.

It is possible that the Antichrist will not be fully aware of the plans of his sponsor, the devil, and will play his role in continuing to maintain the integrity of his kingdom in the face of rebellion by the kings of the earth. It is also possible that he is fully aware of the devil's purpose in rousing the kings of the earth and fights against them in a holding action in anticipation of the return of Christ when *all* will join forces to resist His coming. We may only speculate upon the degree of understanding possessed by the Man of Sin. [400]

As we have related, with the sending of the frog demons,[401] Satan's plan is set into motion. Both God and Lucifer seek to gather the armies of the world in Israel, but for different reasons. God will enable this strategy via the sixth vial judgment.

> Revelation 16:12–14 (KJV 1900)
> 12 And the sixth angel poured out his vial upon the great river Euphrates; and the water thereof was dried up, that the way of the kings of the east might be prepared. 13 And I saw three unclean spirits like frogs *come* out of the mouth of the dragon, and out of the mouth of the beast, and out of the mouth of the false prophet. 14 For they are the spirits of devils, working miracles, *which* go forth unto the kings of the earth and of the whole world, to gather them to the battle of that great day of God Almighty.

Just as God is preparing the way for the kings of the east, Satan is sending his demonic messengers to call the kings of the earth,[402] ostensibly to make war upon the Antichrist, but with the true motive of a convergence upon Israel, the most strategic territory in the world,[403] and the heart of the Antichrist's power,[404] the location of the temple and of his throne [2 Th 2.3-4].

The plans of these kings, the Antichrist and Lucifer will be overturned as the Lord superintends all events to His own purpose, to the everlasting glory of His name.

> Zechariah 12:1–3 (KJV 1900)
> 1 The burden of the word of the LORD for Israel, saith the

LORD, Which stretcheth forth the heavens, and layeth the foundation of the earth, And formeth the spirit of man within him. 2 Behold, I will make Jerusalem a cup of trembling unto all the people round about, When they shall be in the siege both against Judah and against Jerusalem. 3 And in that day will I make Jerusalem a burdensome stone for all people: All that burden themselves with it shall be cut in pieces, Though all the people of the earth be gathered together against it.

The Definition of the Armageddon Campaign

The Battle of Armageddon is more appropriately called the Armageddon Campaign[405], because it includes several battles and events:

1. The Assembling of the Allies of Antichrist at Armageddon[406] [Ps 2.1-6; Joel 3.9-11; Rev 16.12-16]
2. The Siege and Fall of Jerusalem [Micah 4.11-5.1; Zech 12-14]
3. The national regeneration of Israel [Joel 2.28-32; Zech 12.10-14; 13.7-9; Rom 11.25-27]
4. The Second Coming of Christ [Isa 34.1-7; 63.1-3; Mic 2.12-13; Hab 3.3]
5. The Battle of Bozrah/Edom [Isa 34.1-6; 63.1-6; Jer 49.13-14]
6. From the Battle of Bozrah to the Valley of Jehoshaphat[407] [Isa 63.1; Jer 49.20-22; Joel 2.28-32; Zech 14.12-15]
7. -The Victory Ascent upon the Mount of Olives [Joel 3.14-17; Zech 14.3-5; Matt 24.29-31; Rev 19.11-21][408]

The King of the South:

Daniel 11:40a (KJV 1900)
And at the time of the end shall the king of the south push at him:

Each point of the compass is described from the standpoint of its geographic relation to Israel. The king of the south will include an Arab/African alliance,[409] reminiscent of a similar alliance that dominated the world throughout much of the Old Testament era. Beyond these generalities it is not profitable to speculate upon the exact composition of these alliances in the future since they all change over time.

Presumably, this king will strike north towards Jerusalem, since this is the objective suggested by the demonic spirits sent to influence this outcome [Rev 16.13-14].

It appears that the Antichrist and his armies will race across Europe and then head south to mount a counterattack and prevail against the King of the South.

Daniel 11:42–43 (KJV 1900)
[42] He shall stretch forth his hand also upon the countries: and the land of Egypt shall not escape. [43] But he shall have power over the treasures of gold and of silver, and over all the precious things of Egypt: and the Libyans and the Ethiopians *shall be* at his steps.

Here we see Africans of the Southern Confederacy at their defeat by the Antichrist. He now must use military arms to hold together his control of the world, which he will successfully maintain, until the coming of Christ in the heavens to personally intervene to end the war.

On his way from Europe to attack the King of the South, the Antichrist will set up operations in Israel, the Glorious Land.

Daniel 11:41 (NKJV)
He shall also enter the Glorious Land, and many *countries* shall be overthrown; but these shall escape from his hand: Edom, Moab, and the prominent people of Ammon.

The activity of the Antichrist ["he" in vss. 42-43] demonstrates his overwhelming power in the last days. He will meet the challenge of the kings of the North and South decisively, but not without losses in Palestine itself, which will suffer under the attacks of the King of the North and South. These, as well as the counterattack by The Antichrist himself, are referred to as the Siege of Jerusalem [Micah 4.11-5.1; Zech 12-14].

The Kings of the East and North

Daniel 11:44 (KJV 1900)
But tidings out of the east and out of the north shall trouble him: therefore he shall go forth with great fury to destroy, and utterly to make away many.

We have seen the appearance of the Kings of the East earlier in the bowl judgments

Revelation 16:12 (KJV 1900)
And the sixth angel poured out his vial upon the great river Euphrates; and the water thereof was dried up, that the way of the kings of the east might be prepared. [Rev 9.13-19[410]]

Modern history has, from one perspective, consisted of the attempts of the West pushing East to achieve control over the gigantic earth island of Europe and Asia. The beast will, ever so briefly, achieve this objective through treaty and spiritual conquest. In the last days of the Gentile order, supernatural actions on the part of God will result in the Kings of the East moving *West* and crossing the Euphrates with bad intentions towards the Antichrist. It is possible that the Kings of the East will converge on Israel via Edom resulting in the *Battle of Bozrah*.

News regarding this action and the attack upon Israel by the King of the North, perhaps taking advantage of the Antichrist's distraction by the King of the South, will draw the Antichrist and his forces in the South back towards Jerusalem. Joel 2.1-20 and Zechariah 12 describe the attack of the King of the North upon Israel and the *Siege of Jerusalem*.

Joel 2:3 (KJV 1900)
A fire devoureth before them; And behind them a flame burneth: The land is as the garden of Eden before them, And behind them a desolate wilderness; Yea, and nothing shall escape them.

Joel 2:20 (KJV 1900)
But I will remove far off from you the northern army, And will drive him into a land barren and desolate, With his face toward the east sea, And his hinder part toward the utmost sea, And his stink shall come up, and his ill savour shall come up, Because he hath done great things.

After his initial success against the King of the South, the Antichrist will be forced to head back to Israel due to the reports that he has heard.

First the successful initial battle against the King of the South

Daniel 11:42–44 (KJV 1900)
42 He shall stretch forth his hand also upon the countries: and the

land of Egypt shall not escape. 43 But he shall have power over the treasures of gold and of silver, and over all the precious things of Egypt: and the Libyans and the Ethiopians shall be at his steps. 44 But tidings out of the east and out of the north shall trouble him: therefore he shall go forth with great fury to destroy, and utterly to make away many.

Next his forced return to Israel

Daniel 11:44–45 (KJV 1900)
44 But tidings out of the east and out of the north shall trouble him: therefore he shall go forth with great fury to destroy, and utterly to make away many. 45 And he shall plant the tabernacles of his palace between the seas in the glorious holy mountain; yet he shall come to his end, and none shall help him.

The intent of the Antichrist may be to have the unwitting assistance of the kings of the East, South, and North in eliminating the Jews, certainly many Jews will die because of this conspiracy, *but it does not look that way in the text*. It is not essential that the knowledge of the Antichrist and of Satan perfectly align. The Antichrist has desired the worship of the Jews, and many will worship him [Rev 13.8,12,14]. Although he is willing to kill any Jew who resists his claims to deity, it does not appear that he seeks to wipe out the entire nation.

The *devil* wants the annihilation of the Jews and apparently instigates [Rev 16.13-14] the gathering of world's greatest army of all time, comprised of demons and demon indwelt men, to destroy Israel and, at the right moment, to repel, if possible, the return of Christ. The three coalitions [South, North and East] appear to be motivated by a desire to overthrow the rule of Antichrist. Their attacks are said to be against him. Their attempt to accomplish this overthrow will result in the Siege of Jerusalem. It is during this siege that God's redemptive purpose for Israel will be accomplished, and the tables turned upon Satan and his

hosts.
Zechariah 13:8–9 (KJV 1900)
8 And it shall come to pass, that in all the land, saith the LORD, Two parts therein shall be cut off and die; But the third shall be left therein. 9 And I will bring the third part through the fire, And will refine them as silver is refined, And will try them as gold is tried: They shall call on my name, and I will hear them: I will say, It is my people: And they shall say, The LORD is my God.

God's Activity in History

The devil has a plan, but God also has a plan. God uses our own wickedness to punish us and to accomplish His own ends. This is equally true for the devil. It only *appears* that Lucifer has the upper hand: God is working in history and outside of history in the spiritual realm to accomplish his purposes. The question is, are His people too busy fearing the devil to follow the Lord?

> ### The Armageddon Campaign
> - *The Assembling of the Allies of Antichrist at Armageddon [Ps 2.1-6; Joel 3.9-11; Rev 16.12-16]*
> - *The Siege and Fall of Jerusalem [Micah 4.11-5.1; Zech 12-14]*
> - *The National Regeneration of Israel [Joel 2.28-32; Zech 12.10-14; 13.7-9; Rom 11.25-27]*
> - *The Second Coming of Christ [Isa 34.1-7; 63.1-3; Mic 2.12-13; Hab 3.3]*
> - *The Battle of Bozrah/Edom [Isa 34.1-6; 63.1-6; Jer 49.13-14]*
> - *From the Battle of Borzah to the Valley of Jehoshaphat [Isa 63.1; Jer 49.20-22; Joel 2.28-32; Zech 14.12-15]*
> - *The Victory Ascent upon the Mount of Olives [Joel 3.14-17; Zech 14.3-5; Matt 24.29-31; Rev 19.11-21]*

God can use the unfolding of history to punish the rebellious and to test the faithful. *God is using every combination of historical circumstances to demonstrate his own righteousness and mankind's sinfulness.* These ages are also called dispensations. [411] In every dispensation God allows the catastrophe which is the inevitable consequence of unbelieving humanity's failure to adjust to the divine revelation provided to that generation.

DISPENSATION	FAILURE AND JUDGMENT
Innocence	The Fall [Gen 3]
Conscience	The Flood [Gen 6-7]
Law	The Fall of Jerusalem and Diaspora of the Jews [2 Kin 25.1-21]
Grace	The Resurrection of the Church followed by the Onset of the Day of the Lord 1 Th 4.13-5.3]
Kingdom	The Defeat of the Final Rebellion and the White Throne Judgment [Rev 20.7-14]

Figure 15: Dispensations

In these judgments, *believers* receive the opportunity to demonstrate the effectiveness of divinely supplied spiritual assets in each age [Heb 11.32-40]. These assets enable the believer to not only endure suffering but to use suffering as a powerful means of spiritual advance for themselves and the world. The redeemed Israelites of the Tribulation will experience extreme suffering through which they will be sanctified to the glory God.

Zechariah 13:8–9 (KJV 1900)
⁸ And it shall come to pass, *that* in all the land, saith the Lord, Two parts therein shall be cut off *and* die; But the third shall be left therein. ⁹ And I will bring the third part through the fire, And will refine them as silver is refined, And will try them as gold is tried: They shall call on my name, and I will hear them: I will say, It *is* my people: And they shall say, The Lord *is* my God.

For the believer, historical disaster, be it social, economic, environmental, or military, results in pain and *pain always asks a question*: Can the believer use suffering to glorify God and to illustrate the spiritual power that God imparts to those who believe in him; or is pain a sovereign, a monarch at whose disposal we must serve?

The Return of Christ

The return of Christ marks the counter offensive of Christ in the Armageddon Campaign. The return of Christ is the beginning of the end of evil altogether [Dan 9.24]. It is the eschatological exclamation point that answers every skeptic and ends all debate regarding the existence and nature of God. It is the initial act of the vindication of those who follow God through Christ, it is the validation of the scriptures, and it is the victory of the believing remnant of Israel.

Satan has used demonic deception to maneuver the kings of the earth into participating in the destruction of Israel. Satan, having read the Bible, will use these same armies to confront and resist the return of Christ. While Satan plans, God uses these plans to accomplish divine purposes in the Armageddon Campaign.

> "Har-Magedon" [Rev 16.14-16] is situated in the plain of Esdraelon, around the hill of Megiddo, in northern Israel about 20 miles south-southeast of Haifa.[412] It is likely that this word is used symbolically to describe the entire military campaign by which Christ singlehandedly defeats Satan and the Antichrist. Christ is returning not as a peacemaker, but as a warrior. Jesus is not returning to have a conference with the devil, but to slay the wicked.

"Mine eyes have seen the glory of the coming of the Lord; He is trampling out the vintage where the grapes of wrath are stored; He hath loosed the fateful lightning of His terrible swift sword; His truth is marching on."[413]

Revelation 19:11–21 (KJV 1900)
11 And I saw heaven opened, and behold a white horse; and he that sat upon him was called Faithful and True, and in righteousness he doth judge and make war. 12 His eyes were as a flame of fire, and on his head were many crowns; and he had a name written, that no man knew, but he himself. 13 And he was clothed with a vesture dipped in blood: and his name is called The Word of God. 14 And the armies which were in heaven followed him upon white horses, clothed in fine linen, white and clean. 15 And out of his mouth goeth a sharp sword, that with it he should smite the nations: and he shall rule them with a rod of iron: and he treadeth the winepress of the fierceness and wrath of Almighty God. 16 And he hath on his vesture and on his thigh a name written, KING OF KINGS, AND LORD OF LORDS. 17 And I saw an angel standing in the sun; and he cried with a loud voice, saying to all the fowls that fly in the midst of heaven, Come and gather yourselves together unto the supper of the great God; 18 That ye may eat the flesh of kings, and the flesh of captains, and the flesh of mighty men, and the flesh of horses, and of them that sit on them, and the flesh of all men, both free and bond, both

small and great. 19 And I saw the beast, and the kings of the earth, and their armies, gathered together to make war against him that sat on the horse, and against his army. 20 And the beast was taken, and with him the false prophet that wrought miracles before him, with which he deceived them that had received the mark of the beast, and them that worshipped his image. These both were cast alive into a lake of fire burning with brimstone. 21 And the remnant were slain with the sword of him that sat upon the horse, which sword proceeded out of his mouth: and all the fowls were filled with their flesh.

The End of Antichrist

The warfare against Israel ends as the antagonists' become allies and unite against their common enemy Jesus Christ. The world is not the friend of Jesus, nor will they welcome His return. The kings of this world have a master and it is not Jesus Christ. If it were Him, then they would advance His interests, they would obey His commands.

The Antichrist and kings of the world will attempt to resist Christ with a combination of military and demonic power. However, the combined might of what will likely be demonically hybridized people and technology will be no match for Jesus Christ.

Jesus Himself with fight with the armies of the world, the armies who accompany Christ will be only witnesses. He will defeat the massive armies assembled near Jerusalem and singlehandedly cause hundreds of thousands of casualties, likely millions, due to the size of the four armies involved. There will be no negotiations, no quarter given, Christ will administer complete destruction to the participating armies present in the Valley of Jehoshaphat.

> Joel 3:9–16 (KJV 1900)
> 9 Proclaim ye this among the Gentiles; Prepare war, wake up the mighty men, Let all the men of war draw near; let them come up: 10 Beat your plowshares into swords, And your pruninghooks into spears: Let the weak say, I am strong. 11 Assemble yourselves, and come, all ye heathen, And gather yourselves together round about: Thither cause thy mighty ones to come down, O LORD. 12 Let the heathen be wakened, and come up to the valley of Jehoshaphat: For there will I sit to judge all the

heathen round about. 13 Put ye in the sickle, for the harvest is ripe: Come, get you down; for the press is full, the fats overflow; For their wickedness is great. 14 Multitudes, multitudes in the valley of decision: For the day of the LORD is near in the valley of decision. 15 The sun and the moon shall be darkened, And the stars shall withdraw their shining. 16 The LORD also shall roar out of Zion, And utter his voice from Jerusalem; And the heavens and the earth shall shake: But the LORD will be the hope of his people, And the strength of the children of Israel.

The Antichrist and the False Prophet will not be killed but cast alive into the Lake of Fire.

Revelation 19:20 (KJV 1900)
[20] And the beast was taken, and with him the false prophet that wrought miracles before him, with which he deceived them that had received the mark of the beast, and them that worshipped his image. These both were cast alive into a lake of fire burning with brimstone.

The rest of those killed in the battle go to Hades and will remain there until Hades itself is cast into the Lake of Fire [Rev 20.14].

The Lake of Fire will become the permanent abode of both the Antichrist and the False Prophet. Lucifer will be sent temporarily to the bottomless pit, where he will remain until released for a brief time at the end of the 1000-year reign of Christ [Rev 20.3, 7-10]. After this, Satan also will be incarcerated in the Lake of Fire where he will permanently remain.

30
Epilogue: What Are Our Chances?

If we cannot prevent the emergence of the Antichrist, what then is the end game for the believer?

God has not directed believers to be outcome-oriented, but faithfulness-oriented. It is God who controls outcomes; only He has the vision, wisdom, and power to ensure the proper end of the decisions of men and angels, only He can guide every aspect of His creation to achieve His own purposes.

> Isaiah 46:9–10 (KJV 1900)
> 9 Remember the former things of old: For I am God, and there is none else; I am God, and there is none like me, 10 Declaring the end from the beginning, And from ancient times the things that are not yet done, Saying, My counsel shall stand, And I will do all my pleasure:

The believer, who lacks God's sovereignty, omniscience, and omnipotence, is not held responsible for spiritual outcomes but for his own motives, thoughts, decisions, and actions. He will give an account to God, not for what society has done, but for what he himself did with the Word of God.

Christians today tend to focus upon outcomes to the detriment of their own spiritual lives. We want to "grow the local church," create a "Christian government," or "overcome oppression" through direct attacks upon the institutions of society by both legitimate and illegitimate means. Outcome-based thinking tends to cause people to focus upon results rather than the spiritual processes that through God, irresistibly influence institutions and civilization.

Just as God has not charged believers with growing the Church, neither has He charged the Church with preventing the advent of the Antichrist. A commitment to winning the lost *is not the same thing* as a commitment to growing the local church. In the same way, a commitment to spiritual growth, resulting in personal holiness, is not the same as delaying or preventing the advent of the Antichrist. The scriptures demonstrate that the objective of the spiritual life is the individual believer becoming what he is commanded to become in Christ. God has not charged us to promote a specific social, political, or economic configuration of society. What God has demanded is a personal spiritual transformation, culminating in conformity to divine holiness and love.

It is this personal transformation on the part of individual believers that has a transformative effect upon civilization. Therefore, our endgame is: *the effective biblical function of the Church in producing disciples of Jesus Christ who are sanctified and faithful to a sound interpretation of the scriptures.*

The Engine of History

God is concerned about the behavior of peoples and nations.

Acts 10:34–35 (KJV 1900)
34 Then Peter opened his mouth, and said, Of a truth I perceive that God is no respecter of persons: 35 But in every nation he that feareth him, and worketh righteousness, is accepted with him.

God is not God of Christians and Jews only, but of the Gentiles as well [Dan 4.17; Rom 3.29]. He has made it clear that he has expectations of unbelievers and their governments and that he will hold Gentile governments responsible for violations of the dictates of conscience and morality [Prov 14.34; Rom 1.18-19]. It is these very restraints that man wishes to do away with.

Psalm 2:1–3 (KJV 1900)
1 Why do the heathen rage, And the people imagine a vain thing?
2 The kings of the earth set themselves, And the rulers take counsel together, Against the LORD, and against his anointed, saying, 3 Let us break their bands asunder, And cast away their cords from us.

The biblical mechanism in place for the transforming of peoples and nations is the penetrating effect of Christian discipleship upon the consciences and moral climate of unbelieving peoples and nations. It is the cumulative witness of the lips and lives of maturing believers that has this purifying effect upon the institutions of society as unbelievers are won to Christ and/or see the plan of God for marriage, family and the state portrayed in the faithful lives of believers in Jesus Christ. The human conscience is constantly recalibrated by viewing the obedience or disobedience [2 Sam 12.14; Rom 2.17-24; 1 Tim 6.1] of believers. It is in this way that the Christian functions as salt and light within the unbelieving world: either preserving and illuminating biblical morality or by demonstrating that their witness is "good for nothing."

Matthew 5:13–16 (KJV 1900)
13 Ye are the salt of the earth: but if the salt have lost his savour, wherewith shall it be salted? it is thenceforth good for nothing, but to be cast out, and to be trodden under foot of men. 14 Ye are the light of the world. A city that is set on an hill cannot be hid. 15 Neither do men light a candle, and put it under a bushel, but on a candlestick; and it giveth light unto all that are in the house. 16 Let your light so shine before men, that they may see your good works, and glorify your Father which is in heaven.

In this way, God controls history, in part, through the discipleship of members of His body, the Church. Therefore, we may, by looking at the behavior of His Church at any point in history, determine the historical trends likely to flow from its behavior.

Why I am Not Optimistic for the Future of America

Without spiritual revival, the prevailing historical trends will continue until the nation suffers terminal judgment from the justice of God. No nation has ever survived the collapse of the fundamental institutions of marriage, family, and government.

The means of national revival is found in the local church, which produces a steady supply of spiritually mature believers who through the witness of their lives and their lips purify and preserve the nation.

Unfortunately, the local church is malfunctioning in America. The two trends below are evidence of the seriousness of the dysfunction. These trends and others [e.g., racial prejudice] show no signs of abating. Anything is possible, the Lord may rescue us from our spiritual apostasy, but I'm not optimistic.

Trend: Seeking the Kingdom of God via Government

Throughout the history of the world, religious movements have been enamored with the idea of using government as the primary means by which the kingdom of heaven will be instituted. Since the early decades of the 20th century, the evangelical/fundamentalist Christian movement has conspired to do the same. It is committed to the implementation of a purportedly Christian worldview and culture via lobbying, elections, judicial appointments and decisions, legislation, and executive orders. This strategy assumes that government has a *spiritual* mandate not granted to it by scripture [Rom 13.1-4] revealing the lack of *authority* that the Bible retains in these movements. If this policy involves the compromise of biblical principle and the embrace of sinful concepts and alliances, then the disobedience to the Bible is judged to be worth it to implement the Christian Agenda. Consequently, the evangelicals have developed a complex web of lies, evasions and self-deceptions to justify the support of a worldview that is in many ways contrary to scripture. If achieved, there will exist the thinnest veneer of Christian morality justifying an undercurrent of racism, theft and violence and driven by the most powerful economy and military on earth. In view of this, what else could result but the ends sought by Satan since the beginning of the creation?

The rise of government as the vehicle for spiritual advance has been accompanied by the decline of the authority of the scriptures as the rule of life for the believer. *Biblical authority* is the concept that the Bible is the inspired Word of God and as such should be both believed and obeyed. It is not possible to faithfully seek national righteousness via non-spiritual means [i.e., government] and remain committed to the Bible as the highest authority for the believer's faith and practice. Until recently, the evangelical Church could, like the Pharisees, hide behind accurate doctrinal statements to hide their disbelief in the scriptures. However, recent political trends [2016-2021] have revealed the evangelical position for what it is. Consequently, these doctrinal statements are discovered to be meaningless because *theology that is not followed is theology that is not believed*. Nor can those Christian Churches which have not actively participated in this apostasy be considered safe, because, for the most part, they have refused to repudiate the political Church movement and to reveal the precise nature of its abominable departure from the Word of God.[414]

Therefore, because of the Christian movement to build the spiritual kingdom of God through government, I am not optimistic that this generation will effectively resist the devil's stratagems. This failure will result in unnecessary suffering for the nation and the world.

Trend: The Pneumatic Revolt, The Charismatic Movement[415]

When a retrovirus attacks a computer or a human body, it first disables the ability of the system to defend itself, for example, by preventing the creation and use of System Restore Points[416] in a PC, or by the impairment of the immune system of the human body. The charismatic doctrine performs this same function in the Church. This matrix of errors damages biblical authority, weakens Christian discipleship, and promotes ecumenical unity. In doing these things, charismatic doctrine leads *towards* the one World Order and not away from it. I do not believe that Christendom will depart from this doctrine, therefore I am not optimistic that our American generation will prevail against the world forces of this darkness in our generation or the next. As I have said, the Church will ultimately prevail, but that does not mean *your* local church, your community or your nation will do so.

Every local church that is influenced by the Charismatic Movement is not equally subject to its errors and there are charismatic Churches that still stand for the fundamentals of the Christian faith. To the extent that they do embrace the doctrines of that movement, they become carriers of the disease, without significant symptoms themselves, but able to convey the virus to others.

The erosion of the authority[417] of the Word of God among Christians precipitated by the liberalism of the nineteenth century is now maintaining it deadly momentum by the multitude of errors associated with the Charismatic Movement.[418] This movement is now so popular that it is considered synonymous with sound Christian spiritual doctrine and practice. That which was largely considered as both abomination and foolishness just a couple of generations ago is now acceptable.[419] Its doctrines and practices are embraced by all denominations either explicitly or implicitly,[420] despite its being the cause of the expansion of the Word of Faith and Ecumenical movements.

I'm not optimistic because Christendom as well as evangelicalism shows absolutely no inclination to rid of itself of the charismatic doctrines. Since the acceptance of these false doctrines requires the rejection of what the Bible actually teaches, these believers are freed to construct any doctrine that they please without regard for scriptural support. This is precisely what is happening. American Christian organizations have been exporting these errors overseas via missionary efforts for decades. *The Charismatic Movement appears to be a key organizational factor in producing the spiritual apparatus of the New World Order* due to its ability to unite every Christian denomination or local church to every practitioner of spiritual mysticism, Christian or otherwise.

The Solution

The solution to the present situation begins with a revolution of repentance in the pulpits of America. Pastoral repentance from personal sins and from the promotion of false doctrines, or from the failure to identify them to the congregation, is where revival begins. Calling an out-of-town preacher to holler at the people is not the solution. The problem is an epidemic of false teachers and those who are afraid of them, or who profit from their existence.

A genuine pulpit revival will result in the mass exposure of false teachers and the doctrines which distinguish them from true pastors and teachers. Pulpit repentance will move God from a position of judging the Church to working mightily to extend revival from the *Pastors* to the *Congregation*. Only God can overcome the devil. Repentance, now occurring among the Congregation, will result in the restoration of spiritual growth and eventually, strengthened marriages and families in the local church. These believers will become the agents of transformation for the *Community* through the example of their righteous living, their proclamation of the gospel and their disciple making.

In the best-case scenario, repentance will secure divine blessing in a limited [but potentially vast] geography for a limited period of time. The Antichrist is coming, and he will arrive on schedule. However, the appearance of one thousand Antichrists cannot keep the faithful believer from ministering to others, or from his blessings on earth and in heaven.

Appendix 1:
A God Of Forces

Definition

The Antichrist is said to worship a "god of forces or fortresses."

Daniel 11:38–39 (KJV 1900)
38 But in his estate shall he honour the God of forces: and a god whom his fathers knew not shall he honour with gold, and silver, and with precious stones, and pleasant things. 39 Thus shall he do in the most strong holds with a strange god, whom he shall acknowledge *and* increase with glory: and he shall cause them to rule over many, and shall divide the land for gain.

The word Forces/Fortress [OT:4581] means a place of safety, **strength**, refuge, fortress, stronghold.

Psalm 37:39 (KJV 1900)
39 But the salvation of the righteous *is* of the Lord: *He is* their <u>strength</u> in the time of trouble.

Proverbs 10:29 (KJV 1900)
29 The way of the Lord *is* <u>strength</u> to the upright: But destruction *shall be* to the workers of iniquity.

Isaiah 25:4 (KJV 1900)
4 For thou hast been a <u>strength</u> to the poor, A <u>strength</u> to the

needy in his distress, A refuge from the storm, a shadow from the heat, When the blast of the terrible ones *is* as a storm *against* the wall.

Jeremiah 16:19 (KJV 1900)
[19] O Lord, my strength, and my <u>fortress</u>, and my refuge in the day of affliction, the Gentiles shall come unto thee from the ends of the earth, and shall say, Surely our fathers have inherited lies, vanity, and *things* wherein *there is* no profit.

Ezekiel 24:25 (KJV 1900)
[25] Also, thou son of man, *shall it* not *be* in the day when I take from them their <u>strength</u>, the joy of their glory, the desire of their eyes, and that whereupon they set their minds, their sons and their daughters,

These scriptures imply that man, in himself, is of limited strength or ability. Man must choose to rely upon God for strength beyond his own ability, *or he must seek strength from another source*. For the one who believes in God, the Lord becomes his strength, fortress, and refuge.

The Antichrist will reject the true God and seek support from a strange god [Dan 11.39]. The Willful King will rely upon the god who enables him to administer irresistible **strength**, *of whatever kind required*. This quality of strength is seen in the fourth beast of Daniel's vision, the kingdom where the Antichrist first appears as an actor [Dan 7.7-8]. This strength is observed in diplomacy, the ability of the Antichrist to produce what has been nearly impossible in history, the brokering of a peace agreement that secures Israel. He will wield this strength to violently uproot three kings to establish his initial kingdom. He will demonstrate irresistible military power when confronted by the Kings of the South and the North [Dan 11.40.44]. A supernatural entity, whom the Man of Sin will honor as a god, will be the source of this strength.

Of course, this god must be Lucifer, because Antichrist has disdained and rejected all other gods as beneath him [1 Th 2.3-4]. The only god greater than himself would have to be Lucifer. In history, the worship of Lucifer has been a hidden, or occult faith and not a visible part of the parade of false religions which cover the earth. This association with a god of overwhelming power is not inconsistent with Daniel's other prophecies regarding this man and his administration, which projects force in a way unknown to all previous Gentile empires.

This worship of power as an absolute good is consistent with Satan's view of God. It appears that Lucifer believes that God is God primarily because He is stronger than everyone else. The devil tells Eve that she should desire to be like God, receiving secret knowledge and by implication superior authority [Gen 3.4-5]. Lucifer claims that Job serves God because of God's power to protect and to bless him [Job 1.9-11]. He also claims that the only thing preventing him from turning Job against God is God's own powerful intercession on Job's behalf [Job 2.4-5]. The devil tempts Christ by an appeal to His power to turn stones into bread [Mt 4.4]. Indeed, Satan appears to incorrectly identify Deity with power alone. *God is Power and Power is God.* It is therefore not surprising that his "son," the Antichrist, would acquire the same incorrect view.

This Hebrew word *forces/fortresses* is translated into the Greek version of the Old Testament [Septuagint] using the word [G3794] for *stronghold* that we find in a well-known New Testament passage.

2 Corinthians 10:4–5 (KJV 1900)
⁴ (For the weapons of our warfare *are* not carnal, but mighty through God to the pulling down of <u>strong holds</u>;) ⁵ Casting down imaginations, and every high thing that exalteth itself against the knowledge of God, and bringing into captivity every thought to the obedience of Christ;

This New Testament word "stronghold" is NT: 3794[421] which signifies a fortified place, or, by extension, anything upon which one relies. The strongholds in 2 Corinthians *spiritual*, they include, but are not limited to,[422] concepts, ideas, propositions, philosophies, and doctrines that are theological skyscrapers standing in opposition to God and His Word. As such they describe forms of power or strength, in this case, ideological power. strength or power is the main idea behind the Old Testament word [OT: 4581].

This same concept is found in some Old Testament references, where the word for strength is translated *fortress*.

Jeremiah 16:19 (KJV 1900)
¹⁹ O Lord, my strength, and my **fortress**, and my refuge in the day of affliction, the Gentiles shall come unto thee from the ends of the earth, and shall say, Surely our fathers have inherited lies, vanity, and *things* wherein *there is* no profit.

> Nahum 1:7 (KJV 1900)
> ⁷ The Lord *is* good, a **strong hold** in the day of trouble; And he knoweth them that trust in him.

In these verses and others, God is not providing fortresses and strongholds of rock and wood and earth. The point of these scriptures is that God *Himself* is our defense and rock and fortress. Man, who has little strength, finds through faith in God, unlimited *ability* to accomplish His will in the world [Jn 4.5-7; Php 4.13]. There are many ways in which God comes to our defense, but what all the references have in common is the believers' covenant relationship to God and his faith in God's willingness and ability to deliver. This understanding and this faith itself come by way of the Word of God [Rom 10.17].

God as A Fortress and Refuge in the Soul

To successfully execute the spiritual warfare today, spiritual effectiveness is a necessity. The previous chapters have attempted to show that the conspiracy against God and man is a spiritual one. There is no rearrangement of human institutions that will result in the defeat of evil. Victory will only be achieved by believers who have paid the price to become effective spiritual warriors. By this we do not mean the current erroneous charismatic conceptions of spiritual warfare. God is a fortress and a refuge to the believer who can deploy the spiritual resources that God has placed at his disposal.

> Ephesians 6:11–12 (KJV 1900)
> 11 Put on the whole armour of God, that ye may be able to stand against the wiles of the devil. 12 For we wrestle not against flesh and blood, but against principalities, against powers, against the rulers of the darkness of this world, against spiritual wickedness in high places.

The scriptures employ the analogy of fortresses and strongholds to describe spiritual realities. The "whole armor of God" is the panoply of spiritual means that God has provided for the spiritual life: the Word of God, prayer, witness, worship, and fellowship. It is through these spiritual means that the believer achieves and maintains intimacy with God, and by which the spiritual warfare is engaged.

First, God's strength, for protection or any other purpose, is first utilized in our *thinking*. It is in our perception of reality and our actions within that sphere that we succeed or fail spiritually. The devil seeks the overthrow of the believer via the subversion of his thinking [Gen 3.1 sq.]. Likewise, God admonishes the believer to demonstrate the power of the new birth in his thinking.

> Romans 12:2 (KJV 1900)
> 2 And be not conformed to this world: but be ye transformed by the renewing of your mind, that ye may prove what is that good, and acceptable, and perfect, will of God.

Our thinking is the basis of all spiritual warfare. In your thinking you are defeated, and, in your thinking, you achieve spiritual victory.

Accordingly, you cannot fight the spiritual warfare or determine its results strictly from what you can see. Physical events are valid and meaningful, but do not comprise the sum of reality. Spiritual effectiveness cannot be judged solely based on earthly outcomes. Jesus was delivered, but he was crucified, the Jews were delivered from Egypt, but they were delivered into the wilderness. Jacob was delivered from Laban and from Esau, but it cost him many years of his life, Joseph was delivered from slavery and prison, but he first had to go through both slavery and prison. The apostles won the spiritual victory, but most died as martyrs. Part of our failure in calling upon God as our strength and fortress is in looking for empirical evidence rather than by trusting in God through faith. Without faith it is impossible to please God.

> Hebrews 11:32–40 (KJV 1900)
> 32 And what shall I more say? for the time would fail me to tell of Gedeon, and *of* Barak, and *of* Samson, and *of* Jephthae; *of* David also, and Samuel, and *of* the prophets: 33 Who through faith subdued kingdoms, wrought righteousness, obtained promises, stopped the mouths of lions, 34 Quenched the violence of fire, escaped the edge of the sword, out of weakness were made strong, waxed valiant in fight, turned to flight the armies of the aliens. 35 Women received their dead raised to life again: and others were tortured, not accepting deliverance; that they might obtain a better resurrection: 36 And others had trial of *cruel* mockings and scourgings, yea, moreover of bonds and imprisonment: 37 They were stoned, they were sawn asunder, were tempted, were slain with the sword: they wandered about in sheepskins and goatskins;

being destitute, afflicted, tormented; ³⁸ (Of whom the world was not worthy:) they wandered in deserts, and *in* mountains, and *in* dens and caves of the earth. ³⁹ And these all, having obtained a good report through faith, received not the promise: ⁴⁰ God having provided some better thing for us, that they without us should not be made perfect.

When we speak of our God as a fortress, a refuge, and a strong tower, we recognize that God will provide the whatever resources are necessary for spiritual *victory*, regardless of the circumstances. We must, by experience and training, be spiritually prepared to be used by Him. The spiritual life is not our use of God to obtain security and comfort. The successful spiritual combatant is oriented to reality, knowing that we are here for *His* service, which will include hardships.

There is an *invisible fortress* that exists in the soul of the believer, and which enables him to fight and win in the spiritual warfare. This invisible fortress consists of the character of Christ which is developed through the consistent function of the Spirit filled life, which consists of the intake of the Word of God [1 Pet 2.2], the filling of the Spirit [Gal 5.16] and is maintained by obedience to the Word of God[423] [1 Jn 1.7] and confession of sin [1 Jn 1.9]. Spiritual maturity is the fortification of the believer's soul which serves as a temple in which God resides [1 Cor 3.16]. That spiritually reinforced soul possesses the spiritual attributes, fruit of the Spirit [Gal 5.22], that form the basis of a rewarding fellowship with God, an invincible inner life, and powerful human dynamics.[424]

John 14:23 (KJV 1900)
Jesus answered and said unto him, If a man love me, he will keep my words: and my Father will love him, and we will come unto him, and make our abode with him.

Such a soul becomes God's base of operations in the world and the foundation of the believer's protection, spiritual strength, and well-being. John is not speaking in this verse of the indwelling of the Spirit, which is the privilege of the best and worst of believers [1 Cor 12.13b]. He is speaking of the power of a continuing fellowship based upon obedience to God [1 Jn 1.7; Rev 3.20]. The soul of the mature believer becomes a fortress from which God ministers to the believer and through him, to the world.

Lucifer as the God of Fortresses

Lucifer is a god of fortresses [Dan 11.38]. He is god of the rebellion at Babel, whose *tower* was the first stronghold built after the Flood. He was the god [Marduk] of ancient Babylon, a seemingly impregnable city with two sets of double walls.

> "Babylon was a rectangularly shaped city surrounded by a broad and deep water-filled moat and then by an intricate system of double walls.42 The first double-wall system encompassed the main city. Its inner wall was twenty-one feet thick and reinforced with defense towers at sixty-foot intervals while the outer wall was eleven feet in width and also had watchtowers. Later Nebuchadnezzar added another defensive double-wall system (an outer wall twenty-five feet thick and an inner wall twenty-three feet thick) east of the Euphrates that ran the incredible distance of seventeen miles and was wide enough at the top for chariots to pass.43 The height of the walls is not known, but the Ishtar Gate was forty feet high, and the walls would have approximated this size. A forty-foot wall would have been a formidable barrier for enemy soldiers."[425]

Lucifer was the god [Melqart] of the stronghold [Zech 9.2-3] of Tyre which was unassailable until the time of Alexander. Satan is the prototype rebel who has erected fortifications against God to resist his judgments. Many of these structures are physical and many are philosophical and theological.

The concept of the fortress, especially when applied to the efforts of created beings, is related to the concept of warfare and military operations. Physical fortresses enable a superior military defense. Therefore, the god of fortification is also the god of forces or munitions.[426] By engaging God as his enemy, Lucifer has a perceived need for defenses against Him. This attitude is replicated in his fallen human servants who are engaged in perpetual war with one another. Even now, military operations are being used as a *first* resort, including the concepts of perpetual limited wars and low intensity conflict.[427] In the future, Satan will advance the program of the Antichrist via unparalleled military violence. In the time of the Antichrist, after a preliminary period of diplomacy and statecraft, he will strike with unprecedented violence against believing Israel, breaking the negotiated peace which will have existed for only a few years [Dan 9.27 c.f. Mt 24.15-22]. In the process of establishing world hegemony, he will develop enemies [Dan 11.40-44]. His manipulation of these military enemies will result in the Battle of Armageddon [Joel 3.9-11;

Rev 16.12-16].

In Satan's conflict with God, he is active in the creation of invisible, logical fortresses. The advent of the Antichrist is not just another military movement; the advent of the Man of Sin will be a cultural phenomenon which will encompass every human institution. It will also be the culmination of millennia of planning by the secret societies representing the Mystery Religions. Through spiritual deception and spiritual power, he will capture the thinking and imagination of the world.

Revelation 13:4 (KJV 1900)
4 And they worshipped the dragon which gave power unto the beast: and they worshipped the beast, saying, Who is like unto the beast? who is able to make war with him?

2 Corinthians 10:4–5 (NKJV)
4 For the weapons of our warfare *are* not carnal but mighty in God for pulling down <u>strongholds,</u> 5 casting down arguments and every high thing that exalts itself against the knowledge of God, bringing every thought into captivity to the obedience of Christ,

Paul characterizes the weapons of God's opponents <u>as invisible strongholds</u>, *spiritual* structures in the mind and in the soul. These structures consist of arguments and thoughts in 2 Cor 10.5. These spiritual strongholds of doctrines and philosophies are the means of advancing spiritual warfare against God and against his Church. Satan attacks the Church by means of the same philosophical approach that he took with Eve in the garden and that he took with Jesus in the temptation in the wilderness.

Paul indicates that spiritual weapons are required to address these spiritual fortresses and doctrinal skyscrapers. Carnal or fleshly weapons are not sufficient. Government, economics, civil disobedience, violence, community action, human philosophy, none of these are adequate to the task of fighting the spiritual warfare. However, the weapons that God does provide are mighty, and effective for this battle.

Satan has created spiritual strongholds in areas that nullify the spiritual effectiveness of believers. Once these strongholds, these doctrinal and philosophical structures are established and left unchallenged, believers are weakened to the point that they can be eliminated as a factor in the spiritual warfare by relatively simple sins and temptations. In this sense, the devil's fortresses and lofty places behave like computer retroviruses which destroy the ability of the system to repair itself *before* it launches its own deadly attack. The presence of these spiritual fortresses, unchallenged by the Church, has led to a new spiritual dark age.

It is not denied that there are spiritual strongholds in various areas of *overt* sin such as chemical abuse, addictions to ethnic prejudice, sexual sin, food etc. But for these strongholds to flourish, the protective mechanisms of the local church must first be shut down or disabled. Once these protective defenses are turned off by philosophical and doctrinal strongholds, sin can and will run rampant through both the local church and the community.

Partial List of Spiritual [Theological] Strongholds or Fortresses

Spiritual Strongholds in the form of arguments or doctrines can be found in the direct statements of Satan in Scripture:

The Substructure of Luciferian Doctrine

Principle of Deception: Genesis 3.1 If you ever encounter Lucifer, you will not recognize him. Lucifer modifies his appearance and manner to deceive men.

Principle of The Lie: Genesis 3.4-5 Matthew 4.3a Lucifer denies that Jehovah is who He claims to be in scripture. He denies that Jesus is Christ. He claims that God lied to Adam and Eve to prevent their spiritual progress.

Principle of Occult Religion: Genesis 3.4-5 Lucifer represents himself as the benefactor of man, the champion of freedom and the conductor of souls to spiritual evolution and godhood.

Principle of Human Non-Culpability: Genesis 3.4 Lucifer claims that disobedience to God leads not to death but to spiritual evolution.

Principle of Scriptural Misuse: Gen 3.1 Matthew 4.1-10 Satan uses his mastery of the scriptures to deceive man by their misuse. Satan attempted to use God's own words to control Him.

Principle of the Superhero: Matt 4.3-10 Lucifer represents spiritual power, spiritual gifts and spiritual ministry as ours to use as we please.

Principle of Prosperity: Job 1.1-11; 2.3-7 Lucifer argues to God that man serves Him because it is in his best interests to do so. Man serves God to receive blessings and protection alone. The inverse of this argument is that man is entitled to prosperity [health, wealth, and protection] at all times as a servant of God. [Job 2.7-10].

Principle of Pragmatism: Genesis 3.4-5 Matthew 4.8-10 Satan deceives men by the claim that God's plan can be advanced by the violation of His Word. Man is the judge of scripture. His ends justify his means.

Appendix 2: The Rapture

The Rapture is the theological concept that the Body of Christ, the Church, will experience a separate resurrection before that of Tribulational, Old Testament or Millennial groups of believers. This resurrection will occur before the judgment of the unbelieving world, known as the Day of the Lord or the Day of Christ. The Rapture is a doctrine which is not shared by all believers.[428] Eschatology, or the doctrine of last things, can be understood, just as the rest of scripture. Because eschatology can be studied and understood, it is possible to provide a clear defense of the doctrine of the Rapture of the Church.[429]

There is a biblical precedent to the denial of the true doctrine of the resurrection or Rapture of the Church. In Thessalonica, the local church was confused and frightened by those representing themselves as apostles, who taught an incorrect succession of end time events.

> 2 Thessalonians 2:1–3 (KJV 1900)
> 1 Now we beseech you, brethren, by the coming of our Lord Jesus Christ, and by our gathering together unto him, 2 <u>That ye be not soon shaken in mind, or be troubled, neither by spirit, nor by word, nor by letter as from us, as that the day of Christ is at hand.</u> 3 Let no man deceive you by any means: for that day shall not come, except there come a falling away first, and that man of sin be revealed, the son of perdition;

Paul is referring to teachers who had visited the Churches claiming that the day of the judgment of the Lord had already arrived, and that the Thessalonian believers would be swept up in the cataclysms to be visited upon the world by God.

The Day of Christ is defined as follows:

> "The Day of the Lord is a period of time in which God will deal with wicked men directly and dramatically in fearful judgment. Today a man may be a blasphemer of God, an atheist, can denounce God and teach bad doctrine. Seemingly God does nothing about it. But the day designated in Scripture as "the day of the Lord" is coming when God will punish human sin, and He will deal in wrath and in judgment with a Christ-rejecting world. One thing we are sure of, that God in His own way will bring every soul into judgment."[430]

> "What Is the Day of the Lord?

> "In order to understand the nature of the error Paul is correcting, it is necessary to define what is meant by the "day of the Lord." This expression is found often in the Bible. In a word, it is the period of time predicted in the Scripture when God will deal directly with human sin. It includes the tribulation time preceding the second advent of Christ as well as the whole millennial reign of Christ. It will culminate in the judgment of the great white throne. The Day of the Lord is therefore an extended period of time lasting over one thousand years. This is brought out in the events included in the Day of the Lord, presented in connection with the study of 1 Thessalonians 5."[431]

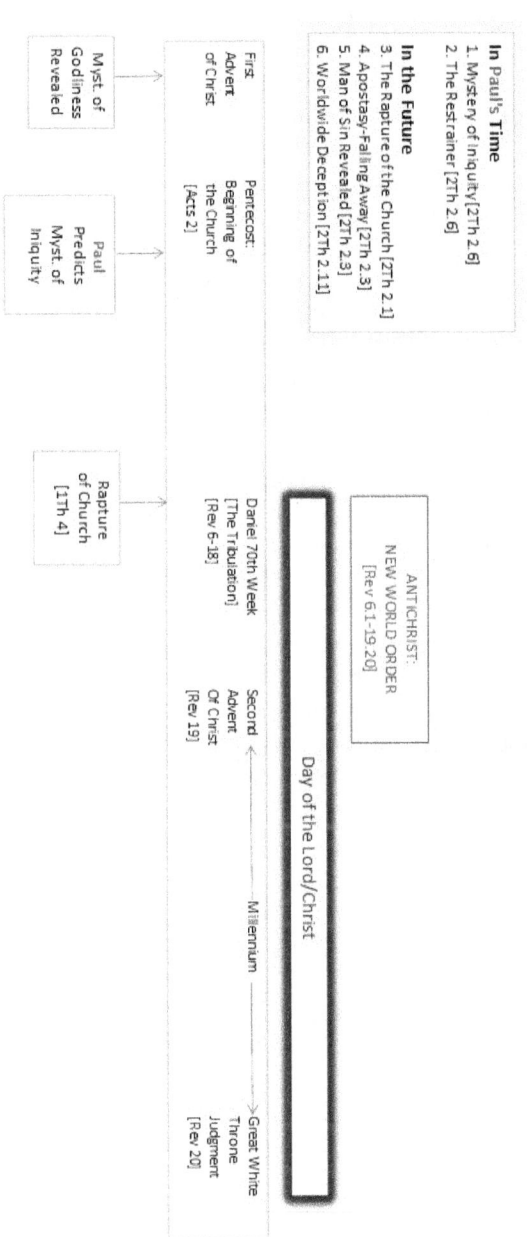

Figure 3 The Day of the Lord and Antichrist

The assertion that the Day of Lord had begun contradicted Paul's earlier teaching to this Church about the Rapture, implying that these believers, as well as their deceased brethren were, at best, of uncertain spiritual status.[432] The promotion of this misaligned prophetic sequence among the people resulted in emotional instability, doctrinal confusion, and loss of focus on how exactly to execute the Christian life at that time. Paul was aggressive in setting the record straight by placing the prophetic timetable into its proper arrangement.

The proper understanding of prophecy is important because God has said that He will do certain things in a particular order. An inaccurate understanding of biblical prophecy may cause the believer to doubt God's knowledge and/or His truthfulness. Furthermore, understanding what God has chosen to reveal in prophecy is critical to understanding the entire scriptural record [Rev 1.3; 19.10; 22.18-19]. Finally, unless the believer can orient himself in time, he will misapply the scriptures to the expectations that God has for his generation. For example, the discipleship of Abraham's generation was not identical to that of Moses, nor was God's expectation of the spiritual walk of Israel under the Law of Moses the same of His commands to the Church.

Paul clarified the order of prophetic events that troubled the Thessalonian believers. These events included the resurrection of the Church or that event called the "Rapture." The Bible distinguishes several resurrections of believers [first in kind] and one of unbelievers [second in kind]. The scriptures also differentiate the resurrection of the Church, or the "Rapture" from the Second Coming of Christ.

Definition of the Rapture

Death vs. Resurrection

Upon physical death, spiritual life continues for the believer, who is conveyed into the presence of Christ.

> 2 Corinthians 5:8 (KJV 1900)
> 8 We are confident, I say, and willing rather to be absent from the body, and to be present with the Lord.

> Philippians 1:21–24 (KJV 1900)
> 21 For to me to live is Christ, and to die is gain. 22 But if I live in the flesh, this is the fruit of my labour: yet what I shall choose I wot not. 23 For I am in a strait betwixt two, having a desire to depart, and to be with Christ; which is far better: 24 Nevertheless to abide in the flesh is more needful for you.

At death, physical life is ended, and the individual believer is carried into the presence of the Lord. Resurrection, by contrast, is the mechanism by which an entire cohort of believers move from one phase of the spiritual life to a permanently glorified and perfected state.

> "…the resurrection is the victory of God and His Christ over the power of death."[433]

Resurrection vs. Reincarnation

> "Reincarnation is the belief that, after death, the soul passes on to another body. By contrast, the Bible declares that, after death, the same physical body is made incorruptible at the resurrection (see RESURRECTION, EVIDENCE FOR). Rather than a series of bodies that die, resurrection makes alive forever the same body that died. Rather than seeing personhood as a soul in a body, resurrection sees each human being as a soul-body unity. While reincarnation is a process of perfection, resurrection is a perfected state. Reincarnation is an intermediate state, while the soul longs to be disembodied and absorbed in God; but, resurrection is an ultimate state, in which the whole person, body and soul, enjoys the goodness of God."

"The differences between resurrection and reincarnation are as follows: [434]

RESURRECTION	REINCARNATION
Happens once into the same body	Occurs many times into a different body
Into an immortal body	Into a mortal body
A perfect state	An imperfect state
An ultimate state	An intermediate state

Figure 16. Resurrection vs. Reincarnation [Geisler]

The Procession of Resurrections

Every believer, regardless of the age or dispensation in which he lived will experience a resurrection, *but not all at the same time.*

1 Corinthians 15:20–23 (KJV 1900)
20 But now is Christ risen from the dead, and become the firstfruits of them that slept. 21 For since by man came death, by man came also the resurrection of the dead. 22 For as in Adam all die, even so in Christ shall all be made alive. 23 But every man in his own order [NT:5001]: Christ the firstfruits; afterward they that are Christ's at his coming.

"order" [NT5001] τάγμα [tagma /tag·mah/] n n. From 5021; TDNT 8:31; TDNTA 1156; GK 5413; AV translates as "order" once. 1 that which has been arranged, thing placed in order. 2 a body of soldiers, a corps. 3 band, troop, class.[435]

Jesus experienced the first true resurrection from the grave: he was resurrected with the result that he will never face death again. The words "in his own order" in verse 23 refers to the resurrections of believers which will follow that of Christ:

> ➢ Christ the first fruits from the grave [1 Cor 15.20, 23]
> ➢ The resurrection of the Church prior to the Tribulation [1 Cor 15.23; c.f. John 14.2-3; and 1 Th 4.16-17; Titus 2.12-13]

> The resurrection of the <u>Old Testament and Tribulation believers</u> at the Second Coming of Christ, [Isa 26.19; Dan 12.2; Zec 14.1-5; Matt 24.29-31; Mk 13.27; Rev 20.4[436]]
> The resurrection of the <u>Millennial believers</u> at the close of the 1000-year reign of Christ [Rev 20.5,11-15].

The Bible refers to the awakening of the *unbelieving* dead also as a resurrection [Jn 5.28-29; Acts 24.15]. According to the scriptures, the resurrection of the unjust is unto damnation.

It is the resurrection of the Church age believers, the first phalanx after Christ (those saved since Pentecost and before the Tribulation/Day of the Lord) that is referred to as the Rapture.

1 Thessalonians 4:16–18 (KJV 1900)
16 For the Lord himself shall descend from heaven with a shout, with the voice of the archangel, and with the trump of God: and the dead in Christ[437] shall rise first: 17 Then we which are alive and remain shall be <u>caught up</u> together with them in the clouds, to meet the Lord in the air: and so shall we ever be with the Lord. 18 Wherefore comfort one another with these words.

What is the Rapture

The Rapture is the theological concept that the Body of Christ, the Church, will experience a separate resurrection from that of other groups of believers [e.g., Old Testament, Tribulational, Millennial] or the unbelieving dead. It is distinguished in scripture from these other resurrections. The Rapture will include both living and deceased individuals. The pre-tribulational version of this doctrine holds that the resurrection will occur before the seventieth week of Daniel the period that commences the judgment of the unbelieving world known as the Day of the Lord or the Day of Christ.

The word "Rapture" is not a Greek word and is not found in the Bible. It comes from the Latin translation of the word translated "caught up" in 1Th 4:17 (NT:726 *harpazo*) which means:

> "**Harpazo.** This is a Greek word which has various meanings. It is not translated by one uniform English word. The meanings are as follows: "to seize, to carry off by force, to claim for one's self eagerly, to snatch out or away." It was used proverbially in the sense of "to rescue from the danger of destruction." It was used also of divine

power transferring a person marvellously and swiftly from one place to another."[438]

The word [harpazo] is used to describe how the Spirit transported Philip from Gaza to Caesarea [Acts 8:39] and Paul being "caught up" into the third heaven [2 Cor. 12:2-4].

The Rapture describes the removal of people from one place to somewhere else. In the context of 1Thessalonians 4, Rapture is the removal of Christians from the earth into the presence of God to receive their eternal inheritance. The Thessalonians feared for the status of their saved loved ones who had already died. Paul reminded them of his original instruction that the resurrection of the Church would be participated in by all those who were members of the body of Christ.[439]

> 1 Thessalonians 4:13–18 (KJV 1900)
> 13 But I would not have you to be ignorant, brethren, concerning them which are asleep, that ye sorrow not, even as others which have no hope. 14 <u>For if we believe that Jesus died and rose again</u>, even so them also which sleep in Jesus will God bring with him. 15 For this we say unto you by the word of the Lord, that we which are alive and remain unto the coming of the Lord shall not prevent them which are asleep. 16 For the Lord himself shall descend from heaven with a shout, with the voice of the archangel, and with the trump of God: <u>and the dead in Christ shall rise first</u>: 17 <u>Then</u> we which are alive and remain shall be caught up together with them in the clouds, to meet the Lord in the air: and so shall we ever be with the Lord. 18 Wherefore comfort one another with these words.

The Rapture is limited to the Church, ["for if we believe that Jesus died and rose again"] it will not include the Old Testament saints, who will be resurrected at the second coming of Christ. Both dead and living believers will experience this resurrection. *The Rapture is not the same as the second coming of Christ*, which occurs approximately seven years later. The doctrine of the Rapture is to be a comfort for the Church [1Thes 4.18] since the Church will not experience the wrath of God during the coming Day of the Lord.

> 1 Thessalonians 5:9–11 (KJV 1900)
> 9 <u>For God hath not appointed us to wrath</u>, but to obtain salvation

by our Lord Jesus Christ, 10 Who died for us, that, whether we wake or sleep, we should live together with him. 11 Wherefore comfort yourselves together, and edify one another, even as also ye do.

Therefore, the Rapture will not include those saved during the Tribulation period.

The Rapture is a Mystery

1 Corinthians 15:51–52 (KJV 1900)
51 <u>Behold, I shew you a mystery</u>; We shall not all sleep, but we shall all be changed, 52 In a moment, in the twinkling of an eye, at the last trump: for the trumpet shall sound, and the dead shall be raised incorruptible, and we shall be changed.

It was no mystery to the believing Jew of the Old Testament era that the Day of the Lord would unleash the wrath of God upon the unbelieving world, both Jew and Gentile [Jer 46.10; Amos 5.14-27; Zeph 1.14-17;];.no mystery that the Messiah would come to earth to establish the eternal Davidic Kingdom [Isa 2.1-3; Jer 23.5; Zech 14.9]. It was no mystery that the Jewish saints would be resurrected to reside in this kingdom forever [Dt 30.3-6; Jer 23.6-8; Eze 37.21-28; Dan 12.2; Mic 4.6-9]. On the other hand, the Church, its advent, duration, and resurrection, was indeed a mystery until revealed by Jesus [John 14.1-3, 15-20] and explained by Paul. The resurrection of the Church had to be a mystery because the Church itself was a mystery [Eph 1.9-14;3.3-6; 5.32; Col 1.26-27]. As a mystery, the Church was unrevealed in the Old Testament and remained unrevealed until the New Testament.

It was Jesus who introduced the fact of His return for the Church in John 14.[440]

John 14:1–3 (KJV 1900)
1 Let not your heart be troubled: ye believe in God, believe also in me. 2 In my Father's house are many mansions: if it were not so, I would have told you. I go to prepare a place for you. 3 And if I go and prepare a place for you, I will come again, and receive you unto myself; that where I am, there ye may be also.

Later in that same passage Jesus would unveil the Church, ["ye in me"] to which his audience of Chapter 14 would soon belong.

John 14:16–20 (KJV 1900)
16 And I will pray the Father, <u>and he shall give you another Comforter, that he may abide with you for ever</u>; 17 Even the Spirit of truth; whom the world cannot receive, because it seeth him not, neither knoweth him: but ye know him; <u>for he dwelleth with you, and shall be in you.</u> 18 I will not leave you comfortless: I will come to you. 19 Yet a little while, and the world seeth me no more; but ye see me: because I live, ye shall live also. 20 <u>At that day ye shall know that I am in my Father, and ye in me, and I in you.</u>

Matthew 16:16–18 (KJV 1900)
16 And Simon Peter answered and said, Thou art the Christ, the Son of the living God. 17 And Jesus answered and said unto him, Blessed art thou, Simon Bar-jona: for flesh and blood hath not revealed it unto thee, but my Father which is in heaven. 18 And I say also unto thee, That thou art Peter, <u>and upon this rock I will build my church</u>; and the gates of hell shall not prevail against it.

Paul explained the translation of Church Age believers in 1 Corinthians 15:51-58 and 1 Thessalonians 4:13-18.

What was unknown to the Old Testament prophets and holy men has now been made known to and through the Church. The unsaved consider it nonsense and a growing number of believers don't believe it either. Fortunately, you do not have to agree with Rapture to participate in it!

The "Day of the Lord/Christ" is not the Rapture

The Church, both those living and dead in Christ, will be rescued from the earth prior to the Day of Christ/Day of The Lord. The uncertainty of the Thessalonians regarding this fact is reflected in both the first [1 Th 4:13 "that ye sorrow not"] and second letter to the Thessalonians [2 Th 2.2 "shaken in mind or be troubled"]. This revived uncertainty was one reason that prompted the writing of 2 Thessalonians. The Church feared that the Day of the Lord was in progress and that the dead in Christ had already been united with Him in heaven or had not risen at all.

The resurrection of the Church is prior to and distinct from the Day of the Lord. God has not chosen to share when the resurrection of the Body of Christ will occur, neither has He provided any signs to signal that the Rapture is coming. The Rapture for the believer will come without warning, in other words, the Rapture is imminent. In a similar way, the day of the Lord will suddenly occur for unbelievers. The similarity does not make the events the same.

In 2 Thessalonians 2, Paul is relating the events immediately prior to and during the beginning of the lengthy period known as the "Day of the Lord." In 1 Thessalonians 5.1-3 the apostle relates that the Day of the Lord will be unanticipated by the unbelieving world. For whatever reason [2 Th 2.11-12], the sudden disappearance of the Church will not be recognized by the unbelieving world as having any relation to the events that follow. The period following the translation of the Church [the Rapture] is the Day that will come as a "thief in the night" *from the standpoint of the Christ rejecting world that will be caught off guard by its appearance*. The apostle's consolation to the Thessalonian believers confirms that the departure of the Church will occur prior to the dire events of the day of the Lord [1 Th 4.13-18 cf. 2 Th 2.1-5].

2 Thessalonians 2:1–5 (KJV 1900)
1 Now we beseech you, brethren, by the coming of our Lord Jesus Christ, and by our gathering together unto him, 2 That ye be not soon shaken in mind, or be troubled, neither by spirit, nor by word, nor by letter as from us, <u>as that the day of Christ is at hand</u>. 3 Let no man deceive you by any means: <u>for that day shall not come</u>, except there come a falling away first, and that man of sin be revealed, the son of perdition;

Order of Events in the Thessalonian Epistles

Paul taught the Thessalonian Church the relative timing of end time events.

1 Thessalonians 5:1 (KJV 1900)
1 But of the times and the seasons, brethren, ye have no need that I write unto you.

2 Thessalonians 2:5 (KJV 1900)
5 Remember ye not, that, when I was yet with you, I told you these things?

He could not tell them in absolute terms when these events would occur. He could and did let them know the relative order of their occurrence.

2 Thessalonians 2:1–5 (KJV 1900)
1 Now we beseech you, brethren, by the coming of our Lord Jesus Christ, and by our gathering together unto him, 2 That ye be not soon shaken in mind, or be troubled, neither by spirit, nor by word, nor by letter as from us, <u>as that the day of Christ is at hand</u>. 3 Let no man deceive you by any means: <u>for that day shall not come</u>, except there come a falling away first, and that man of sin be revealed, the son of perdition; 4 Who opposeth and exalteth himself above all that is called God, or that is worshipped; so that he as God sitteth in the temple of God, shewing himself that he is God. 5 Remember ye not, that, when I was yet with you, I told you these things?

"[T]he coming of the Lord Jesus Christ, and by our gathering together unto him" 2 Th 2.1

First in the sequence of events, "*the coming of our Lord Jesus Christ, and by our gathering together unto him*" [c.f. 1 Th 4.14-17]. Understanding this statement requires the analysis of the rest of this passage in 2 Thessalonians 2. It will be shown that, for a variety of reasons, the removal of the Body of Christ, the Church, must precede the unfolding the events of the Day of the Lord, which the false prophets proclaimed was already in progress. The presence of the Thessalonian believers upon the earth was itself a proof that the Day of the Lord had not yet occurred.

Who will be "gathered unto Him" and who will not? There is in 1 Thessalonians 5 a clear delineation between the "**they**," and "**them**" that will undergo the wrath of God during the Day of the Lord, and the "<u>ye</u>, <u>we</u>, <u>us</u>" that will not.

1 Thessalonians 5:1–11 (KJV 1900)
¹ But of the times and the seasons, brethren, ye have no need that I write unto you. ² For yourselves know perfectly that the day of the Lord so cometh as a thief in the night. ³ For when **they** shall say, Peace and safety; then sudden destruction cometh upon **them**, as travail upon a woman with child; and **they** shall not escape. ⁴ But <u>ye</u>, brethren, are not in darkness, that that day should

overtake you as a thief. ⁵ Ye are all the children of light, and the children of the day: we are not of the night, nor of darkness. ⁶ Therefore let us not sleep, as *do* others; but let us watch and be sober. ⁷ For **they** that sleep sleep in the night; and **they** that be drunken are drunken in the night. ⁸ But let us, who are of the day, be sober, putting on the breastplate of faith and love; and for an helmet, the hope of salvation. ⁹ For God hath not appointed us to wrath, but to obtain salvation by our Lord Jesus Christ, ¹⁰ Who died for us, that, whether we wake or sleep, we should live together with him. ¹¹ Wherefore comfort yourselves together, and edify one another, even as also ye do.

Children of the day, children of the night. The time of judgment is characterized as night, whereas believers are children of the day. The end of the day marks the beginning of the night.

Amos 5:20 (KJV 1900)
20 Shall not the day of the LORD be darkness, and not light?
Even very dark, and no brightness in it?

Paul interprets this symbolism for them, explaining that they were not appointed to wrath [darkness] but to salvation [1 Th 5.9; 2 Th 2.13]. God will not allow the Church to be exposed to His own wrath, the wrath which will be expressed during the Day of the Lord, the wrath from which they were spared by the blood of Christ.

1 Thessalonians 5:9–11 (KJV 1900)
9 For God hath not appointed us to wrath, but to obtain salvation by our Lord Jesus Christ, 10 Who died for us, that, whether we wake or sleep, we should live together with him. 11 Wherefore comfort yourselves together, and edify one another, even as also ye do.

Regarding the Wrath of God. The suffering that is a consequence of the sin of Adam: all those effects of the Fall such as violence, war, accidents, natural disasters, persecutions, deprivations, sickness, and death must be contrasted with the coming judgments of the Day of the Lord of which God is the direct source. All believers are subject to the first category of suffering, but are exempt from the second, for the same reason that believers are not subject to hell fire [Jn 5.22, 24 c.f. Rev 5.5-7; 6.1 sq. Jn 3.18-19; Rom 5.1; 8.1].

The Rapture is a source of comfort. Paul repeatedly communicated the reality of the resurrection of the Church as a rescue from judgment and therefore a source of comfort to believers [1 Th 4.18; 5.9-11; 2 Th 2.13]. Edification by proper teaching is a comfort for the obedient Christian [1 Th 2.11]. 1 Thessalonians 4:18 instructs believers to comfort one another by reinforcing a proper understanding of the future. For the follower of Christ, a proper eschatology is a source of comfort. Paul is *not* commanding believers to console one another with the news that they would go through the terrors of the Day of the Lord. *The Day of the Lord is no mystery.* The Body of Christ is not associated in scripture with the day of judgment to come upon the world. The Day of the Lord or of Christ is a phase of history that has been predicted throughout the Old Testament. The Church, by contrast, is a mystery that was unrevealed in the Old Testament. In the Day of the Lord, God resumes His focus upon unredeemed Israel, which will undergo judgment during the second half of the Daniel's seventieth week [Matt 24.15-21; Joel 2.1-11; Zech 14.1-5]. Even under national disaster, God will provide a witness [Mt 24.14; Rev 7.13-17; 14.1-6], and many will respond to the gospel during this period, also known as the Great Tribulation and the time of Jacob's Trouble.[441] The removal of the Body of Christ from the earth is followed by the resumption of God's plan to save a remnant in Israel from the midst of the catastrophic judgments of the Tribulation.

"[F]or that day shall not come, except there come a falling away first" 2 Th 3b.

Secondly, the resurrection of the Church is followed by a falling away of many from Christendom. This apostasy will be hastened by the removal of the restraining influence of the Spirit of God, who is operating in a powerful way through the Body of Christ upon civilization.

> 2 Thessalonians 2:6–7 (KJV 1900)
> 6 And now ye know <u>what withholdeth</u> that he might be revealed in his time. 7 For the mystery of iniquity doth already work: <u>only he who now letteth will let, until he be taken out of the way</u>.
>
> 2 Thessalonians 2:6–7 (NASB95)
> 6 And you know <u>what restrains him now</u>, so that in his time he

will be revealed. 7 For the mystery of lawlessness is already at work; only <u>he who now restrains will do so until he is taken out of the way.</u>

The neuter "what" in verse 6 is the Church. The masculine "he" in verse 7 is the Holy Spirit who creates and empowers the Church, living within every genuine believer of that age.

It is the Spirit operating through the Church that restrains[442] the operation of the Mystery of Iniquity, keeping the world from being as evil as it can be. With the removal of the Body of Christ from the earth via the Rapture, the falling away, or apostasy of the mass of unredeemed humanity remaining upon the earth will occur.

"Falling away" is the Greek word *apostasia* [NT: 646[443]] from which we get the term "apostasy." The Holy Spirit is predicting that some will depart from the teaching or doctrine of the Christian faith. This is what is signified by the words "the faith"

> Jude 3 (KJV 1900)
> 3 Beloved, when I gave all diligence to write unto you of the common salvation, it was needful for me to write unto you, and exhort you that ye should earnestly contend for <u>the faith</u> which was once delivered unto the saints.

"The Faith" means the system of biblical teaching identified as true Christianity. Thus, the falling away is from genuine or true Christian teaching.

To fall away from the faith therefore means walking away from the authority of the teachings of the Bible, to no longer submit to their authority or even to acknowledge their truth.

A person who fails to submit to the Word of God but who acknowledges the Word of God as truth, is sinning, or out of fellowship and needs to establish or re-establish right relations with the Lord.

These people in 2 Thessalonians 2.3, who remain upon the earth immediately after the Rapture, are apostates, they have turned their backs upon the Christian Faith as valid and authoritative. The question that logically follows is whether these people were ever saved?

The apostates mentioned in 2 Thessalonians 2.3 are discussed again in vss. 9-12

> *The Mystery of Iniquity, the spirit of Antichrist, is the overarching conspiracy which finds its origin in prehistory. It began with the fall of Lucifer and his efforts to precipitate a rebellion amongst the angelic host. This was the origin of the fallen angels and the spiritual conflict that spilled into human history at the Garden of Eden. The Mystery of Iniquity continued in human history and will continue, until it is ended by the judgment of the Antichrist, the False Prophet and at last Lucifer himself.*

2 Thessalonians 2:9–12 (KJV 1900)
Even him, whose coming is after the working of Satan with all power and signs and lying wonders, 10 And with all deceivableness of unrighteousness in them that perish; <u>because they received not the love of the truth, that they might be saved</u>. 11 And for this cause God shall send them strong delusion, that they should believe a lie: 12 <u>That they all might be damned who believed not the truth</u>, but had pleasure in unrighteousness.

These people were in the local church: listening to the sermons, giving money, taking communion, attending Sunday School, participating in ministry, sending their kids to Christian schools: they held the "right" political views, but they were never saved. Many of them probably claimed to be saved, but they were not because verses 10 and 12 say that they were not saved. These people were once in the local church, just like the antichrists of 1 John 2.18 started out in the Church. The visible Church has always had professors of faith who were not possessors of true faith. The very definition of Christendom [the visible Church] is the amalgamation of these two groups, the professors of faith and the genuine body of Christ, the true Church. It is Christendom that becomes the host for these fallen persons and the "Lie" of which they will become heralds. It is the frequent, accurate and systematic teaching and preaching of the Word of God that will either drive them out or draw them in to true faith in Christ.

Because of their unbelief, these people will be victimized by a triple deception. The first deception is accomplished by the false teachers, who will deceive these lost individuals into believing "the Lie." This is the lie that Jesus is not the Christ. This is "the lie" that began with Satan's suggestion to Eve and will culminate in a worldwide cult of faith in a false Messiah. The final and greatest false prophet will be the beast of the earth, who will be the herald of the Antichrist. This man will perform the lying signs and wonders that will cause the world to believe that the Antichrist is the Messiah.

The second deception of these apostates is called the "deceivableness of unrighteousness." This is the spiritual state of suggestibility and the self-delusion which attends a commitment to wickedness. The individual dedicated to unrighteousness is out of touch with reality. Such a person is in extreme danger.

The third deception in 2 Thessalonians 2.11-12 will occur when God Himself sends them a "strong delusion," specifically, a delusion that is efficient or effective, a delusion that works. The word "delusion" means deception. God is going to allow their decision to fall away to have the fullest possible consequences by sending strong delusion to ensure that this decision results in the most terrible consequences.

2 Thessalonians 2:12–13 (KJV 1900)
12 <u>That they all might be damned</u> who believed not the truth, but had pleasure in unrighteousness. 13 But we are bound to give thanks alway to God for you, brethren beloved of the Lord, <u>because God hath from the beginning chosen you to salvation</u> through sanctification of the Spirit and belief of the truth:

"[A]nd that man of sin be revealed, the son of perdition;" 2 Th 2.3c

These events: the removal of the Restrainer by the Rapture of the Church, and the apostasy or falling away of everyone left upon the earth, precipitate the ***third*** event, the appearance of the Man of Sin, the Antichrist. The purpose of this book is to describe the person of Antichrist, the conditions which lead to his appearance upon the world stage, and his brief career. The "New World Order" is the objective of human history from Lucifer's perspective as he implements the earthly phase of the Mystery of Iniquity. The Antichrist, the Son of Perdition will execute Lucifer's plan for his rule of the earth. The appearance of the Man of Sin, an individual predicted and described in the Old Testament, occurs after the Rapture of the mystery Body of Christ, the Church.

> 2 Thessalonians 2:3–4 (KJV 1900)
> 3 Let no man deceive you by any means: <u>for that day shall not come</u>, [The Day of the Lord, which false teachers claimed had already arrived] except there come a falling away first, and that man of sin be revealed, the son of perdition; 4 Who opposeth and exalteth himself above all that is called God, or that is worshipped; so that he as God sitteth in the temple of God, shewing himself that he is God.

These two events, the Apostasy and the appearing of the Antichrist *follow* the return of Christ for the Church, the Rapture. These same two events *are themselves; a part of the judgment God will send upon the wicked.* Next, we will demonstrate that the Rapture is distinct from the Second Coming of Christ.

The Second Coming of Christ is Not the Same as the Rapture[444]

The Central Passages

Rapture

John 14:1-3; 1 Corinthians 15:51-58 and 1 Thessalonians 4:13-18.

Second Coming

Zechariah 14:1- 21; Matthew 24:29-31; Mark 13:24-27; Luke 21:25-27 and Revelation 19.

No Visible Signs Preceding the Rapture

The Second Coming is preceded by signs, but the Rapture is imminent, occurring without signs. The Old and New Testaments prophesy and document the signs associated with the Day of the Lord and the Second Advent [Ac 2:19-20 See also Joel 2:30-31; Isa 13:9-10; Joel 2:10; Lk 21:11, 25-26]. Many signs and terrible wonders will have occurred in the months before the Second Advent. The return of Christ to the earth will be heralded by several immediate signs in the heavens.

> Luke 21:25–27 (KJV 1900)
> 25 And there shall be signs in the sun, and in the moon, and in the stars; and upon the earth distress of nations, with perplexity; the sea and the waves roaring; 26 Men's hearts failing them for fear, and for looking after those things which are coming on the earth: for the powers of heaven shall be shaken. 27 <u>And then</u> shall they see the Son of man coming in a cloud with power and great glory.

> Matthew 24:29–30 (KJV 1900)
> 29 <u>Immediately after the tribulation of those days</u> shall the sun be darkened, and the moon shall not give her light, and the stars shall fall from heaven, and the powers of the heavens shall be shaken: 30 And then shall appear the sign of the Son of man in heaven: and then shall all the tribes of the earth mourn, and they shall see the Son of man coming in the clouds of heaven with power and great glory.

There is no mention of signs in the heavens before the Rapture. The Rapture occurs suddenly and without warning of any kind. The Rapture is imminent, specifically because there are no prophesied events which must occur before the coming of Christ, in the air, for the Church.[445]

> "(6) The *sequel* of the Tribulation. The signs of Matthew 24 (and numerous other passages) were given to Israel concerning the second coming of Christ; no signs, however, were given to the Church to anticipate the Rapture (which means it will come suddenly, as pretribulationists have affirmed). [446]"

> "The Church was told to live in the light of the imminent coming of the Lord to translate them in His presence (John 14:2–3; Acts 1:11; 1 Cor. 15:51–52; Phil. 3:20; Col. 3:4; 1 Thess. 1:10; 1 Tim. 6:14; James 5:8; 2 Pet. 3:3–4)."[447]

The Church at Philadelphia is told by the apostle John to anticipate a sudden return of Jesus for the Church.

Revelation 3:10–12 (KJV 1900)
10 Because thou hast kept the word of my patience, <u>I also will keep thee from the hour of temptation, which shall come upon all the world, to try them that dwell upon the earth</u>. 11 <u>Behold, I come quickly</u>: hold that fast which thou hast, that no man take thy crown. 12 Him that overcometh will I make a pillar in the temple of my God, and he shall go no more out: and I will write upon him the name of my God, and the name of the city of my God, which is new Jerusalem, which cometh down out of heaven from my God: and I will write upon him my new name. [Rev 22:7, 12, 20. 1:3. 22:10]

"The Lord's coming for them is compared to an imminent event, one which will come suddenly without announcement. In view of this expectation they are to hold fast to their testimony for Christ in order to receive their reward at His coming. The expression "quickly" is to be understood as something which is sudden and unexpected, not necessarily immediate.

"In this passage the Rapture of the Church is in view. The coming of Christ to establish a kingdom on earth is a later event following the predicted time of tribulation which is unfolded in the book of Revelation itself. By contrast, the coming of Christ for His Church is portrayed here as elsewhere in the book as an event which is not separated from us by any series of events, but is one of constant expectation in the daily walk of the believer in this age. This promise was historically true as directed to the church at Philadelphia. If the church at Philadelphia foreshadows a future period of church history just as other churches seem to do, the promises given to this church can be taken as given to all churches bearing a true witness for Christ even down to the present day."[448]

No Judgments before the Rapture

The roughly seven years of catastrophe which occur before the return of Christ to the earth is the beginning of the Day of the Lord. It is the time of God's judgment against the unbelieving world. The Day of the Lord includes all the judgments of Rev 6-19 as well as Christ's establishment of His kingdom upon the earth.[449] The Day of the Lord is a well-documented prophecy of the Old Testament scriptures and does not envision the resurrection of the Church, which was a mystery in that dispensation [Eph 3.3-6; Col 1.25-27]. The second coming of Christ itself is a judgment against the world [Rev 19.11-21].

Besides the disappearance of believers from the earth, the Rapture is an invisible event. The resurrection of the Church is portrayed in scripture not as a culmination of judgments but a rescue by which the Church is delivered from the wrath to come.

In the Rapture Jesus is coming to rescue, in the Second Advent He is coming to administer judgment.

No Kingdom Established at the Rapture

Passages referencing the Second Coming of Christ often include the establishment of the Messianic Kingdom [Zec 14:9 See also Da 2:44; 7:13-14; Rev 11:15]

> Matthew 25:31 [NKJV]
> "When the Son of Man comes in His glory, and all the holy* angels with Him, then He will sit on the throne of His glory. 32 All the nations will be gathered before Him, and He will separate them one from another, as a shepherd divides his sheep from the goats. 33 And He will set the sheep on His right hand, but the goats on the left. 34 Then the King will say to those on His right hand, 'Come, you blessed of My Father, inherit the kingdom prepared for you from the foundation of the world:

No kingdom references are associated with the coming of Christ for the Church.

Glorified Bodies Are a Part of the Rapture

A Rapture passage mentions glorified bodies, but the Second Advent passages make no mention of glorified bodies.

> 1 Corinthians 15:51–52 (KJV 1900)
> 51 Behold, I shew you a mystery; We shall not all sleep, but we shall all be changed, 52 In a moment, in the twinkling of an eye, at the last trump: for the trumpet shall sound, and the dead shall be raised incorruptible, and we shall be changed.

Believers Meet Christ in the Air in the Rapture

The Rapture passage in 1 Thessalonians 4 mentions meeting in the air. The Second Coming passages do not mention a meeting in the air.

1 Thessalonians 4:16–17 (KJV 1900)
16 For the Lord himself shall descend from heaven with a shout, with the voice of the archangel, and with the trump of God: and the dead in Christ shall rise first: 17 Then we which are alive and remain shall be caught up together with them in the clouds, to meet the Lord in the air: and so shall we ever be with the Lord.

A commentary on the Book of Matthew describes the gathering of believers during the Tribulation from the four points of the compass, across the inhabited earth.

> "**He will** then **send His angels forth** to regather **His elect from the four winds**, which relates to the earth (cf. Mark 13:27), **from one end of the heavens to the other.** This involves the gathering of those who will have become believers during the Seventieth Week of Daniel and who will have been scattered into various parts of the world because of persecution (cf. Matt. 24:16). This gathering will probably also involve all Old Testament saints, whose resurrection will occur at this time, so that they may share in Messiah's kingdom (Dan. 12:2–3, 13)."[450] [emphasis in the original]

The next passage describes not the removal of believers from the earth, but the removal [*taking*] of unbelievers at the end of the Tribulation via judgment. At that time the Church is already absent from the world.

Luke 17:26–37 (KJV 1900)
26 And as it was in the days of Noe, so shall it be also in the days of the Son of man. 27 They did eat, they drank, they married wives, they were given in marriage, until the day that Noe entered into the ark, and the flood came, and destroyed them all. 28 Likewise also as it was in the days of Lot; they did eat, they drank, they bought, they sold, they planted, they builded; 29 But the same day that Lot went out of Sodom it rained fire and brimstone from heaven, and destroyed them all. 30 Even thus shall it be in the day when the Son of man is revealed. 31 In that day, he which shall be

upon the housetop, and his stuff in the house, let him not come down to take it away: and he that is in the field, let him likewise not return back. 32 Remember Lot's wife. 33 Whosoever shall seek to save his life shall lose it; and whosoever shall lose his life shall preserve it. 34 I tell you, in that night there shall be two men in one bed; the <u>one shall be taken</u>, and the other shall be left. 35 Two women shall be grinding together; the <u>one shall be taken</u>, and the other left. 36 Two men shall be in the field; the <u>one shall be taken</u>, and the other left. 37 And they answered and said unto him, <u>Where, Lord?</u> And he said unto them, Wheresoever <u>the body is</u>, thither will <u>the eagles</u>[451] be gathered together.

The Role of the Angels

At the Second Coming, the angels are the ones who will gather the elect. [452]

Matthew 24:31 (KJV 1900)
31 And he shall send his angels with a great sound of a trumpet, and they shall gather together his elect from the four winds, from one end of heaven to the other.

At the Rapture Jesus is the direct agent of the gathering.

1 Thessalonians 4:16–17 (KJV 1900)
16 For the Lord himself shall descend from heaven with a shout, with the voice of the archangel, and with the trump of God: and the dead in Christ shall rise first: 17 Then we which are alive and remain shall be caught up together with them in the clouds, to meet the Lord in the air: and so shall we ever be with the Lord.

The "Mystery" Nature of the Rapture

Paul speaks of the Rapture as a 'mystery', that is, a truth not revealed until it was disclosed by the apostles (Col. 1:26).

1 Corinthians 15:51–52 (KJV 1900)
51 Behold, I shew you <u>a mystery</u>; We shall not all sleep, but we shall all be changed, 52 In a moment, in the twinkling of an eye, at

the last trump: for the trumpet shall sound, and the dead shall be raised incorruptible, and we shall be changed.

The Rapture is a newly revealed mystery, distinct from the Second Advent of Christ, that has been prophesied throughout the Old Testament.

The Rapture is distinguished from the Second Coming of Christ by the scriptures. These are two separate resurrections impacting two different cohorts of believers. One is imminent and not preceded by signs. The other is preceded by many signs. One occurs before the Day of the Lord and the other occurs during it. One is an act of rescue and the other an act of retribution.

About the Restrainer

2 Thessalonians 2:6–7 (KJV 1900)
6 And now ye know <u>what</u> withholdeth that he might be revealed in his time. 7 For the mystery of iniquity doth already work: only <u>he</u> who now letteth will let, until he be taken out of the way.

The Mystery of Lawlessness [Iniquity] is operating by means of the working of Satan [2 Th 2.9; Jn 8.41; Eph 2.2; Rev 13.1-4]. Something else is restraining [withholdeth…letteth…let[453]] the full expression of the Mystery of Iniquity/Lawlessness. It is a "thing" as it is referred to in the neuter[454] in verse 6 "what withholdeth." It is also a person, referred to as "He who now letteth"[455] in verse 7, and "He be taken out of the way.[456]"

It is helpful first to recognize that the Mystery of Iniquity is a force that *requires* restraining.

As evil as the world is today, it is not nearly as evil as it can be or as it will be. Today, Satan administers a world system that works in coordinated fashion with the human sin nature to promote every category of rebellion against the law of God.

1 John 2:16 (KJV 1900)
16 For <u>all</u> that is in the world, the lust of the flesh, and the lust of the eyes, and the pride of life, is not of the Father, but is of the world.

The *organizing principle of iniquity* is *not* generally known, it is a Mystery.[457] The Mystery of Iniquity is present and active in the world, but it cannot be seen for what it truly is by the overwhelming majority of mankind who have been deceived into thinking that they are not violating Gods' law, but simply doing what they wish to do.

Ephesians 2:2 (KJV 1900)
2 Wherein in time past ye walked according to <u>the course of this world</u>, according to <u>the prince</u> of the power of the air, <u>the spirit that now worketh</u> in the children of disobedience:

During the Church age, the devil has been at war with God and His Church, attempting to limit the advance of God's plan for history. In doing this, he is making preparation for *his* son, the Antichrist, and the kingdom which he is planning to provide to him.

Revelation 13:2b (KJV 1900)
and the dragon gave him his power, and his seat, and great authority.

The Mystery of Iniquity or Lawlessness is the demonic conspiracy against Christ and against divine law [Ps 2]. Although it has functioned since the fall of Satan [Isa 7], it was undisclosed until the writers of the New Testament revealed it. The Mystery of Iniquity is a multifaceted attack upon God and humanity by Satan and his angels. The theological imperative of the Mystery of Iniquity is the use of deception to promote a Lie, that Lie being that Jesus is not the Christ. This concept is the centerpiece of a demonic worldview which will form the basis of Antichrist's kingdom.

The Mystery of Iniquity, therefore, has as one of its objectives the overthrow of the doctrine of Christ, the Mystery of Godliness, and the system of righteousness that belongs to Christ, originating in His own holy Person [1 Jn 1.5].

1 Timothy 3:16 (KJV 1900)
16 And without controversy great is the <u>mystery of godliness</u>: <u>God</u> was manifest in the flesh, justified in the Spirit, seen of angels, preached unto the Gentiles, believed on in the world, received up into glory.

Psalm 2:1–3 (KJV 1900)
1 Why do the heathen rage, And the people imagine a vain thing?
2 The kings of the earth set themselves, And the rulers take

counsel together, <u>Against</u> the LORD, and <u>against</u> his anointed, saying, 3 Let us break their bands asunder, And cast away their cords from us.

When the restraint of 2 Thessalonians 2.6-7 is removed, the unnamed theology which opposes Christ and His righteous rule will be named and the Lie which forms its basis will become the rallying point for the new spiritual dynasty to be inaugurated in the last days.

Revelation 13:5–9 (KJV 1900)
5 And there was given unto him a mouth speaking great things and blasphemies; and power was given unto him to continue forty *and* two months. 6 And he opened his mouth in blasphemy against God, to blaspheme his name, and his tabernacle, and them that dwell in heaven. 7 And it was given unto him to make war with the saints, and to overcome them: and power was given him over all kindreds, and tongues, and nations. 8 And all that dwell upon the earth shall worship him, whose names are not written in the book of life of the Lamb slain from the foundation of the world. 9 If any man have an ear, let him hear.

Just as *deception* characterized the function of the Mystery of Iniquity in the Church age, *blasphemy* will characterize its function after the restraining power has been removed.

The foundation of the Mystery of Iniquity is the theology, the doctrine of Lucifer concerning his own self-concept and aspirations. Just as there is a Mystery of Godliness [1 Tim 3.16] that pertains to God's Person and His Program for mankind, so the Mystery of Lawlessness describes Lucifer's idea of himself and his program for the heavens and the earth.

In 2 Thessalonians 2, as in 1 Thessalonians 5, Paul makes a distinction between the destiny of the lost and that of the saved. The lost will enter the Day of the Lord which shall overtake them like a thief in the night; the saved will be rescued from this judgment into the presence of the Lord [1 Th 4.17] where they will be delivered from the time of testing [*wrath* 1 Th 5.9-11] that will come upon the world.

The appearing of the Antichrist, and the progress of Satan's plan for humanity is being restrained. It is the progress of the Mystery of Iniquity as a world transforming spiritual force that is being limited and its destructive power constrained by another superior force. Even with this restraint, the Mystery of Lawlessness is still advancing the devil's agenda in the world. What is restraining it?

2 Thessalonians 2:6 (KJV 1900)
6 And now ye know what withholdeth that he might be revealed in his time.

We have amply established that the Mystery of Iniquity is a complex spiritual strategy. However, the Mystery of Iniquity is not an intellectual exercise. It is also a mighty supernatural force, energized by Satan and his demonic host. It is the mind of Lucifer imposed upon the fallen creation with the authority and strength to accomplish its aims in history. It is the plan which since the Flood has been supervised upon the earth by Mystery Babylon. Its name, Mystery of Iniquity connotes the management of the sinful natures of men and fallen angels to prosecute a successful revolution against God. The Mystery of Iniquity was the blueprint by which Mystery Babylon instigated the spiritual corruption of Israel, the assassination of John the Baptist and of Christ Himself. It is through this power that society's institutions are debased from God's original intent to institutions suitable to the designs of the New World Order.

A spiritual power can only be restrained by a greater spiritual power. A great error of modern Christianity is the attempt to address spiritual issues via secular means. Spiritual problems cannot be solved via political means. Nor can they be resolved through violence. The appeal of this incorrect approach to Christians is that it allows an *appearance* of spiritual battle, while the believer remains lazily cocooned in various categories of carnality. True spiritual warfare requires spiritual strength which is always accompanied by personal righteousness and justice.

Matthew 12:29 (KJV 1900)
29 Or else how can one enter into a strong man's house, and spoil his goods, except he first <u>bind</u> the strong man? and then he will spoil his house.

The restraining power is a spiritual power, rather than the power of the state or of the people. In 2 Thessalonians 2.6 the restraining power is a "thing." What is this thing that can restrain the power of Lucifer's vision for this world?

The only *thing* strong enough to restrain the devil would be Christ, specifically, His spiritual body of which he is the Head, the Church. The Church is the total population of born-again individuals united via the baptism of the Spirit [1 Cor 12.13]. The Church came into existence via this new ministry of the Spirit inaugurated at Pentecost in Acts 2 and continues until the resurrection of the body of Christ or the Rapture, which is yet future. The Church, the body of which Christ is the Head, restrains the full expression of the Mystery of Iniquity and therefore the emergence of the Antichrist. The Church is a bride, or a "she," but it is also a body, an "it."

> Ephesians 1:22–23 (KJV 1900)
> 22 And hath put all things under his feet, and gave him to be the head over all things to the Church, 23 <u>Which is his body</u>, the fulness of him that filleth all in all.

The spiritual body of Christ, the Church, is the mechanism which restrains the free function of the Mystery of Iniquity and therefore the Man of Sin. This means the true Church, not the millions of false believers who are mingled with them in Christendom.

The Church, in its totality, possesses God's life, God's power, God's wisdom and God's gifts. It is the body of which Christ is the Head.

The Church accomplishes many of God's purposes on the earth, despite what the fumbling and bungling of Christendom portrays to the world. Christendom is the outward *professing* Church. It is not the Body of Christ, though it claims to be. It consists of both believers and unbelievers, saints, and antichrists

Because the body of Christ is the body of Christ, it cannot fail, because Christ as its Head cannot fail.

> 1 John 4:4 (KJV 1900)
> ⁴ Ye are of God, little children, and have overcome them: because greater is he that is in you, than he that is in the world.

The Body of Christ is one aspect of the Restrainer, but there is another.

> 2 Thessalonians 2:7 (KJV 1900)
> ⁷ For the mystery of iniquity doth already work: only **he** who now letteth *will let*, until he be taken out of the way.

The "what" is now described as a "He." He is God Himself. No human being or human organization could restrain the cumulative power of evil for one moment, let alone the entire period of the Church age.

No government possesses spiritual power or a spiritual mandate and therefore does not qualify as the restrainer even if you could refer to a government as a 'He'.

No angel or combination of angels is powerful enough to restrain this world system and its temporary ruler Lucifer.

That leaves God Himself. God is active in the Church as the Third Person, the Holy Spirit.

The Holy Spirit:

- *Creates* the Church through regeneration [Titus 3.5] and Spirit baptism [1 Corinthians 12.13a]
- *Empowers* the Church through indwelling [Romans 8.9] and filling [1 Corinthians 12.13b]
- *Equips* the Church [1 Corinthians 12.4-11]
- *Instructs* the Church [John 16.12-15]
- *Guides* the Church [Galatians 5.16]

2 Thessalonians 2:7 (KJV 1900)
7 For the mystery of iniquity doth already work: only he who now letteth *will let*, until he be taken out of the way.

The body of Christ consists of spiritually regenerated individuals, who have been given the highest spiritual position, endowed with supernatural ministry gifts, and provided unlimited access to divine omnipotence through the Spirit *for the purpose* of glorifying God through obedience to the scriptures.

By contrast, Lucifer's core *human* organization consists of unregenerate persons [Jude 4] whom he empowers [Eph 2.2], who receive direct and indirect instruction from demons [1 Timothy 4.1] for the purpose of secretly introducing a theology of lawlessness into the world [1 John 2.22; Jude 4]. They possess intelligence, skill, and the uncanny ability to impersonate true Christians [Rom 16.17-18; 1 John 4.1].

The Holy Spirit working in the Church successfully restrains the full evil potential of the Mystery of Iniquity until it [the Church] is taken out of the way at the Rapture. At that time two conflicting historical trends will collide: one is the Day of the Lord and the other, the Mystery of Iniquity.

In conclusion, the translation, or Rapture of the Church sets into motion the events prophesied as the Day of the Lord, when God's judgment and wrath will be poured out upon unredeemed humanity. The supernatural exit of the Church will unleash the full potential of Mystery Babylon, resulting in a massive spiritual deception, and an apostasy from Christianity. The Antichrist will be revealed after his ascent to worldwide political influence. The events that begin in Revelation 6 are the outworking of the conflict between his kingdom aspirations and the wrath of God which is systematically visited upon the world at that time.

Appendix 3: Dispensations

Dispensation: Definition[458]

> "Etymology. A dispensation may be defined as "a distinguishable economy in the outworking of God's purpose."7 The English word dispensation comes from the Greek word oikonomia, which means "stewardship." This word is used in Luke 16:2, 3, 4; 1 Corinthians 9:17; Ephesians 1:10; 3:2, 9; Colossians 1:25; 1 Timothy 1:4.[459]

> "The "dispensation" (oikonomia) is an arrangement or administration.[460]

A dispensation is an economy [administration, government] but also an age [a distinguishable period of time].

> "To view the Bible dispensationally is to view God's plan for history, including future prophecy, from His perspective"[461]

Dispensation: Elements of

- ➢ Distinctive Revelation
- ➢ Testing
- ➢ Failure
- ➢ Judgment
- ➢ A continuation of certain ordinances

- An annulment of other regulations
- Fresh introduction of new principles
- Progressive revelation of God's plan for history[462]

Dispensations: Number

At least three

- Old Testament [Exodus 19.5]
- New Testament [Matt 26.26-28]
- Kingdom [Rev 20:1-4]

Perhaps as many as seven:

- Innocence [Gen 1.28-3.6];
- Conscience [Gen 3.7-8.14];
- Human Government [Gen 8.15-11.9];
- Promise [Gen 11.10-Ex.18.27];
- Law/Israel [Ex 19-Jn 14.30];
- Grace/Church [Acts 2.1-Rev 19.21];
- Kingdom [Rev 20.1-15].

Identifying A Change in Dispensations

- A change in God's governmental relationship with man (though a dispensation does not have to be composed entirely of completely new features)
- A resultant change in man's responsibility
- Corresponding revelation necessary to effect the change (which is new and is a stage in the progress of revelation through the Bible.)[463]

Dispensations and Covenants

Dispensations include Covenants but also other elements such as progressive revelation, failure, judgment, continuity of certain regulations and the establishment of new practices.

Dispensation	Covenant
Innocence Gen 1:28-3:6	Edenic Covenant Gen 1:28-30; 2:15-17
Conscience Gen 4:1-8:14	Adamic Covenant Gen 3:14-19
Human Government Gen 8:15-11:9	Noahic Covenant Gen 8:20-9:17
Promise Gen 11:10-Ex 18:27	Abrahamic Covenant Gen 12:1-3; 15:1-21; 1:.1-21; 26:2-5; 28:10-17
Law Ex 19:1-Acts 1:26	Mosaic Covenant Ex 20-23; Deuteronomy
Grace Ac 2:1-Rev 19:21	New Covenant Matt 26:27-28; Luke 22:20; 2 Cor 3:6
Kingdom/Millennium Rev 20:1-15	Abrahamic/Palestinian/Davidic/New Covenants Dt 30:1-10; 2 Sam 7:4-17 Jer 31:31-37

Figure 16: Dispensations and Covenants

What Distinguishes Dispensationalism from Other Systems of Interpretation

- ➢ Consistent literal interpretation of Scripture
- ➢ Distinction between God's plan for Israel and the Church
- ➢ The glory of God as the goal of history

ABOUT THE AUTHOR

Richard G. Walker is a Bible teacher and writer. He has published two doctrinal books: "The Spiritual Gift of Tongues" and "The Baptism of the Holy Spirit." His next projects include the book "Black Nations in Scripture" [December 2022] and volume two of this work "Antichrist and the New World Order [July 2023]. His blog and video studies may be found at www.aricherwalk.com. Richard is married to Cynthia; they have three adult children and one who is with the Lord.

Works Cited

Ahmed, Nafeez Mosaddeq. 2002. *The War on Freedom: How and Why America Was Attacked, September 11th, 2001.* Joshua Tree: Media Messenger Books.

Alexander, Michelle. 2012. *The New Jim Crow: Mass Incarceration in the Age of Colorblindness. Revised edition.* . New York: New Press.

Alnor, Jackie. 1998. "Evangelism: Groups Battle over Catholic Outreach." *Christianity Today.* March 2. Accessed June 28, 2017. http://www.christianitytoday.com/ct/1998/march2/8t3070.html?start=2. .

B. Blayney, Thomas Scott, and R.A. Torrey with John Canne, Browne,. n.d. *The Treasury of Scripture Knowledge, vol. 1* . London: Samuel Bagster and Sons.

Bailey, Alice A. n.d. *Externalisation of the Hierarchy.* Lucis Publishing Companies. Kindle Edition.

Barbieri, Louis A. Jr. 1985. *"Matthew," in The Bible Knowledge Commentary: An Exposition of the Scriptures, ed. J. F. Walvoord and R. B. Zuck, vol. 2* . Wheaton: Victor Books.

Britannica, The Editors of Encyclopaedia. n.d. ""Dialectic". Encyclopedia Britannica." *Encyclopedia Britannica, .* Accessed June 21, 2019. https://www.britannica.com/topic/dialectic-logic.

Bullinger, Ethelbert W. n.d. *The Companion Bible: Being the Authorized Version of 1611 with the Structures and Notes, Critical, Explanatory and Suggestive and with 198 Appendixes.* Bellingham: Faithlife.

Burgon, John William. 1971. *The Revision Revised.* New York: Dover Publications Inc., Public Domain, Kindle Version.

Burns, Cathy. 1994. *Hidden Secrets of the Eastern Star: The Masonic Connection.* Mt. Carmel: Sharing.

Butler, Smedley D, and Dragan Nikolic. 2014. *War Is a Racket: The Antiwar Classic by America's Most Decorated Soldiee.*

Center, Pew Research. 2005. "Myths of the Modern MegaChurch." *Pew Research Center.* May 23. Accessed June 21, 2017. http://www.pewforum.org/2005/05/23/myths-of-the-modern-megaChurch/.

Chafer, Lewis Sperry. 1951. *Dispensationalism.* Dallas: Dallas Seminary Press.

—. n.d. *Satan.* Public Domain Books, Kindle Edition.

—. 1936. *The Kingdom in History and Prophecy.* Chicago: The Bible Institute Colportage Ass'n.

Clark, Gordon H. n.d. "Gordon H. Clark Foundation." *Faith and Reason.* Accessed June 14, 2017. http://gordonhclark.reformed.info/faith-and-reason-by-gordon-h-clark/.

Clarke, Adam. 2006. *Adam Clarke's Commentary, Electronic Database.* Biblesoft.

Cloud, David W. 1999. *Evangelicals and Rome.* Way of Life Literature.

—. 2005. *Faith vs. The Modern Bible Versions.* Port Huron: Way of Life Literature.

—. 2006. *New Evangelicalism: Its History, Characteristics, and Fruit. .* Port Huron: Way of Life Literature.

—. 2006. *The Pentecostal-Charismatic Movements: Their History and Error.* Way of Life.

Constable, Thomas L. 1985. *"2 Thessalonians," in The Bible Knowledge Commentary: An Exposition of the Scriptures, ed. J. F. Walvoord and R. B. Zuck, vol. 2 .* Wheaton: Victor Books.

Council of Trent. n.d. "Documents – Paul III Council of Trent-6 – Our Catholic Faith." *Our Catholic Faith.* Accessed December 13, 2019. https://ourcatholicfaith.org/documents-paul-iii-council-of-trent-6/.

Dialectics, Hegel's. n.d. "Hegel's Dialectics." *Stanford Encyclopedia of Philosophy.* Accessed June 25, 2019. https://plato.stanford.edu/entries/hegel-dialectics/.

Dictionary, Masonic. n.d. "Masonic Dictionary." *s.v.* "Initiation" Masonic Dictionary [source: 100 Words in Masonry]. Accessed November 5, 2017. http://www.masonicdictionary.com/initiation.html.

Duignan, Brian. 2018. "Postmodernism Encyclopædia Britannica, October 25, 2018. https://www.britannica.com/topic/postmodernism-philosophy. Accessed June 24, 2019." *Encyclopædia Britannica.* October 25. https://www.britannica.com/topic/postmodernism-philosophy.

Dyer, Charles H. 1985. *"Ezekiel," in The Bible Knowledge Commentary: An Exposition of the Scriptures, ed. J. F. Walvoord and R. B. Zuck, vol. 1.* Wheaton: Victor.

Edwards, Jonathan. 1752. "Works of Jonathan Edwards Volume 2-Sermon 56: True Grace Distinguished From The Experience of Devils." *Christian Classics Ethereal Library.* September 28.

Accessed July 2, 2022. https://ccel.org/ccel/edwards/works2/works2.iii.v.html.

Elwell, Walter A., and Barry J. Beitzel. 1988. *Baker Encyclopedia of the Bible.* Grand Rapids: Baker Book House.

Enns, Paul P. 1989. *The Moody Handbook of Theology (Chicago, IL: Moody Press, 1989), .* Chicago: Moody Press.

Erdmann, Martin. 2016. *Ecumenical Quest for a World Federation: The Churches' Contribution to Marshal Public Support for World Order and Peace, 1919-1945.* Greenville: Verax Vox Media.

Fausset, Andrew Robert. 2006. *FAUSSET'S Bible DICTIONARY Electronic Database. .* Biblesoft Inc.

Finkenrath, G., ed. Coenen, Lothar, Beyreuther, Erich, and Bietenhard, Hans. 1986. *"Secret, Mystery" in New International Dictionary of New Testament Theology .* Grand Rapids: Zondervan Publishing House.

Fuller, David Otis and Wilkinson, Benjamin George. 2000. *Which Bible?* Grand Rapids: Grand Rapids International Publications.

Geisler, Norman L. 1999. *"Reincarnation" Bakeer Encyclopedia of Christian Apologetics, Baker Reference Library.* Grand Rapids: Baker Books.

Gerhard Peters, John T. Woolley,. n.d. "George Bush, Address Before a Joint Session of the Congress on the State of the Union Online." *The American Presidency Project .* Accessed December 19, 2018. https://www.presidency.ucsb.edu/node/265956.

Grundmann, Walter. 1964-. *Walter Grundmann, "Δύναμαι, Δυνατός, Δυνατέω, Ἀδύνατος, Ἀδυνατέω, Δύναμις, Δυνάστης, Δυναμόω, Ἐνδυναμόω," ed. Gerhard Kittel, Geoffrey W. Bromiley, and Gerhard Friedrich, Theological Dictionary of the New Testament.* Grand Rapids: Eerdmans.

Hall, Manley P. n.d. "The Secret Teaching of All Ages (1928)." *sacredtexts.com.* Accessed October 17, 2018. http://www.sacred-texts.com/eso/sta/sta04.htm.

Hanegraaff, Hank. 1997. *Christianity in Crisis.* Eugene: Harvest Houst.

—. 2001. *Counterfeit Revival.* Nashville: Thomas Nelson.

Hannah, John. 2009. *An Uncommon Union.* Grand Rapids: Zondervan.

Hays, S. A. 2018. "Transhumanism." *Encyclopedia Britannica.* June 12. Accessed July 10, 2022. https://www.britannica.com/topic/transhumanism.

Henry, Carl F.H. 1988. *"Bible, Authority of The," Baker Encyclopedia of the Bible.* Grand Rapids: Baker Book House.

Hills, Edward F. 1984. *The King James Version Defended. 4th ed.* Des Moines: CRP.

Hislop, Alexander. 1998. *The Two Babylons.* . Chino: Chick Publications.

n.d. "Hitler Speech at the Berlin Sports Palace (January 30, 1941)." *Jewish Virtual Library.* Accessed December 15, 2018. Hitler Speech at the Berlin https://www.jewishvirtuallibrary.org/hitler-speech-at-the-berlin-sports-palace-january-30-1941.

Hoehner, Harold W. 1985. *"Ephesians" in The Bible Knowledge Commentary: An Exposition of the Scriptures, ed. J. F. Walvoord and R. B. Zuck, vol. 2.* Wheaton: Victor Books.

Hunt, Dave. 1994. *A Woman Rides the Beast: The Roman Catholic Church and the Last Days. Dave Hunt. A Woman Rides the Beast: The Roman Catholic Church and the Last Days. (Harvest House Publishers, Eugene Oregon, 1994)* . Eugene: Harvest House Publishers.

Ice, Thomas. 1995. "The Biblical Basis for the Pretribulational Rapture," in *Basic Theology Applied.* Victor Books.

—. n.d. ""What is Replacement Theology," ." *www.pre-trib.org.* Accessed February 29, 2012. http://www.pre-trib.org/data/pdf/Ice-WhatisReplacementThe.pdf .

II, Vatican Council. n.d. "Vatican Council II, Decree on Ecumenism 3, II, 24;." *Catholic Information Network.* Accessed March 1, 2012. http://www.cin.org/v2ecum.html .

Vatican II. 1964. "Unitatis Redintegratio-Chapter I Catholic Principles On Ecumenism." *The Vatican.* November 21. Accessed December 9, 2018. http://www.vatican.va/archive/hist councils/ii vatican council/documents/va-ii decree 19641121 unitatis-redintegratio en.html.

Jamieson, Robert, A. R. Fausset, and David Brown. 1997. . *Commentary Critical and Explanatory on the Whole Bible.* Oak Harbor: Logos Research Systems, Inc.

Johnson, Phil. n.d. *A Beginners Guide to Postmodernism.* Accessed June 24, 2019. https://www.gracechurch.org/sermons/10244 .

Josephus, Flavius, and Whiston, William The Works of Josephus: Complete and Unabridged. (Peabody: Hendrickson, 1987). Book 6 Chapter 2. 1987. *The Works of Josephus: Complete and Unabridged. (Peabody: Hendrickson, 1987). Book 6 Chapter 2.* Peabody: Hendrickson.

Kittel, Gerhard, Geoffrey W. Bromiley, and Gerhard Friedrich, eds. 1964- . *Theological Dictionary of the New Testament.* Grand Rapids: Eerdmans.

KJV. 2009. *The Holy Bible King James Electronic Edition of the 1900 Authorized Version.* Bellingham WA: Logos Research Systems Inc.

LaHaye, Tim, Thomas Ice,. 2001. *Charting the End Times. Tim LaHaye Prophecy Library.* Eugene: Harvest House Publishers.

Lindsell, Harold. 1978. *Battle for the Bible.* Zondervan.

Louw, Johannes P., Nida, Eugene Albert. 1996. *Greek-English Lexicon of the New Testament: Based on Semantic Domains.* New York: United Bible Societies.

MacArthur, John F. Kindle Edition. *Strange Fire: The Danger of Offending the Holy Spirit with Counterfeit Worship.* Nashville: Thomas Nelson.

MacArthur, John, John Ankerberg, and R. C. Sproul. n.d. "Grace To You." *Irreconcilable Differences Catholics, Evangelicals and the New Quest for Unity Parts 1-3.* Accessed April 28, 2017. https://www.gty.org/library/sermons-library/GTY54/irreconcilable-differences-catholics-evangelicals-and-the-new-quest-for-unity-parts-13.

Machen, J. Gresham. n.d. *Christianity and Liberalism.* Kindle Edition. . Christianity and Liberalism (Kindle Locations 2454-2455). Kindle Edition.

Mackey, Albert Gallatin. 1882. *The Symbolism of Freemasonry / Illustrating and Explaining Its Science and Philosophy, Its Legends, Myths and Symbols* . Amazon Kindle.

Manhattan, Avro. 1953. *, Terror Over Yugoslavia: The Threat to Europe.* Watts.

Manser, Martin H. 2009. *Dictionary of Bible Themes: The Accessible and Comprehensive Tool for Topical Studies* . London: Martin Manser.

McCoy, Alfred W. 2003. *The Politics of Heroin: CIA Complicity in the Global Drug Trade: Afghanistan, Southeast Asia, Central America, Colombia. Rev. ed.* . Chicago: Lawrence Hill Books: Distributed by Independent Publishers Group.

McGowan, Dave. 2014. *"Weird Scenes Inside the Canyon: Laurel Canyon, Covert Ops & the Dark Heart of the Hippy Dream",* . Head Press.

Merriam Webster Dictionary, n.d. "s.v. "Esoteric" Merriam Webster Dictionary." *Merriam Webster Dictionary.* https://www.merriam-webster.com/dictionary/esoteric.

Miller, Stephen R. 1994. *"Daniel," vol. 18, The New American Commentary.* Nashville: Broadman & Holman Publishers.

Mohler Jr., Albert R. 2001. "Standing Together, Standing Apart: Cultural Co-Belligerence Without Theological Compromise, , R. Albert Mohler Jr., December 25, 2001." *The Southern Baptist Journal of*

Theology.

Mohler, Albert. 2010. "The Inerrancy of Scripture: The Fifty Years War...and Counting." *www.albertmohler.com.* August 16. Accessed November 12, 2017. https://albertmohler.com/2010/08/16/the-inerrancy-of-scripture-the-fifty-years-war-and-counting/ [Accessed November 12, 2017].

Mounce, Robert H. 1977. *The Book of Revelation, New International Commentary-New Testament.* Grand Rapids: Eerdmans.

Nielsen. 2019. "Nielsen. "FROM CONSUMERS TO CREATORS THE DIGITAL LIVES OF BLACK CONSUMERS," n.d. ." *www.walterkaitz.org.* January. https://www.walterkaitz.org/wp-content/uploads/2019/01/nielsen-from-consumers-to-creators.pdf.

NKJV. 1982. *The New King James Version.* Nashville: Thomas Nelson.

Online, Etymology Dictionary. n.d. " s.v. "Occult" ." *Etymology Dictionary Online.* Accessed April 11, 2017. http://www.etymonline.com/index.php?term=occult .

Pache, Rene. 1951. ""The Ecumenical Movement Part 4: Moving toward the Super-Church." *Galaxie Software.* Accessed June 28, 2017. http://www.galaxie.com/article/bsac108-430-06.

—. 1950. "The Ecumenical Movement Part 1 ." *Galaxie Software.* Accessed June 14, 2014. http://www.galaxie.com/article/bsac107-427-10.

—. 1951. "The Ecumenical Movement Part 2." *Galaxie Software.* Accessed June 22, 2017. http://www.galaxie.com/article/bsac107-428-05. .

Pentecost, Dwight J. eds. Walvoord, J.F. and Zuck, R.B. 1985. *"Daniel."* In *The Bible Knowledge Commentary: An Exposition of the Scriptures.* Wheaton: Victor Books.

Pentecost, Dwight, J. 1964. *Things to Come: A Study in Biblical Eschatology.* Grand Rapids: Academie Books.

Pink, Arthur W. The Antichrist, Arthur Pink Collection Book 1, (p. 7, 8). Prisbrary Publishing. Kindle Edition. n.d. *The Antichrist, Arthur Pink Collection Book 1.* Prisbrary Publishing. Kindle Edition.

Pope, Francis. 2014. *Pope Francis Sends Video Message to Kenneth Copeland - Lets Unite - YouTube."* . February 22. Accessed June 15, 2017. https://www.youtube.com/watch?v=uA4EPOfic5A.

Rice, John R. 1976. *The Charismatic Movement.* Sword of the Lord.

Riplinger, G.A. 1993. *New Age Bible Versions.* (Shelbyville: Bible & Literature Missionary Foundation.

Robbins, John W. 1998. "BLEATING WOLVES THE MEANING OF EVANGELICALS AND CATHOLICS TOGETHER." *A Paper Presented at The Trinity Foundation Conference on Christianity and Roman Catholicism.* The Trinity Foundation.

Robertson, A.T. 1933. *Word Pictures in the New Testament.* Nashville: Broadman Press.

Ryrie, Charles C. 2001. *First and Second Thessalonians.* Chicago: Moody

Press.

Ryrie, Charles Caldwell. 1995. *Dispensationalism. Revised and Expanded.* Chicago: Moody Press.

Schaff, Philip and David Schley Schaff, History of the Christian Church, vol. 2 (New York: Charles Scribner's Sons, 1910),. 1910. *History of the Christian Church, vol. 2 (New York: Charles Scribner's Sons, 1910), .* New York: Charles Scribner's Sons.

Scofield, C. I. ed. 1917. *The Scofield Reference Bible: The Holy Bible Containing the Old and New Testaments .* New York, London, Toronto, Melbourne, Bombay: Oxford University Press.

Scott, Peter Dale. Dallas '63: The First Deep State Revolt Against the White House (Forbidden Bookshelf Book 17) . Kindle Edition: Open Road Media.

Seiss, Joseph A. 2006. *The Apocalypse: Exposition of the Book of Revelation.* Electronic Database, Biblesoft Inc. Electronic Database. Copyright © 1998, 2003, 2006 by Biblesoft, Inc. All rights reserved.).

Sharlet, Jeff. n.d. *The Family, The Secret Fundamentalism at the Heart of American Power.* HarperCollins e-books. Kindle Edition.

Smietana, Bob. 2015. "International Mission Board Drops Ban onSpeaking in Tongues-New Rules also loosen restrictions on baptism, divorce, and parents of teenagers." *Christianity Today,.* May 14. Accessed August 20, 2018. https://www.christianitytoday.com/ct/2015/may-web-only/imb-ban-speaking-in-tongues-baptism-baptist-missionary.html .

Soanes, Catherine and Stevenson, Angus eds.,*"Desecrate" in Concise Oxford English Dictionary* . Oxford: Oxford University Press, 2004.

Spence, O. Tallmadge. 1978. *Charismatism: Awakening or Apostasy.* Greenville: Bob Jones University Press.

Spence, Tallmadge O. 1978. *Charismatism.* Greenville: Bob Jones University Press.

Spurgeon, Chaerles H. 2016. "Battle with Apollyon 2." *Sermon Audio.* April 19. Accessed July 2, 2022. Charles H. Spurgeon, "Battle w https://www.sermonaudio.com/sermoninfo.asp?SID=41916722 310 .

Strong, James. 1995. *Enhanced Strong's Lexicon.* Woodside Bible Fellowship.

Sutton, Antony C. 2002. *America's Secret Establishment: An Introduction to the Order of Skull & Bones.* Walterville: Auflage, Updated Reprint, Trine Day.

Swanson, James. 1997. *Dictionary of Biblical Languages with Semantic Domains: Greek (New Testament)* . Oak Harbor: Logos Research Systems, Inc.

Teilhard de Chardin, Pierre. 2008. *The Phenomenon of Man.* . New York 2008: Harper Perennial Modern Thought.

Thieme, Robert B. Jr. 1974. *Armageddon.* Houston: R.B. Thieme Jr.

—. 2002. *Christian Suffering.* Houston: Robert B. Thieme Jr.

Thieme, Robert B. Jr. 1972. *The Edification Complex of the Soul.*

Houston: Robert B. Thieme Jr.

Thieme, Robert B., and Wayne F. Hill. 1999. *The Divine Outline of History: Dispensations and the Church.* Houston: R.B. Thieme, Jr. Bible Ministries.

Thompson, Charles. n.d. "Charles Thomson's design for the Great Seal of the United States, 1782;." *Reports of Committees of Congress; Records of the Continental and Confederation Congresses and the Constitutional Convention, 1774-1789, Record Group 360; National Archives.* Accessed November 28, 2021. https://www.ourdocuments.gov/doc.php?flash=false&doc=5.

Thompson, Paul. 2006. *The Terror Timeline: Year by Year, Day by Day, Minute by Minute; a Comprehensive Chronicle of the Road to 9/11 - and America's Response.* New York: Regan.

Trent, Paul III The Council of. n.d. "Documents-The Council of Trent 6." *Our Catholic Faith.* Accessed December 13, 2019. https://ourcatholicfaith.org/documents-paul-iii-council-of-trent-6/.

Various. n.d. "Evangelicals & Catholics Together: The Christian Mission in the Third Millennium by Various | Articles | First Things." *First Things.* Accessed June 22, 2017. https://www.firstthings.com/article/1994/05/evangelicals-catholics-together-the-christian-mission-in-the-third-millennium.

Vergil, J. B. Greenough. 1900. "Vergil. Bucolics, Aeneid, and Georgics Of Vergil." *Perseus Project.* Accessed November 28, 2021. http://www.perseus.tufts.edu/hopper/text?doc=Perseus:abo:p

hi,0690,001:4 .

Vergilius, Maro P. n.d. "The Eclogues, Eclogue ." *The Internet Classics Archive.* Accessed November 28, 2021. http://classics.mit.edu/Virgil/eclogue.4.iv.html.

Vincent, Marvin Richardson. 1887. *Word Studies in the New Testament, vol. 2* . New York: Charles Scribner's Sons .

Vinge, Vernor. 1993. "What is the Sinbgularity." *www.kurzweilai.net.* March 30. Accessed December 2, 2021. https://www.kurzweilai.net/the-technological-singularity.

Wagner, Martin L. 2000. *Freemasonry Interpreted.* New York: A&B Publishers Group.

Walker, Richard G. 2009. "While Men Slept, Roman Catholic Ecclesiology, Eschatology and the Ecumenical Movement." *Masters Degree Papers.* Richard G. Walker.

Walvoord, John F. 2007. *The Thessalonian Epistles* . Galaxie Software.

—. 2008. *Daniel: The Key To Prophetic Revelation.* Galaxie Software.

Walvoord, John F. ed. Walvoord, J.F. and Zuck R.B. 1985. *"Revelation," in The Bible Knowledge Commentary: An Exposition of the Scriptures, vol. 2* . Wheaton: Victor Books.

Walvoord, John F. 2008. *The Revelation of Jesus Christ.* Galaxie Software.

Webb, Gary. 1998. *Dark Alliance: The CIA, the Contras, and the Crack Cocaine Explosion.* New York: Seven Stories Press.

Webster, Mirriam. 2017. *"Seduce"*. October 21. https://www.Merriam-Webster.com.

Wiersbe, Warren W. The Bible Exposition Commentary, vol. 2. 1996. *The Bible Exposition Commentary, vol. 2 .* Wheaton: Victor Books.

Wikipedia. n.d. "The Joint Declaration on the Doctrine of Justification." *Wikipedia.* Accessed June 15, 2015. https://en.wikipedia.org/wiki/Joint_Declaration_on_the_Doctrine_of_Justification. .

—. n.d. *Ubermensch.* Accessed November 5, 2017. https://en.wikipedia.org/wiki/Übermensch Accessed November 5, 2017.

Wooley, John T. and Peters Gerhard. n.d. "George Bush, The President's News Conference on the Persian Gulf Crisis." *The American Presidency Project.* Accessed December 19, 2018. https://www.presidency.ucsb.edu/node/265638.

Wooley, John T. and Peters, Gerhard. n.d. "Franklin D. Roosevelt, Address for Navy and Total Defense Day ." *The American Presidency Project.* Accessed December 19, 2018. https://www.presidency.ucsb.edu/node/210207.

—. n.d. "Franklin D. Roosevelt, Address on Armistice Day, Arlington National Cemetery." *The American Presidency Project.* Accessed December 2, 2021. https://www.presidency.ucsb.edu/node/209352.

—. n.d. "Jimmy Carter, Visit of Lieutenant General Obasanjo of Nigeria Toasts of the President and Lieutenant General Obasanjo at a Dinner Honoring the Nigerian Head of State." *The American

Presidency Project. Accessed December 19, 2018. https://www.presidency.ucsb.edu/node/242820.

—. n.d. "William J. Clinton, Remarks at the Welcoming Ceremony for Prime Minister Romano Prodi of Italy ." *The American Presidency Project.* Accessed December 2, 2021. https://www.presidency.ucsb.edu/node/226235.

Woolley, John T. and Peters, Gerhard. n.d. "Richard Nixon, toasts of the President and President Medixi of Brazil." *The American Presidency Project.* Accessed December 19, 2018. https://www.presidency.ucsb.edu/node/240363.

Wuest, Kenneth S. 1997. *Wuest's Word Studies from the Greek New Testament: For the English Reader .* Grand Rapids: Eerdmans.

Wylie, James Aitken. n.d. *The History of Protestantism.* Kindle Edition: Kirk Press.

Wylie, James. n.d. *The Papacy Is The Antichrist (PROOF) Illustrated: A DEMONSTRATION.* Delmarva Publications Kindle Edition.

Zylstra, Sarah Eekhoff. 2016. ""Pope Francis Quiet on Catholic Persecution of Protestants in Mexico"." *Christianity Today.* February. Accessed July 9, 2017. http://www.christianitytoday.com/news/2016/february/pope-francis-catholic-persecution-protestant-mexico-chiapas.html.

Antichrist and the New World Order

---

[1] The period between Pentecost and the resurrection of the Church. See Appendix III: Dispensations
[2] See Appendix III Dispensations
[3] In this book, the terms Lucifer, Satan, the devil, and the serpent pertain to the same person, the chief of the fallen angels [Isa 14.12-14, Lk 4.1-13; 10.18; Rev 20.1-2]
[4] Dan 7.25; Rev 13.7
[5] Rev 5-19

[6] John 3:16–18 (KJV 1900) 16 For God so loved the world, that he gave his only begotten Son, that whosoever believeth in him should not perish, but have everlasting life. 17 For God sent not his Son into the world to condemn the world; but that the world through him might be saved. 18 He that believeth on him is not condemned: but he that believeth not is condemned already, because he hath not believed in the name of the only begotten Son of God. (KJV 2009).

[7] "Again, Satan is revealed as directing and empowering the children of disobedience: "And you hath he quickened, who were dead in trespasses and sins; wherein in times past ye walked according to the course of this age, according to the prince of the power of the air, the spirit that now worketh in the children of disobedience" (Eph. 2:1, 2). The real force of this passage, also, is dependent upon the meaning of one word; the word "worketh" being the same as is used in Phil. 2:13, where God is said to impart His wisdom and strength to the believer: "For it is God that worketh in you both to will and to do of his good pleasure." Additional light may be had as to the reality of this relationship from the following passages in which the same original word is used: "And there are diversities of operations, but it is the same God that worketh all in all" (I Cor. 12:6); "But all these (gifts) worketh that one and the selfsame Spirit, dividing to every man severally as he will" (I Cor. 12:11); "And what is the exceeding greatness of His power to usward who believe, according to the working of His mighty power, which He wrought in Christ when He raised Him from the dead, and set Him at His own right hand in the heavenlies" (Eph. 1:19-20); "For He that wrought effectually in Peter to the apostleship of the circumcision, the same was mighty in me toward the Gentiles" (Gal. 2:8); "Whereunto I also labor, striving according to His working, which worketh in me mightily" (Col. 1:29); "Now unto Him that is able to do exceeding abundantly above all that we ask or think, according to his power that worketh in us" (Eph. 3:20). It is also said in regard to the energizing power of Satan, using the same original word: "For the mystery of iniquity doth already work" (II Thes. 2:7); "For when we were in the flesh, the motions of sins, which were by the law, did work in our members to bring forth fruit unto death" (Rom. 7:5). In the last two passages quoted, the meaning is, like the preceding passages, of an imparted energy, and is, therefore, most suggestive. It may then be concluded from the testimony of Scripture that Satan imparts his wisdom and strength to the unbelieving in the same manner as the power of God is imparted to the believer by the Holy Spirit. Chafer, Lewis Sperry. *Satan* (Kindle Locations 411-427). Public Domain Books. Kindle Edition. (Chafer, Satan n.d.)
[8] Teilhard de Chardin, Pierre. *The Phenomenon of Man*. (New York: Harper Perennial Modern Thought, 2008) (Teilhard de Chardin 2008)
[9] "What Is the Singularity? [Vernor Vinge]
The acceleration of technological progress has been the central feature of this century. I argue in

this paper that we are on the edge of change comparable to the rise of human life on Earth. The precise cause of this change is the imminent creation by technology of entities with greater than human intelligence... I think it's fair to call this event a singularity ("the Singularity" for the purposes of this paper). It is a point where our old models must be discarded and a new reality rules. As we move closer to this point, it will loom vaster and vaster over human affairs till the notion becomes a commonplace. Yet when it finally happens it may still be a great surprise and a greater unknown. In the 1950s there were very few who saw it: Stan Ulam [28] paraphrased John von Neumann as saying: One conversation centered on the ever accelerating progress of technology and changes in the mode of human life, which gives the appearance of approaching some essential singularity in the history of the race beyond which human affairs, as we know them, could not continue." Vinge, Vernor. "What Is the Singularity?," March 30, 1993. https://www.kurzweilai.net/the-technological-singularity [Accessed December 2, 2021]. (Vinge 1993)

[10] See Chapter 4 for the definitions of the Mystery of Iniquity or Lawlessness and Mystery Babylon
[11] How this is possible in view of all the "good" in the world we will address shortly.
[12] *The spiritual purpose of the New World Order is its main purpose.* The social, economic, and political motives assigned to the perceived creators of this Order are unsatisfying because they do not explain why people who *already* control the world and its wealth wish to gain even greater control of it. The spiritual motive of the New World Order cannot be perceived by most students of history because of their rejection of the Bible and/or their misperception of the true nature of reality.
[13] **Abraham Vereide** (October 7, 1886 - May 16, 1969) a Norwegian-born Methodist minister and founder of International Christian Leadership (ICL) group, also known as "The Family" or "The Fellowship."

"Thereafter, Abram would spend his days arranging the spiritual affairs of the wealthy. <u>It would be another decade—ten years spent cultivating not just Seattle's big men but those of the nation—before Abram would coin a phrase for his vision: the "new World Order." By then, 1945</u>, he'd moved to Washington, D.C., and he cut a different figure than he had as a preacher." Sharlet, Jeff. *The Family, The Secret Fundamentalism at the Heart of American Power* 90. HarperCollins e-books. Kindle Edition. (Sharlet n.d.)

President Medici of Brazil [1971]

"Our friendship has undergone the tests of both war and of peace, and the United States always knows that it will find in Brazil a loyal and independent ally. Brazil cannot display indifference and apathy in the presence of new events and new circumstances, in the presence of a reality which is ever changing and above which we must rise in order to build a new World Order in the spheres of political, diplomatic, economic, financial, and monetary activity.

We must approach this new world without preconceived ideas and without inflexible positions.

Antichrist and the New World Order

And what seems imperative to us is that this new World Order must also bring about an entirely new phase of peace, justice, and progress for all the members of the family of nations." (Woolley n.d.) [emphasis added-rw]

Richard Nixon, Toasts of the President and President Medici of Brazil. Online by Gerhard Peters and John T. Woolley, The American Presidency Project https://www.presidency.ucsb.edu/node/240363 [Accessed December 19, 2018].

Lieutenant General Obasanjo of Nigeria [1977]

"We are encouraged to know that the United States is committed to work towards the creation of a more just world economic system, because we also desire the elimination of a situation in which nations of the world are prominently categorized as industrialized and developing states, haves and have-nots. I am happy that we are both committed to the creation of a new World Order which will take due cognizance of the interdependence between states, a world in which nation states will relate to one another on the basis of equality, understanding, and mutual respect." (J. T. Wooley, Jimmy Carter, Visit of Lieutenant General Obasanjo of Nigeria Toasts of the President and Lieutenant General Obasanjo at a Dinner Honoring the Nigerian Head of State n.d.)[emphasis added-rw]

Jimmy Carter, Visit of Lieutenant General Obasanjo of Nigeria Toasts of the President and Lieutenant General Obasanjo at a Dinner Honoring the Nigerian Head of State. Online by Gerhard Peters and John T. Woolley, The American Presidency Project https://www.presidency.ucsb.edu/node/242820 [Accessed December 19, 2018].

George Bush [1991]

"What is at stake is more than one small country; it is a big idea: a new World Order, where diverse nations are drawn together in common cause to achieve the universal aspirations of mankind -- peace and security, freedom, and the rule of law. Such is a world worthy of our struggle and worthy of our children's future." (Gerhard Peters n.d.)

George Bush, Address Before a Joint Session of the Congress on the State of the Union Online by Gerhard Peters and John T. Woolley, The American Presidency Project https://www.presidency.ucsb.edu/node/265956 [Accessed December 19, 2018].

"I listened to that `Aziz meeting, and all he tried to do is obfuscate, to confuse, to make everybody think this had to do with the West Bank, for example. And it doesn't. It has to do with the aggression against Kuwait -- the invasion of Kuwait, the brutalizing of the people in Kuwait. And it has to do with a new World Order. And that World Order is only going to be enhanced if this newly-activated peacekeeping function of the United Nations proves to be effective. That is the only way the new World Order will be enhanced."] (J. T. Wooley n.d.) [emphasis added-rw

George Bush, The President's News Conference on the Persian Gulf Crisis Online by Gerhard Peters and John T. Woolley, The American Presidency Project
https://www.presidency.ucsb.edu/node/265638 [Accessed December 19, 2018].
[14] **Adolph Hitler**

"The German people follows its leadership with determination, confident in its armed forces and ready to bear what fate demands. The year 1941 will be, I am convinced, the historical year of a great European New Order. The program could not be anything else than the opening up of the world for all, the breaking down of individual privileges, the breaking of the tyranny of certain peoples, and better still, of their financial autocrats.

"Finally this year will help to assure the basis for understanding between the peoples, and thereby, for their reconciliation. I do not want to miss pointing out what I pointed out on 3rd of September [1940] in the German Reichstag, that if Jewry were to plunge the world into war, the role of Jewry would be finished in Europe. They may laugh about it today, as they laughed before about my prophecies. The coming months and years will prove that I prophesied rightly in this case too. But we can see already how our racial peoples which are today still hostile to us will one day recognize the greater inner enemy, and that they too will then enter with us into a great common front. The front of Aryan mankind against Jewish-International exploitation and destruction of nations." [emphasis added-rw]
"Hitler Speech at the Berlin Sports Palace (January 30, 1941)."
https://www.jewishvirtuallibrary.org/hitler-speech-at-the-berlin-sports-palace-january-30-1941 Accessed December 15, 2018. (Hitler Speech at the Berlin Sports Palace (January 30, 1941). n.d.)

President Franklin Delano Roosevelt [1941]

"Hitler has often protested that his plans for conquest do not extend across the Atlantic Ocean. His submarines and raiders prove otherwise. So does the entire design of his new World Order.

"For example, I have in my possession a secret map made in Germany by Hitler's Government—by the planners of the new World Order. It is a map of South America and a part of Central America, as Hitler proposes to reorganize it. Today in this area there are fourteen separate countries. But the geographical experts of Berlin have ruthlessly obliterated all existing boundary lines; they have divided South America into five vassal states, bringing the whole continent under their domination. And they have also so arranged it that the territory of one of these new puppet states includes the Republic of Panama and our great life line—the Panama Canal."That is his plan. It will never go into effect. "This map, my friends, makes clear the Nazi design not only against South America but against the United States as well.
Your Government has in its possession another document, made in Germany by Hitler's Government. It is a detailed plan, which, for obvious reasons, the Nazis did not wish and do not

wish to publicize just yet, but which they are ready to impose, a little later, on a dominated world— if Hitler wins. It is a plan to abolish all existing religions- Catholic, Protestant, Mohammedan, Hindu, Buddhist, and Jewish alike. The property of all Churches will be seized by the Reich and its puppets. The cross and all other symbols of religion are to be forbidden. The clergy are to be forever liquidated, silenced under penalty of the concentration camps, where even now so many fearless men are being tortured because they have placed God above Hitler.

"In the place of the Churches of our civilization, there is to be set up an International Nazi Church- a Church which will be served by orators sent out by the Nazi Government. And in the place of the Bible, the words of Mein Kampf will be imposed and enforced as Holy Writ. And in thelace of the cross of Christ will be put two symbols—the swastika and the naked sword." (J. T. Wooley, Franklin D. Roosevelt, Address for Navy and Total Defense Day n.d.)

Franklin D. Roosevelt, Address for Navy and Total Defense Day. Online by Gerhard Peters and John T. Woolley, The American Presidency Project https://www.presidency.ucsb.edu/node/210207 Accessed December 19, 2018.

[15] "The movement to implement a New World Order, led by British and American statesmen such as John Foster Dulles, and specialists associated with the Round Table Group such as Phillip Kerr made no secret of their desire to use ecumenical, liberal Christianity to be the vehicle by which the New World Order would be brough to being."
Erdmann, Martin. *Ecumenical Quest for a World Federation: The Churches' Contribution to Marshal Public Support for World Order and Peace, 1919-1945*, (Verax Vox Media, Greenville, South Carolina 2016). 90-109. (Erdmann 2016)

[16] Charles Thomson's design for the Great Seal of the United States, 1782; Reports of Committees of Congress; Records of the Continental and Confederation Congresses and the Constitutional Convention, 1774-1789, Record Group 360; National Archives https://www.ourdocuments.gov/doc.php?flash=false&doc=5 Accessed November 28, 2021. (C. Thompson n.d.)

[17] Franklin D. Roosevelt, Address on Armistice Day, Arlington National Cemetery. Online by Gerhard Peters and John T. Woolley, The American Presidency Project https://www.presidency.ucsb.edu/node/209352 Accessed December 2, 2021 (J. T. Wooley, Franklin D. Roosevelt, Address on Armistice Day, Arlington National Cemetery n.d.)

[18] William J. Clinton, Remarks at the Welcoming Ceremony for Prime Minister Romano Prodi of Italy Online by Gerhard Peters and John T. Woolley, The American Presidency Project https://www.presidency.ucsb.edu/node/226235 Accessed December 2, 2021 (J. T. Wooley, William J. Clinton, Remarks at the Welcoming Ceremony for Prime Minister Romano Prodi of Italy n.d.)

[19] Perseus Project, Vergil. Bucolics, Aeneid, and Georgics Of Vergil. J. B. Greenough. Boston. Ginn & Co. 1900. (Vergil 1900)
http://www.perseus.tufts.edu/hopper/text?doc=Perseus:abo:phi,0690,001:4 Accessed November 28, 2021.

[20] Maro, P. Vergilius. "The Eclogues, Eclogue IV.5-10" (Vergilius n.d.)
http://classics.mit.edu/Virgil/eclogue.4.iv.html Accessed November 28, 2021

[21] Not the Sibylline Oracles, which were written centuries later.

[22] See the suggestive image of her upon the Sistine Ceiling painted by Michaelangelo.
https://en.wikipedia.org/wiki/Cumaean_Sibyl#/media/File:CumaeanSibylByMichelangelo.jpg

[23] The New Age Movement reveals an explicitly spiritual element that is often omitted from references to the New World Order. It provides a partial revelation of a more accurate conception of what is to come than the analysis of current events alone. For example:

"[36] I have indicated somewhat the intended work of the first group from the angle of telepathic interplay (Telepathy and the Etheric Vehicle). The method of communication between the Members of the Hierarchy has to be externalised, eventually, upon earth and this is one of the tasks of the group. It might be of service to you if I outlined a little more clearly what is the purpose of the new seed groups, in terms of the new age civilisation and culture so that the practical results might be visioned with clarity and some new ideals emerge as to the quality of the coming new World Order." (Bailey n.d.) [emphasis added] Bailey, Alice A. *Externalisation of the Hierarchy*. (Location 670). Lucis Publishing Companies. Kindle Edition.

[24] Chapter 24-Section: An Example of Political Babylon

[25] Lk 4.5-7; Jn 12.31; 2 Cor 4.4

[26] "The unregenerate are, then, unconscious of their position in the arms of Satan, and blind in their thoughts toward the gospel of mercy and favor, —their only hope for time or eternity. Satan, like a fond mother, is bending over those in his arms, breathing into their minds the quieting balm of a "universal fatherhood of God" and a "universal brotherhood of man;" suggesting their worthiness before God on the ground of their own moral character and physical generation; feeding their tendency to imitate the true faith by great humanitarian undertakings and schemes for the reformation of individuals and the betterment of the social order. God's necessary requirements of regeneration are carefully set aside, and the blinded souls go on without hope, "having the understanding darkened, being alienated from the life of God through the ignorance that is in there (sic), because of the blindness of their heart" (Eph. 5:18)."

Chafer, Lewis Sperry. *Satan* (Kindle Locations 448-454). Public Domain Books. Kindle Edition. (Chafer, Satan n.d.)

[27] *The New King James Version*. (Nashville: Thomas Nelson, 1982). (NKJV 1982)

[28] "Dialectic, also called dialectics, originally a form of logical argumentation but now a philosophical concept of evolution applied to diverse fields including thought, nature, and history.

"Among the classical Greek thinkers, the meanings of dialectic ranged from a technique of refutation in debate, through a method for systematic evaluation of definitions, to the investigation and classification of the relationships between specific and general concepts. From the time of the Stoic philosophers until the end of the European Middle Ages, dialectic was more or less closely identified with the discipline of formal logic. More recently, Immanuel Kant denoted by "transcendental dialectic" the endeavour of exposing the illusion involved in attempting to use the categories and principles of the understanding beyond the bounds of phenomena and possible experience. G.W.F. Hegel identified dialectic as the tendency of a notion to pass over into its own negation as the result of conflict between its inherent contradictory aspects. Karl Marx and Friedrich Engels adopted Hegel's definition and applied it to social and economic processes."

Britannica, The Editors of Encyclopaedia. "dialectic". Encyclopedia Britannica, https://www.britannica.com/topic/dialectic-logic. [Accessed June 21, 2019]. (Britannica n.d.)

"Hegel's dialectics" refers to the particular dialectical method of argument employed by the 19th Century German philosopher, G.W.F. Hegel (see entry on Hegel), which, like other "dialectical" methods, relies on a contradictory process between opposing sides. Whereas Plato's "opposing sides" were people (Socrates and his interlocutors), however, what the "opposing sides" are in Hegel's work depends on the subject matter he discusses. In his work on logic, for instance, the "opposing sides" are different definitions of logical concepts that are opposed to one another. In the Phenomenology of Spirit, which presents Hegel's epistemology or philosophy of knowledge, the "opposing sides" are different definitions of consciousness and of the object that consciousness is aware of or claims to know. As in Plato's dialogues, a contradictory process between "opposing sides" in Hegel's dialectics leads to a linear evolution or development from less sophisticated definitions or views to more sophisticated ones later. The dialectical process thus constitutes Hegel's method for arguing against the earlier, less sophisticated definitions or views and for the more sophisticated ones later. Hegel regarded this dialectical method or "speculative mode of cognition" (PR §10) as the hallmark of his philosophy, and used the same method in the Phenomenology of Spirit [PhG], as well as in all of the mature works he published later—the entire Encyclopaedia of Philosophical Sciences (including, as its first part, the "Lesser Logic" or the Encyclopaedia Logic [EL]), the Science of Logic [SL], and the Philosophy of Right [PR].".
"Hegel's Dialectics (Stanford Encyclopedia of Philosophy).". (Dialectics n.d.) https://plato.stanford.edu/entries/hegel-dialectics/ Accessed June 25, 2019.

[29] Jn 3.16; 6.35; 8.12; 10.11; 11.25; 14.6

[30] Eccl 1.14-18; 12.12 c.f. Jn 5.39-40

[31] Chapter 9, His Character-The Lawless One

[32] Antony Sutton Provides an illustration:

"For Hegelians, the State is almighty, and seen as "the march of God on earth." Indeed, a State religion. Progress in the Hegelian State is through contrived conflict: the clash of opposites makes for progress. If you can control the opposites, you dominate the nature of the outcome. We trace the extraordinary Skull and Bones influence in a major Hegelian conflict: Naziism vs. Communism. Skull and Bones members were in the dominant decision-making positions - Bush, Harriman, Stimson, Lovett, and so on - all Bonesmen, and instrumental in guiding the conflict through use of "right" and "left." They financed and encouraged the growths of both philosophies and controlled the outcome to a significant extent. This was aided by the "reductionist" division in science, the opposite of historical "wholeness." By dividing science and learning into narrower and narrower segments, it became easier to control the whole through the parts." [Note: see also the Author's Preface to Sutton's book-rw].
Sutton, Antony C., *America's Secret Establishment: An Introduction to the Order of Skull & Bones*. (Auflage, Updated Reprint. Walterville: Trine Day, 2002). 14 (Sutton 2002)

[33] Although the new birth results in a new life, nature, and a new power; it is by a proper discipleship that believers are moved to live out the righteousness and the justice that characterize the indwelling Christ [Jn 14.20; 15.4]. It is through the actions of believers living in obedience to the scriptures that the institutions within which these believers' function are purified and stabilized [Mt 5.14]. There is a scriptural means by which evil may be resisted in the world. For the believer, social justice solutions begin with personal sanctification: when Christians do right, we change the world.

What is *not* being said here is that believers can avoid this world and its conflicts by hiding behind a truncated gospel which proclaims the good news but fails to live by it. What is rejected here is the replacement of divine good with human good, which is the best that human systems can offer, if even this.

[34] Lewis Sperry Chafer, *Satan* (New York: Gospel Publishing House, 1909), 82–83. (Chafer, Satan n.d.)

[35] If the roles and relations of the Persons of the Godhead are not what the scriptures say them to be, who then is the new god created by these churches?
John 16:13–15 (KJV 1900)13 Howbeit when he, the Spirit of truth, is come, he will guide you into all truth: for he shall not speak of himself; but whatsoever he shall hear, that shall he speak: and he will shew you things to come. 14 He shall glorify me: for he shall receive of mine, and shall shew it unto you. 15 All things that the Father hath are mine:[the Son] therefore said I, that he [the Spirit] shall take of mine, and shall shew it unto you. [emphasis added]

[36] Chapter 23, Section: An Example of Religious Babylon

[37] Christendom is the entire realm of Christian profession, consisting of all sects, denominations and movements that call themselves Christian. Thus, Christendom consists of both empty professors and true possessors of faith in Christ. Christendom is the visible church.

[38] "Postmodernism And Modern Philosophy

"Postmodernism is largely a reaction against the intellectual assumptions and values of the modern period in the history of Western philosophy (roughly, the 17th through the 19th century). Indeed, many of the doctrines characteristically associated with postmodernism can fairly be described as the straightforward denial of general philosophical viewpoints that were taken for granted during the 18th-century Enlightenment, though they were not unique to that period. The most important of these viewpoints are the following.

"1. There is an objective natural reality, a reality whose existence and properties are logically independent of human beings—of their minds, their societies, their social practices, or their investigative techniques. Postmodernists dismiss this idea as a kind of naive realism. Such reality as there is, according to postmodernists, is a conceptual construct, an artifact of scientific practice and language. This point also applies to the investigation of past events by historians and to the description of social institutions, structures, or practices by social scientists.

2. The descriptive and explanatory statements of scientists and historians can, in principle, be objectively true or false. The postmodern denial of this viewpoint—which follows from the rejection of an objective natural reality—is sometimes expressed by saying that there is no such thing as Truth...

Brian Duignan. "Postmodernism." Encyclopædia Britannica, October 25, 2018. https://www.britannica.com/topic/postmodernism-philosophy. Accessed June 24, 2019. (Duignan 2018)

Also, "A Beginner's Guide to Postmodernism" by Phil Johnson
https://www.graceChurch.org/sermons/10244 Accessed June 24, 2019, (Johnson n.d.)

[39] We will discover that it is the Antichrist who will implement the true World Order about which we are writing. All efforts to establish that order today are in fact efforts to create the environment that will enable the emergence of the Antichrist, who will himself inaugurate the New World Order.
[40] Appendix II The Rapture, Section: About the Restrainer
[41] 1 Cor 12.13, 27; Eph 5.30
[42] Appendix II
[43] By the Baptism of the Spirit, we do not mean the charismatic conception of a second work of grace whereby the believer receives an experience sometime after the new birth. This is a false view of the doctrine of Spirit baptism. The Baptism of the Spirit is unexperienced and occurs at the moment of faith in Christ [1 Cor 12.13a]. In Acts, when the ministry of the Spirit created the Church, the Body of Christ, everyone received all the ministries of the Spirit, including Spirit Baptism into Christ at the moment they believed the Gospel [Acts 10.44]. The result of the scriptural Baptism of the Spirit is union with Christ and through it union to all other members of the Church. This union with Christ is highly significant and results in many advantages. Doctrinally, the Baptism of the Spirit is distinct from the Indwelling, Filling and Sealing of the Spirit. It is also separate from the spiritual gift of tongues/languages, which ceased with the end of the apostles.
[44] 2 Cor 11.2; Eph 5.22-32; Rev 19.7-9; 21.9; 22.17
[45] "The last hour (ἐσχάτη ὥρα). The phrase only here in the New Testament. On John's use of ὥρα hour, as marking a critical season, see John 2:4; 4:21, 23; 5:25, 28; 7:30; 8:20; 12:23, 27; 16:2, 4, 25, 32. The dominant sense of the expression *last days*, in the New Testament, is that of a period of suffering and struggle preceding a divine victory. See Acts 2:17; Jas. 5:3; 1 Pet. 1:20. Hence the phrase here does not refer to the end of the world, but to the period preceding a crisis in the advance of Christ's kingdom, a changeful and troublous period, marked by the appearance of "many antichrists."
Marvin Richardson Vincent, *Word Studies in the New Testament, vol. 2* (New York: Charles Scribner's Sons, 1887), 337. (Vincent 1887)
[46] "manifested" 28.36 φανερόωb; ἐμφανίζωb; φαίνομαιb; φωτίζωb; φανέρωσις, εως f; φωτισμόςb, οῦ m: to cause something to be fully known by revealing clearly and in some detail—'to make known, to make plain, to reveal, to bring to the light, to disclose, revelation.
Johannes P. Louw and Eugene Albert Nida, *Greek-English Lexicon of the New Testament: Based on Semantic Domains* (New York: United Bible Societies, 1996), 337–338. (Louw 1996)
[47] Age, in this case meaning the interval between the first and second advents of Christ.
[48] Johannes P. Louw and Eugene Albert Nida, *Greek-English Lexicon of the New Testament: Based on Semantic Domains* (New York: United Bible Societies, 1996), 542. (Louw 1996)
[49] James Swanson, *Dictionary of Biblical Languages with Semantic Domains: Greek (New Testament)* (Oak Harbor: Logos Research Systems, Inc., 1997). (Swanson 1997)
[50] James Strong, *Enhanced Strong's Lexicon* (Woodside Bible Fellowship, 1995).
[51] Johannes P. Louw and Eugene Albert Nida, *Greek-English Lexicon of the New Testament: Based on Semantic Domains* (New York: United Bible Societies, 1996), 542.
[52] "antichrist" 500 ἀντίχριστος [antichristos /an·tee·khris·tos/] n m. From 473 and 5547; TDNT 9:493; TDNTA 1322; GK 532; Five occurrences; AV translates as "antichrist" five times. 1 the adversary of the Messiah.
James Strong, *Enhanced Strong's Lexicon* (Woodside Bible Fellowship, 1995). (Strong 1995)
[53] Dan 9.21-27; 2 Th 2; Rev 6.1-2

[54] Mt 24.5; Jn 5.42-43; Rev 13.4, 8
[55] Day of the Lord Jer 30.7; Da 12.1; Zech 14.2-3; Mt 24.9-21
[56] Abrahamic Covenant Gen 12.1-3; 13.14-17; 15.1-20; 17.1-10
[57] Davidic Covenant 2 Sam 7.11-17
[58] James Strong, *Enhanced Strong's Lexicon* (Woodside Bible Fellowship, 1995).
[59] By this we mean the virgin conception and birth of Jesus and not the conception or birth of Mary.
[60] Ps 110.1
[61] This does not mean that Satan *believes* that Jesus is not the Christ. It means that this is the doctrine that he professes and will continue to maintain via his chief human representatives, here identified as antichrists. Satan knows that his doctrine is a lie [Mt 4.3 "If thou be the Son of God" (first class condition: "If, and you are"); Mk 1.24]
[62] Fuller, David Otis, and Benjamin George Wilkinson. *Which Bible?* (Grand Rapids, Mich.: Grand Rapids International Publications, 2000) (Fuller 2000)

Hills, Edward F. *The King James Version Defended*. 4th ed. (Des Moines, Iowa: CRP, 1984). (Hills 1984)

Burgon, John William. *The Revision Revised*. [Kindle Version] (Burgon 1971)Cloud, David W. *Faith vs. The Modern Bible Versions*. (Port Huron, Michigan: Way of Life Literature, 2005). (Cloud, Faith vs. The Modern Bible Versions 2005)

Riplinger, G. A. *New Age Bible Versions*. (Shelbyville, Tenn: Bible & Literature Missionary Foundation, 1993 (Riplinger 1993)

[63] *Translators*, such as those who translated the KJV, *are not inspired by God*. However, it is God who is responsible that the Bible remains eternally available as an accurate record of His revelation. It is the process of selecting the best original manuscript family and conveying that revelation from the original language manuscripts to their modern language translations where the mischief happens.

[64] "The testimony of Frank Gaebelein in 1960: "...we must not blink at the evidence that there is a strong current among some evangelicals, a subtle erosion of the doctrine of the infallibility of the Scripture that is highly illogical as well as dangerous" (Christianity Today, May 9, 1960, p. 647).

"The testimony of Carl Henry, 1976: "A GROWING VANGUARD OF YOUNG GRADUATES OF EVANGELICAL COLLEGES WHO HOLD DOCTORATES FROM NON-EVANGELICAL DIVINITY CENTERS NOW QUESTION OR DISOWN INERRANCY and the doctrine is held less consistently by evangelical faculties. ... Some retain the term and reassure supportive constituencies but nonetheless stretch the term's meaning" (Carl F.H. Henry, pastor senior editor of Christianity Today, "Conflict Over Biblical Inerrancy," Christianity Today, May 7, 1976)

"In 1976, Richard Quebedeaux added the following details:

""Most people outside the evangelical community itself are totally unaware of the profound changes that have occurred within evangelicalism during the last several years--in the movement's understanding of the inspiration and authority of Scripture, in its social concerns, cultural attitudes and ecumenical posture, and in the nature of its emerging leadership. ... evangelical theologians have begun looking at the Bible with a scrutiny reflecting THEIR WIDESPREAD ACCEPTANCE OF THE PRINCIPLES OF HISTORICAL AND LITERARY CRITICISM ... The position--affirming that Scripture is

inerrant or infallible in its teaching on matters of faith and conduct but not necessarily in all its assertions concerning history and the cosmos—IS GRADUALLY BECOMING ASCENDANT AMONG THE MOST HIGHLY RESPECTED EVANGELICAL THEOLOGIANS. ... these new trends ... indicate that evangelical theology is becoming more centrist, more open to biblical criticism and more accepting of science and broad cultural analysis. ONE MIGHT EVEN SUGGEST THAT THE NEW GENERATION OF EVANGELICALS IS CLOSER TO BONHOEFFER, BARTH AND BRUNNER THAN TO HODGE AND WARFIELD ON THE INSPIRATION AND AUTHORITY OF SCRIPTURE" (Richard Quebedeaux," The Evangelicals: New Trends and Tensions," Christianity and Crisis, Sept. 20, 1976, pp. 197-202). [emphasis in the original]""
Above quotations from: David W. Cloud. *New Evangelicalism: Its History, Characteristics, and Fruit.* (Way of Life Literature, 2006) (Cloud, New Evangelicalism: Its History, Characteristics, and Fruit. 2006)

[65] T.D. Jakes https://www.youtube.com/watch?v=22xL2E10JJE Accessed October 21, 2017

[66] Joel Osteen https://www.youtube.com/watch?v=KwL1DThtxYg Accessed October 21, 2017

[67] Carleton Pearson http://www.houstonpress.com/news/carlton-pearson-6577423 Accessed October 21, 2017

[68] "deceiver" 4108 πλάνος [planos /plan·os/] adj. Of uncertain affinity; TDNT 6:228; TDNTA 857; GK 4418; Five occurrences; AV translates as "deceiver" four times, and "seducing" once. 1 wandering, roving. 2 misleading, leading into error. 2A a vagabond, "tramp", imposter. 2B corrupter, deceiver. James Strong, *Enhanced Strong's Lexicon* (Woodside Bible Fellowship, 1995).

[69] We will address the similarities and differences between false teachers and erroneous teachers in upcoming pages of this chapter.

[70] "confess" 3670 ὁμολογέω [homologeo /hom·ol·og·eh·o/] v. From a compound of the base of 3674 and 3056; TDNT 5:199; TDNTA 687; GK 3933; 24 occurrences; AV translates as "confess" 17 times, "profess" three times, "promise" once, "give thanks" once, "confession is made" once, and "acknowledgeth" once. 1 to say the same thing as another, i.e. to agree with, assent. 2 to concede. 2A not to refuse, to promise. 2B not to deny. 2B1 to confess. 2B2 declare. 2B3 to confess, i.e. to admit or declare one's self guilty of what one is accused of. 3 to profess. 3A to declare openly, speak out freely. 3B to profess one's self the worshipper of one. 4 to praise, celebrate.
James Strong, *Enhanced Strong's Lexicon* (Woodside Bible Fellowship, 1995).

[71] "Seduce." Merriam-Webster.com. Merriam-Webster, n.d. Web. 21 Oct. 2017. (Webster 2017)

[72] Eve is addressed here rather than Adam because Adam was not deceived by Satan. Adam knowingly chose to disobey God at the request of his wife and was also condemned.
1 Timothy 2:14 (KJV 1900) And Adam was not deceived, but the woman being deceived was in the transgression.

[73] Isa 14.4, 16-17 c.f. Rev 13.6-7

[74] Jesus came to the Jews offering the fulfillment of the Old Testament promises concerning the Kingdom [Mt 4.17 c.f. Jn 1.11]. The rejection of the Kingdom was demonstrated by the crucifixion of the King. Anticipating this rejection, Jesus described in parables another form of the Kingdom, a kingdom in mystery, existing between the two Advents of Christ. [see Chafer, Lewis Sperry. *The Kingdom in History and Prophecy*. (Chicago: The Bible Institute Colportage Ass'n, 1936).53-56] (Chafer, The Kingdom in History and Prophecy. 1936)

"The Davidic [Millennial] Kingdom promised to redeemed Israel is postponed. In the interim there exists a mystery entity, the Church, which is un-prophesied and unforeseen in the Old Testament, consisting mostly of Gentiles. There is also, between the advents, the prophesied period called the Tribulation wherein God punishes the unbelieving world. The Jews are persecuted during the second half of this seven-year period, called the *Time of Jacob's Trouble* [ibid. 101-102]
[75] [Mt:] 13:17 The O.T. prophets saw in one blended vision the rejection and crucifixion of the King (see "Christ, sacrifice," Gen. 4:4; Heb. 10:18, note), and also His glory as David's Son (Zech. 12:8, note), but "what manner of time the Spirit of Christ which was in them did signify when it testified beforehand the sufferings of Christ and the glory that should follow," was not revealed to them—only that the vision was not for themselves (1 Pet. 1:10–12). <u>That revelation Christ makes in these parables. A period of time is to intervene between His sufferings and His glory. That interval is occupied with the "mysteries of the kingdom of heaven" here described.</u>" [emphasis added rw]
C. I. Scofield, ed., *The Scofield Reference Bible: The Holy Bible Containing the Old and New Testaments* (New York; London; Toronto; Melbourne; Bombay: Oxford University Press, 1917), 1015. (Scofield 1917)
[76] Concerning Christendom

"13:3 The seven parables of Mt. 13, called by our Lord "mysteries of the kingdom of heaven" (v. 11), taken together, describe the result of the presence of the Gospel in the world during the present age, that is, the time of seed-sowing which began with our Lord's personal ministry, and ends with the "harvest" (vs. 40–43). Briefly, that result is the mingled tares and wheat, good fish and bad, in the sphere of Christian profession. It is Christendom."
C. I. Scofield, ed., *The Scofield Reference Bible: The Holy Bible Containing the Old and New Testaments* (New York; London; Toronto; Melbourne; Bombay: Oxford University Press, 1917), 1014. (Scofield 1917)
[77] See Appendix II
[78] [Mt:]13.24…The "world" here is both geographical and ethnic—the earth-world, and also the world of men. The wheat of God at once becomes the scene of Satan's activity. Where children of the kingdom are gathered, there, "among the wheat" (vs. 25, 38, 39), Satan "sows" "children of the wicked one," who profess to be children of the kingdom, and in outward ways are so like the true children that only the angels may, in the end, be trusted to separate them (vs. 28–30, 40–43). So great is Satan's power of deception that the tares often really suppose themselves to be children of the kingdom (Mt. 7:21–23). Many other parables and exhortations have this mingled condition in view (e.g. Mt. 22:11–14; 25:1–13, 14–30; Lk. 18:10–14; Heb. 6:4–9). Indeed, it characterizes Matthew from Chapter 13 to the end. The parable of the wheat and tares is not a description of the world, but of that which professes to be the kingdom.
C. I. Scofield, ed., *The Scofield Reference Bible: The Holy Bible Containing the Old and New Testaments* (New York; London; Toronto; Melbourne; Bombay: Oxford University Press, 1917), 1015
[79] 1 Tim 4.1-3; 2 Tim 3.5-8; 2 Pet 2.1-22; Jude 4
[80] "manifest" 5319 φανερόω [phaneroo /fan·er·o·o/] v. From 5318; TDNT 9:3; TDNTA 1244; GK

5746; 49 occurrences; AV translates as "make manifest" 19 times, "appear" 12 times, "manifest" nine times, "show" three times, "be manifest" twice, "show (one's) self" twice, "manifestly declare" once, and "manifest forth" once. 1 to make manifest or visible or known what has been hidden or unknown, to manifest, whether by words, or deeds, or in any other way. 1A make actual and visible, realised. 1B to make known by teaching. 1C to become manifest, be made known. 1D of a person. 1D1 expose to view, make manifest, to show one's self, appear. 1E to become known, to be plainly recognised, thoroughly understood. 1E1 who and what one is.
James Strong, *Enhanced Strong's Lexicon* (Woodside Bible Fellowship, 1995).

[81] "try" 1381 δοκιμάζω, δοκιμασία [dokimazo /dok·im·ad·zo/] v. From 1384; TDNT 2:255; TDNTA 181; GK 1507 and 1508; 23 occurrences; AV translates as "prove" 10 times, "try" four times, "approve" three times, "discern" twice, "allow" twice, "like" once, and "examine" once. 1 to test, examine, prove, scrutinise (to see whether a thing is genuine or not), as metals. 2 to recognise as genuine after examination, to approve, deem worthy.
James Strong, *Enhanced Strong's Lexicon* (Woodside Bible Fellowship, 1995).

[82] Mt 1.10; Mk 1.23; 3.11; 5.2; 6.7; 7.25; 9.25; Lk 6.18; 8.29 Also the Apostles Acts 5.16; 8.7

[83] Chapter 22

[84] Johannes P. Louw and Eugene Albert Nida, *Greek-English Lexicon of the New Testament: Based on Semantic Domains* (New York: United Bible Societies, 1996), 757.

[85] Rom 6.19; 2 Tim 2.19; 1 Jn 3.4 Gk.

[86] Gen 3.4-5; Eze 28.14-18; Rev 12.7-9; 19.19-20.3; 20.7-10

[87] See Appendix II

[88] 3. Practically wherever it occurs in the NT mystērion is found with vbs. denoting → revelation or → proclamation, i.e. mystērion is that which is revealed (cf. TDNT IV 819). It is a present-day secret, not some isolated fact from the past which merely needs to be noted, but something dynamic and compelling.
G. Finkenrath, "Secret, Mystery," ed. Lothar Coenen, Erich Beyreuther, and Hans Bietenhard, *New International Dictionary of New Testament Theology* (Grand Rapids, MI: Zondervan Publishing House, 1986), 504. (Finkenrath 1986).

[89] Johannes P. Louw and Eugene Albert Nida, *Greek-English Lexicon of the New Testament: Based on Semantic Domains* (New York: United Bible Societies, 1996), 344.

[90] Isa 53.5, 6; 2 Cor 5.21; Gal 3.13; 1 Tim 2.6

[91] "So, too, did the "mystery of godliness" work. Even at this initial stage of the two mysteries we trace a resemblance between them. Let us think how long the Gospel worked before it issued in the incarnation of the Son of God. For ages and for generations Christianity was a hidden mystery. The redemption of men by means of the incarnation of the Son of God was a secret profoundly hidden in the councils of God in eternity, and even after time had begun its course it long remained a secret unknown to the world. Bit by bit this mystery revealed itself. First, the idea of incarnation was dimly made known. In the first promise, mention was made of the "seed of the woman," and on this obscure intimation was built the hope of a Deliverer, and that hope descended the ages with the race. The idea of expiation was next revealed in the appointment of sacrifice, which also, with the hope which is expressed and sustained, came down the stream of time. Next a complete system of ceremonial worship was instituted, to reveal the coming redemption in the amplitude of its blessings. Still the veil was upon it. It stood before the world in type. There arose an illustrious

series of august personages, who were forerunners or types of Christ. They exhibited to the Church the offices which her incarnate Saviour was to fill, and the work He was to execute. There stood up an order of prophetical men who prefigured Him as the Great Teacher; there stood up an order of sacrificial men who prefigured Him as the One Priest. There stood up an order of kingly men who prefigured Him as a Monarch, and a Monarch who was to be higher and mightier than any of the monarchs of earth. The Kings of the House of Judah foreshadowed Him as sprung of a royal stock, and the heir of a throne which all nations should serve, and before which all kings should bow. Thus did the "mystery of godliness" work, unfolding and still unfolding itself as the ages passed on –the type growing ever the clearer, and the prophecy ever the fuller – till at last the "mystery" stepped out from behind the veil, and stood before the world, perfected, finished, and fully revealed in the person of Jesus of Nazareth, the Christ – "God manifest in the flesh;" and centering in His person, and flowing out from it, through His life and ministry and death, as rays from the sun, were all the glorious doctrines of the Gospel.

Wylie, James. *The Papacy Is The Antichrist (PROOF) Illustrated*: A DEMONSTRATION (Kindle Locations 2692-2911). www.DelmarvaPublications.com. Kindle Edition. (J. Wylie n.d.).

[92] "According to Scripture, the relation of the unbelieving to Satan is far more vital than a mere pleasure-seeking allegiance. On two occasions Jesus spoke of the unsaved as the "children of Satan" (Matt. 13:38; Jno. 8:44), and Paul so addressed Elymas, the sorcerer, according to Acts 13:10. The same class is also twice called the "children of disobedience" (Eph. 2:2; Col. 3:6), and once it is called the "children of wrath" (Eph. 2:3).

"It is evident that these are descriptions of the same class of people, since both terms are employed together in Eph. 5:6: "Let no man deceive you: for because of these things cometh the wrath of God upon the children of disobedience." The exact cause of that wrath is stated in Rom. 1:18 (R. V.): "For the wrath of God is revealed from heaven against all ungodliness and unrighteousness of men, who hinder the truth in unrighteousness;" the word "hinder" being the same as is used in 2 Thes. 2:7, where the Holy Spirit is said to be restraining the working of lawlessness in this age. Therefore, the willing neglect and disregard for the testimony of God by the world, has allied them with Satan, and placed them under the wrath of God, which must find its righteous execution in due time if grace is not accepted.

"Again, Satan is revealed as directing and empowering the children of disobedience: "And you hath he quickened, who were dead in trespasses and sins; wherein in times past ye walked according to the course of this age, according to the prince of the power of the air, the spirit that now worketh in the children of disobedience" (Eph. 2:1, 2). The real force of this passage, also, is dependent upon the meaning of one word; the word "worketh" being the same as is used in Phil. 2:13, where God is said to impart His wisdom and strength to the believer: "For it is God that worketh in you both to will and to do of his good pleasure." Additional light may be had as to the reality of this relationship from the following passages in which the same original word is used: "And there are diversities of operations, but it is the same God that worketh all in all" (1 Cor. 12:6); "But all these (gifts) worketh that one and the selfsame Spirit, dividing to every man severally as he will" (1 Cor. 12:11); "And what is the exceeding greatness of His power to usward who believe, according to the working of His mighty power, which He wrought in Christ when He raised Him from the dead, and set Him at His own right hand in the heavenlies" (Eph. 1:19–20); "For He that wrought effectually in Peter to the apostleship of the circumcision, the same was mighty in me toward the Gentiles" (Gal.

2:8); "Whereunto I also labor, striving according to His working, which worketh in me mightily" (Col. 1:29): "Now unto Him that is able to do exceeding abundantly above all that we ask or think, according to his power that worketh in us" (Eph. 3:20). It is also said in regard to the energizing power of Satan, using the same original word: "For the mystery of iniquity doth already work" (2 Thes. 2:7); "For when we were in the flesh, the motions of sins, which were by the law, did work in our members to bring forth fruit unto death" (Rom. 7:5). In the last two passages quoted, the meaning is, like the preceding passages, of an imparted energy, and is, therefore, most suggestive.

"It may then be concluded from the testimony of Scripture that Satan imparts his wisdom and strength to the unbelieving in the same manner as the power of God is imparted to the believer by the Holy Spirit. There is, however, no revelation as to the comparative degree of strength imparted by each. It should be further noted in this connection that this impartation of energizing power from Satan is not toward a limited few who might be said, because of some strange conduct, to be possessed of a demon; but is the common condition of all who are yet unsaved, and are, therefore, still in the "power of darkness.""
Lewis Sperry Chafer, *Satan* (New York: Gospel Publishing House, 1909), 45–47. (Chafer, Satan n.d.)
[93] The Day of the Lord is a period of time in which God will deal with wicked men directly and dramatically in fearful judgment. Today a man may be a blasphemer of God, an atheist, can denounce God and teach bad doctrine. Seemingly God does nothing about it. But the day designated in Scripture as "the day of the Lord" is coming when God will punish human sin, and He will deal in wrath and in judgment with a Christ-rejecting world. One thing we are sure of, that God in His own way will bring every soul into judgment.
Walvoord, John F., *The Thessalonian Epistles* (Galaxie Software, 2007), 49–50. (J. F. Walvoord, The Thessalonian Epistles 2007)
[94] Ibid., 73.
[95] See Appendix II-Section: Order of Events in the Thessalonian Epistles
[96] See Appendix III
[97] Chapter 9
[98] Pentecost, J. Dwight. "Daniel." In *The Bible Knowledge Commentary: An Exposition of the Scriptures*, edited by J. F. Walvoord and R. B. Zuck. (Wheaton, IL: Victor Books, 1985). Dan 9.24. (D. J. Pentecost 1985)
[99] Jer 31.31-34; Heb 10.12-18; Rev 21.1-8
[100] Rom 4.25; 1 Pet 2.24; 3.18
[101] Rom 5.1-2; 1 Cor 5.19-21
[102] "righteousness" 7406 צֶדֶק (sě·děq): n.masc.; ≡ Str 6664; TWOT 1879a—1. LN 88.12–88.23 righteousness, justice, rightness, i.e., the act. of doing what is required according to a standard (Ps 7:9[EB 8]); 2. LN 88.39–88.45 honesty, fairness, accuracy, i.e., an act. which is proper according to a standard, and not deviant in any way (Lev 19:36); 3. LN 12.1–12.42 Righteousness, i.e., a title of the LORD (Jer 23:6; 33:16); 4. LN 56.20–56.34 justice, i.e., the act. of fairly deciding what is right in a legal case, without prejudice (Dt 16:20), note: further study may yield more domains.
James Swanson, *Dictionary of Biblical Languages with Semantic Domains: Hebrew* (Old Testament) (Oak Harbor: Logos Research Systems, Inc., 1997). (Swanson 1997)
[103] Eph 5.26-27; 1 John 3:2; Rom. 8:29
[104] Pentecost, J. Dwight. "Daniel." In *The Bible Knowledge Commentary: An Exposition of the*

Scriptures, edited by J. F. Walvoord and R. B. Zuck. (Wheaton, IL: Victor Books, 1985). Daniel 10:20-11:1

[105] "desolate" 85.84 ἔρημοςα, ov: pertaining to an absence of residents or inhabitants in a place—'uninhabited, deserted.' γενηθήτω ἡ ἔπαυλις αὐτοῦ ἔρημος 'may his house become uninhabited' Ac 1:20; ἀφίεται ὑμῖν ὁ οἶκος ὑμῶν ἔρημος 'your house will be left uninhabited' Mt 23:38. Johannes P. Louw and Eugene Albert Nida, *Greek-English Lexicon of the New Testament: Based on Semantic Domains* (New York: United Bible Societies, 1996), 731.

[106] Josephus, Flavius, and William Whiston. *The Works of Josephus: Complete and Unabridged.* (Peabody: Hendrickson, 1987). Book 6 Chapter 2. (Josephus 1987)
Although Titus was responsible for the destruction of the "city and the sanctuary" of Daniel 9.26; he is not the personage described as "he" in Daniel 9.27.

[107] The Age of Israel: From the giving of the Law of Moses to the first Pentecost after the Ascension of Jesus, approximately 1500 years.

[108] God has revealed His program for the Church which was previously a mystery (Rom. 16:25; Gal. 3:23; Eph. 3:3, 5).
Enns, Paul P., *The Moody Handbook of Theology* (Chicago, IL: Moody Press, 1989), 106. (Enns 1989). See also Eph 3.3-9; 5.32; Col 1.26

[109] Chapter 13

[110] Rom. 16:25; Gal. 3:23; Eph. 3:3, 5

[111] "According to Daniel 9:26 the Anointed One was not "cut off" in the 70th "seven"; He was cut off after the 7 and 62 "sevens" had run their course. This means that there is an interval between the 69th and 70th "sevens." Christ's crucifixion, then, was in that interval, right after His Triumphal Entry, which concluded the 69th "seven." This interval was anticipated by Christ when He prophesied the establishing of the Church (Matt. 16:18). This necessitated the setting aside of the nation Israel for a season in order that His new program for the Church might be instituted. Christ predicted the setting aside of the nation (Matt. 21:42–43). The present Church Age is the interval between the 69th and 70th "sevens."

"Amillenarians teach that Christ's First Advent ministry was in the 70th "seven," that there was no interval between the 69th and 70th "sevens," and that the six actions predicted in Daniel 9:24 are being fulfilled today in the Church. This view, however, (a) ignores the fact that verse 26 says "after the 62 sevens, ' "not" in the 70th seven, '" (b) overlooks the fact that Christ's ministry on earth was three and one-half years in length, not seven, and (c) ignores the fact that God's six actions pertain to Daniel's "people" (Israel) and His "Holy City" (Jerusalem), not the Church."
J. Dwight Pentecost, "Daniel," in *The Bible Knowledge Commentary: An Exposition of the Scriptures*, ed. J. F. Walvoord and R. B. Zuck, vol. 1 (Wheaton, IL: Victor Books, 1985), 1363–1364.

[112] "people" 5971 עַם, עָם ['am /am/] n m. From 6004; TWOT 1640a, 1640e; GK 6638 and 6639; 1861 occurrences; AV translates as "people" 1836 times, "nation" 17 times, "people + 1121" four times, "folk" twice, "Ammi" once, and "men" once. 1 nation, people. 1A people, nation. 1B persons, members of one's people, compatriots, country-men. 2 kinsman, kindred.
James Strong, *Enhanced Strong's Lexicon* (Woodside Bible Fellowship, 1995).

[113] Joel 2.11, 31; Zeph 1.14; 1 Th 5.1-10; Rev 6.16-17

[114] Rev 10.5-7; 11.15; 13.1 see also Figure 4

[115] "The covenant he will make will evidently be a peace covenant, in which he will guarantee Israel's safety in the land. This suggests that Israel will be in her land but will be unable to defend herself for she will have lost any support she may have had previously. Therefore she will need and welcome the peacemaking role of this head of the confederation of 10 European (Roman) nations. In offering this covenant, this ruler will pose as a prince of peace, and Israel will accept his authority. But then in the middle of that "seven," after three and one-half years, he will break the covenant. According to 11:45, he will then move from Europe into the land of Israel." J. Dwight Pentecost, "Daniel," in *The Bible Knowledge Commentary: An Exposition of the Scriptures*, ed. J. F. Walvoord and R. B. Zuck, vol. 1 (Wheaton, IL: Victor Books, 1985), 1364–1365.

"In a word, the prophecy is that there will be a future compact or covenant between a political ruler designated as the prince that shall come in verse 26 with the representatives of the Jewish people. Such an alliance will obviously be an unholy relationship and ultimately to the detriment of the people of Israel, however promising it may be at its inception… The fulfillment of this prophecy necessarily involves the reactivation of the Mosaic sacrificial system in a temple in Judea. The present occupation of Jerusalem by Israel may be a preparatory step to the re-establishment of the Mosaic system of sacrifices. Obviously, sacrifices cannot be stopped and a temple cannot be desecrated unless both are in operation… The final period of seven years begins with the introduction of a covenant relationship between the future "prince that shall come" and "the many," the people of Israel. This covenant is observed for the first half of the future seven-year period; then the special liberties and protections granted Israel are taken away; and Israel becomes persecuted in their time of great tribulation. The beginning of the last three and one-half years of the seventy sevens of Daniel is marked by the desecration of the future temple, the stopping of the sacrifices, and the desolation of the Jewish religion. It is this period referred to by Christ as the great tribulation in Matthew 24:15–26."
Walvoord, John F., *Daniel: The Key To Prophetic Revelation* (Galaxie Software, 2008), 234–237. (J. F. Walvoord, Daniel: The Key To Prophetic Revelation 2008).
See Also
Stephen R. Miller, "Daniel," vol. 18, *The New American Commentary* (Nashville: Broadman & Holman Publishers, 1994), 271–272. (Miller 1994)

[116] There is at least a 2000-year gap between Daniel 11.35 and 11.36. See: J. Dwight Pentecost, "Daniel," in *The Bible Knowledge Commentary: An Exposition of the Scriptures*, ed. J. F. Walvoord and R. B. Zuck, vol. 1 (Wheaton, IL: Victor Books, 1985), 1370–1371.

[117] Rom 4.6-22; 2 Cor 5.21

[118] Rom 6.1-2

[119] 2 Cor 5.17; Gal 6.15

[120] Rom 8.9; 1 Cor 3.16

[121] Chapter 8-The Son of Perdition. There are two named Sons of Perdition: Judas and the Antichrist. Judas was indwelt by Lucifer [Jn 22.3]. The Antichrist, who will receive his power and everything else from the Dragon, or Lucifer [Rev 13.2-4], is called the Beast from the Bottomless Pit [Rev 11.7] while Apollyon, a spiritual entity who is Lucifer, is titled the Lord of that same Abyss [Rev 9.2-3, 11].

[122] Satan is opposed to all of humanity, not just believers. It is by deception that he convinces unbelievers that his New World Order has a meaningful place for them, since he knows full well

that his and their doom is certain. Satan's program for the unbeliever is an eternal "kingdom" in hell. Satan is not your friend.

[123] desecrate /ˈdɛsɪkreɪt/
verb treat (a sacred place or thing) with violent disrespect.
DERIVATIVES desecration noun desecrator noun
ORIGIN 17th century: from DE- (expressing reversal) + a shortened form of CONSECRATE.
Catherine Soanes and Angus Stevenson, eds., *Concise Oxford English Dictionary* (Oxford: Oxford University Press, 2004). (Soanes 2004).

[124] "Perdition" 684 ἀπώλεια [apoleia /ap·o·li·a/] n f. From a presumed derivative of 622; TDNT 1:396; TDNTA 67; GK 724; 20 occurrences; AV translates as "perdition" eight times, "destruction" five times, "waste" twice, "damnable" once, "to die + 1519" once, "perish + 1498 + 1519" once, and "pernicious" once. 1 destroying, utter destruction. 1A of vessels. 2 a perishing, ruin, destruction. 2A of money. 2B the destruction which consists of eternal misery in hell.
James Strong, *Enhanced Strong's Lexicon* (Woodside Bible Fellowship, 1995).

[125] "3. The specific theological sense of these words in the NT is brought out by Jn. and Paul. Just as sōtēria (salvation) and zōē aiōnios (eternal life) connote sure and lasting salvation, so apollymi and apōleia mean "definitive destruction, not merely in the sense of the extinction of physical existence, but rather of an eternal plunge into Hades and a hopeless destiny of death"" (A. Oepke, TDNT I 396). (Kittel 1964-)
C. H-Hahn, "Destroy, Perish, Ruin," ed. Lothar Coenen, Erich Beyreuther, and Hans Bietenhard, *New International Dictionary of New Testament Theology* (Grand Rapids, MI: Zondervan Publishing House, 1986), 464.

[126] "Apollyon" This word has the same meaning as NT:684
20.31 ἀπόλλυμι; ἀπώλεια, ας f; λυμαίνομαι: to destroy or to cause the destruction of persons, objects, or institutions—'to ruin, to destroy, destruction.'
Johannes P. Louw and Eugene Albert Nida, *Greek-English Lexicon of the New Testament: Based on Semantic Domains* (New York: United Bible Societies, 1996), 231.

[127] Mt 7.14; Rom 9.22; Heb 10.39

[128] In Chapter 16 it will be established that in scripture the Beast represents a kingdom, a person, and a spiritual entity [Apollyon]. Distinguishing between these identities clarifies prophecies concerning him.

[129] APOLLYON [ə pŏl′yən] (Gk. Apollyōn, from apollýō "destroy"). An angel, the "prince" of the "scorpions" of the bottomless pit (Rev. 9:11). The Greek name constitutes a "derogatory reference to the Greek god Apollo and those emperors [e.g., Domitian] who claimed a special relationship to him" R. H. Mounce, *The Book of Revelation. NICNT* (1977), 198. (Mounce 1977)
Myers, Allen C., *The Eerdmans Bible Dictionary* (Grand Rapids, MI: Eerdmans, 1987), 66.
Regarding Apollo see:
Encyclopaedia Britannica, 1952 ed., s.v. "Apollo." Chicago: Encyclopaedia Britannica, 1952.
Wikipedia contributors, "Apollo," Wikipedia, The Free Encyclopedia,
https://en.wikipedia.org/w/index.php?title=Apollo&oldid=813586485 Accessed December 8, 2017.

[130] "destroy:" apollumi Johannes P. Louw and Eugene Albert Nida, Greek-English Lexicon of the New Testament: Based on Semantic Domains (New York: United Bible Societies, 1996) 20.31

[131] Revelation 6:1–2 (KJV 1900) 1 And I saw when the Lamb opened one of the seals, and I heard, as

it were the noise of thunder, one of the four beasts saying, Come and see. 2 <u>And I saw, and behold a white horse: and he that sat on him had a bow; and a crown was given unto him: and he went forth conquering, and to conquer.</u> [emphasis added]

[132] Chafer, Lewis Sperry. "Angelology Part 2." Bibliotheca Sacra 99, no. 393 (1942). 12

"The demons had a ruler over them whose Hebrew name is Abaddon and whose Greek name is Apollyon. Both words mean "destroyer." Though Satan is sometimes portrayed as an angel of light (2 Cor. 11:14), here Satan and his demons are seen for what they really are, destroyers of people" Walvoord, John F., "Revelation," in *The Bible Knowledge Commentary: An Exposition of the Scriptures*, ed. J. F. Walvoord and R. B. Zuck, vol. 2 (Wheaton, IL: Victor Books, 1985), 953.

"John accepts the reality of a personal devil. This enemy has many different names in Scripture: Satan (adversary, enemy), the devil (accuser), Abaddon or Apollyon (destroyer), the prince of this world, the dragon, etc. Whatever name you call him, keep in mind that his chief activity is to oppose Christ and God's people." Wiersbe, Warren W., *The Bible Exposition Commentary, vol. 2* (Wheaton, IL: Victor Books, 1996), 505–506. (Wiersbe 1996)

Jamieson, Robert, A. R. Fausset, and David Brown. *Commentary Critical and Explanatory on the Whole Bible*. (Oak Harbor, WA: Logos Research Systems, Inc., 1997). Rev 9.11 (Jamieson 1997).

"The devil, on account of his hateful nature, and those accursed dispositions which reign in him, is called Satan, the adversary, Abaddon and Apollyon, the great destroyer, the wolf, the roaring lion, the great dragon, the old serpent." Edwards, Jonathan, The Works of Jonathan Edwards Volume 2: "Sermon V 56 .True Grace Distinguished From The Experience Of Devils." Christian Classics Ethereal Library, https://ccel.org/ccel/edwards/works2/works2.iii.v.html Accessed July 2, 2022. (Edwards 1752)

Charles H. Spurgeon, "Battle with Apollyon 2" SermonAudio https://www.sermonaudio.com/sermoninfo.asp?SID=41916722310 Accessed July 2, 2022. (Spurgeon 2016)

[133] Pink's argument is included here because of its ingenuity. We will argue in Chapter 16 that the Antichrist or the Beast is identified in scripture simultaneously as a person, a kingdom, and a spiritual entity. Thus, the reference to the Son of Perdition is a reference to both Judas and the Beast's relation to Apollyon or Perdition. Both men share the distinction of having been the only men recorded in scripture as being indwelt by Lucifer himself.

[134] This issue is also addressed in Chapter 16: Section-The Beast Identified with World Government

[135] Pink, Arthur W. *The Antichrist*, Arthur Pink Collection Book 1, (p. 7, 8). Prisbrary Publishing. Kindle Edition. (Pink n.d.)

[136] "lawless" 459 ἄνομος [anomos /an·om·os/] adj. From 1 (as a negative particle) and 3551; TDNT 4:1086; TDNTA 646; GK 491; 10 occurrences; AV translates as "without law" four times, "transgressor" twice, "wicked" twice, "lawless" once, and "unlawful" once. 1 destitute of (the Mosaic) law. 1A of the Gentiles. 2 departing from the law, a violator of the law, lawless, wicked James Strong, *Enhanced Strong's Lexicon* (Woodside Bible Fellowship, 1995).

[137] "Quote by Hermes Trismegistus: 'As above, so below, as within, so without…'" https://www.goodreads.com/quotes/6667328-as-above-so-below-as-within-so-without-as-the.

Accessed November 26, 2020.

[138] Jer 5.1-5; Rom 1.19-21; 2.14-15; 1 Pet 2.12

[139] For example, the widespread adoption of the Charismatic doctrine has resulted in many believers who cannot interpret the scriptures and are therefore susceptible to increasingly faulty Bible teaching, such as the Word of Faith doctrine, and the Ecumenical Movement.

[140] "anti" 473 ἀντί [anti /an·tee/] prep. A primary particle; TDNT 1:372; TDNTA 61; GK 505; 22 occurrences; AV translates as "for" 15 times, "because + 3639" four times, "for ... cause" once, "therefore + 3639" once, and "in the room of" once. 1 over against, opposite to, before. 2 for, instead of, in place of (something). 2A instead of. 2B for. 2C for that, because. 2D wherefore, for this cause.
James Strong, *Enhanced Strong's Lexicon* (Woodside Bible Fellowship, 1995).

[141] "iniquity" 6406 עֲוְלָה ('ăw·lā(h)): n.fem. or poss.masc.; ≡ Str 5766; TWOT 1580a—LN 88.12–88.23 wickedness, evil, injustice, crime, i.e., be in a state of not being right or just, often with a focus that these wrongs are harmful or damaging to others...
James Swanson, *Dictionary of Biblical Languages with Semantic Domains: Hebrew (Old Testament)* (Oak Harbor: Logos Research Systems, Inc., 1997).

[142] James Swanson, *Dictionary of Biblical Languages with Semantic Domains: Hebrew (Old Testament)* (Oak Harbor: Logos Research Systems, Inc., 1997).

[143] Identifying Lucifer as the originator of revolution.

[144] merchandise = traffic, or going about, as in 28:18. Hence it meant calumniator (slanderer), in a moral sense.
Bullinger, Ethelbert W. *The Companion Bible: Being the Authorized Version of 1611 with the Structures and Notes, Critical, Explanatory and Suggestive and with 198 Appendixes*. Bellingham, WA: Faithlife, 2018. Ezekiel 28.16 (Bullinger n.d.)

[145] In a *fourth* instance, the devil even tempted Jesus with the issue of unauthorized authority three times at the beginning of His ministry: the use of unauthorized power [Mt 4.2-3], the suggestion that he use unauthorized privilege [Mt 4.6] and the temptation of unauthorized position [Mt 4.8-9].

[146] The Davidic Covenant of 2 Sam 7 wherein David is promised an eternal succession and kingdom, presupposes an eternal king, land, and people.

[147] Teilhard de Chardin, Pierre. *The Phenomenon of Man*. (New York: Harper Perennial Modern Thought, 2008).

[148] The image presented by God to Nebuchadnezzar did not address the duration, but the *sequence* of the Gentile nations from his own time until the end of the Times of the Gentiles. If it did address time, then the iron legs and feet of iron and clay would have to account for literally thousands of years. Other scriptures must be consulted to understand the time dimensions of the fourth kingdom of his dream and the fourth beast of Daniel's vision in chapter 7 of his book.

[149] Matthew 22.15-22; Romans 13.3-7; 1 Peter 2.13-14;

[150] Ps 2; Eph 2.1-2; Rev 17.1-4

[151] Jn 12.31; 14.30; 1 Cor 4.4

[152] Daniel Chapter 8: Two years after the vision of chapter 7, in the third year of Belshazzar of Babylon. The vision focuses upon the second and third beasts, this time represented by a Ram and a Goat. Daniel is given a vision with a more immediate fulfillment. The Babylonian Empire would soon end, and the times of the Medes and Persians would begin. This prophecy focuses upon a notable horn which arises from one of the four horns of the male goat, or the Grecian Empire. In a double fulfillment, it represents Antiochus IV Epiphanes [Reign: 175-164 B.C.], but the

interpretation supplied by the angel Gabriel indicates that this is also a prophecy about another person far in the future. Therefore, in this vision Daniel was shown the proximate future concerning the Gentile nations and a second look [Dan 7.19-26-the first look] at the most significant personage of the times of the Gentiles, the Antichrist.

[153] Daniel 2; 7; Luke 21.24; Rom 11.25

[154] Thieme, R. B., and Wayne F. Hill. *The Divine Outline of History: Dispensations and the Church.* (Houston: R.B. Thieme, Jr. Bible Ministries, 1999). 6-7 (R. B. Thieme 1999)

[155] Gen 3; Job 1; Matt 4.1-11; Eph 3.10

[156] Rev 13.4, 15-18; 14.9-11

[157] "change" (#10731 definition #5 [hafel construction])
James Swanson, *Dictionary of Biblical Languages with Semantic Domains: Aramaic (Old Testament)* (Oak Harbor: Logos Research Systems, Inc., 1997).

[158] This truth can easily be construed as a justification for the believer to absent himself from citizenship responsibilities, or to harden his heart against real suffering in the world. The true Christian's righteous function in divinely ordained institutions such as marriage, family and government are means by which God's righteousness and grace are extended to the unbelieving world. The believer in the world is to be salt and light, a north star pointing to divine righteousness and justice among men and women. The gospel of salvation through Jesus Christ is illuminated by Christian sanctification in the world. The gospel and citizenship are not mutually exclusive but are logically complementary. A good Christian is a good citizen [Pr 14.34].

[159] See Appendix 1: A God of Forces

[160] See Walvoord, John F. *Daniel: The Key To Prophetic Revelation.* (Galaxie Software, 2008). Chapter 11 (J. F. Walvoord, Daniel: The Key To Prophetic Revelation 2008)

[161] The state exists to enforce a code of morality through its laws. Christians as citizens should be concerned about just laws and their just enforcement. The dangers to which the Church is susceptible are: 1. Confusing the Kingdom of God with a manmade political vision such as a Christian State, 2. Becoming defenders of wickedness due to being unequally yoked in political organizations 3. Dividing local churches by emphasis upon political allegiance rather than upon allegiance to the scriptures.

[162] "marvelous" 6381 פלא [pala' /paw·law/] v. A primitive root; TWOT 1768; GK 7098; 71 occurrences; AV translates as "(wondrous", "marvellous ...) work" 18 times, "wonders" nine times, "marvellous" eight times, "wonderful" eight times, "... things" six times, "hard" five times, "wondrous" three times, "wondrously" twice, "marvellously" twice, "performing" twice, and translated miscellaneously eight times. 1 to be marvellous, be wonderful, be surpassing, be extraordinary, separate by distinguishing action. 1A (Niphal). 1A1 to be beyond one's power, be difficult to do. 1A2 to be difficult to understand. 1A3 to be wonderful, be extraordinary. 1A3A marvellous (participle). 1B (Piel) to separate (an offering). 1C (Hiphil). 1C1 to do extraordinary or hard or difficult thing. 1C2 to make wonderful, do wondrously. 1D (Hithpael) to show oneself wonderful or marvellous.
James Strong, *Enhanced Strong's Lexicon* (Woodside Bible Fellowship, 1995).

[163] Kenneth Copeland- https://www.youtube.com/watch?v=FluPJNWvUBU Accessed July 11, 2018
Creflo Dollar- https://www.youtube.com/watch?v=X4LirHMPlnM Accessed July 11, 2018 *Also*, https://www.youtube.com/watch?v=-NV1plklvhg
John Hagee: https://www.youtube.com/watch?v=1bv05U--rY8 Accessed July 11, 2018

A Variety of Other Teachers- https://www.youtube.com/watch?v=sPoQixUloZk Accessed July 11, 2018
[164] Eph 2.1-3; 2 Cor 4.4; 1 Jn 5.19
[165] "Lucifer" https://www.imdb.com/title/tt4052886/ Accessed July 11, 2018
[166] 2 Th 2.4; 1 Jn 4.3; 2 Jn 7; Rev 13.1
[167] Walvoord demonstrates that this passage does not automatically validate the assertion that the Antichrist will be a Jew.

"One of the more important arguments supporting the conclusion that this king is a Jew is found in the opening phrase of verse 37, "neither shall he regard the God of his fathers." As Gaebelein states, "The King, Antichrist shall not regard the God of his fathers. Here his Jewish descent becomes evident. It is a Jewish phrase 'the God of his fathers' and beside this, to establish his fraudulent claim to be the King Messiah, he must be a Jew."44 Gaebelein and others upholding this view, however, overlook a most decisive fact that the word for "God" here is Elohim, a name for God in general, applying both to the true God and to false gods. If the expression had been the usual one when referring to the God of Israel, the Jehovah of his fathers, the identification would be unmistakable. Very frequently in Scripture, the God of Israel is described as Jehovah, "the Lord God" of their fathers (cf. Ex 3:15–16; 4:5; Deu 1:11, 21; 4:1; 6:3; 12:1; 26:7; 29:25; Jos 18:3; Judg 2:12; 2 Ki 21:22; 1 Ch 29:20; 2 Ch 7:22; 11:16; 13:18; 15:12; 19:4; 20:6; 21:10; 24:24; 28:9; 29:5; 30:7, 19; 34:33; 36:15; Ezra 7:27; 8:28). Although Daniel uses "God (Elohim) of my fathers" in Daniel 2:23 in view of this common usage elsewhere in Scripture, for Daniel to omit the word Jehovah or Lord, (KJV) in a passage where a specific name for the God of Israel would be necessary, becomes significant. The expression should be rendered "the gods of his fathers," that is, any god, as most revisions translate it.
Walvoord, John F., *Daniel: The Key To Prophetic Revelation* (Galaxie Software, 2008), 273–274.
[168] Gen 3.14-15 c.f. Rom 16.20; 1 Jn 3.8
[169] *Mystery* Babylon is real, but its intent is hidden, sometimes even from its own adherents and leaders [e.g., Rev 17.16-17]. The current ecumenical efforts to produce a world Church and government are designed to position the existing religious and political institutions for an ultimate bulldozing before the establishment of the mystical New World Order where all worship is directed to Lucifer and his son, the Antichrist.
[170] See Appendix I
[171] "occult" occult (adj.) 1530s, "secret, not divulged," from Middle French occulte and directly from Latin occultus "hidden, concealed, secret," past participle of occulere "cover over, conceal," from assimilated form of ob "over" (see ob-) + a verb related to celare "to hide,"
Etymology Dictionary Online, http://www.etymonline.com/index.php?term=occult Accessed April 11, 2017 (Online n.d.).
[172] Isa 13.6-11; Joel 2.10, 31; Mt 25.29
[173] Appendix II
[174] Stars appear to reference messengers: either human or angelic Rev 1.20 c.f., Rev 12.7
[175] "Caught Up" Same Greek word as in 1 Th 4.17 with reference to the Church, but here with reference to Jesus:
18.4 ἁρπάζω: to grab or seize by force, with the purpose of removing and/or controlling—'to seize, to snatch away, to take away.
Johannes P. Louw and Eugene Albert Nida, *Greek-English Lexicon of the New Testament: Based on*

Semantic Domains (New York: United Bible Societies, 1996), 220.

[176] John F. Walvoord, "Revelation," in The Bible Knowledge Commentary: An Exposition of the Scriptures, ed. J. F. Walvoord and R. B. Zuck, vol. 2 (Wheaton, IL: Victor Books, 1985), 957.

[177] Page 229

[178] It is very likely that the persecution of Rev 12.13-17 is against *redeemed* Israelites and not against Jews in general.

The rescue of Rev 12.6, 13-17 will pertain to a portion of Israel, which remnant is warned by Jesus in the gospels:

Matthew 24:15–21 (KJV 1900)
15 When ye therefore shall see the abomination of desolation, spoken of by Daniel the prophet, stand in the holy place, (whoso readeth, let him understand:) 16 Then let them which be in Judaea flee into the mountains: 17 Let him which is on the housetop not come down to take any thing out of his house: 18 Neither let him which is in the field return back to take his clothes. 19 And woe unto them that are with child, and to them that give suck in those days! 20 But pray ye that your flight be not in the winter, neither on the sabbath day: 21 For then shall be great tribulation, such as was not since the beginning of the world to this time, no, nor ever shall be.

This warning is provided to those Jews who had responded to the gospel by faith and were born again. This message will not have any impact upon unredeemed Israel, who will see the Antichrist as a savior, not as an enemy [Rev 13.8, 11-12].

Romans 9:6–8 (KJV 1900)
6 Not as though the word of God hath taken none effect. <u>For they are not all Israel, which are of Israel</u>: 7 Neither, because they are the seed of Abraham, are they all children: but, In Isaac shall thy seed be called. 8 That is, <u>They which are the children of the flesh, these are not the children of God: but the children of the promise</u> are counted for the seed.

2 Thessalonians 2:8–12 (KJV 1900)
8 And then shall that Wicked be revealed, whom the Lord shall consume with the spirit of his mouth, and shall destroy with the brightness of his coming: 9 Even him, whose coming is after the working of Satan with all power and signs and lying wonders, 10 And with all deceivableness of unrighteousness in them that perish; <u>because they received not the love of the truth, that they might be saved</u>. 11 <u>And for this cause God shall send them strong delusion, that they should believe a lie</u>: 12 That they all might be damned who believed not the truth, but had pleasure in unrighteousness.

John specifically identifies the objects of the wrath of the Dragon:

Revelation 12:13–17 (KJV 1900)
13 And when the dragon saw that he was cast unto the earth, he persecuted the woman which brought forth the man child. 14 And to the woman were given two wings of a great eagle, that she might fly into the wilderness, into her place, where she is nourished for a time, and times, and half a time, from the face of the serpent. 15 And the serpent cast out of his mouth water as a flood after the woman, that he might cause her to be carried away of the flood. 16 And the earth helped

the woman, and the earth opened her mouth, and swallowed up the flood which the dragon cast out of his mouth. 17 <u>And the dragon was wroth with the woman, and went to make war with the remnant of her seed, which keep the commandments of God, and have the testimony of Jesus Christ.</u>

In fact, approximately three years later, prior to the Siege of Jerusalem, there will be many Jews living in Jerusalem, apparently unmolested by the Antichrist. Therefore, the objects of the wrath of the devil may be initially limited to redeemed Israel and exclude their apostate brethren. God will protect the Woman, or the elect remnant of Israel [Rom 9.6; 11.1-11, 26] while she is hiding during the last half of the tribulation. In fact, He will do more than protect Israel, He will go on the offensive against the devil. In the meanwhile, unbelieving Jews will continue to respond to the gospel throughout the duration of the Tribulation

[179] Dan 9.27; Matt 24.15-22; 2 Th 2.3-10
[180] Revelation 17:1-17 [Joseph A. Seiss-The Apocalypse]

"A "mountain," or prominent elevation on the surface of the earth, is one of the common Scriptural images, symbols, or representatives of a kingdom, regal dominion, empire, or established authority. So David, speaking of the vicissitudes which he experienced as the king of Israel, says: "Lord, by Thy favor Thou didst make my mountain to stand strong"-margin, "settled strength for my mountain;" meaning his kingdom and dominion. (Ps 30:7). So the Lord in His threat against the throne and power of Babylon said: "I am against thee, O destroying mountain, which destroyest all the earth; and I will stretch out mine hand upon thee, and will roll thee down from the rocks, and will make thee a burnt mountain" (Jer 51:25). So the kingdom of the Messiah is likened to "a stone, which became a great mountain, and filled the whole earth" (Dan 2:35). And this is exactly the sense in which the angel uses the word here, as he himself tells us… The seven imperial mountains on which she rides must therefore fill up the whole interval; or there was a time, and the most of her history, when she did not ride at all, which is not the fact. Seven is itself the number of fulness, which includes the whole of its kind. The reference here is to kings, to mountains of temporal dominion, to empires. It must therefore take in all of them…Of these seven regal mountains, John was told "the five are fallen," dead, passed away, their day over; "the one is," that is, was standing, at that moment, was then in sway and power; "the other is not yet come, and when he shall come, he must continue a little time." What regal mountain, then, was in power at the time John wrote? There can be no question on that point; it was the Roman Empire. Thus, then, we ascertain and identify the sixth in the list, which shows what sort of kings the angel meant. Of the same class with this, and belonging to the same category, there are five others-five which had then already run their course and passed away. But what five imperial mountains like Rome had been and gone, up to that time? Is history so obscure as not to tell us with unmistakable certainty? Preceding Rome the world had but five great names or nationalities answering to imperial Rome, and those scarce a schoolboy ought to miss.

"They are Greece, Persia, Babylon, Assyria, and Egypt; no more, and no less. And these all were imperial powers like Rome. Here, then, are six of these regal mountains; the seventh is not yet come. When it comes it is to endure but a short time. This implies that each of the others continues a long time; and so, again, could not mean the dictators, decemvirs, and military tribunes of the early history of Rome, for some of them lasted but a year or two. Thus, then, by the clearest, most direct, and most natural signification of the words of the record, we are brought to the identification of these seven mountain kings as the seven great world-powers, which stretch from the beginning of our present world to the end of it. Daniel makes the number less; but he started with his own times, and looked only down the stream. Here the account looks backward as well as forward. What is first in Daniel is the third here, and that which is the sixth here is the fourth in Daniel. Only in the commencing point is there any difference. The visions of Daniel and the visions of John are from the same Divine Mind, and they perfectly harmonize, only that the latest are the amplest.

"By these seven great powers then, filling up the whole interval of this world's history, this great Harlot is said to be carried. On these she rides, according to the vision. It is not upon one alone, nor upon any particular number of them, but upon all of them, the whole seven-headed Beast, that she sits. These seven powers, each and all, support the Woman as their joy and pride; and she accepts and uses them, and sways their administrations, and rides in glory by means of them. They are her devotees, lovers, and most humble servants; and she is their patronizing and most noble lady, with a mutuality of favors and intercommunion belonging to her designation. This is the picture as explained by the angel. But, to say that the Roman Catholic Papacy was thus carried, nurtured, and sustained by the ancient empires of Greece, Persia, Babylon, Assyria, and Egypt, would be a great lie on history."

Seiss, Joseph A., *The Apocalypse: Exposition of the Book of Revelation*, (Electronic Database. Copyright © 1998, 2003, 2006 by Biblesoft, Inc. All rights reserved.) (Seiss 2006).

[181] Rev 17.12-13 c.f. Dan 2.40-42

[182] The Beast [Antichrist] is said to ascend from the bottomless pit in Rev 17.8. Either he was there all along, as Pink claims [see Chapter 8], or he [Antichrist] is indwelt by the one who is identified as the King of the Abyss, who is Lucifer or Apollyon.

[183] Except that upon the Dragon the *heads* are crowned, symbolizing his dominion over all of history, while the Beast has the *horns* crowned, indicating his sovereignty in the seventh kingdom of the end times. These crowned horns are the kings of that era [the ten toes] who subject themselves to the Beast Rev 17.12-13.

[184] Chapter 8-The Son of Perdition

[185] Gen 3; Isa 14.12-14; Eze 28.14-18

[186] From Chapter 1: "This book attempts to remind the believer of what can be done to ensure the successful prosecution of God's program in his own time. The advent of the Antichrist and the ultimate implementation of his World Order has been prophesied and will occur on schedule. However, the plan of God requires that each generation of believers execute the divine game plan in their own geography and historical context to secure the ultimate victory. Every believer, regardless of his place in history, has a contribution to make to the resolution of this ancient conflict. Understanding what Satan is specifically attempting to accomplish is an aid to the believer as he watches and engages the historical trends of his time."

[187] 1 John 5:4–5 (KJV 1900) For whatsoever is born of God overcometh the world: and this is the victory that overcometh the world, even our faith. 5 Who is he that overcometh the world, but he that believeth that Jesus is the Son of God?

[188] Gen 10.5, 20, 31; Rom 13.1-4

[189] Chapter 9-Section: Where Does Morality Originate

[190] "change" (#10731 definition #5 [hafel construction])

James Swanson, *Dictionary of Biblical Languages with Semantic Domains: Aramaic* (Old Testament)

(Oak Harbor: Logos Research Systems, Inc., 1997).

[191] The Freemasons, the Builders, said by some to be the depository of the Mystery Religions, travel to the East with the tools of the craft of Masonry, to rebuild ([v3] bricks, mortar [v4] "Go, let us build") that which was destroyed by God. The magazine of the Scottish Rite of Freemasonry was titled The "New Age" for over eighty years.

[192] 2 Thessalonians 2:3–4 (KJV 1900) 3 Let no man deceive you by any means: for that day shall not come, except there come a falling away first, and that man of sin be revealed, the son of perdition; 4 Who opposeth and exalteth himself above **all** that is called God, or that is worshipped; so that he as God sitteth in the temple of God, shewing himself that he is God. [emphasis added]

[193] Ex 22.21; Lev 25.17; Dt 24.14; Judg 2.18; Job 36.15; Ps 9.9; 10.18; Ps 62.10; 103.6; 146.7; Prov 22.22; Isa 1.17; 5:7; 33.15; Jer 7.6; Zech 7.8-12; Mal 3.5; Acts 7.24

[194] Prov 11.10-1; 14.34; 28.12; Mt 5.13-16

[195] Chapter 23-Section: An Example of Religious Babylon, The Ecumenical Movement

[196] Volume II of this work [2023] will provide a complete explanation of the issue of the Charismatic Movement. Many godly believers are a part of charismatic Churches.

The problem with this movement is that it is necessary to disregard the scriptures to justify many of its practices. It is the partial disregard of the scripture [for example, in the doctrine of speaking in tongues] that has *enabled* the worldwide influence of the Word of Faith movement, the rapid advance of ecumenical cooperation and other problems. You cannot advance the Plan of God by violating the Word of God.

[197] "Bible, Authority of the. View that the Bible is the Word of God and as such should be believed and obeyed."

"The Bible is authoritative because it is divinely authorized; in its own terms, "all Scripture is God-breathed" (2 Tm 3:16 NIV). According to this passage the whole OT (or any element of it) is divinely inspired. Extension of the same claim to the NT is not expressly stated, though it is more than merely implied. The NT contains indications that its content was to be viewed, and was in fact viewed, as no less authoritative than the OT. The apostle Paul's writings are catalogued with "other scriptures" (2 Pt 3:15, 16). Under the heading of Scripture, 1 Timothy 5:18 cites Luke 10:7 alongside Deuteronomy 25:4 (cf. 1 Cor 9:9). The Book of Revelation, moreover, claims divine origin (1:1–3) and employs the term "prophecy" in the OT meaning (22:9, 10, 18). The apostles did not distinguish their spoken and written teaching but expressly declared their inspired proclamation to be the Word of God (1 Cor 4:1; 2 Cor 5:20; 1 Thes 2:13)."

"The historic evangelical position is summed up in the words of Frank E. Gaebelein, general editor of The Expositors' Bible Commentary: "the divine inspiration, complete trustworthiness, and full authority of the Bible." Scripture is authoritative and fully trustworthy because it is divinely inspired. Lutheran theologian Francis Pieper directly connected the authority of the Bible with its inspiration: "The divine authority of Scripture rests solely on its nature, on its theopneusty"—that is, its character as 'God breathed.' " J.I. Packer commented that every compromise of the truthfulness of the Bible must at the same time be regarded as a compromise of its authority: "To assert biblical inerrancy and infallibility is just to confess faith in (i) the divine origin of the Bible and (ii) the truthfulness and trustworthiness of God. The value of these terms is that they conserve the principles of biblical authority; for statements that are not absolutely true and reliable could not be absolutely authoritative." Packer reinforced that argument by demonstrating that Christ, the apostles, and the early Church all agreed that the OT was both absolutely trustworthy and

authoritative. Being a fulfillment of the OT, the NT is no less authoritative. Christ entrusted his disciples with his own authority in their teaching so the early Church accepted their teaching. As God's revelation, Scripture stands above the limitations of human assertion."
Carl F.H. Henry, "Bible, Authority of The," *Baker Encyclopedia of the Bible* (Grand Rapids, MI: Baker Book House, 1988), 296, 298, 299 (Henry 1988).

[198] Dale Coulter, *Pope Francis And The Future Of Charismatic Christianity* 2-20-14 https://www.firstthings.com/blogs/firstthoughts/2014/02/we-know-pope-francis Accessed December10, 2017
Andrea Gagliarducci, *Evangelizing Evangelicals – Why Pope Francis Loves To Meet With Charismatic Movements* https://www.catholicnewsagency.com/news/evangelizing-evangelicals-why-pope-francis-loves-to-meet-with-charismatic-movements-66914 Accessed December 10, 2017.

[199] "E. J. Young provides a suitable definition of inerrancy: "By this word we mean that the Scriptures possess the quality of freedom from error. They are exempt from the liability to mistake, incapable of error. In all their teachings they are in perfect accord with the truth"30 Ryrie provides a syllogism for logically concluding the biblical teaching of inerrancy: "God is true (Rom. 3:4); the Scriptures were breathed out by God (2 Tim. 3:16); therefore, the Scriptures are true (since they came from the breath of God who is true)."31
"In defining inerrancy it is also important to state what it does not mean. It does not demand rigidity of style and verbatim quotations from the Old Testament. "The inerrancy of the Bible means simply that the Bible tells the truth. Truth can and does include approximations, free quotations, language of appearances, and different accounts of the same event as long as those do not contradict."32 At the Chicago meeting in October 1978, the International Council on Biblical Inerrancy issued the following statement on inerrancy: "Being wholly and verbally God-given, Scripture is without error or fault in all its teaching, no less in what it states about God's acts in creation, about the events of world history, and about its own literary origins under God, than in its witness to God's saving grace in individual lives."33
"In a final definition it is noted that inerrancy extends to the original manuscripts: "Inerrancy means that when all the facts are known, the Scriptures in their original autographs and properly interpreted will be shown to be wholly true in everything they teach, whether that teaching has to do with doctrine, history, science, geography, geology, or other disciplines or knowledge."34
Enns, Paul P., *The Moody Handbook of Theology* (Chicago, IL: Moody Press, 1989), 167.

[200] See Luke 4.5-7

[201] "wounded" 4969 σφάζω [sphazo /sfad·zo/] v. A primary verb; TDNT 7:925; TDNTA 1125; GK 5377; 10 occurrences; AV translates as "slay" eight times, "kill" once, and "wound" once. 1 to slay, slaughter, butcher. 2 to put to death by violence. 3 mortally wounded.
James Strong, *Enhanced Strong's Lexicon* (Woodside Bible Fellowship, 1995).

[202] Both are perfect passive participles of *sphazo*

[203] Corresponding to Jesus before his crucifixion.

[204] "Unitatis Redintegratio."
http://www.vatican.va/archive/hist_councils/ii_vatican_council/documents/vat-ii_decree_19641121_unitatis-redintegratio_en.html. 1.4. Accessed November 5, 2018.

[205] Depending upon how one identifies the seventh kingdom and whether the Man of Sin has any function within it. If he does, then the reference to special occult power applies to that head as well as the eighth. We have already stated that the kingdoms of the earth are and have always been

involved spiritually with Mystery Babylon [Ps 2; Rev 17.2].

[206] "terrible" 1763 דחל [dâchal /deh·khal/] v. Corresponding to 2119; TWOT 2672; GK 10167; Six occurrences; AV translates as "fear" twice, "dreadful" twice, "terrible" once, and "afraid" once. 1 to fear. 1A (P'al). 1A1 to fear. 1A2 terrible (pass participle). 1B (Pael) to cause to be afraid, make afraid.
James Strong, *Enhanced Strong's Lexicon* (Woodside Bible Fellowship, 1995).

[207] Ps 2; Jer 51.7; Dan 7.1-8; 1 Cor 10.20-21; Rev 17.1-2

[208] In Chapter 25 we will provide an example of Mystery Babylon in action in the Rap Music industry. A book could be written of the efforts of that industry to promote the coming religion of the New World Order and to proclaim it's disdain for Christ.

[209] Key, but not the only witness, as God has provided man with the witness of nature [Rom 1.19-21] and of conscience [Rom 2.14-15]. Satan will re-explain the first and re-calibrate the latter.

[210] The main proposition made to Eve by the serpent is an implication: that if God misled you about the Tree of Knowledge and about the issue of death, perhaps He is not who He claims to be.

[211] Jesus was crucified because He claimed to be God, which His accusers denied [Mk 14.61-64]

[212] This is not an attempt to argue the true scriptural doctrine of divine election, but to address the presence of a divine plan working itself out in human history.

[213] Key, but not the only agency.
"The policy of the Roman government, the fanaticism of the superstitious people, and the self-interest of the pagan priests conspired for the persecution of a religion which threatened to demolish the tottering fabric of idolatry; and they left no expedients of legislation, of violence, of craft, and of wickedness untried, to blot it from the earth."
Philip Schaff and David Schley Schaff, History of the Christian Church, vol. 2 (New York: Charles Scribner's Sons, 1910), 40. (Schaff 1910)

[214] Philip Schaff and David Schley Schaff, History of the Christian Church, vol. 2 (New York: Charles Scribner's Sons, 1910), 41–42.

[215] "Galerius, the real author of the persecution, brought to reflection by a terrible disease, put an end to the slaughter shortly before his death, by a remarkable edict of toleration, which he issued from Nicomedia in 311, in connexion with Constantine and Licinius. In that document he declared, that the purpose of reclaiming the Christians from their wilful innovation and the multitude of their sects to the laws and discipline of the Roman state, was not accomplished; and that he would now grant them permission to hold their religious assemblies provided they disturbed not the order of the state. To this he added in conclusion the significant instruction that the Christians, "after this manifestation of grace, should pray to their God for the welfare of the emperors, of the state, and of themselves, that the state might prosper in every respect, and that they might live quietly in their homes."1"
Philip Schaff and David Schley Schaff, History of the Christian Church, vol. 2 (New York: Charles Scribner's Sons, 1910), 71.

[216] "Unfortunately, the successors of Constantine from the time of Theodosius the Great (383–395) enforced the Christian religion to the exclusion of every other; and not only so, but they enforced orthodoxy to the exclusion of every form of dissent, which was punished as a crime against the state."
Philip Schaff and David Schley Schaff, *History of the Christian Church, vol. 2* (New York: Charles Scribner's Sons, 1910), 73.

[217] The Roman Catholic Church was never the sole manifestation of Christianity in the world, or

even in Europe.

[218] "The Roman Catholic Church came into being as a consequence of a "perfect storm" of political and theological developments. It could be argued that Constantine saw the potency of the Christian movement as a force capable of uniting or at least slowing the dissolution of the Empire. There were theological controversies such as Arianism, which highlighted the need for greater doctrinal precision and the definition of heresy. In this process of uniting Church and state, each would take upon itself the characteristics of the other: The state would strengthen the concept of the divine right of rule,[6] the Church would become preoccupied with the maintenance of the visible apparatus of religion and religious authority as well as the legal enforcement of its decrees." Richard G. Walker, *While Men Slept,* n.d.

[219] "Skeptical writers have endeavored to diminish its moral effect by pointing to the fiendish and hellish scenes of the papal crusades against the Albigenses and Waldenses, the Parisian massacre of the Huguenots, the Spanish Inquisition, and other persecutions of more recent date. Dodwell expressed the opinion, which has been recently confirmed by the high authority of the learned and impartial Niebuhr, that the Diocletian persecution was a mere shadow as compared with the persecution of the Protestants in the Netherlands by the Duke of Alva in the service of Spanish bigotry and despotism. Gibbon goes even further, and boldly asserts that "the number of Protestants who were executed by the Spaniards in a single province and a single reign, far exceeded that of the primitive martyrs in the space of three centuries and of the Roman empire." The victims of the Spanish Inquisition also are said to outnumber those of the Roman emperors.1" Philip Schaff and David Schley Schaff, *History of the Christian Church, vol. 2* (New York: Charles Scribner's Sons, 1910), 78.

[220] Gen 9.7 c.f. Gen 10.5, 20, 31-31; Acts 17.26

[221] The persecutions proceeded first from the Jews, afterwards from the Gentiles, and continued, with interruptions, for nearly three hundred years. History reports no mightier, longer and deadlier conflict than this war of extermination waged by heathen Rome against defenseless Christianity. Philip Schaff and David Schley Schaff, *History of the Christian Church, vol. 2* (New York: Charles Scribner's Sons, 1910), 33.
[Schaff's affinity for the Catholic Church results in his tendency to somewhat understate the wickedness of that institution, particularly in its persecution of Christians. See footnote immediately above.-rw]

[222] "Maecenas counselled Augustus: "Honor the gods according to the custom of our ancestors, and compel2 others to worship them. Hate and punish those who bring in strange gods."" "The senate and emperor, by special edicts, usually allowed conquered nations the free practice of their worship even in Rome; not, however, from regard for the sacred rights of conscience, but merely from policy, and with the express prohibition of making proselytes from the state religion; hence severe laws were published from time to time against transition to Judaism." Philip Schaff and David Schley Schaff, *History of the Christian Church, vol. 2* (New York: Charles Scribner's Sons, 1910), 42.

[223] Rom 16.20; 1 Cor 6.3; Rev 20.10

[224] Acts 16.16-19

[225] In this he resembles John the Baptist, a Levite who performed a similar function for Christ.

[226] "privily shall bring in" 3919 παρεισάγω [pareisago /par·ice·ag·o/] v. From 3844 and 1521; TDNT 5:824; TDNTA 786; GK 4206; AV translates as "privily bring in" once. 1 to introduce or bring in

secretly or craftily.
James Strong, *Enhanced Strong's Lexicon* (Woodside Bible Fellowship, 1995).
[227] "power" 37.35 ἐξουσία ᵃ, ας f: the right to control or govern over—'authority to rule, right to control.' ἴσθι ἐξουσίαν ἔχων ἐπάνω δέκα πόλεων 'go with the authority to rule over ten cities' Lk 19:17
Johannes P. Louw and Eugene Albert Nida, *Greek-English Lexicon of the New Testament: Based on Semantic Domains* (New York: United Bible Societies, 1996), 475.
[228] Rev 13.8
[229] Even our pictures of Jesus in our churches and homes have done more damage than good by providing a false image of who God is. Their purpose is not spiritual [since they are direct violations of scripture] but are idolatrous artifacts of cultural warfare.
[230] Appendix II Section: About the Restrainer
[231] occult (adj.) 1530s, "secret, not divulged," from Middle French occulte and directly from Latin occultus "hidden, concealed, secret," past participle of occulere "cover over, conceal," from assimilated form of ob "over" (see ob-) + a verb related to celare "to hide,"
Etymology Dictionary Online, http://www.etymonline.com/index.php?term=occult [accessed 04/11/2017]
[232] A discussion of this information may be found in Chapter 19-Section: The True Origin of the Doctrine of the Superman as well as in Appendix I
[233] "The word "world" is aiōn (αἰων), which Trench defines as follows: "All that floating mass of thoughts, opinions, maxims, speculations, hopes, impulses, aims, aspirations, at any time current in the world, which it may be impossible to seize and accurately define, but which constitute a most real and effective power, being the moral, or immoral atmosphere which at every moment of our lives we inhale, again inevitably to exhale,—all this is included in the aiōn (αἰων) (age), which is, as Bengel has expressed it, the subtle informing spirit of the kosmos (κοσμος) or world of men who are living alienated and apart from God." The Germans have a word for it, the zeitgeist or spirit of the age."
Kenneth S. Wuest, *Wuest's Word Studies from the Greek New Testament: For the English Reader* (Grand Rapids: Eerdmans, 1997), Ro 12:2. (Wuest 1997)
[234] Esoteric: 1.a. designed for or understood by the specially initiated alone. 1.b. requiring or exhibiting knowledge that is restricted to a small group
Merriam Webster Dictionary, https://www.merriam-webster.com/dictionary/esoteric Accessed February 11, 2022.
[235] Elements of Demonic Despotism: Dan 2.2; 3.4-6 c.f. Rev 13.7, 15-16. This concept will be addressed in Volume 2 of this work [2023].
[236] "The perpetuation of warfare.
"Cost of National Security: Counting How Much the U.S. Spends Per Hour."
https://www.nationalpriorities.org/cost-of/ Accessed December 22, 2018.
[237] God has not given believers the ability to discern who is and is not so indwelt, nor would it matter if we specifically knew. The key factor is the near universal commitment to the agenda of the devil, regardless of other considerations.
[238] The Roman Catholic Church has been a nurturing factor in the development of many of these erroneous Christian systems that have captivated the world including the Charismatic Movement and its symbiotic parasite the Word of Faith Movement. The Catholic led Ecumenical Movement is

drawing in every other variety of spiritual error in the name of spiritual unity to create a single spiritual organism under its leadership. See Chapter 23- Section: "An Example of Religious Babylon: The Ecumenical Movement"

[239] Jn 3.29; Eph 5.25-27; 1 Cor 12.12-13 ;2 Cor 11.2

[240] Each retains his character: redeemed man does not become God, nor is the deity of God diminished by this union. The Church is *not* another incarnation of Christ, but his spiritual union with the redeemed of this age.

[241] Rom 6.3 c.f. Rom 6.1-10; 1 Cor 12.13a

[242] "The baptism of the Holy Spirit is unique to the Church Age. The basic reference is 1 Corinthians 12:13, which states, "For by one Spirit we were all baptized into one body, whether Jews or Greeks, whether slaves or free, and we were all made to drink of one Spirit." That this ministry of the Spirit began at Pentecost can be seen by comparing Acts 1:5, which indicates the baptizing work is still future, with Acts 11:15, which indicates the "beginning" of this work was at Pentecost in Acts 2. The baptizing work did not occur in the Old Testament; it is unique to the Church Age which began at Pentecost.

"The baptism of the Holy Spirit includes all believers in this age. The emphasis that "all" are baptized by the Holy Spirit is stated in several passages. In 1 Corinthians 12:13 it indicates "we were all baptized." In Romans 6 all who were baptized (v. 3) are those who have been united to Christ (v. 5), hence, all believers. In Galatians 3:27–28 it indicates "all of you" were baptized into Christ and became "one in Christ," no matter whether they were Jew or Greek, slave or free, male or female." Enns, Paul P., *The Moody Handbook of Theology* (Chicago, IL: Moody Press, 1989), 266–267.

[243] Jn 7.17; 16.13; Rom 12.1-2; 2 Tim 2.15

[244] Eph 5.8; Php 2.15; Rev 1.20

[245] However Adam and Eve chose to understand this offer, it appears to have been the devil's intent.

[246] "A mark (χαραγμα [charagma]). Old word from χαρασσω [charassō], to engrave, in Acts 17:29 of idolatrous images, but in Rev. (13:16, 17; 14:9, 11; 16:2; 19:20; 20:4) of the brand of the beast on the right hand or on the forehead or on both. Deissmann (Bible Studies, pp. 240ff.) shows that in the papyri official business documents often have the name and image of the emperor, with the date as the official stamp or seal and with χαραγμα [charagma] as the name of this seal" A.T. Robertson, *Word Pictures in the New Testament* (Nashville, TN: Broadman Press, 1933), Re 13:16. (Robertson 1933).

[247] Revelation 13:16

"He causeth all (same use of ποιεω [poieō] as in 12 and 15). Note article here with each class (the small and the great, etc.). That there be given them (ἱνα δωσιν αὐτοις [hina dōsin autois]). Same use of ἱνα [hina] after ποιεω [poieō] as in 12 and 15, only here with indefinite plural δωσιν [dōsin] (second aorist active subjunctive), "that they give themselves," as in 10:11; 12:6; 16:15. A mark (χαραγμα [charagma]). Old word from χαρασσω [charassō], to engrave, in Acts 17:29 of idolatrous images, but in Rev. (13:16, 17; 14:9, 11; 16:2; 19:20; 20:4) of the brand of the beast on the right hand or on the forehead or on both. Deissmann (Bible Studies, pp. 240ff.) shows that in the papyri official business documents often have the name and image of the emperor, with the date as the official stamp or seal and with χαραγμα [charagma] as the name of this seal. Animals and slaves were often branded with the owner's name, as Paul (Gal. 6:17) bore the stigmata of Christ. Ptolemy Philadelphus compelled some Alexandrian Jews to receive the mark of Dionysus as his devotees (3

Macc. 3:29). The servants of God receive on their foreheads the stamp of the divine seal (Rev. 7:3). Charles is certain that John gets his metaphor from the τεφιλλιν [tephillin] (phylacteries) which the Jew wore on his left hand and on his forehead. At any rate, this "mark of the beast" was necessary for life and all social and business relations. On the right hand, that is in plain sight."
A.T. Robertson, *Word Pictures in the New Testament* (Nashville, TN: Broadman Press, 1933), Re 13:16.
[248] Masonic Dictionary, http://www.masonicdictionary.com/initiation.html Accessed November 5, 2017 (Dictionary n.d.).
[249] Wikipedia: Initiation, https://en.wikipedia.org/wiki/Initiation Accessed November 5, 2017
[250] Wikipedia: Initiation [Theosophy], https://en.wikipedia.org/wiki/Initiation%28Theosophy%29 Accessed November 5, 2017
[251] **Übermensch**

"The Übermensch (German for "Beyond-Man", "Superman", "Overman", "Superhuman", "Hyperman", "Hyperhuman"; German pronunciation: [ˈʔyːbɐmɛnʃ]) is a concept in the philosophy of Friedrich Nietzsche. In his 1883 book Thus Spoke Zarathustra (German: Also sprach Zarathustra), Nietzsche has his character Zarathustra posit the Übermensch as a goal for humanity to set for itself. It is a work of philosophical allegory, with a structural similarity to the Gathas of Zoroaster/Zarathustra.

This-worldliness

"Nietzsche introduces the concept of the Übermensch in contrast to his understanding of the other-worldliness of Christianity: Zarathustra proclaims the Übermensch to be the meaning of the earth and admonishes his audience to ignore those who promise other-worldly hopes in order to draw them away from the earth.[5][6] The turn away from the earth is prompted, he says, by a dissatisfaction with life—a dissatisfaction that causes one to create another world in which those who made one unhappy in this life are tormented. The Übermensch is not driven into other worlds away from this one.

"Zarathustra declares that the Christian escape from this world also required the invention of an eternal soul which would be separate from the body and survive the body's death. Part of other-worldliness, then, was the abnegation and mortification of the body, or asceticism. Zarathustra further links the Übermensch to the body and to interpreting the soul as simply an aspect of the body.

Death of God and the creation of new values

"Zarathustra ties the Übermensch to the death of God. While this God was the ultimate expression of other-worldly values and the instincts that gave birth to those values, belief in that God nevertheless did give meaning to life for a time. 'God is dead' means that the idea of God can no longer provide values. With the sole source of values no longer capable of providing those values, there is a real chance of nihilism prevailing.

"Zarathustra presents the Übermensch as the creator of new values. In this way, it appears as a solution to the problem of the death of God and nihilism. If the Übermensch acts to create new values within the moral vacuum of nihilism, there is nothing that this creative act would not justify. Alternatively, in the absence of this creation, there are no grounds upon which to criticize or justify any action, including the particular values created and the means by which they are promulgated.

"In order to avoid a relapse into Platonic idealism or asceticism, the creation of these new values cannot be motivated by the same instincts that gave birth to those tables of values. Instead, they must be motivated by a love of this world and of life. Whereas Nietzsche diagnosed the Christian value system as a reaction against life and hence destructive in a sense, the new values which the Übermensch will be responsible for will be life-affirming and creative (see Nietzschean affirmation). Wikipedia: =Übermensch, https://en.wikipedia.org/wiki/Übermensch Accessed November 5, 2017. (Wikipedia, Ubermensch n.d.)

[252] Gen 3.1b "And he said unto the woman..."

[253] Zane C. Hodges, "*The Greek Text of the King James Version*", Bibliotheca Sacra 125:500 (October 1968)

Zane C. Hodges, "*Modern Textual Criticism and The Majority Text: A Response,*" Journal of the Evangelical Theological Society 21:2, (June 1978)

Zane C. Hodges, "*Rationalism and Contemporary New Testament Textual Criticism,*" Bibliotheca Sacra 128:509 (Jan 1971)

[254] A Beginners Guide to Postmodernism, Phil Johnson, Audio Recording, http://teampyro.blogspot.com/2010/01/primer-on-postmodernism.html Accessed November 12, 2017

[255] *The Inerrancy of Scripture: The Fifty Years' War . . . and Counting*, Albert Mohler, https://albertmohler.com/2010/08/16/the-inerrancy-of-scripture-the-fifty-years-war-and-counting/ Accessed November 12, 2017, (Mohler 2010)

Harold Lindsell, "The Battle for the Bible" (Zondervan, 1978) (Lindsell 1978)

Biblical Inspiration, David Cloud Way of Life Literature, https://www.wayoflife.org/database/biblical_inspiration.html Accessed November 12, 2017

Neo-Orthodoxy, http://www.theopedia.com/neo-orthodoxy Accessed November 12, 2017

[256] "lest" 7153 פֶּן (pĕn): c.; ≡ Str 6435; TWOT 1780—1. LN 89.55–89.64 lest, so that not, i.e., a marker of a negative purpose, implying some apprehension or worry of a possible future event (Ge 3:22; Ps 2:12); 2. LN 89.139–89.140 or, otherwise, i.e., a marker of an alternative relation (Ex 5:3); 3. LN 71.1–71.10 might, would, i.e., a marker of a mode of possibility of an event (1Sa 27:11); 4. LN 69.2–69.6 not, i.e., a marker that negates a statement (Dt 4:23), note: further study may yield more domains

Swanson, James. *Dictionary of Biblical Languages with Semantic Domains: Hebrew (Old Testament)*. Oak Harbor: Logos Research Systems, Inc., 1997.

[257] The world is being prepared for the promise of this initiation in the explosion of films which feature super-powered individuals. I would expect that these powers will increasingly be identified with spiritual rather than natural origins. In any case, the new age movement has long anticipated what they call a new stage in human evolution. The quality of this leap forward is anticipated to be

technological, psychological and spiritual in character. These television programs and movies create a familiarity and expectation in the minds of the people of the world regarding that which the Antichrist and False Prophet will promise and to a degree, fulfill in this initiation.

[258] "**transhumanism**, social and philosophical movement devoted to promoting the research and development of robust human-enhancement technologies. Such technologies would augment or increase human sensory reception, emotive ability, or cognitive capacity as well as radically improve human health and extend human life spans. Such modifications resulting from the addition of biological or physical technologies would be more or less permanent and integrated into the human body."

"One prominent strain of transhumanism argues that social and cultural institutions—including national and international governmental organizations—will be largely irrelevant to the trajectory of technological development. Market forces and the nature of technological progress will drive humanity to approximately the same end point regardless of social and cultural influences. That end point is often referred to as the "singularity," a metaphor drawn from astrophysics and referring to the point of hyperdense material at the centre of a black hole which generates its intense gravitational pull. Among transhumanists, the singularity is understood as the point at which artificial intelligence surpasses that of humanity, which will allow the convergence of human and machine consciousness. That convergence will herald the increase in human consciousness, physical strength, emotional well-being, and overall health and greatly extend the length of human lifetimes." Hays, S. A.. "transhumanism." Encyclopedia Britannica, June 12, 2018. https://www.britannica.com/topic/transhumanism. (Hays 2018)

[259] Isa 47.7-12; Jer 51.7; Rev 17.2, 4

[260] Rev 17.3, 5, 8-14, 16-17

[261] Dan 2.38; Isa 13.19; 47.5

[262] Jer 51.13; Rev 17.1, 15

[263] Isa 13; Jer 50.8-13, 39-40; 51.26

[264] [Or, eastward, as ch. 13:11. 2 Sam. 6:2. with 1 Chr. 13:6.] But comp. ch. 12:8.
The Holy Bible: King James Version, Electronic Edition of the 1900 Authorized Version. (Bellingham, WA: Logos Research Systems, Inc., 2009).

[265] UR
"Of the Chaldees (Gen 11:28,31; 15:7; Neh 9:7), from which Terah, Abraham, and Lot were called. In Mesopotamia (Acts 7:2). Now Mugheir (a ruined temple of large bitumen bricks, which also "mugheir" means, namely, Um Mugheir "mother of bitumen") on the right bank of the Euphrates, near its junction with the Shat el Hie from the Tigris; in Chaldaea proper. Called Hur by the natives, and on monuments Ur. The most ancient city of the older Chaldaea. Its bricks bear the name of the earliest monumental kings, "Urukh king of Ur"; his kingdom extended as far N. as Niffer. The royal lists on the monuments enumerate Babylonian kings from Urukh (2230 B.C., possibly the Orchanus of Ovid, Met. 4:212) down to Nabonid (540 B.C.) the last. The temple was sacred to 'Urki, the moon goddess; Ilgi son of Urukh completed it. For two centuries it was the capital, and always was held sacred. One district was "Ibra," perhaps related to "Hebrew," Abraham's designation. Ur was also a cemetery and city of tombs, doubtless because of its sacred character, from whence the dead were brought to it from vast distances for 1,800 years. Eupolemos (in Eusebius, Praep. Ev. 9:17) refers to Ur as "the moon worshipping (kamarine; kamar being Arabic for moon) city." The derivation from

Ur, "fire," led to the Koran and Talmud legends that Abraham miraculously escaped out of the flames into which Nimrod or other idolatrous persecutors threw him. Ur lies six miles distant from the present coarse of the Euphrates, and 125 from the sea; though it is thought it was anciently a maritime town, and that its present inland site is due to the accumulation of alluvium (?). The buildings are of the most archaic kind, consisting of low mounds enclosed within an enceinte, on most sides perfect, an oval space 1,000 yards long by 800 broad. The temple is thoroughly Chaldaean in type, in stages of which two remain, of brick partly sunburnt, partly baked, cemented with bitumen.

Fausset, Andrew Robert. *FAUSSET'S Bible DICTIONARY* Electronic Database. Copyright © 1998, 2003, 2006 by Biblesoft, Inc. All rights reserved (Fausset 2006)

BABEL; BABYLON

"Babel (Hebrew) means Babylon; so that "the tower" should be designated "the tower of Babel." Capital of the country Shinar (Genesis), **Chaldea** (later Scriptures). The name as given by Nimrod (Gen 10:10), the founder, means (Bab-il), "the gate of the god Il," or simply "of God." Afterward the name was attached to it in another sense (Providence having ordered it so that a name should be given originally, susceptible of another sense, signifying the subsequent divine judgment), Gen 11:9; Babel from baalal , "to confound; .... because the Lord did there confound the language of all the earth," in order to counteract their attempt by a central city and tower to defeat God's purpose of the several tribes of mankind being "scattered abroad upon the face of the whole earth," and to constrain them, as no longer "understanding one another's speech," to disperse...."

Fausset, Andrew Robert. *FAUSSET'S Bible DICTIONARY* Electronic Database. Copyright © 1998, 2003, 2006 by Biblesoft, Inc. All rights reserved (Fausset 2006)

[266] Josh 24.2 c.f. Acts 17.16; 1 Cor 10.19-20; Rev 9.20

[267] Isaiah 13:19 And Babylon, the glory of kingdoms, the beauty of the Chaldees' excellency, shall be as when God overthrew Sodom and Gomorrah.

"[And Babylon] The great city of Babylon was at this time rising to its height of glory, while the Prophet Isaiah was repeatedly denouncing its utter destruction. From the first of Hezekiah to the first of Nebuchadnezzar, under whom it was brought to the highest degree of strength and splendour, are about one hundred and twenty years. I will here very briefly mention some particulars of the greatness of the place, and note the several steps by which this remarkable prophecy was at length accomplished in the total ruin of it.

"It was, according to the lowest account given of it by ancient historians, a regular square, forty-five miles in compass, enclosed by a wall two hundred feet high and fifty broad; in which there were a hundred gates of brass. Its principal ornaments were the temple of Belus, in the middle of which was a tower of eight stories of building, upon a base of a quarter of a mile square, a most magnificent palace, and the famous hanging gardens, which were an artificial mountain, raised upon arches, and planted with trees of the largest as well as the most beautiful sorts.

"Cyrus took the city by diverting the waters of the Euphrates which ran through the midst of it, and entering the place at night by the dry channel. The river being never restored afterward to its proper course, overflowed the whole country, and made it little better than a great morass; this and the great slaughter of the inhabitants, with other bad consequences of the taking of the city, was the first step to the ruin of the place. The Persian monarchs ever regarded it with a jealous eye; they kept it under, and took care to prevent its recovering its former greatness. Darius

Hystaspes not long afterward most severely punished it for a revolt, greatly depopulated the place, lowered the walls, and demolished the gates. Xerxes destroyed the temples, and with the rest the great temple of Belus, Herod. iii. 159, Arrian. Exp. Alexandri, lib. vii. The building of Seleucia on the Tigris exhausted Babylon by its neighbourhood, as well as by the immediate loss of inhabitants taken away by Seleucus to people his new city, Strabo, lib. xvi.

"A king of the Parthians soon after carried away into slavery a great number of the inhabitants, and burned and destroyed the most beautiful parts of the city, Valesii Excerpt. Diodori, p. 377. Strabo (ibid.) says that in his time great part of it was a mere desert; that the Persians had partly destroyed it; and that time and the neglect of the Macedonians, while they were masters of it, had nearly completed its destruction. Jerome (in loc.) says that in his time it was quite in ruins, and that the walls served only for the inclosure for a park or forest for the king's hunting. Modern travelers, who have endeavoured to find the remains of it, have given but a very unsatisfactory account of their success. What Benjamin of Tudela and Pietro della Valle supposed to have been some of its ruins, Tavernier thinks are the remains of some late Arabian building. Upon the whole, Babylon is so utterly annihilated, that even the place where this wonder of the world stood cannot now be determined with any certainty!

Adam Clarke's Commentary, Electronic Database. Copyright © 1996, 2003, 2005, 2006 by Biblesoft, Inc. All rights reserved.) Isaiah 13.19 (Clarke 2006)

[268] In Isaiah 14, a prophecy concerning Babylon and its king is mingled with a prophecy concerning one who's aspirations are superimposed upon the earthly kingdom and betray a supernatural and prehistoric ambition not possible for a mortal king.

Isaiah 14:4 (KJV 1900)
4 That thou shalt take up this proverb against the king of Babylon, and say, How hath the oppressor ceased! the golden city ceased!

Isaiah 14:12–14 (KJV 1900)
12 How art thou fallen from heaven, O Lucifer, son of the morning! How art thou cut down to the ground, which didst weaken the nations! 13 For thou hast said in thine heart, I will ascend into heaven, I will exalt my throne above the stars of God: I will sit also upon the mount of the congregation, in the sides of the north: 14 I will ascend above the heights of the clouds; I will be like the most High.

Lucifer

"light bringer", "the morning star": Isaiah 14:12 (helel , "spreading brightness".) Symbol of the once bright but now fallen king of Babylon. The title belongs of right to Christ (Revelation 22:16), therefore about to be assumed by antichrist, of whom Babylon is type and mystical Babylon the forerunner (Revelation 17:4-5). The language is primarily drawn from that of Satan himself, the spirit that energized the pagan world power Babylon, that now energizes the apostate Church, and shall at last energize the last secular antichrist..."

Fausset, Andrew Robert. FAUSSET'S Bible DICTIONARY Electronic Database. Copyright © 1998, 2003, 2006 by Biblesoft, Inc. All rights reserved. Art. Lucifer

Lucifer is identified with Babylon. The aims of Lucifer coincide with those of Babylon, which said "I am and no other" [Isa 45.22 c.f. Isa 14.14].

[269] Dan 9.24; Mt 4.5

[270] "Beginning with verse 36, a sharp break in the prophecy may be observed, introduced by the expression the time of the end in verse 35. Up to this point, the prophecy dealing with the Persian and Grecian Empires has been fulfilled minutely and with amazing precision. Beginning with verse 36, however, an entirely different situation obtains. No commentator claims to find precise fulfillment in the remainder of this chapter. Although Zockler and others attempt to relate Daniel 11:36–45 to Antiochus, many students of Scripture have recognized from antiquity that another king must be in view. Ibn-Ezra, for example, identified this king with Constantine the Great; Rashi and Calvin referred him to the Roman Empire as a whole; and Jerome, Theodoret, and Luther, among others, identified him with the New Testament Antichrist. In contrast to the preceding section, there is no specific correspondence to history. Accordingly, scholars who regard this as genuine Scripture, usually regard this section as future and unfulfilled."
Walvoord, John F., *Daniel: The Key To Prophetic Revelation* (Galaxie Software, 2008), 270.

[271] Zech 8.3

[272] Rev 18.2, 10, 16, 18-19 etc.

[273] "Kurzweil: Essays" Kurzweil's Law (aka "the law of accelerating returns") January 12, 2004, by Ray Kurzweil https://www.kurzweilai.net/kurzweils-law-aka-the-law-of-accelerating-returns Accessed June 25, 2022. See also "Moore's Law" https://en.wikipedia.org/wiki/Moore%27s_law Accessed June 25, 2022.

[274] "colon" "noun, plural co·lons for 1, co·la [koh-luh] for 2.
the sign (:) used to mark a major division in a sentence, to indicate that what follows is an elaboration, summation, implication, etc., of what precedes;" Dictionary.com
https://www.dictionary.com/browse/colon Accessed July, 16, 2022

[275] Chapter 29, section-The Armageddon Campaign

[276] Pg. 148

[277] Ex. Isa 47.1-5; Jer 50.14-15, 42; 51.33

[278] Pink, Arthur Walkington. *The Antichrist: [A Study of Satan's Christ]*. (Blackburg, VA: Wilder Publications, 2008).

[279] Manly P. Hall
"There are, however, but few mature minds in the world; and thus it was that the philosophic-religious doctrines of the pagans were divided to meet the needs of these two fundamental groups of human intellect--one philosophic, the other incapable of appreciating the deeper mysteries of life. To the discerning few were revealed the esoteric, or spiritual, teachings, while the unqualified many received only the literal, or exoteric, interpretations. In order to make simple the great truths of Nature and the abstract principles of natural law, the vital forces of the universe were personified, becoming the gods and goddesses of the ancient mythologies. While the ignorant multitudes brought their offerings to the altars of Priapus and Pan (deities representing the procreative energies), the wise recognized in these marble statues only symbolic concretions of great abstract truths.
"In all cities of the ancient world were temples for public worship and offering. In every community also were philosophers and mystics, deeply versed in Nature's lore. These individuals were usually banded together, forming seclusive philosophic and religious schools. The more important of these groups were known as the Mysteries. Many of the great minds of antiquity were initiated into these secret fraternities by strange and mysterious rites, some of which were extremely cruel.

Alexander Wilder defines the Mysteries as "Sacred dramas performed at stated periods. The most celebrated were those of Isis, Sabazius, Cybele, and Eleusis." After being admitted, the initiates were instructed in the secret wisdom which had been preserved for ages. Plato, an initiate of one of these sacred orders, was severely criticized because in his writings he revealed to the public many of the secret philosophic principles of the Mysteries.

"Every pagan nation had (and has) not only its state religion, but another into which the philosophic elect alone have gained entrance. Many of these ancient cults vanished from the earth without revealing their secrets, but a few have survived the test of ages and their mysterious symbols are still preserved. Much of the ritualism of Freemasonry is based on the trials to which candidates were subjected by the ancient hierophants before the keys of wisdom were entrusted to them."

Hall, Manly P. The Secret Teaching of All Ages, (1928) http://www.sacred-texts.com/eso/sta/sta04.htm Accessed October 17, 2018 p. 21 (Hall n.d.)

Albert G. Mackey

"Before proceeding to an examination of those Mysteries which are the most closely connected with the masonic institution, it will be as well to take a brief view of their general organization. The secret worship, or Mysteries, of the ancients were always divided into the lesser and the greater; the former being intended only to awaken curiosity, to test the capacity and disposition of the candidate, and by symbolical purifications to prepare him for his introduction into the greater Mysteries. The candidate was at first called an aspirant, or seeker of the truth, and the initial ceremony which he underwent was a lustration or purification by water. In this condition he may be compared to the Entered Apprentice of the masonic rites, and it is here worth adverting to the fact (which will be hereafter more fully developed) that all the ceremonies in the first degree of masonry are symbolic of an internal purification. In the lesser Mysteries24 the candidate took an oath of secrecy, which was administered to him by the mystagogue, and then received a preparatory instruction,25 which enabled him afterwards to understand the developments of the higher and subsequent division. He was now called a Mystes, or initiate, and may be compared to the Fellow Craft of Freemasonry. In the greater Mysteries the whole knowledge of the divine truths, which was the object of initiation, was communicated. Here we find, among the various ceremonies which assimilated these rites to Freemasonry, the aphanism, which was the disappearance or death; the pastos, the couch, coffin, or grave; the euresis, or the discovery of the body; and the autopsy, or full sight of everything, that is, the complete communication of the secrets. The candidate was here called an epopt, or eye-witness, because nothing was now hidden from him; and hence he may be compared to the Master Mason, of whom Hutchinson says that "he has discovered the knowledge of God and his salvation, and been redeemed from the death of sin and the sepulchre of pollution and unrighteousness." Albert Gallatin Mackey. The Symbolism of Freemasonry / Illustrating and Explaining Its Science and Philosophy, Its Legends, Myths and Symbols (Kindle Locations 411-426). (Mackey 1882)

Albert Pike

"Socrates said, in the Phaedo of Plato: "It well appears that those who established the Mysteries, or secret assemblies of the initiated, were no contemptible personages, but men of great genius, who in the early ages strove to teach us, under enigmas, that he who shall go to the invisible regions without being punfied[sic],will be precipitated into the abyss; while he who arrives there, purged of the stains of this world, and accomplished in virtue, will be admitted to the dwelling-place of the Deity. The initiated are certain to attain the company of the Gods." Pretextatus, Proconsul of Achaia, a man endowed with all the virtues, said, in the 4th century, that to deprive the Greeks of those Sacred Mysteries which bound together the whole human race, would make life insupportable. Initiation was considered to be a mystical death; a descent into the infernal regions, where every pollution, and the stains and imperfection's of a corrupt and evil life were purged away by fire and water; and the perfect Epopt was then said to be regenerated, new-born, restored to a renovated existence of life, light, and purity; and placed under the Divine Protection." Pike, Albert. Morals and Dogma of the Ancient and Accepted Scottish Rite of Freemasonry," 1871. 248-249

[280] "'Thee,' says Martianus Capella, in his hymn to the Sun, 'dwellers on the Nile adore as Serapis, and Memphis worships as Osiris: in the sacred rites of Persia thou art Mithras, in Phrygia, Atys, and Libya bows down to thee as Ammon, and Phœnician Byblos as Adonis; thus the whole world adores thee under different names.'"
Pike, Albert., *Morals and Dogma*, (1871) 587-588 cited in Hall, Manly P. *The Secret Teaching of All Ages*, (1928) http://www.sacred-texts.com/eso/sta/sta04.htm [Accessed October 17, 2018] 28.

[281] "The Egyptian secret school of philosophy was divided into the Lesser and the Greater Mysteries, the former being sacred to Isis and the latter to Serapis and Osiris. Wilkinson is of the opinion that only the priests were permitted to enter the Greater Mysteries. Even the heir to the throne was not eligible until he had been crowned Pharaoh, when, by virtue of his kingly office, he automatically became a priest and the temporal head of the state religion. (See Wilkinson's Manners and Customs of the Egyptians.) A limited number were admitted into the Greater Mysteries: these preserved their secrets inviolate."
Hall, Manly P. *"Secret Teachings of All Ages: The Ancient Mysteries and Secret Societies Which Have Influenced Modern Masonic Symbolism."* http://www.sacred-texts.com/eso/sta/sta04.htm. Accessed November 14, 2018.

[282] Gen 15.16; Gen 18:17-19.29; Isa 13.19-20; 23.1; Nahum; etc.

[283] Prov 11.10-11; 14.34; Mt 13.13-16

[284] The primary source of the calibration of the conscience is nature or the Creation Rom 1.18-21.

[285] "But the language applied to the New Testament Babylon, as the reader cannot fail to see, naturally leads us back to the Babylon of the ancient world. As the Apocalyptic woman has in her hand A CUP, wherewith she intoxicates the nations, so was it with the Babylon of old. Of that Babylon, while in all its glory, the Lord thus spake, in denouncing its doom by the prophet Jeremiah: "Babylon hath been a GOLDEN CUP in the Lord's hand, that made all the earth drunken: the nations have drunken of her wine; therefore the nations are mad" (Jer 51:7). Why this exact similarity of language in regard to the two systems? The natural inference surely is, that the one stands to the other in the relation of type and antitype. Now, as the Babylon of the Apocalypse is characterised by the name of "MYSTERY," so the grand distinguishing feature of the ancient Babylonian system was the Chaldean "MYSTERIES," that formed so essential a part of that system. And to these mysteries, the very language of the Hebrew prophet, symbolical though of course it is, distinctly alludes, when he speaks of Babylon as a "golden CUP." To drink of "mysterious

beverages," says Salverte, was indispensable on the part of all who sought initiation in these Mysteries. These "mysterious beverages" were composed of "wine, honey, water, and flour." From the ingredients avowedly used, and from the nature of others not avowed, but certainly used, there can be no doubt that they were of an intoxicating nature; and till the aspirants had come under their power, till their understandings had been dimmed, and their passions excited by the medicated draught, they were not duly prepared for what they were either to hear or to see." Hislop, Alexander. *The Two Babylons*. (Chino, CA: Chick Publications, 1998). 9 (Hislop 1998)

"But the testimony of Clement of Alexandria and others is that they [the Mysteries-rw] were based upon the adulterous and incestuous acts of Zeus and Demeter, and commemorated the obscenity and indecencies of these deities, which were enacted in realistic form before the neophyte...In the great Dionysiac festival in Athens, the phallus was solemnly carried in procession. The mystic chest or box answers to the yoni as the phallys to the linga of the Hindoos. (Encl. Brit., Vol 8, p.120, 9th Ed.). The password or token of recognition of those initiated into the Eleusinian mysteries was 'I have fasted, I have drunk the cup, I have received from the box, having done, I put it into the basket and out of the basket into the chest" (Clement, Exhor. To the Heathen Chap. 2)" Wagner, Martin L. *Freemasonry Interpreted*. (New York: A&B Publishers Group, 2000). (Wagner 2000)

[286] "Every initiated witch must be involved with astrology and other occult practices and must participate in the "Great Rite" which is ritual sexual intercourse invoking the forces of the universe and drawing down the moon"

Burns, Cathy. *Hidden Secrets of the Eastern Star: The Masonic Connection*. (Mt. Carmel, Pa: Sharing, 1994). 175 (Burns 1994)

[287] Jn 8.44; Eph 2.1-3; 1Jn 5.19

[288] Rev 14.8; 17.2

[289] Kenneth S. Wuest, *Wuest's Word Studies from the Greek New Testament: For the English Reader, vol. 2* (Grand Rapids: Eerdmans, 1997), 207.

[290] Also: Abomination-Men taking upon themselves the prerogatives of God: Dan 9.27; 11.31; 12.11; Mt 24.15; Mk 13.14; Rev 17.4-5 [Mother of Harlots]

[291] The Religion Book: Places, Prophets, Saints, and Seers. s.v. "ecumenism." http://encyclopedia2.thefreedictionary.com/ecumenism Accessed June 12 2017

[292] Britannica, T. Editors of Encyclopaedia. "ecumenism." Encyclopedia Britannica, https://www.britannica.com/topic/ecumenism. Accessed July 18, 2018

[293] http://saddleback.com/connect/ministry/the-peace-plan Accessed June 13, 2017 Also, Way of Life Literature: Rick Warren's P.E.A.C.E. Plan
https://www.wayoflife.org/database/peaceplan.html Accessed June 13, 2017

[294] The Columbia Electronic Encyclopedia®. S.v. "Social Gospel." http://encyclopedia2.thefreedictionary.com/Social+Gospel Accessed June 12, 2017

[295] Chapter I Catholic Principles On Ecumenism
"Unitatis Redintegratio.".

http://www.vatican.va/archive/hist_councils/ii_vatican_council/documents/vat-ii_decree_19641121_unitatis-redintegratio_en.html. I.2 [Accessed December 9, 2018] (V. II 1964)
[296] https://www.catholic.com/magazine/print-edition/can-non-christians-be-saved [Accessed June 13, 2017]. Also http://www.vatican.va/archive/hist_councils/ii_vatican_council/documents/vat-ii_decl_19651028_nostra-aetate_en.html Accessed June 13, 2017
[297] The theology of Roman Catholicism lends itself to the ecumenical effort since it claims to be the only "help towards" salvation.
United States Catholic Conference Inc., *Catechism of the Catholic Church for the United States of America, Second Edition*, (New York; Doubleday, 1994) 234-235
[298] http://www.catholicnewsagency.com/news/evangelizing-evangelicals-why-pope-francis-loves-to-meet-with-charismatic-movements-66914/
Also
https://cruxnow.com/Church-in-the-usa/2016/10/17/pentecostal-promotes-pope-calls-walking-ecumenism/ Accessed June 13, 2017
[299] http://www.nsc-chariscenter.org/about-ccr/ Accessed June 13, 2017
[300] Spence, O. Tallmadge. *Charismatism: Awakening or Apostasy*, (Bob Jones University Press, 1978). 115 (T. O. Spence 1978)
[301] "The Ecumenical Movement Part 1 -- By: Rene Pache | Galaxie Software." http://www.galaxie.com/article/bsac107-427-10. Accessed June 14, 2017.
[302] Hunt, Dave,. *A Woman Rides the Beast: The Roman Catholic Church and the Last Days*. (Eugene Oregon: Harvest House Publishers, 1994). 416-420
[303] https://www.oikoumene.org/en/what-we-do/wcc-un-office-new-york Accessed June 13, 2017.
[304] "This liberty of interpretation is also evident from the fact that the preparation of the various ecumenical conferences has been entrusted each time to hundreds of theologians representing the main theological points of view: Unitarians, liberals, Barthians, evangelicals, Greek Orthodox, etc. Thus the ecumenical movement places itself on an entirely different basis than that of faith in the plenary inspiration of the scriptures. Elie Gounelle, one of the leaders of French ecumenicalism, writes in this regard: "It would be impossible to impose on everyone in a universal Church the errors and the superstitions of that literalism which accompanies belief in plenary inspiration.... We know that the ecumenical leaders respect, in their place, the sacred rights of scientific and historical criticism."9"
"The Ecumenical Movement Part 1 -- By: Rene Pache | Galaxie Software." Accessed June 14, 2017. http://www.galaxie.com/article/bsac107-427-10.
[305] Acts 20.29-31; Gal 1.18; 1Tim 4.1-3; Tit 1.10-11; 2 Pet 2.1; 2 Jn 7-11; Rev 2.2, 6, 14-16, 20-22
[306] "The Ecumenical Movement Part 1 -- By: Rene Pache | Galaxie Software." Accessed June 14, 2017. http://www.galaxie.com/article/bsac107-427-10.
[307] This is seen in the ecumenical character of Rick Warren's P.E.A.C.E. Plan. He clearly assents to the Vatican II ecumenical emphasis upon pluralism and service-orientation. The following is a quote from Rick Warren at the Pew Forum in 2005:
"You know, 500 years ago, the first Reformation with Luther and then Calvin, was about beliefs. I think a new reformation is going to be about behavior. The first Reformation was about creeds; I think this one will be about deeds. I think the first one was about what the Church believes; I think

this one will be about what the Church does.

"The first Reformation actually split Christianity into dozens and then hundreds of different segments. I think this one is actually going to bring them together. Now, you're never going to get Christians, of all their stripes and varieties, to agree on all of the different doctrinal disputes and things like that, but what I am seeing them agree on are the purposes of the Church. And I find great uniformity in the fact that I see this happening all the time. Last week I spoke to 4,000 pastors at my Church who came from over 100 denominations in over 50 countries. Now, that's wide spread. We had Catholic priests, we had Pentecostal ministers, we had Lutheran bishops, we had Anglican bishops, we had Baptist preachers. They're all there together and you know what? I'd never get them to agree on communion or baptism or a bunch of stuff like that, but I could get them to agree on what the Church should be doing in the world."

"ELSA WALSH, THE NEW YORKER: So are you saying doctrine won't be important or is not important if you bring together all these –

MR. WARREN: No, no. I think, though, it's what Augustine said: "In the essentials, unity; in the non-essentials, liberty; and in all things, charity." And I think that's how evangelicals and Catholics can get together. And I don't know if you know this or not, but fundamentalists and Pentecostals don't like each other, okay? They don't. But they could get together. "In the essentials, unity; in the non-essentials, liberty; in all things, charity."

SARAH WILDMAN, THE AMERICAN PROSPECT: I'll try to be quick, although I think my two or three questions are sort of unconnected. What about people who don't have Jesus in their lives, if you could address that sort of generally, and then also, do you see this Reformation involving conversion? And then also, how do you see people responding to this in the wake of, say, the tsunami this year? How dose the purpose-driven life connect to natural disaster?

MR. WARREN: Before you go to the third, let me answer those two. First, on the answer to the first one, everybody is betting their life on something. Every one of you are betting your life on something. You're all doing it. Every one of you are betting your life on something. I'm betting my life that Jesus was right when he said, "No one comes to the Father but by me." **Now, I may be wrong**, but I'm betting my life that he knew more about it than I do. And that's all I can say. [emphasis added]

"Myths of the Modern MegaChurch | Pew Research Center.".
http://www.pewforum.org/2005/05/23/myths-of-the-modern-megaChurch/. Accessed June 21, 2017. (Center 2005)

[308] "But if any one fact is clear, on the basis of this evidence, it is that the Christian movement at its inception was not just a way of life in the modern sense, but a way of life founded upon a message. It was based, not upon mere feeling, not upon a mere program of work, but upon an account of facts. In other words it was based upon doctrine."
Machen, J. Gresham. *Christianity and Liberalism* (Kindle Locations 316-319). Kindle Edition. (Machen n.d.)

"The growth of ignorance in the Church is the logical and inevitable result of the false notion that

Christianity is a life and not also a doctrine;" ibid. (Kindle Locations 2454-2455).
[309] "Much of the responsibility for the growing partnership with Catholicism lies with certain leaders in the charismatic movement. Charismatics were the first to hold joint Protestant-Catholic conferences and to accept one another as Christians. About 10 million Catholics in America and 72 million in 163 countries worldwide now [1994-rw] "speak in tongues." That alleged ability was taken as proof by other Charismatics that Catholics must be born again."
Hunt, Dave. *A Woman Rides the Beast: The Roman Catholic Church and the Last Days*. (Eugene Oregon: Harvest House Publishers, 1994). 430
[310] The cry of "paper pope" has been shouted at evangelical Protestants ever since the Reformation. Today, however, one observes with amazement and with sorrow that in the very orthodox circles where the twentieth-century battle for biblical authority has been most courageously fought, voices are being raised against the inerrancy of Holy Writ. Biblical Seminary in New York, an evangelical center, where brilliant pioneering techniques of inductive Bible study were developed, saw the 1963 publication of Dewey M. Beegle's The Inspiration of Scripture, in which that faculty member having embraced Neo-Orthodox, dialectic presuppositions as to the nature of truth—imposes them on Scripture, denies its inerrancy, and makes the incredible claim that evangelicals by a "mental readjustment" can now retain inspiration without inerrancy and thereby rejoin mainline Protestant-ecumenical theology.
"Guest Editorial -- By: John Warwick Montgomery | Galaxie Software."
http://www.galaxie.com/article/jets08-4-01?highlight=inerrancy%20and%20ecumenism. Accessed June 14, 2017.
[311] "Having now named and pinpointed what Fundamentalism is we would like to address ourselves in the same manner to ecumenicity. We hold in our hands a stenographic report of Dr. E. Stanley Jones' address which we heard given February 3, 1937, in St. Paul's Methodist Church of Cedar Rapids, Iowa…In the same message he named the goal and purpose of ecumenicity. The goal and purpose was to establish "the kingdom of God on earth." To establish this he kept emphasizing, to use his own words, "We are in the death clutch of the old order and in the birth of a new." He further said, "We must take off all reserve and believe in the kingdom of God on earth." Again he said, "We mean that here and now we are going to make a new order — and let God invade us," Again he said, "Are you big enough to do this? We must make our social order truly Christian."
"Fundamentalists And Ecumenicity -- By: Richard V. Clearwaters | Galaxie Software." Accessed June 14, 2017. http://www.galaxie.com/article/cenq02-1-03?highlight=ecumenism%20and%20the%20kingdom%20of%20god.

"In the 1930's this same concept of ecumenism and the Kingdom of God on earth, was embellished by the idea that the New World Order itself would be the mechanism by which the Kingdom of God Would be introduced and that the ecumenical movement w would be heralds of this necessity."
Erdmann, Martin. *Ecumenical Quest for a World Federation: The Churches' Contribution to Marshal Public Support for World Order and Peace, 1919-1945*, (Verax Vox Media, Greenville S.C. 2016). 84-80
[312] "According to many Protestant writers, Roman Catholicism is seriously mistaken in making faith a mere intellectual assent to certain dogmas. Faith, true faith in Christ, these writers say, is a personal trust rather than a cold intellectual belief. On the other side, the Catholic Encyclopedia (in loc. cit., p. 752, 1913 ed.) states "Non-Catholic writers have repudiated all idea of faith as

intellectual assent." The truth of the matter, however, seems to be more complicated than these brief characterizations suggest.

"These complications include the uncritical assumption that personality should be divided into intellect, will and emotion rather than into id, ego and superego. Granted the Freudian division may have an evil odor, but its very recognition of an evil nature in man could be closer to the biblical view than the other division allows. For the older division is not self-evidently scriptural. At any rate, those who use it often assume that intellect, will and emotion may be equated with specific biblical terms, when a study of the Bible shows that this is not so.

THE HEAD AND THE HEART

"The key term of biblical psychology, particularly in the Old Testament where the fundamental principles are laid down, is the term heart. When contemporary Christians, often in evangelistic preaching, contrast the head and the heart, they are in effect equating the heart with the emotions. Such an antithesis between head and heart is nowhere found in Scripture. In the Psalms and the Prophets the heart designates the focus of personal life. It is the organ of conscience, of self-knowledge, indeed of all knowledge. One may very well say that the Hebrew heart is the equivalent of the English word self..."

"...But this is not Christianity. Christianity includes the primacy of the intellect and the sovereign claims of truth. There is no distinction between the head and the heart, no depreciation of intellectual belief. Christianity cannot exist without the truth of certain definite historical propositions."

"Faith and Reason by Gordon H. Clark | The Gordon H. Clark Foundation." Accessed June 14, 2017. http://gordonhclark.reformed.info/faith-and-reason-by-gordon-h-clark/. (Clark n.d.)

[313] 1 Cor 14.14-15 Is the unfruitful mind the desired state of worship?

1. God fully expects our commitment and love for Him to originate in our minds. He demands the mental focus of man upon Himself: Mt 22.37; Ps 7.9 c.f., Rev 2.23
2. The spiritual identity of a person is demonstrated by his thinking: 1Sam 16.7; Ps 14.1; Pr 27.19; Mt 12.34;
3. Thinking is an essential factor in spiritual function, without it there is no understanding, no faith, and no godliness: Ps 119.9, 11; Prov 4.23; Rom 12.1-2; Php 4.8; Col 3.2
4. The Word of God, the Holy Spirit and the Human Mind may combine to produce Spiritual Understanding: 1Cor 2.9-12, 16
5. The target of Gods communication with man is the human mind: Jeremiah 31.33 c.f. Heb 4.12; Heb 8.10-11

[314] "Unity taken by faith. In spite of the foregoing it is understood that the boasted unity has not yet been realized. From a logical point of view it is impossible to have unity without truth, since truth is not contradictory. Thus the issue cannot be a human one: the Holy Spirit it is who will bring to pass the unity desired. One must believe in unity, then, as a miracle which God will perform.

"W. A. Visser't Hooft writes concerning this: "Such is the dilemma which dominates the existence of the council—the member Churches together are not yet capable of being the united Church of God, but neither are they able to regard the other Churches affiliated with the council as outside of the Church of God. Incapable of union, they are equally incapable of separating from one another. They know that there is no unity without truth, but they know equally well that the truth requires

unity. Does the dilemma have a solution? There is only one solution, faith…. Its point of departure is the certainty that the unity of the Church is the responsibility of the Lord of the Church."
"The Ecumenical Movement Part 1 -- By: Rene Pache | Galaxie Software.".
http://www.galaxie.com/article/bsac107-427-10. Accessed June 14, 2017
315 Ibid pg. 365
316 "Pope Francis Sends Video Message to Kenneth Copeland - Lets Unite - YouTube." Accessed June 15, 2017. https://www.youtube.com/watch?v=uA4EPOfic5A. (Pope 2014)

Also,

"Much of the responsibility for the growing partnership with Catholicism lies with certain leaders in the charismatic movement. Charismatics were the first to hold joint Protestant-Catholic conferences and to accept one another as Christians. About 10 million Catholics in America and 72 million in 163 countries worldwide now [1994-rw] "speak in tongues." That alleged ability was taken as proof by other Charismatics that Catholics must be born again."
Dave Hunt. *A Woman Rides the Beast: The Roman Catholic Church and the Last Days*. (Harvest House Publishers, Eugene Oregon, 1994) 430 (Hunt 1994).
Also,

"In spite of their gross theological error, charismatics demand acceptance within mainstream evangelicalism. And evangelicals have largely succumbed to those demands, responding with outstretched arms and a welcoming smile. In so doing, mainstream evangelicalism has unwittingly invited an enemy into the camp. The gates have been flung open to a Trojan horse of subjectivism, experientialism, ecumenical compromise, and heresy. Those who compromise in this way are playing with strange fire and placing themselves in grave danger."
MacArthur, John F.. Strange Fire: The Danger of Offending the Holy Spirit with Counterfeit Worship (p. xiv). Thomas Nelson. Kindle Edition. (J. F. MacArthur Kindle Edition)
317 John MacArthur. "What's So Dangerous About the Emerging Church?" Accessed June 17, 2017. https://www.gty.org/library/sermons-library/GTY107. See also: David W. Cloud. *The Emerging Church Is Coming*. (Way of Life Literature, 2009).
318 Scripture can be debased by misconstruing their meaning, or by the consistent misapplication of their truth. False religion may be introduced piecemeal by the gradual introduction of destructive heresies, or more directly by carpet bombing Christianity via a direct attack upon the infallibility and inerrancy of the bible ["hath *God* said?" Gen 3.1]. False religion also results from an unwillingness to properly apply a true doctrine, for example: Churches which fail to teach the biblical concept of sanctification with respect to racial prejudice and discrimination.
319 International Mission Board Drops Ban on Speaking in Tongues-New rules also loosen restrictions on baptism, divorce, and parents of teenagers.
Bob Smietana, Christianity Today, MAY 14, 2015. https://www.christianitytoday.com/ct/2015/may-web-only/imb-ban-speaking-in-tongues-baptism-baptist-missionary.html Accessed August 20, 2018. (Smietana 2015)

Also

McKissic wants SBC to address 'tongues' in Baptist Faith & Message,

Robert Marus, Associated Baptist Press https://www.baptiststandard.com/archives/2006-archives/mckissic-wants-sbc-to-address-tongues-in-baptist-faith-aamp-message/ Accessed August 20, 2018.

[320] Standing Together, Standing Apart: Cultural Co-Belligerence Without Theological Compromise, The Southern Baptist Journal of Theology, R. Albert Mohler Jr., December 25, 2001, (Mohler Jr. 2001)

This article is an example of the principle of compromising doctrine, while claiming not to, in the interest of impacting culture, as if God needed the help of those who openly reject His Word. Mohler concludes his paper with the following thought on "co-belligerency:"

"Seventh, we must be ready to stand together in cultural co-belligerence, rooted in a common core of philosophical and theological principles, without demanding confessional agreement or pretending that this has been achieved. We must contend for the right of Christian moral witness in secular society."

The late John Robbins commented upon the concept of co-belligerency in a paper entitled "Bleating Wolves-The Meaning of Evangelicals and Catholics Together"

"[Charles] Colson goes on to say, **after asserting that Protestants and Romanists have fundamental doctrines in common**, that we should put aside the remaining minor doctrines and unite to fight secularism. Why Colson finds secularism a greater threat than false religions, I do not know. The greatest enemies of Christianity have always been false religions. It was not secularists who crucified Christ; it was false religionists. It was not secularists who persecuted Christians in the first century; it was false religionists. It was not secularists who ruined ancient Israel; it was false religionists. The ancient prophets denounced the false religions of their times. Quite frankly, friends, the eighteenth century Enlightenment did less harm to Christianity than Romanism or twentieth century modernism. Colson, being a political animal, calls for a united front against the barbarians scaling the walls. He denies that the barbarians are already within the walls, that barbarians ruled and ruined virtually all the Churches for a thousand years – and for the past 500 years, most of the Churches professing to be Christian. If we are going to make alliances for political purposes, why should Christians not ally themselves with secularists to protect ourselves against the growing power of the Roman State-Church? But of course all such alliances – whether with false religionists or secularists – are forbidden by Scripture. Had Charles Colson lived in the first century, he would have scolded Paul for criticizing and cursing the Judaizers. After all, the Judaizers agreed on most fundamental doctrines with the Galatians and even with Paul, and their help was needed to fight the pagan barbarians assaulting Western civilization. What was Paul thinking? Surely he should have agreed at least to **a co-belligerency** (to use the late Francis Schaeffer's phrase) with the Judaizers against the pagans. Instead, Paul cursed the Judaizers over some minor point of doctrine like justification and divided the fledgling and struggling Church, even though the Judaizers believed in God, the deity of Christ, his birth of a virgin, his return to Earth, and the authority of the Scriptures. We have no reason to doubt that the Judaizers believed the fundamental doctrines that Colson says Romanists and Protestants have in common. Paul, judged by Colson's standards, was a divisive fool. Paul not only did not seek a co-belligerency with the Judaizers, he did not seek to co-evangelize the world with them. Paul missed the opportunity to construct a united front in the culture wars of his day. Had Paul done so, Western Civilization might

have been saved and the Roman Empire might never have fallen to the barbarians scaling the walls. If we accept Colson's premises and argument, we must conclude that Edward Gibbon and the pagan Romans were right, and Augustine was wrong: The fall of Rome was indeed the fault of the Christians." [emphasis mine rw]
BLEATING WOLVES THE MEANING OF EVANGELICALS AND CATHOLICS TOGETHER A Paper Presented at The Trinity Foundation Conference on Christianity and Roman Catholicism October 8, 1998 John W. Robbins. (Robbins 1998)

[321] David W. Cloud. *Evangelicals and Rome*. (Way of Life Literature, 1999).7-41 (Cloud, Evangelicals and Rome 1999)

[322] David W. Cloud. *New Evangelicalism: Its History, Characteristics, and Fruit*. (Way of Life Literature, 2006). (Cloud, New Evangelicalism: Its History, Characteristics, and Fruit. 2006)

[323] This event will not signal the end of the activity of the Holy Spirit upon the earth, but a change in His dispensational ministry. Just as the formation of the Church at Pentecost was a change in the ministry of the Spirit from that of the Age of Israel [1 Cor 12.13], so also the absence of the Body of Christ will result in yet another change in His operations here on earth. The immediate result of this change will be the escalation of the Satan's plans to install a visible earthly kingdom.

[324] "delusion v11" 31.8 πλανάω; πλάνηα, ης f: (figurative extensions of meaning of πλανάω 'to cause to wander off the path,' not occurring in the NT) to cause someone to hold a wrong view and thus be mistaken—'to mislead, to deceive, deception, to cause to be mistaken.'2 Johannes P. Louw and Eugene Albert Nida, *Greek-English Lexicon of the New Testament: Based on Semantic Domains* (New York: United Bible Societies, 1996), 364–366.

[325] "The Ecumenical Movement Part 2 -- By: Rene Pache | Galaxie Software." Accessed June 22, 2017. http://www.galaxie.com/article/bsac107-428-05. 371-373 (Pache, The Ecumenical Movement Part 2 1951).

[326] The Joint Declaration on the Doctrine of Justification (JDDJ) is a document created, and agreed to, by the Catholic Church's Pontifical Council for Promoting Christian Unity (PCPCU) and the Lutheran World Federation in 1999, as a result of extensive ecumenical dialogue. It states that the Churches now share "a common understanding of our justification by God's grace through faith in Christ."[1] To the parties involved, this essentially resolves the five-hundred-year-old conflict over the nature of justification which was at the root of the Protestant Reformation. The World Methodist Council has also adopted the document. [2][3]
"Joint Declaration on the Doctrine of Justification - Wikipedia." Accessed June 15, 2017. https://en.wikipedia.org/wiki/Joint_Declaration_on_the_Doctrine_of_Justification. (Wikipedia, The Joint Declaration on the Doctrine of Justification n.d.)
Also,

"Evangelicals & Catholics Together: The Christian Mission in the Third Millennium by Various | Articles | First Things." Accessed June 22, 2017.
https://www.firstthings.com/article/1994/05/evangelicals-catholics-together-the-christian-mission-in-the-third-millennium. (Various n.d.)

[327] Canon 7. If anyone says that all works done before justification, in whatever manner they may be done, are truly sins, or merit the hatred of God; that the more earnestly one strives to dispose himself for grace, the more grievously he sins, let him be anathema.

Canon 9. If anyone says that the sinner is justified by faith alone,[114] meaning that nothing else is required to cooperate in order to obtain the grace of justification, and that it is not in any way necessary that he be prepared and disposed by the action of his own will, let him be anathema. Canon 11. If anyone says that men are justified either by the sole imputation of the justice of Christ or by the sole remission of sins, to the exclusion of the grace and the charity which is poured forth in their hearts by the Holy Ghost,[116] and remains in them, or also that the grace by which we are justified is only the good will of God, let him be anathema.

Canon 12. If anyone says that justifying faith is nothing else than confidence in divine mercy,[117] which remits sins for Christ's sake, or that it is this confidence alone that justifies us, let him be anathema. "Documents – Paul III Council of Trent-6 – Our Catholic Faith." Accessed December 13, 2019. https://ourcatholicfaith.org/documents-paul-iii-council-of-trent-6/. (Council of Trent n.d.)

Also

"Decree Concerning Justification & Decree Concerning Reform | EWTN." Accessed December 13, 2019. https://www.ewtn.com/catholicism/library/decree-concerning-justification--decree-concerning-reform-1496.

[328] Maintaining Catholic Doctrine in Ecumenism

"Now that we have briefly set out the conditions for ecumenical action and the principles by which it is to be directed, we look with confidence to the future. This Sacred Council exhorts the faithful to refrain from superficiality and imprudent zeal, which can hinder real progress toward unity. Their ecumenical action must be fully and sincerely Catholic, that is to say, faithful to the truth which we have received from the apostles and Fathers of the Church, in harmony with the faith which the Catholic Church has always professed, and at the same time directed toward that fullness to which Our Lord wills His Body to grow in the course of time."
Vatican Council II, Decree on Ecumenism 3, II, 24; Catholic Information Network, http://www.cin.org/v2ecum.html Accessed March 1, 2012. (V. C. II n.d.)[emphasis added]

[329] The Catholic Church has literal centuries of experience in this practice, demonstrated at the Diet of Augsburg [1530]

"During the slow incubation of the Refutation, seven men were chosen (13th August) on each side, to meet in conference and essay the work of conciliation.[1324] They made rapid progress up to a certain point; but the moment they touched the essentials of either faith, they were conclusively stopped. The expedient was tried of reducing the commission to three on each side, in the hope that with fewer members there would be fewer differences. The chief on the Protestant side was Melancthon, of whom Pallavicino says that "he had a disposition not perverse, although perverted, and was by nature as desirous of peace as Luther was of contention."[1325] Well did Melancthon merit this compliment from the pen of the Catholic historian. For the sake of peace he all but sacrificed himself, his colleagues, and the work on which he had spent so many years of labor and prayer. His concessions to the Romanists in the Commission were extraordinary indeed. He was willing to agree with them in matters of ceremony, rites, and feasts. In other and more important points, such as the mass, and justification by faith, findings were come to in which both sides acquiesced, being capable of a double interpretation. The Papists saw that they had only to bide their time to be able to put their own construction on these articles, when all would be right." [emphasis added]

Wylie, James Aitken. *The History Of Protestantism* (Kindle Locations 18122-18133). Kirk Press. Kindle Edition.) (J. A. Wylie n.d.)

[330] "Equivocation - Wikipedia.". https://en.wikipedia.org/wiki/Equivocation Accessed June 17, 2017.

[331] "In the past, whenever a single visible Church has succeeded in gaining control, it has used its power to suppress the liberty of non-adherents. The entire history of the Roman Church should teach us this menace. Today the same threat to religious liberty is already perceptible. So-called "proselyting" is to be outlawed in principle. The Orthodox Church professor Zander writes, accordingly, that ecumenical love is based on certain theological and practical presuppositions one of which is abstention from all proselyting. To quote, "The principle which causes us to abstain from efforts at proselyting is founded on the conviction...that every Christian resembles a leaf growing on its own tree, and that his transfer into another Church always causes the destruction of a certain organic unity which to that point had nourished his religious being."28
"The Ecumenical Review takes up the same question in these words: "Many evangelical leaders have been wondering for some time whether the day had not arrived for a slowing or cessation of the process of growth at the expense of the ancient Churches [that is, the Greek Orthodox and Roman, probably also the Protestant state-Churches] and its replacement by a policy of consolidation."29 "The time has surely arrived when Churches which have joined the World Council of Churches should repudiate proselytism or any endeavors to expand at each other's expense."30
"All this simply means that it will not be possible any more to preach the gospel in the lands or regions where a member Church of the ecumenical movement is in control, no matter whether that Church is liberal, asleep or obviously insufficient. It also signifies that in the countries where the "sister Church" of Rome is in the majority, as in Spain or South America, the mouths of evangelicals must be stopped, and they must be delivered over to their persecutors."
"The Ecumenical Movement Part 4: Moving toward the Super-Church -- By: Rene Pache | Galaxie Software." Accessed June 28, 2017. http://www.galaxie.com/article/bsac108-430-06 (Pache, "The Ecumenical Movement Part 4: Moving toward the Super-Church 1951)

[332] "Evangelism: Groups Battle over Catholic Outreach | Christianity Today." Jackie Alnor Accessed June 28, 2017. http://www.christianitytoday.com/ct/1998/march2/8t3070.html?start=2. (Alnor 1998)

[333] "Irreconcilable Differences: Catholics, Evangelicals, and the New Quest for Unity, Parts 1-3." Accessed June 28, 2017. https://www.gty.org/library/sermons-library/GTY54/irreconcilable-differences-catholics-evangelicals-and-the-new-quest-for-unity-parts-13. (MacArthur, Ankerberg and Sproul n.d.)[see segment #3 rw]

[334] "Pope Tells New Bishops to Build Unity; Division Is Work of the devil – Franciscan Media." Accessed July 9, 2017. https://www.franciscanmedia.org/pope-tells-new-bishops-to-build-unity-division-is-work-of-the-devil/.

[335] "Pope Francis Quiet on Catholic Persecution of Protestants in Mexico" Sarah Eekhoff Zylstra Christianity Today." Accessed July 9, 2017. http://www.christianitytoday.com/news/2016/february/pope-francis-catholic-persecution-protestant-mexico-chiapas.html. (Zylstra 2016)

[336] This does not mean that members of the body of Christ are incapable of human good, sin and evil, but that the Spirit filled activity of the true Church cannot produce these works [1 Jn 3.6-10].

[337] Dt 31.16; Lev 17.7; Judg 8.27; 1 Ch 5.25; Eze 16.28; 23.36-37; Hos 3.1

[338] [Regarding Ezekiel 28.16, 18] One of the elements of Satan's sin was his widespread **dishonest trade**. The word for trade comes from the verb rāḵal which means "to go about from one to

another." Ezekiel had used that noun in speaking of Tyre's commercial activities (Ezek. 28:5). Does this mean Satan was operating a business? Obviously not. Instead, Ezekiel was comparing the human "prince" of Tyre and his satanic "king." So Ezekiel used a word that could convey a broad meaning. Satan's position in heaven involved broad contact with many elements of God's creation much as the prince of Tyre's position enabled him to contact many nations. [emphasis in the original]
Charles H. Dyer, "Ezekiel," in *The Bible Knowledge Commentary: An Exposition of the Scriptures*, ed. J. F. Walvoord and R. B. Zuck, vol. 1 (Wheaton, IL: Victor Books, 1985), 1284. (Dyer 1985)

[339] "sorceries" 53.100 φαρμακεία

Johannes P. Louw and Eugene Albert Nida, *Greek-English Lexicon of the New Testament: Based on Semantic Domains* (New York: United Bible Societies, 1996), 544.

[340] Christendom is the visible Christian presence in the world, consisting of true and false believers, true and false doctrines. Although Christendom includes the true Church, the true Church can be influenced, *but not controlled* by Mystery Babylon, because the Head of the Church, [the Body] is Christ [Eph 4.15; 5.23; Col 1.18]. That being said, *many* false pastors and teachers have insinuated themselves into Christendom of today [1 Jn 2.18-19; 4.1; Jude 4].

[341] "fornication" 88.271 πορνεύω; ἐκπορνεύω; πορνεία, ας f: to engage in sexual immorality of any kind, often with the implication of prostitution—'to engage in illicit sex, to commit fornication, sexual immorality, fornication, prostitution.'
Louw, J. P., & Nida, E. A. (1996). *Greek-English lexicon of the New Testament: based on semantic domains* (electronic ed. of the 2nd edition.). New York: United Bible Societies.

[342] Although this is no mystery to the Church, it is still a mystery to the vast majority of fallen men.

[343] The government is able, to an extent, to *restrain* evil is due to its original design by God for this purpose, which it performs even in its fallen state. Evil is also restrained by the conscience, which, though also fallen, is constantly recalibrated by general revelation in creation and special creation via the people of God.

[344] Franklin Roosevelts speech continued in part as follows:

"For example, I have in my possession a secret map made in Germany by Hitler's Government—by the planners of the new World Order. It is a map of South America and a part of Central America, as Hitler proposes to reorganize it. Today in this area there are fourteen separate countries. But the geographical experts of Berlin have ruthlessly obliterated all existing boundary lines; they have divided South America into five vassal states, bringing the whole continent under their domination. And they have also so arranged it that the territory of one of these new puppet states includes the Republic of Panama and our great life line—the Panama Canal. [emphasis added-rw]
"That is his plan. It will never go into effect.
"This map, my friends, makes clear the Nazi design not only against South America but against the United States as well.
"Your Government has in its possession another document, made in Germany by Hitler's Government. It is a detailed plan, which, for obvious reasons, the Nazis did not wish and do not wish to publicize just yet, but which they are ready to impose, a little later, on a dominated world—if Hitler wins. It is a plan 'to abolish all existing religions- Catholic, Protestant, Mohammedan, Hindu, Buddhist, and Jewish alike. The property of all Churches will be seized by the Reich and its puppets. The cross and all other symbols of religion are to be forbidden. The clergy are to be

forever liquidated, silenced under penalty of the concentration camps, where even now so many fearless men are being tortured because they have placed God above Hitler.

"In the place of the Churches of our civilization, there is to be set up an International Nazi Church- a Church which will be served by orators sent out by the Nazi Government. And in the place of the Bible, the words of Mein Kampf will be imposed and enforced as Holy Writ. And in the place of the cross of Christ will be put two symbols—the swastika and the naked sword.

The god of Blood and Iron will take the place of the God of Love and Mercy. Let us well ponder that statement which I have made tonight."

"Address for Navy and Total Defense Day. | The American Presidency Project." Accessed December 14, 2018. https://www.presidency.ucsb.edu/documents/address-for-navy-and-total-defense-day.

Richard M. Nixon said the following:

"You remember V-J Day and V-E Day. I recall that on V-J Day I was in New York City, in Times Square, with my wife, and the wonderful elation that we all felt about the war--it was over. And then came the United Nations and all the hope for a new World Order, and we thought, now we are going to have real peace." [emphasis added-rw]

Richard M. Nixon. "Remarks in Ashland, Kentucky. | The American Presidency Project." Accessed December 14, 2018. https://www.presidency.ucsb.edu/documents/remarks-ashland-kentucky.

George H. W. Bush said the following:

"We stand today at a unique and extraordinary moment. The crisis in the Persian Gulf, as grave as it is, also offers a rare opportunity to move toward an historic period of cooperation. Out of these troubled times, our fifth objective -- a new World Order -- can emerge: a new era -- freer from the threat of terror, stronger in the pursuit of justice, and more secure in the quest for peace. An era in which the nations of the world, East and West, North and South, can prosper and live in harmony. A hundred generations have searched for this elusive path to peace, while a thousand wars raged across the span of human endeavor. Today that new world is struggling to be born, a world quite different from the one we've known. A world where the rule of law supplants the rule of the jungle. A world in which nations recognize the shared responsibility for freedom and justice. A world where the strong respect the rights of the weak. This is the vision that I shared with President Gorbachev in Helsinki. He and other leaders from Europe, the Gulf, and around the world understand that how we manage this crisis today could shape the future for generations to come." [emphasis added-rw]

"Address Before a Joint Session of the Congress on the Persian Gulf Crisis and the Federal Budget Deficit | The American Presidency Project." Accessed December 14, 2018. https://www.presidency.ucsb.edu/documents/address-before-joint-session-the-congress-the-persian-gulf-crisis-and-the-federal-budget.

[345] DAVIDIC COVENANT [see 2 Samuel 7.12-16, Ps 89; 110]

"The kingdom concept reaches its zenith in the Davidic Covenant, which predicts the future millennial reign of David's greater Son, the Messiah.

"NATURE OF THE COVENANT

"In 2 Samuel 7 God promised David the following: "(1) David is to have a child, yet to be born, who shall succeed him and establish his kingdom. (2) This son (Solomon) shall build the temple instead of David. (3) The throne of his kingdom shall be established forever. (4) The throne will not be taken away from him (Solomon) even though his sins justify chastisement. (5) David's house, throne, and kingdom shall be established forever."1
"Solomon, the son of David, would be established on the throne of Israel, and God promised the blessings of the Davidic Covenant would be continued through Solomon. The essence of the Davidic Covenant is given in 2 Samuel 7:16 and contains four important elements. (1) House. This refers to the royal dynasty of David; God promised David a continuing posterity that would be of the royal line of David. This promise verified that the lineage of David would not be destroyed but would issue in Messiah who would reign over the earth. (2) Kingdom. The word kingdom involves a people and a dominion over whom the king will rule; it is the sphere of the king's rulership. It is a political kingdom. (3) Throne. The throne suggests the authority and the power of the king in his rule. (4) Forever. Forever emphasizes that the right to rule will never be taken from the family of David; moreover, the posterity of David will never cease to rule over the house of Israel."
Enns, Paul P., *The Moody Handbook of Theology* (Chicago, IL: Moody Press, 1989), 61–62.
[346] Gen 9.1, 7 c.f. 11.4, 8
[347] There has been no world encompassing state since Babel. Each subsequent empire has failed to conquer the world and even these identified themselves in terms of their national and ethnic states of origin. The fourth kingdom [specifically that era corresponding to the feet of iron and clay] will achieve world domination to a greater extent than any since Babel and will assume an international character. It too will be vetoed by God by the judgments of the Tribulation, followed by the personal return of Christ who will permanently incarcerate its leaders, the Antichrist, and the False Prophet.
[348] "terrible" 1763 דְּחַל [dâchal /deh·khal/] v. Corresponding to 2119; TWOT 2672; GK 10167; Six occurrences; AV translates as "fear" twice, "dreadful" twice, "terrible" once, and "afraid" once. 1 to fear. 1A (P'al). 1A1 to fear. 1A2 terrible (pass participle). 1B (Pael) to cause to be afraid, make afraid.
James Strong, *Enhanced Strong's Lexicon* (Woodside Bible Fellowship, 1995).
[349] Chapter 22: Section-Babylon as the Great Cities of Man
[350] "What is at stake is more than one small country; it is a big idea: a new World Order, where diverse nations are drawn together in common cause to achieve the universal aspirations of mankind -- peace and security, freedom, and the rule of law. Such is a world worthy of our struggle and worthy of our children's future."
President George H.W. Bush "Address Before a Joint Session of the Congress on the State of the Union | The American Presidency Project." Accessed December 11, 2018.
https://www.presidency.ucsb.edu/documents/address-before-joint-session-the-congress-the-state-the-union-1.
[351] "troubled" 7192 פָּעַם (pā·'ăm): v.; ≡ Str 6470; TWOT 1793—1. LN 57.71–57.124 (qal) endow, bestow, grant, formally, push or impel, i.e., to give an object or benefit to someone (Jdg 13:25+); 2. LN 25.223–25.250 (nif) be troubled, be disturbed, i.e., be in a mental state of distress and worry relating to a situation (Ge 41:8; Ps 77:5[EB 4]; **Da 2:3+**); (hitp) be troubled (**Da 2:1+**)

James Swanson, *Dictionary of Biblical Languages with Semantic Domains: Hebrew* (Old Testament) (Oak Harbor: Logos Research Systems, Inc., 1997).
[352] "brake them to pieces" 10182 דְּקַק (deqăq): v.; ≡ DBLHebr 1990 Str 1855; TWOT 2681—LN 19.43–19.54 (peal pf. 3mp.) be crushed, be in state of being broken to pieces (BDB); or transitive they crush (Holladay, KB) (Da 2:35+); (hafel) crush, smash, pulverize (**Da 2:34, 40(2×)**,44, 45; 6:25[EB 24]; 7:7, 19, 23+)
James Swanson, *Dictionary of Biblical Languages with Semantic Domains: Aramaic* (Old Testament) (Oak Harbor: Logos Research Systems, Inc., 1997).
[353] Atomic Weight: "the average weight of an atom of an element, formerly based on the weight of one hydrogen atom taken as a unit or on 1/16 (0.0625) the weight of an oxygen atom, but after 1961 based on 1/12 the weight of the carbon-12 atom. Abbreviation : at. wt."
"Atomic Weight | Define Atomic Weight at Dictionary.Com." Accessed December 10, 2018. https://www.dictionary.com/browse/atomic-weight.
[354] Specific Gravity" "the ratio of the density of any substance to the density of some other substance taken as standard, water being the standard for liquids and solids, and hydrogen or air being the standard for gases.
"Specific Gravity | Define Specific Gravity at Dictionary.Com." Accessed December 10, 2018. https://www.dictionary.com/browse/specific-gravity?s=t.
[355] "brass or copper" 10473 נְחָשׁ (neḥāš): n.masc.; ≡ DBLHebr 5703, 5733 Str 5174; TWOT 2858—LN 2.54 (most versions) bronze metal or possibly copper material (Da 2:32, 35, 39, 45; 4:12[EB 15],20[EB 23]; 5:4, 23; 7:19+) note: brass (ASV, KJV), is not a technically accurate term in modern usage for bronze as a composite metal
James Swanson, *Dictionary of Biblical Languages with Semantic Domains: Aramaic* (Old Testament) (Oak Harbor: Logos Research Systems, Inc., 1997).
[356] 2022 numbers
[357] "What Is a Genome? - Genetics Home Reference - NIH." Accessed December 12, 2018. https://ghr.nlm.nih.gov/primer/hgp/genome.
[358] But not at the same time. Antichrist and the False Prophet will be immediately dispatched to the Lake of Fire upon the return of Christ to the Earth. Lucifer will be confined to the Abyss for one thousand years and then sent to the Lake of Fire.
[359] Gen 12.1-3; 15:1-21; 17.1-21; 26.2-5; 28.10-17
[360] Although the kingdom will begin with redeemed individuals only, those believers alive in the world at the time of the return of Christ will have offspring who will be born as sinners into the world, in need of salvation. At the end of the Millennial period, there will be the final judgment, the great white throne, at which all unbelievers of every age will be committed to the Lake of Fire forever [Rev 20.11-15]. The eternal state will then be inaugurated with elect persons [angels and men] only [Rev 21].
[361] "John stated that what he was seeing is the first resurrection. Posttribulationists refer to this as proof that the Church will not be Raptured before the Tribulation and that no resurrection has taken place prior to this point in fulfillment of God's prophetic program. It should be obvious, however, that in no sense could this be the number-one resurrection chronologically because historically Christ was the first to rise from the dead with a transformed, resurrected body. There was also the resurrection "of many" (Matt. 27:52–53) which took place when Christ died. In what sense then can this resurrection in Revelation 20:5 be "first"?

"As the context which follows indicates, "the first resurrection" (vv. 5–6) contrasts with the last resurrection (vv. 12–13), which is followed by "the second death" (vv. 6, 14). It is first in the sense of before. All the righteous, regardless of when they are raised, take part in the resurrection which is first or before the final resurrection (of the wicked dead) at the end of the Millennium. This supports the conclusion that the resurrection of the righteous is by stages. Christ was "the Firstfruits" (1 Cor. 15:23), which was preceded by the token resurrection of a number of saints (Matt. 27:52–53). Then will occur the Rapture of the Church, which will include the resurrection of dead Church saints and the translation of living Church saints (1 Thes. 4:13–18). The resurrection of the two witnesses will occur in the Great Tribulation (Rev. 11:3, 11). Then the resurrection of the martyred dead of the Great Tribulation will occur soon after Christ returns to earth (20:4–5). To these may be added the resurrection of Old Testament saints which apparently will also occur at this time, though it is not mentioned in this text (cf. Isa. 26:19–21; Ezek. 37:12–14; Dan. 12:2–3)." Walvoord, John F., "Revelation," in *The Bible Knowledge Commentary: An Exposition of the Scriptures*, ed. J. F. Walvoord and R. B. Zuck, vol. 2 (Wheaton, IL: Victor Books, 1985), 980.

[362] https://www.imdb.com/title/tt4052886/ Accessed June 27 2022

[363] "THE INFRASTRUCTURE OF A GARRISON STATE

"If I could bring my parents back from the dead right now, I know that this country in its present state would boggle their minds. They wouldn't recognize it. If I were to tell them, for instance, that just three men—Bill Gates, Jeff Bezos, and Warren Buffett—now possess as much wealth as the bottom half of the US population, of 160 million Americans, they would never believe me.
"How, for instance, could I begin to explain to them the ways in which, in these years, money flowed ever upward into the pockets of the immensely wealthy and then down again into what became 1 percent elections that would finally ensconce a billionaire and his family in the White House? How would I explain to them that, while leading congressional Democrats and Republicans couldn't say often enough that this country was uniquely greater than any that ever existed, none of them could find the funds—some $5.6 trillion, for starters—necessary for our roads, dams, bridges, tunnels, and other crucial infrastructure? This on a planet where what the news likes to call "extreme weather" is increasingly wreaking havoc on that same infrastructure."
https://www.thenation.com/article/americas-war-on-terror-has-cost-taxpayers-5-6-trillion/ Accessed June 23, 2018

[364] "Hip-Hop Continued to Dominate the Music Business in 2018 - Rolling Stone." Accessed December 22, 2019. https://www.rollingstone.com/music/music-news/hip-hop-continued-to-dominate-the-music-business-in-2018-774422/.   Accessed December 22, 2019

[365] "Goldman Sachs Bets On Hip Hop And Millennials For Music Revival." Accessed December 22, 2019. https://www.forbes.com/sites/korihale/2019/02/06/goldman-sachs-bets-on-hip-hop-and-millennials-for-music-revival/#62f9ee666f17.   Accessed December 22, 2019

[366] Nielsen. "FROM CONSUMERS TO CREATORS THE DIGITAL LIVES OF BLACK CONSUMERS," n.d. https://www.walterkaitz.org/wp-content/uploads/2019/01/nielsen-from-consumers-to-creators.pdf. (Nielsen 2019)

[367] With the notable exception of the independent [*indie*] music marketplace.

[368] For example, the creation of a drug crisis in order to promote a justification for a legislative revolution entitled "law and order," or the creation of laws leading to mass incarceration of black people and the inevitable degrading or the rights of all Americans.
Alexander, Michelle. *The New Jim Crow: Mass Incarceration in the Age of Colorblindness*. Revised

edition. New York: New Press, 2012. (Alexander 2012).

Webb, Gary. *Dark Alliance: The CIA, the Contras, and the Crack Cocaine Explosion*. Seven Stories Press 1st ed. New York: Seven Stories Press, 1998. (Webb 1998)

[369] Like the rock/folk movement in the 1960's. McGowan, David, *"Weird Scenes Inside the Canyon: Laurel Canyon, Covert Ops & the Dark Heart of the Hippy Dream"*, (Headpress, 2014) (McGowan 2014).

[370] See the Billboard Top R&B and Hip Hop Artists for Year end 2019 and research their artistic production. https://www.billboard.com/charts/year-end/top-r-and-b-hip-hop-artists

[371] Our footnotes throughout this book cite examples. Blacks have been and continue to be subject to legal injustices in areas such as constitutional interpretation; criminal justice, policing, voting laws, medical apartheid, job discrimination, as well as discrimination in housing, lending, public education etc. which have been both de jure and de facto, by the imposition of unjust laws and the failure to enforce existing laws. These actions have created a network of legalized injustice that must ultimately enslave all Americans.

[372]*Lecrae Breaks New Ground as Christian Rapper, Looks to Kanye West for Inspiration*, http://www.billboard.com/articles/columns/the-juice/6274191/lecrae-breaks-new-ground-as-christian-rapper-looks-to-kanye-west   Accessed May 24, 2017.

[373] The fact that apostate Israel is a part of Mystery Babylon is a reason that the Antichrist does not appear as the enemy of all Israel, even after the Abomination of Desolation. This marker, at the midpoint of the Tribulation is when all unbelievers must choose between their previous religious affiliations under Mystery Babylon or the pure worship of Lucifer via his son the Antichrist. All true believers as well as unbelievers unwilling to make this transition will be subject to capital punishment [Rev 13.7, 15 see also Mt 24.15-26]. Apostate Israel will survive the destruction of Mystery Babylon by worshipping the Antichrist [Rev 13.8].This does not mean that Satan [as distinct from Antichrist] means the Jews well, whether saved or apostate. Satan's plan is as always, the destruction of Jews to invalidate God's promises to redeemed Israel. The point here is that the scriptures do not depict the *Antichrist* as intending to destroy apostate Israel.

[374] Chapter 3-Section: Binary Traps

[375] FRED. SEYLER in BENGEL calculates that papal Rome, between A.D. 1540 and 1580, slew more than nine hundred thousand Protestants. Robert Jamieson, A. R. Fausset, and David Brown, Commentary Critical and Explanatory on the Whole Bible, vol. 2 (Oak Harbor, WA: Logos Research Systems, Inc., 1997), 595.

[376] See Foxe's Book of Martyrs, Chapter II: The Ten Primitive Persecutions

[377] The Most Persecuted Religion in the World, http://www.huffingtonpost.com/kelly-james-clark/christianity-most-persecuted-religion_b_2402644.html   Accessed May 24, 2017

[378] Avro Manhattan, *Terror Over Yugoslavia: The Threat to Europe*, (Watts, 1953) (Manhattan 1953)

[379] Rev 13.14-16

[380] The withdrawal of Christians from society and its institutions is not a spiritual solution. Spiritual warfare includes the personal witness of righteousness and justice by believers everywhere. Spiritual victory is not won by secular means but Christians purify civilization by their testimony in marriage, family, the community, and government.

[381] Rom 12.1-2; 1 Th 4.3; 1 Pet 2.15

[382] Chapter 18

[383] Chapter 22

[384] Chapter 25-Section: Wealth Transfer
[385] Butler, Smedley D, and Dragan Nikolic. *War Is a Racket: The Antiwar Classic by America's Most Decorated Soldier*, 2014. (Butler 2014).
[386] Who is paying for the war on terror and who is profiting from it? The "war on terror" is a massive modern wealth transfer mechanism which also powerfully advances the agenda of the devil in the New World Order, simultaneously accomplishing all four key objectives:

1. **Wealth Transfer** [from the Public to Mystery Babylon]
2. **Corruption of Values** of Common People [Intoxication with the wine of her fornication]
3. **Promotion of Luciferian Religion** [Moving towards Externalization of the NWO]
4. **Political End Game** [to Enable the Appearing of the Antichrist]

[387] https://www.theguardian.com/commentisfree/2015/jun/03/us-isis-syria-iraq Accessed June 24, 2018
[388] https://www.thenation.com/article/americas-war-on-terror-has-cost-taxpayers-5-6-trillion/ Accessed June 23, 2018
[389] https://www.history.com/topics/patriot-act Accessed June 23, 2018
https://www.epic.org/privacy/terrorism/hr3162.html
[390] "Management of the drug traffic takes a variety of forms: from denial of this important power source to competing powers (the first and most vital priority), to exploitation of it to strengthen the existing state. There now exists abundant documentation that, at least since World War II, the US Government has exploited the drug traffic to finance and staff covert operations abroad. Perhaps the most conspicuous example is the massive paramilitary army organized and equipped by the CIA in Laos in the 1960s, for which drugs were the chief source of support. This alliance between the CIA and drug-financed forces has since been repeated in Afghanistan (1979), Central America (1982–87), and most recently Kosovo (1998)." Scott, Peter Dale. Dallas '63: *The First Deep State Revolt Against the White House* (Forbidden Bookshelf Book 17) (Kindle Locations 529-534). Open Road Media. Kindle Edition. (Scott n.d.).

McCoy, Alfred W. *The Politics of Heroin: CIA Complicity in the Global Drug Trade: Afghanistan, Southeast Asia, Central America, Colombia*. Rev. ed. Chicago: Lawrence Hill Books: Distributed by Independent Publishers Group, 2003. (McCoy 2003).

Webb, Gary. *Dark Alliance: The CIA, the Contras, and the Crack Cocaine Explosion*. Seven Stories Press 1st ed. New York: Seven Stories Press, 1998. (Webb 1998).

See the "Dark Alliance" Newspaper Articles
http://www.narconews.com/darkalliance/shock/day1main.htm Accessed June 24, 2018
[391] Ahmed, Nafeez Mosaddeq. *The War on Freedom: How and Why America Was Attacked, September 11th, 2001*. Joshua Tree, Calif: Media Messenger Books, 2002. (Ahmed 2002).

Thompson, Paul. *The Terror Timeline: Year by Year, Day by Day, Minute by Minute; a Comprehensive Chronicle of the Road to 9/11 - and America's Response*. New York, NY: Regan, 2006. (P. Thompson 2006).
[392] This recapitulation section is influenced by the book entitled "Satan" by Lewis Sperry Chafer, cited below.

[393] "Second, the Satanic system, according to Scripture, is wholly evil. This is a hard saying; and is usually denied by those who do not realize that all Scripture estimates are made from the standard of the holiness of God; and that the Satanic system, of itself and apart from the influence of God and His people, has never improved their own moral condition, but that they are individually under condemnation before God (Jno. 3:18); their borrowed interest in morality and charity being a poor commendation, in view of their fallen and Christ-rejecting attitude before God.
Chafer, Lewis Sperry. *Satan* (Kindle Locations 511-515). Public Domain Books. Kindle Edition.
[394] "Though the unsaved are moral, educated, refined, or religious, they are not righteous in God's sight; for the charge here brought against them is that "there is none righteous, no, not one;" and "all have sinned and come short of the glory of God."" [Rom 3.10, 23]
Chafer, Lewis Sperry. *Satan* (Kindle Locations 522-524). Public Domain Books. Kindle Edition.

"These judgments are made from the view-point of the purity and holiness of God. In His sight the highest moral, educational, and religious ideals that the unregenerate world can comprehend are but a part of the confusion and darkness of this age when coupled with a rejection of His testimony in regard to His Son as their atoning Saviour. Thus, it is presented from the Scripture that the present age and its great federation is, in God's sight, most unholy." Ibid. (Kindle Locations 536-539).
[395] Chapter 3-Section: Binary Traps
[396] "How then does the Roman Catholic Church inherit the combined political and religious authority of Israel? Amillennial theology removes Israel from the eschatological prophecies and transfers her blessings to the Church. This transfer is performed via allegorical or spiritualizing interpretation of the scripture and one of its most prominent illustrations, Replacement Theology or Supersessionism is how the birthright of Jacob was snatched back by Esau.

Thomas Ice writes the following regarding Replacement Theology:

"Walt Kaiser tells us that replacement theology, "declared that the Church, Abraham's spiritual seed, had replaced national Israel in that it had transcended and fulfilled the terms of the covenant given to Israel, which covenant Israel had lost because of disobedience."

"Scholars have noted at least four contributing factors to the development of Replacement Theology:
    1. Decreasing Jewish influence in the Local church
    2. The destructions of Jerusalem in A.D. 70 and 135
    3. Jewish-Christian hostilities
    4. The churches' appropriation of the Jewish scriptures29

Thomas Ice, "What is Replacement Theology," http://www.pre-trib.org/data/pdf/Ice-WhatisReplacementThe.pdf (accessed February 29, 2012) (Ice, "What is Replacement Theology," n.d.).

Replacement Theology uses the following scriptures to argue that the Church has replaced Israel Gal 6:16; Romans 2:28-29; 9:6; 1 Pet 2.9-10; Php 3:3; Eph 2.11-19; Jer 31 c.f. Heb 8.8-13 etc. Michael J. Vlach (Vlach, Has the Church Replaced Israel in God's Plan, 13-17[396])quotes a star studded cast of scholars who see these scriptures as evidence of the replacement of Israel by the Church: Wayne Grudem, George Ladd, Douglass Moo, and Anthony A. Hoekema, among others" Walker, Richard G., *While Men Slept, Roman Catholic Ecclesiology, Eschatology and the Ecumenical Movement* n.d. (Walker 2009).

[397] "The Final Solution (German: Endlösung) or the Final Solution to the Jewish Question (German: die Endlösung der Judenfrage, pronounced [di: ˈɛntˌløːzʊŋ deːɐ̯ ˈjuːdn̩ˌfʁaːɡə]) was a Nazi plan for the extermination of the Jews during World War II. The "Final Solution of the Jewish Question" was the official code name for the murder of all Jews within reach, which was not limited to the European continent.[1] This policy of deliberate and systematic genocide starting across German-occupied Europe was formulated in procedural and geo-political terms by Nazi leadership in January 1942 at the Wannsee Conference near Berlin,[2] and culminated in the Holocaust, which saw the killing of 90 percent of Jewish Poles,[3] and two thirds of the Jewish population of Europe.[4]" https://en.wikipedia.org/wiki/Final_Solution Accessed July 21, 2018

[398] Chapter 14

[399] For a discussion of the meaning of this passage see: Walvoord, John F. *Daniel: The Key To Prophetic Revelation.* Galaxie Software, 2008. Chapter 11

[400] "While the meaning of this symbolic presentation is clear, there is a major problem involved in what the demons do. The coming world government in the Great Tribulation will be established by the power of Satan (13:2). Here, however, Satan, the world ruler, and the false prophet unite in inciting the nations of the world to gather for the final world war. Actually the war is a form of rebellion against the world ruler. Why then should satanic forces be let loose to destroy the world empire which has just been created?

"The answer seems to be in the events which follow. Satan, knowing that the second coming of Christ is near, will gather all the military might of the world into the Holy Land to resist the coming of the Son of Man who will return to the Mount of Olives (Zech. 14:4). Though the nations may be deceived in entering into the war in hope of gaining world political power, the satanic purpose is to combat the armies from heaven (introduced in chap. 19) at the second coming of Christ.

"The war is said to continue right up to the day of the Second Coming and involves house-to-house fighting in Jerusalem itself on the day of the Lord's return (Zech. 14:1–3). The reference to "the battle" (ton polemon, Rev. 16:14) is probably better translated "the war" (NASB). Thus it is better to speak of "the war of Armageddon" (see v. 16) rather than the "the battle of Armageddon." The war will be going on for some time, but the climax will come at Christ's second coming. "Armageddon" comes from the Greek Harmagedōn, which transliterates the Hebrew words for Mount (har) of Megiddo. That mountain is near the city of Megiddo and the plain of Esdraelon, the scene of many Old Testament battles."

Walvoord, John F., "Revelation," in *The Bible Knowledge Commentary: An Exposition of the Scriptures*, ed. J. F. Walvoord and R. B. Zuck, vol. 2 (Wheaton, IL: Victor Books, 1985), 968.

[401] An interesting speculation is the meaning of the form of frogs. One reference calls the frog demons an "antitype" of the frogs sent in Ex 8. [Jamieson Fausset and Brown].
The Biblical Illustrator says the following, in part:

Exodus 8:1-14
"IV. THE PURPOSES FOR WHICH THE CREATURES CAME.
1. On account of pride (ver. 2). God still abhors pride, and ever will. Can chastise the proud in a similar way. Can send disease to the pretty face; take away the idols, money, dress, friends;

weakness to either body or mind; death to the unbroken circle. "Walk humbly with thy God."
2. <u>On account of superstition</u>. Because the rising of the sun made wild beasts retire, the Egyptians looked on them as emblems of the sun's power. <u>Because the croaking of frogs helped travellers in a desert to discover waters, the Egyptians held them in some reverence. Regarded the frog also as sacred to the Nymphs and Muses. Called attendants upon the deities of streams and fountains</u>. To correct this wrong and extravagant notion about frogs, the Lord sent them over all the land. We should be careful about the objects we love and hate, esteem and disesteem, revere and abhor."
[emphasis added]
(from The Biblical Illustrator Copyright © 2002, 2003, 2006 Ages Software, Inc. and Biblesoft, Inc.)

Therefore, the drying of the Euphrates, a major ecological event, may have been easily construed by the kings of the earth as a religious portent, during a time of continuing judgments from the Lord. Satan may have used demonic entities to stimulate and nurture the foreboding cause by such a supernatural event, perhaps to goad the kings into taking offensive action against one another.

[402] Jer 49.13; Obad 1-2? See "Definition of the Armageddon Campaign" pg. 244.

[403] "It has been said that the nation which controls the Bosporus and the Suez Canal commands three continents-Europe, Asia and Africa. The Bosporus technically is the twenty-mile strait between the Black Sea and the Sea of Mamara; but the strategic area actually includes the entire body of water from the Mediterranean to the Black Sea and forms part of the boundary between Europe and Asia. It becomes more apparent with the pass of time that Palestine, located between the Bosporus and the Suez Canal, is a focal point for military and economic strategy throughout the world."
R.B. Thieme Jr. *Armageddon*, (R.B. Thieme Jr. Houston 1974) 1 (R. B. Thieme, Armageddon 1974)

[404] "[Daniel] 11:40a. The events in verses 40–45 will transpire at the time of the end, that is, they will occur in the second half of the 70th "seven" of years. Him refers back to the king introduced in verse 36. In verses 40–45 every occurrence of "he" (seven times), "him" (four times), and "his" (three times) refers to this coming king. He will have entered into a covenant with the people of Israel, binding that nation as a part of his domain (9:27). Any attack, then, against the land of Israel will be an attack against him with whom Israel will be joined by covenant."
J. Dwight Pentecost, "Daniel," in *The Bible Knowledge Commentary: An Exposition of the Scriptures*, ed. J. F. Walvoord and R. B. Zuck, vol. 1 (Wheaton, IL: Victor Books, 1985), 1371.

[405] "Rev 16.12-16 is the only passage in which the word "Armageddon" is mentioned. The context of these verses specifies certain events, personalities, nations and geographical localities which are identified with "the battle [POLEMOS] of the great day of God Almighty." The presence of POLEMOS in Revelation 16 rather than MACHE which usually denotes "battle" or "individual combat" indicates that the events described are part of a war or campaign. A campaign involves a military invasion into an unfriendly territory in an effort to locate enemy forces and peoples for the purpose of annihilation, subjugation or enslavement; therefore a campaign is composed of a series of battles in a specific geographical location, fought in chronological succession or simultaneously. Inasmuch as this titanic struggle occurs in one country, Palestine, the translation of POLEMOS as "campaign" is preferred to "war" or "battle."
R.B. Thieme Jr. *Armageddon*, (R.B. Thieme Jr. Houston 1974) 8.

[406] **Armageddon**. Hebrew word in Revelation 16:16 meaning "Mt Megiddo." It is generally thought that the term refers to the town of Megiddo, strategically located between the western coastal area and the broad Plain of Jezreel in northern Palestine. The area of Megiddo was important

commercially and militarily and was the scene of many important battles in Israel's history. There the Lord routed Sisera before the armies of Deborah and Barak (Jgs 4; 5); Gideon was victorious over the Midianites and Amalekites (Jgs 6); King Saul and his army were defeated by the Philistines (1 Sm 31); and King Josiah was slain in battle by the Egyptian army of Pharaoh Neco (2 Kgs 23:29). Because of that long history the name seems to have become <u>symbolic of a battlefield</u>. [emphasis rw] Such identification was evidently the thought in the mind of the apostle John in the Book of Revelation

Elwell, Walter A., and Barry J. Beitzel. *Baker Encyclopedia of the Bible*. (Grand Rapids, MI: Baker Book House, 1988). Art. Armageddon (Elwell 1988).

[407] Parallel to Zec 14:2, 3, 4, where the "Mount of Olives" answers to the "Valley of Jehoshaphat" here. The latter is called "the valley of blessing" (*Berachah*) (2 Ch 20:26). It lies between Jerusalem and the Mount of Olives and has the Kedron flowing through it.

Jamieson, Robert, A. R. Fausset, and David Brown. *Commentary Critical and Explanatory on the Whole Bible*. Oak Harbor, WA: Logos Research Systems, Inc., 1997. Joel 3.2 (Jamieson 1997)

[408] LaHaye, Tim, Thomas Ice, and Tim LaHaye. *Charting the End Times. Tim LaHaye Prophecy Library*. Eugene, OR: Harvest House Publishers, 2001. 63 (LaHaye 2001) [The basic concept and several bullet points are taken from here. Some adaptations have been made to the information rw.]

[409] "The king mentioned in [Daniel] 11:36–39 is now attacked by "the king of the south" and "the king of the north." Earlier in this chapter, the king of the south is uniformly Egypt and refers to the warfare of the third and second centuries B.C. which has already been fulfilled. Here the king of the south is clearly the leader of a political and military force that comes from the south of the Holy Land, but the probability is that it involves much more than only Egypt and can be identified as the African army. There is no mention whatever of such campaigns in the Maccabean books or by Livy, Polybius, and Appian. No such warfare is described in history."

Walvoord, John F., *Daniel: The Key To Prophetic Revelation* (Galaxie Software, 2008), 277.

[410] "[Rev] 9:16. The loosing of the four angels (not the same as the four angels of 7:1) resulted in releasing an army of 200 million ... mounted troops. Most interpreters do not take the number literally, though there is good evidence that all other numbers in Revelation are literal. Even if taken symbolically, this figure clearly represents an overwhelming military force. Years ago Red China claimed to have an army of 200 million (cf. Time, May 21, 1965, p. 35).

"Some interpreters say these millions are demons, but demons are not normally marshaled as a military force. The fact that John heard the number, as obviously he could not visually count 200 million men, seems to lend credence to the concept that this is literal and predicts that an army will come from the East crossing the dried-up Euphrates River (16:12).

"Great dams have already been placed across the Euphrates River to divert water for irrigation so that at times the riverbed is dry or partially so. A large invasion from the East and North in the end times is predicted in Daniel 11:44."

Walvoord, John F., "Revelation," in *The Bible Knowledge Commentary: An Exposition of the Scriptures*, ed. J. F. Walvoord and R. B. Zuck, vol. 2 (Wheaton, IL: Victor Books, 1985), 953.

[411] "Definitions:

"A dispensation is God's distinctive method of governing mankind or a group of men during a period of human history, marked by a crucial event, test, failure, and judgment. From the divine stand point, it is a stewardship, a rule of life, or a responsibility for managing God's affairs in His house. From the historical standpoint, it is a stage in the progress of revelation." [Paul David Niven]

Ryrie, Charles C., *Dispensationalism [Revised and Expanded]*, (Chicago, Moody Press,1995) 30

"Definitions

Erich Sauer states it this way:

A new period always begins only when from the side of God a change is introduced in the composition of the principles valid up to that time; that is, when from the side of God three things concur:

1. A continuance of certain ordinances valid until then;
2. An annulment of other regulations until then valid;
3. A fresh introduction of new principles not before valid.

To summarize: Dispensationalism views the world as a household run by God. In His household-world God is dispensing or administering its affairs according to His own will and in various stages of revelation in the passage of time. These various stages mark off the distinguishably different economies in the outworking of His total purpose, and these different economies constitute the dispensations. The understanding of God's differing economies is essential to a proper interpretation of His revelation within those various economies."
Charles C. Ryrie, Dispensationalism, Biblesoft, 1995 (C. C. Ryrie 1995)

[412] Charting the End Times, LaHaye, Tim; Ice, Thomas (Harvest House, 2001) 63

[413] *Battle Hymn of the Republic.* Lyrics-Julia Ward Howe, 1861; Music-William Steffe, 1856; arranged by James E. Greenleaf, C. S. Hall, and C. B. Marsh, 1861

[414] Donald Trump, American Pastors and the Reason Nations Fail
https://aricherwalk.com/2017/09/11/donald-trump-and-american-pastors-the-reason-nations-fail/ Accessed January 18, 2022.

[415] This issue will be addressed in more detail in Volume Two [Summer 2023]. See the following books for extensive discussion of the Charismatic Movement and its impact upon the modern Church.

MacArthur, John. Strange Fire: The Danger of Offending the Holy Spirit with Counterfeit Worship. Nashville, Tennessee: Thomas Nelson, 2013.

The Pentecostal-Charismatic Movement: Its History and Error, David W. Cloud (Way of Life Literature, 2006) (Cloud, The Pentecostal-Charismatic Movements: Their History and Error 2006)

Hanegraaff, Hank. *Counterfeit Revival*, (Thomas Nelson, 2001) (Hanegraaff, Counterfeit Revival 2001)

[416] "System protection (if turned on) is a feature that allows you to perform a system restore that takes your PC back to an earlier point in time, called a system restore point."https://www.tenforums.com/tutorials/4588-system-restore-windows-10-a.html Accessed July 22, 2018

[417] "We see it common in enthusiasts, that they depreciate this written rule and set up the light within or some other rule above it" Edwards, Works of Jonathan Edwards vol. 2. 267 cited in

Hanegraaff, Counterfeit Revival 123

"Counterfeit revival worship leader John Wimber, in a message on supernatural healing, expressed concern that evangelical Christians today are placing far too much emphasis on Scripture: "Evangelicals all over the country are worshipping the book. They have God the Father, God the Son and God the Holy Book. Thy took the very workings of the Holy Spirit and placed it in the Book." Ibid. 123

Also, On the Issue of the Authority of Scripture: See John MacArthur, ["Strange Fire"] Chapter 11 "The Spirit and the Scriptures"

MacArthur, John F. Strange Fire: The Danger of Offending the Holy Spirit with Counterfeit Worship, Thomas Nelson. Kindle Edition, 2013. p. 213-218

[418] See below

Aberrant doctrines concerning Faith 59-97
Prosperity Teachings: 179-217
Teachings Regarding Healing: 233-271

Hanegraaff, Hank. *Christianity in Crisis*, (Harvest House, 1997). (Hanegraaff, Christianity in Crisis 1997).

On the Issue of the Authority of Scripture

MacArthur, John F. Strange Fire: The Danger of Offending the Holy Spirit with Counterfeit Worship, Thomas Nelson. Kindle Edition, 2013. 213-230

On the Issue of Tongues

Rice, John R. The Charismatic Movement, Sword of the Lord, 1976 Chapters VIII & IX. (Rice 1976)

Cloud, David W. The Pentecostal-Charismatic Movements: Their History and Error, (Way of Life, 2006) 256-296.

On the Issue of the Trinity

"History has already suffered a "God the Father Only" [referencing the *filioque* of the third council of Toledo in 589-rw] and "Jesus Only" error. Now in Neo-Pentecostalism we are suffering a "Holy Ghost Only" error. Not only is there an overemphasis upon the Holy Spirit, but also modern Pentecostalism has embraced anti-trinitarian doctrine as well as Romanism.
"In these latter days, because of the extreme excesses and lack of Biblical authority and biblical separation, we can see these movements going on into total schism from the Trinity-view, headed towards a spiritualism and even occultism. It is not necessary to deny the doctrine of the Trinity, theologically, although that is equally involved. A movement may achieve the same thing by an

unbalanced teaching of the Holy Spirit. The existential principle that is working in Neo-Pentecostalism and being applied in a Pentecostal context, is resulting in a dangerous direction towards demonism."
Spence, O. Tallmadge. Charismatism: Awakening or Apostasy, (Greenville, Bob Jones University Press, 1978). 63 (O. T. Spence 1978).

[419] "For example, some of the early leaders of Dallas Theological Seminary "did not hesitate to call Pentecostalism both a cult and a satanic agency, a view not uncommon among evangelicals in the 1920s" (John Hannah, An Uncommon Union (Grand Rapids: Zondervan, 2009), 327n61)." (Hannah 2009)

MacArthur, John F. Strange Fire: The Danger of Offending the Holy Spirit with Counterfeit Worship (263). Thomas Nelson. Kindle Edition.

International Mission Board Drops Ban on Speaking in Tongues-New rules also loosen restrictions on baptism, divorce, and parents of teenagers. Bob Smietana, Christianity Today, MAY 14, 2015 https://www.christianitytoday.com/ct/2015/may-web-only/imb-ban-speaking-in-tongues-baptism-baptist-missionary.html Accessed July 24, 2018.

McKissic wants SBC to address 'tongues' in Baptist Faith & Message, By Robert Marus, Associated Baptist Press https://www.baptiststandard.com/archives/2006-archives/mckissic-wants-sbc-to-address-tongues-in-baptist-faith-aamp-message/

[420] "In spite of their gross theological error, charismatics demand acceptance within mainstream evangelicalism. And evangelicals have largely succumbed to those demands, responding with outstretched arms and a welcoming smile. In so doing, mainstream evangelicalism has unwittingly invited an enemy into the camp. The gates have been flung open to a Trojan horse of subjectivism, experientialism, ecumenical compromise, and heresy. Those who compromise in this way are playing with strange fire and placing themselves in grave danger."
MacArthur, John F. Strange Fire: The Danger of Offending the Holy Spirit with Counterfeit Worship (p. xiv). Thomas Nelson. Kindle Edition.
Also,

"A leading facilitator in the charismatic renewal was a South African Pentecostal named David du Plessis…In 1936 du Plessis was given a prophecy that would guide him for the next fifty years of his life. According to the Dictionary of Pentecostal and Charismatic Movements, the prophecy came through "an illiterate English evangelist" named Smith Wigglesworth…Although the content of the prophecy has been enhanced and embellished over time, it essentially predicted that du Plessis "was to leave home and take the Pentecostal message to the far corners of the earth, for God was going to perform a work which would dwarf the Pentecostal movement.
"Wigglesworth's prophecy so captivated du Plessis that he became obsessed with orchestrating its fulfillment by unifying Christianity. The "intoxicating vision to unite the worlds Pentecostals and ultimately world Christians" eventually led him to enlist as a delegate to the Word Council of Churches. It was there that he earned the title "Mr. Pentecost.

""… the crown of his ecumenical achievements" was the "development of the Roman Catholic-Pentecostal Dialogue…His most lasting legacy in terms of charismatic renewal may well have been

his impact on the life of Demos Shakarian, whom he encouraged to persevere in developing the Full Gospel Business Men's Fellowship International...Through the visionary example of du Plessis, Shakarian came to see how he could use the FGBMFI to spread the message of endtime restorationism [of Pentecostal gifts-RW] and denominational unity worldwide."
Hanegraaff, Hank. *Counterfeit Revival*, (Thomas Nelson, 2001)157-158.

[421] "stronghold" 3794 ὀχύρωμα [ochuroma /okh·oo·ro·mah/] n n. From a remote derivative of 2192 (meaning to fortify, through the idea of holding safely); TDNT 5:590; TDNTA 752; GK 4065; AV translates as "strong hold" once. 1 a castle, stronghold, fortress, fastness. 2 anything on which one relies. 2A of the arguments and reasonings by which a disputant endeavours to fortify his opinion and defend it against his opponent.
James Strong, *Enhanced Strong's Lexicon* (Woodside Bible Fellowship, 1995).

[422] Strongholds can also pertain to the domain of the flesh, or sin nature, which though invisible, exercises an overwhelming power [Gal 5.17].

[423] Here is where the dispensationally accurate application of the Word by believers creates spiritual momentum. Categories of application include worship, prayer, fellowship, evangelism, disciple making, citizenship, marriage, family, etc.

[424] Thieme, Robert B. Jr. *The Edification Complex of the Soul*. 1972 (R. B. Thieme 1972).
Thieme, Robert B. Jr. *Christian Suffering*. 2002 (R. B. Thieme, Christian Suffering 2002).

[425] Stephen R. Miller, Daniel, vol. 18, *The New American Commentary* (Nashville: Broadman & Holman Publishers, 1994), 140. (Miller 1994)

[426] But in his estate. or, But in his stead. Heb. But as for the almighty God, in his seat he shall honour, yea, he shall honour a god whom, etc. 1 Ti. 4:1. forces. or, munitions. Heb. Mauzzim, or, gods protectors. Saints and angels, who were invoked as intercessors and protectors, had miracles ascribed to them, their relics worshipped and their shrines and images adorned with costly offerings.
B. Blayney, Thomas Scott, and R.A. Torrey with John Canne, Browne, *The Treasury of Scripture Knowledge, vol. 1* (London: Samuel Bagster and Sons, n.d.), 556.

[427] "Cost of National Security: Counting How Much the U.S. Spends Per Hour." Accessed December 22, 2018. https://www.nationalpriorities.org/cost-of/. (B. Blayney n.d.)

[428] "Historic" Premillennialism: "The Tribulation
Enns, Paul P, *The Moody Handbook of Theology* (Chicago, IL: Moody Press, 1989), 387–388.
"Amillennialism: Second coming of Christ; "Resurrection of the dead.
Enns, Paul P, *The Moody Handbook of Theology* (Chicago, IL: Moody Press, 1989), 381–382.

[429] "The Rapture. The term Rapture comes from the Latin translation, meaning "caught up," in 1 Thessalonians 4:17. The Rapture, which is distinguished from the second coming of Christ, is taught in John 14:1–3; 1 Corinthians 15:51–57; and 1 Thessalonians 4:13–18. Prior to the advent of the Tribulation, Christ will descend from heaven, catching up the Church to be with Himself while the Tribulation is unleashed on an unrepentant and unbelieving world.

"The pretribulation Rapture is espoused for a number of reasons.80 (1) The nature of the Tribulation. The seventieth week of Daniel—the Tribulation—is an outpouring of the wrath of God throughout the seven years (Rev. 6:16–17; 11:18; 14:19; 15:1; 16:1, 19); it is described as God's judgment (Rev. 14:7; 15:4; 16:5–7; 19:2) and God's punishment (Isa. 24:21–22). (2) The scope of the Tribulation. The whole earth will be involved (Isa. 24:1, 3, 4, 5, 6, 21; 34:2). It also involves

God's chastisement of Israel (Jer. 30:7; Dan. 9:24). If this is the nature and scope of the Tribulation, it is inconceivable that the Church will be on earth to experience the wrath of God. (3) The purposes of the Tribulation. The divine intentions of the Tribulation will be to judge people living on earth (Rev. 6:10; 11:10; 13:8, 12, 14; 14:6; 17:8) and to prepare Israel for her King (Ezek. 36:18–32; Mal. 4:5–6). Neither of these pertain to the Church. (4) The unity of the Tribulation. The Tribulation is the seventieth week of Daniel; Daniel 9:24 makes it clear that it has reference to Israel. (5) The exemption of the Tribulation. The Church is the bride of Christ, the object of Christ's love, not His wrath (Eph. 5:25). It would be a contradiction of the very relationship of Christ and the Church for the Church to go through the punishments of the Tribulation. Specific statements affirming the Church will be kept from the Tribulation (cf. Rom. 5:9;81 1 Thess. 5:9; 2 Thess. 2:13; Rev. 3:10).82 (6) The sequel of the Tribulation. The signs of Matthew 24 (and numerous other passages) were given to Israel concerning the second coming of Christ; no signs, however, were given to the Church to anticipate the Rapture (which means it will come suddenly, as pretribulationists have affirmed). "The Church was told to live in the light of the imminent coming of the Lord to translate them in His presence (John 14:2–3; Acts 1:11; 1 Cor. 15:51–52; Phil. 3:20; Col. 3:4; 1 Thess. 1:10; 1 Tim. 6:14; James 5:8; 2 Pet. 3:3–4).[83"]

Enns, Paul P. *The Moody Handbook of Theology* (Chicago, IL: Moody Press, 1989), 390–391.

[430] Walvoord, John F., *The Thessalonian Epistles* (Galaxie Software, 2007), 49–50. (J. F. Walvoord, The Thessalonian Epistles 2007)

[431] Walvoord, John F., *The Thessalonian Epistles* (Galaxie Software, 2007), 73.

[432] The erroneous message which all these voices echoed was that the day of the Lord had arrived; the Thessalonians were in it. But if this were so, the believers were wondering, how could Paul speak of the Lord's return as preceding the day of the Lord? (1 Thes. 1:10) And what about those promises that they would not see God's wrath? (1 Thes. 1:10; 5:9) It is clear that Paul had taught them a pretribulational Rapture. Their confusion arose because they could not distinguish their present troubles from those of the day of the Lord.

Thomas L. Constable, "2 Thessalonians," in The Bible Knowledge Commentary: An Exposition of the Scriptures, ed. J. F. Walvoord and R. B. Zuck, vol. 2 (Wheaton, IL: Victor Books, 1985), 717. (Constable 1985).

[433] Walter Grundmann, "Δύναμαι, Δυνατός, Δυνατέω, Ἀδύνατος, Ἀδυνατέω, Δύναμις, Δυνάστης, Δυναμόω, Ἐνδυναμόω," ed. Gerhard Kittel, Geoffrey W. Bromiley, and Gerhard Friedrich, Theological Dictionary of the New Testament (Grand Rapids, MI: Eerdmans, 1964–), 304. (Grundmann 1964-).

[434] Norman L. Geisler, "Reincarnation," *Baker Encyclopedia of Christian Apologetics*, Baker Reference Library (Grand Rapids, MI: Baker Books, 1999), 643. (Geisler 1999)

[435] James Strong, Enhanced Strong's Lexicon (Woodside Bible Fellowship, 1995).

[436] "Rev 20.5: This is not the first resurrection in *time*: Jesus was resurrected, the Church is resurrected by this point. This is a resurrection of the first *kind*. Jn 5.28-29 illustrates two resurrections one of life and another of judgment. The first kind is unto life and the second unto judgment. The Rapture is a resurrection of the first kind as the one in this verse. The resurrection of the second kind [undo damnation] occurs 1000 years later at the great white throne judgment.

[437] This expression "in Christ" in every one of its many instances in the New Testament refers only to the saints of this dispensation. As far as the expression "the dead in Christ" indicates, only those in Christ are raised. Of course, all the saints are in Christ in the sense that Christ is their substitute,

but the question is whether they are in the body of Christ, baptized into His body, as the Scriptures picture.

"The doctrine of the resurrection of the Old Testament saints, as it is revealed in the Old Testament itself, relates the event to the second coming of Christ to establish His kingdom. By way of illustration, Daniel 12:1 deals with the great tribulation. Daniel 12:2 speaks of many being raised from the dust of the earth. If that is a genuine resurrection, it is a clear indication that according to Daniel the resurrection of the Old Testament saints occurs after the tribulation. The resurrection of the Church, however, occurs before the tribulation. There is no explicit teaching anywhere in the Bible that reveals that the Old Testament saints are resurrected at the time the Church is resurrected. In other words, the two events are never brought together in any passage of Scripture. The best explanation of the expression "dead in Christ" is to refer it to the Church alone."

Walvoord, John F., *The Thessalonian Epistles* (Galaxie Software, 2007), 46.

[438] Wuest's Word Studies from the Greek New Testament: For the English Reader, Wuest, Kenneth S., (Grand Rapids: Eerdmans, 1997).

[439] "This expression "in Christ" in every one of its many instances in the New Testament refers only to the saints of this dispensation. As far as the expression "the dead in Christ" indicates, only those in Christ are raised. Of course, all the saints are in Christ in the sense that Christ is their substitute, but the question is whether they are in the body of Christ, baptized into His body, as the Scriptures picture.

"The doctrine of the resurrection of the Old Testament saints, as it is revealed in the Old Testament itself, relates the event to the second coming of Christ to establish His kingdom. By way of illustration, Daniel 12:1 deals with the great tribulation. Daniel 12:2 speaks of many being raised from the dust of the earth. If that is a genuine resurrection, it is a clear indication that according to Daniel the resurrection of the Old Testament saints occurs after the tribulation. The resurrection of the Church, however, occurs before the tribulation. There is no explicit teaching anywhere in the Bible that reveals that the Old Testament saints are resurrected at the time the Church is resurrected. In other words, the two events are never brought together in any passage of Scripture. The best explanation of the expression "dead in Christ" is to refer it to the Church alone."

Walvoord, John F., *The Thessalonian Epistles* (Galaxie Software, 2007), 46.

[440] The Rapture. Although John does not provide an explicit statement concerning the Rapture as does Paul, John undoubtedly refers to the Rapture in John 14:1–3. The Rapture is related to the Church, and Jesus was speaking to the nucleus of disciples that would compose the small beginnings of the Church in Acts 2. Because the disciples were grieving at the imminent departure of Christ in John 14, He encouraged them by reminding them (as the infant Church) that He was going to prepare dwelling places for them in His Father's home. His promise to return and take them to Himself (John 14:3) is understood as parallel to Paul's statement in 1 Thessalonians 4:13–18.

Enns, Paul P., *The Moody Handbook of Theology* (Chicago, IL: Moody Press, 1989), 141.

[441] (2) The scope of the Tribulation. The whole earth will be involved (Isa. 24:1, 3, 4, 5, 6, 21; 34:2). It also involves God's chastisement of Israel (Jer. 30:7; Dan. 9:24). If this is the nature and scope of the Tribulation, it is inconceivable that the Church will be on earth to experience the wrath of God. (3) The purposes of the Tribulation. The divine intentions of the Tribulation will be to judge people living on earth (Rev. 6:10; 11:10; 13:8, 12, 14; 14:6; 17:8) and to prepare Israel for her King (Ezek.

36:18–32; Mal. 4:5–6). Neither of these pertain to the Church. (4) The unity of the Tribulation. The Tribulation is the seventieth week of Daniel; Daniel 9:24 makes it clear that it has reference to Israel. (5) The exemption of the Tribulation. The Church is the bride of Christ, the object of Christ's love, not His wrath (Eph. 5:25). It would be a contradiction of the very relationship of Christ and the Church for the Church to go through the punishments of the Tribulation. Specific statements affirming the Church will be kept from the Tribulation (cf. Rom. 5:9;81 1 Thess. 5:9; 2 Thess. 2:13; Rev. 3:10).82

Enns, Paul P., *The Moody Handbook of Theology* (Chicago, IL: Moody Press, 1989), 391.

[442] See "About the Restrainer" later in this chapter for a more detailed examination of this subject.

[443] Apostasia, translated "apostasy," does not mean merely disbelieving but rather an aggressive and positive revolt (Acts 21:21; Hebrews 3:12). Ryrie, Charles C., First and Second Thessalonians, Chicago Moody Press, 1959, 1987, 2001.) (C. C. Ryrie 2001)

[444] Main divisions paraphrased from: Ice, Thomas, "*The Biblical Basis for the Pretribulational Rapture*," in Basic Theology Applied, (Victor Books 1995) 269 (Ice, "The Biblical Basis for the Pretribulational Rapture," in Basic Theology Applied 1995)

[445] This means that the return of some Jews to the land of Israel, in unbelief, is not a requisite for the return of Christ for the Church.

[446] Pentecost, *Things to Come*, 203.

[447] Enns, Paul P., *The Moody Handbook of Theology* (Chicago, IL: Moody Press, 1989), 391.

[448] Walvoord, John F., *The Revelation of Jesus Christ* (Galaxie Software, 2008), 87–88.

[449] "day of the LORD"

"The occasion of God's final intervention in human affairs to punish sin, restore the faithful of his people and establish his rule over the nations. It is linked with the Messianic hope and will be fulfilled at Jesus Christ's return. This future consummation is anticipated in historical acts of judgment and, although its time is unknown, it will be heralded and accompanied by signs and by great upheavals in nature.

The day of the LORD as a day of judgment
Of universal judgment Isa 24:21-22 See also Zep 1:14-18
Of judgment on the nations Isa 13:9-11; Jer 46:10 See also Job 20:28-29; Isa 13:4-6 God's judgment on Babylon
God's judgment on Egypt: Isa 19:16-17; Eze 30:3-4; Isa 27:1; Joel 3:12-14; Ob 15 God's judgment on Edom; Zep 3:8; Ro 2:16; Rev 6:15-17
Of judgment on faithless Israel Am 5:18-20 See also Isa 2:12; Joel 1:15; 2:1-2; Mt 7:22-23; Jn 12:48; Ro 2:5

The establishment of God's kingdom on the day of the LORD
God's kingdom will be universal and everlasting Zec 14:9 See also Da 2:44; 7:13-14; Rev 11:15
God will be the object of universal worship Isa 19:19-24; Zep 3:9-10; Zec 14:16
God's rule will be centred on a restored Jerusalem Isa 2:2-4 pp Mic 4:1-3; Zec 2:10-12; Rev 22:3
The fulfilment of Messianic hope on the day of the LORD Isa 4:2 See also Isa 11:10; Jer 30:9; Hos 3:5; Am 9:11; Zec 9:9; 12:10
Manser, Martin H., *Dictionary of Bible Themes: The Accessible and Comprehensive Tool for Topical Studies* (Martin Manser, London, 2009). (Manser 2009).

[450] Louis A. Barbieri, Jr., "Matthew," in *The Bible Knowledge Commentary: An Exposition of the*

Scriptures, ed. J. F. Walvoord and R. B. Zuck, vol. 2 (Wheaton, IL: Victor Books, 1985), 78. (Barbieri 1985)

[451] "eagles" 4.42 ἀετός, οῦ m—'eagle, vulture.' ἐδόθησαν τῇ γυναικὶ αἱ δύο πτέρυγες τοῦ ἀετοῦ τοῦ μεγάλου 'they gave the woman two wings of a large eagle' Re 12:14; ὅπου ἐὰν ᾖ τὸ πτῶμα, ἐκεῖ συναχθήσονται οἱ ἀετοί 'wherever there is a dead body, there the vultures will gather' Mt 24:28.

[452] Referring to Matthew 24.31: "He will then send His angels forth to regather His elect from the four winds, which relates to the earth (cf. Mark 13:27), from one end of the heavens to the other. This involves the gathering of those who will have become believers during the Seventieth Week of Daniel and who will have been scattered into various parts of the world because of persecution (cf. Matt. 24:16). This gathering will probably also involve all Old Testament saints, whose resurrection will occur at this time, so that they may share in Messiah's kingdom (Dan. 12:2–3, 13)."
Louis A. Barbieri, Jr., "Matthew," in *The Bible Knowledge Commentary: An Exposition of the Scriptures*, ed. J. F. Walvoord and R. B. Zuck, vol. 2 (Wheaton, IL: Victor Books, 1985), p. 78.

[453] "withholdeth, letteth, let" 13.150 κατέχωa: to prevent someone from doing something by restraining or hindering—'to prevent, to hinder, to restrain, to keep from.' ἀνθρώπων τῶν τὴν ἀλήθειαν ἐν ἀδικίᾳ κατεχόντων 'the people whose evil ways keep the truth from being known' Ro 1:18.
Johannes P. Louw and Eugene Albert Nida, *Greek-English Lexicon of the New Testament: Based on Semantic Domains* (New York: United Bible Societies, 1996), 164.

[454] pres. act. part. sing. acc. neut. of *katecho* [G2722]

[455] pres. act. part. sing. nom. masc. of katecho [G2722]

[456] aor. mid. subj. third person singular of *ginomai* [G1096]

[457] It is not a mystery to the Church since Paul and the other New Testament writers have explained it to the elect.

[458] "The word *dispensation* is twofold in its import: (1) It may refer to a dispensing or an administration or (2) to an abrogation of standards or existing laws—such are the dispensations practiced by the Church of Rome. It is obvious that the controversy among theologians is concerned only with the former. The word *dispensation* is Latin in its origin, being derived from *dispensatio*—economical management or superintendence—and has its equivalent in the Greek *oikonomia*, meaning, in this specific usage, 'stewardship' or 'economy' as to special features of divine government in the various ages. To quote the *Century Dictionary* bearing on the theological import of the word: "(a) The method or scheme by which God has at different times developed his purpose, and revealed himself to man; or the body of privileges bestowed, and duties and responsibilities enjoined, in connection with that scheme or method of revelation: as the Old or Jewish *dispensation*; the New Gospel *dispensation*. (b) A period marked by a particular development of the divine purpose and revelation: as the *patriarchal dispensation* (lasting from Adam to Moses); the Mosaic *dispensation* (from Moses to Christ); the Christian *dispensation*." The *Century Dictionary* also quotes one pertinent sentence from *Bibliotheca Sacra* of sixty-two years ago: "The limits of certain dispensational periods were revealed in Scripture" (XLV, 237). In the light of this material, the definition advanced by the late Dr. C. I. Scofield (*Scofield Reference Bible*, p. 5), namely, "A dispensation is a period of time during which man is tested in respect of obedience to some *specific* revelation of the will of God," is hardly entitled to the criticism which is aimed against it."

Chafer, Lewis Sperry. *Dispensationalism.* (Dallas, Texas: Dallas Seminary Press, 1951) 8 (Chafer, Dispensationalism 1951).

[459] Enns, Paul P., *The Moody Handbook of Theology* (Chicago, IL: Moody Press, 1989), 517. This definition is found originally in Ryrie, Charles C. Dispensationalism. (1995) 28

[460] Harold W. Hoehner, "Ephesians," in *The Bible Knowledge Commentary: An Exposition of the Scriptures*, ed. J. F. Walvoord and R. B. Zuck, vol. 2 (Wheaton, IL: Victor Books, 1985), 618. (Hoehner 1985).

[461] LaHaye, Tim, and Thomas Ice, *Charting the End Times. Tim LaHaye Prophecy Library.* (Eugene, OR: Harvest House Publishers, 2001). 82

[462] Ryrie, Charles C. *Dispensationalism* (1995) 25-26 summarized in LaHaye, Tim, Thomas Ice, and Tim LaHaye. *Charting the End Times.* Tim LaHaye Prophecy Library. Eugene, OR: Harvest House Publishers, 2001. 82

[463] Ryrie, Charles Caldwell. *Dispensationalism. Revised and Expanded.* Chicago: Moody Press, 1995.34.

www.ingramcontent.com/pod-product-compliance
Lightning Source LLC
Chambersburg PA
CBHW071107160426
43196CB00013B/2496